D1192911

IBM PC and Compatibles

An Introduction to the Operating System, BASIC Programming, and Applications

Fourth Edition

Dr. Larry Joel Goldstein

Brady
New York

Copyright © 1989 by Simon & Schuster, Inc.
All rights reserved,
including the right of reproduction
in whole or in part in any form

 BRADY

Simon & Schuster, Inc.
Gulf+Western Building
One Gulf+Western Plaza
New York, NY 10023

Distributed by Prentice Hall Trade

Manufactured in the United States of America

1 2 3 4 5 6 7 8 9 10

Library of Congress Cataloging-in-Publication Data

Goldstein, Larry Joel.
    IBM PC and compatibles : an introduction to the operating system,
BASIC programming, and applications / Larry Joel Goldstein. -- 4th
ed.
        p. cm.
    Rev. ed. of: IBM PC. 3rd ed. 1986.
    Includes index.
    1. IBM Personal Computer--Programming. 2. BASIC (Computer
program language) I. Goldstein, Larry Joel. IBM PC. II. Title
QA76.8.I2594G64 1989
005.265--dc20   89-7150
                                                           CIP

ISBN 0-13-449521-7

LIMITS OF LIABILITY AND DISCLAIMER OF WARRANTY

The author and the publisher of this book have used their best efforts in preparing this book and the programs contained in it. These efforts include the development, research, and testing of the theories and programs to determine their effectiveness. The author and publisher make no warranty of any kind, express of implied, with regard to these programs or the documentation contained in this book. The author and publisher shall not be liable in any event for incidental or consequential damages in connection with or arising out of, the furnishing, performance, or use of these programs.

List of Registered Trademarks

IBM PC, XT, AT, and PS/2–International Business Machines Corporation
MS-DOS, GWBASIC, QuickBASIC–Microsoft Corporation
Compaq, Compaq Advanced Graphics System–Compaq Computer Corporation
1-2-3–Lotus Development Corporation
Applesoft–Apple Computer Corporation
Turbo BASIC–Borland International Corporation
Zenith–Zenith Data Systems, Inc.
Hewlett-Packard–Hewlett Packard, Inc.
AST Research–AST Research, Inc.
Tandy–Tandy Corporation
NEC–NEC America, Inc.
Epson–Epson America
Wyse–Wyse Technology, Inc.
Olivetti–Olivetti USA

DEDICATION

For Sandy

Who fills my life with all that's worthwhile.

CONTENTS

Preface to the Fourth Edition

It is a relatively rare event that a trade book is reissued in a second edition, let alone a fourth edition. However, in the world of personal computing, the pace of change is swift. And the enthusiastic reception afforded the earlier editions has led to the following updated and expanded version.

The chapters on MS-DOS have been expanded and updated to include a discussion of the latest in peripheral devices as well as the latest computers belonging to the IBM PC-compatible family, including the PS/2 line and the 80386 computers.

In revising the chapters on GWBASIC, I have succumbed to the tendency of most authors to add much and delete little. I hope that I can be pardoned in this situation, since there seems to be so much more to say as the years go by. In this edition, I have added:

- Further discussion of structured programming and problem-solving via programming.

- Expanded discussion of debugging.

- Data structures in BASIC.

- Additional material on sorting.

- A discussion of searching techniques.

In addition, I have rewritten many of the discussions throughout the book often in response to reader and reviewer suggestions.

Since the book is meant as a teaching tool, I have included exercises of two sorts. The **Test Your Understanding** questions are found within the bodies of sections and are meant to involve the reader by testing your understanding of material as it is covered. The answers to these exercises are found at the end of the section. At the end of most sections are lists of exercises that provide further practice in the material of the section. Some of the exercises require short answers (a line or two) while others require you to write whole programs. To get the most out of this book, you should definitely try to work at least a few of the exercises of each set.

I hope you enjoy learning from this book as much as I have enjoyed writing it.

Writing a book is a more complex task than the man in the street realizes. In order to proceed from idea to completed book, the author requires the cooperation and dedication of many people. For this project, it was my good fortune to have the assistance of some of the best: At Goldstein Software, Holly Martinez managed the desktop publishing of this book. At Brady Books, Ozzievelt Owens did a skillful job of editing my manuscript, Mia McCroskey managed the production, and Milissa Koloski and Susan Hunt, who acted as editors and sponsors of the project. To all of them I extend a heartfelt thank you. Also, I want to thank you, the reader, for your interest and attention. I hope that this book provides you with both information and enjoyment.

In spite of our best efforts, some errors may have crept into the book. If you spot any, please let me know so that they can be corrected in future printings.

Larry Joel Goldstein
Silver Spring, Maryland

Part One

Introduction

One

A First Look at Computers

Introduction

In the past decade, personal computers have become common tools on the job, in schools, and in the home. They allow their users to perform a tremendous variety of tasks more efficiently than they could previously be performed, if they could be accomplished at all. These personal computers are changing the way we think, work, and learn. To help you appreciate the all-pervasive nature of personal computers, let me cite a single statistic. By 1984, less than a decade after the invention of the first personal computer, more than 60 percent of all office workers had access to a personal computer.

In 1981, IBM introduced its first entry into the personal computer market. The original IBM PC has enjoyed extraordinary popularity and is in use in millions of homes, schools, and businesses. IBM has responded to the success of its PC by introducing an entire line of personal computers, from the PC XT and PC AT to the new, more compact PS/2 series. All these models vary significantly in accessories, computing power, and, of course, price. IBM's personal computer line has become the de facto standard of microcomputing. In the last few years there have been more than 100 personal computers that are, to some degree, IBM "clones"—clones of the original PC lines and the new PS/2 lines alike. These clones are compatible with the IBM machines in the sense that they can run most IBM PC software programs unaltered.

As of this writing, more than two-thirds of all personal computers are either IBMs or are compatible with the IBM PC. Among the major IBM-compatible computer manufacturers are: Compaq, Tandy, and Epson. In fact they have outgrown the status of simple clone manufacturers and have become major players in the race to build ever faster, ever more powerful PCs. Most recently a group of these IBM-compatible manufacturers have collaboratively developed specifications for an Extended Industry Architecture (EISA). The EISA group proposes to establish an alternative standard to the proprietary architecture of IBM's high-end PS/2 computers. This group, also known as "The Gang of Nine" includes Compaq Computer Corporation, Zenith Data Systems, Hewlett-Packard Company, AST Research, Inc., Tandy Corporation, NEC America, Inc., Epson America, Inc., Wyse Technology, and Olivetti U.S.A.

This book is an introduction to personal computing on the entire range of IBM personal computers. It is divided into three parts. The first is an introduction to the hardware of these systems and some of the options available for expanding their capabilities. It is designed to teach computer novices how computers work and guide them through the technical terminology and the high-tech wizardry that are part and parcel of the personal computer field. The second part instructs the beginner in the MS-DOS operating system, the control program that manages IBM personal computers. This part will teach you to run applications programs under DOS and to perform the rudimentary tasks necessary to personal computing, such as making copies of files and formatting diskettes.

The third part of the book is an introduction to programming in BASIC on the IBM personal computers. In this part, I will teach you to write programs in BASIC. Moreover, this part contains many interesting applications programs that you can use on your own computer. These programs are useful as well as instructional. You may first study them as they appear in the text and then type them into your computer to run them. Alternatively, you may purchase these programs on diskette and thereby save yourself the trouble of typing them in and dealing with the inevitable typographical errors that will arise.

This book is designed as a text, to be used either for self-study or in a classroom setting. Accordingly, it contains questions for you to answer. You should attempt to answer these questions and test your answers on your computer. It is only by being an active learner that you will get the most from this text.

What Is a Personal Computer?

The personal computer is not a toy. It is a genuine computer with most of the features of its big brothers, the so-called "mainframe" computers, which still cost several million dollars. A personal computer can be equipped with enough capacity to handle the accounting and inventory control tasks of most small businesses. It can also perform computations for engineers and scientists, and it can even be used to keep track of home finances and personal clerical chores. It would be quite impossible to give a complete list of the possible applications of personal computers. However, the following list can suggest the range of possibilities:

For the business person

Accounting
Record keeping
Clerical chores
Inventory
Cash management
Payroll
Graph and chart preparation

Word processing
Data analysis
Networking

For the home

Record keeping
Budget management
Investment analysis
Correspondence
Energy conservation
Home security
On-line information retrieval
Tax return preparation

For the student

Computer literacy
Preparation of term papers
Analysis of experiments
Preparation of graphs and charts
Project schedules
Storage and organization of notes

For the professional

Billing
Analysis of data
Report generation
Correspondence
Stock market data access
Scientific/engineering calculations

For recreation

Computer games
Computer graphics
Computer art

As you can see, the list is quite extensive. If your interests aren't listed, don't worry! There's plenty of room for those of you who are just plain curious about computers and wish to learn about them as a hobby.

Parts of a Computer

At the heart of every computer is a **central processing unit** (or CPU), which performs the commands you specify. This unit carries out arithmetic, makes logical decisions, and so forth. In essence, the CPU is the "brain" of the computer. The **memory** of a computer allows it to "remember" or store numbers, words, and paragraphs, as well as the list of commands you wish the computer to perform. The **input unit** allows you to send information to the computer; the **output unit** allows the computer to send information to you or to your printer. The relationship of these four basic components of a computer are shown in Figure 1-1.

In a personal computer, the CPU is a single semiconductor chip, about an inch long. The CPUs used in the IBM personal computers are manufactured by Intel Corporation. The CPU of the original IBM PC and PC/XT, as well as many of the entry-level model clones currently available, is an 8088 microprocessor. In the IBM PC AT, its clones, and certain computers in the PS/2 family, the CPU is a faster, more powerful chip, an 80286 microprocessor. In today's top-of-the-line IBM-compatible personal computers, the CPU is a very powerful microprocessor, an 80386 microprocessor. Already in prototype are the 80486 microprocessors, which will provide desktop computers with the power of Mainframe computers.

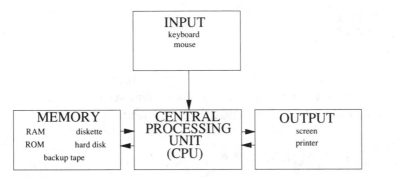

Figure 1-1.
**The main
components of
a computer.**

As a computer novice, it is not necessary for you to know anything about the electronics of the CPU. You may view the CPU as a magical device that somehow manages to carry out instructions that direct the computer to do certain things.

The main input device of a personal computer is the **keyboard**. We will discuss the special features of the keyboard in Chapter 2. For now, think of the keyboard as a typewriter. By typing symbols on the keyboard, you are inputting them to the computer.

The IBM Personal Computer has a number of output devices. The most basic is the **video monitor** or **video display** used to display text and graphics. You may also use a printer to provide paper output. In computer jargon, printed output is called **hard copy**.

There are four types of memory most commonly used in a personal computer: ROM, RAM, diskette, and hard disk (or fixed disk). Each of these types of memory has its own advantages and disadvantages. Microcomputers attempt to make memory as versatile as possible by using several kinds of memory, thereby allowing them to take advantage of the good features of each.

ROM

ROM stands for "read-only memory." The computer can read ROM but cannot write anything in it. ROM is reserved for certain very important programs necessary to the operation of the machine. For example, every time you turn on the computer, it automatically runs a series of programs to test the operations of the various components of the system. These diagnostic programs (as well as others) are recorded in ROM at the factory and you cannot change them.

RAM

RAM stands for "random-access memory." This type of immediate memory is **volatile**. The computer reads from and writes to RAM. The programs you run are loaded into RAM; the data you enter or change is stored in RAM. However, as soon as the computer is turned off, all the contents of RAM are erased. Therefore, RAM may not be used to store data or programs permanently and this explains the need for disks as a medium for storage of programs and data. Nevertheless, RAM is used as the computer's main working storage because of its great speed. (It takes only about a millionth of a second to store or retrieve a character to or from RAM.)

Diskette Drives

A diskette drive (see Figure 1-2) reads and writes information on diskettes, used for program and data storage (see Figure 1-3). Diskettes resemble phonograph records; they are often called "floppy disks" since the oldest types of diskettes were flexible. A diskette can hold anywhere from 360,000 characters to 1,440,000 characters, depending on the type of diskette. (See below for a discussion of the various types of diskettes and their capacities.) A diskette is a **removable storage medium**; that is, you can remove diskettes from a diskette drive and replace them with others. This means that a diskette drive can allow you to access a potentially infinite collection of data, at the expense of swapping diskettes.

All personal computers come equipped with at least one diskette drive. We will discuss how to use such drives later in this chapter.

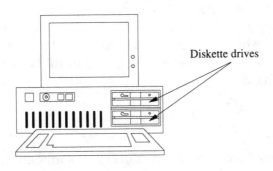

Diskette drives

Figure 1-2.
A diskette drive.

Program XYZ
Version 1.05

Figure 1-3.
A diskette.

Hard Disks

A hard disk (or fixed disk), also called a Winchester disk, stores information on a hard platter that is sealed within either the drive unit itself or a hard plastic cartridge (see Figure 1-4). It is not generally removeable.

Winchester disks are a more costly storage medium than a diskette. However, they allow the most rapid access to your data and can store from 20 million to a billion characters of data.

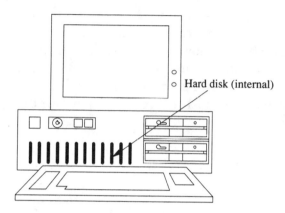

Hard disk (internal)

Figure 1-4.
A hard disk drive.

Math Coprocessors

The microprocessor of a personal computer has circuitry capable of performing arithmetic operations with the following limitations: Built-in arithmetic is limited to whole numbers and, in fact, the microprocessor's circuitry is limited to the size of the whole numbers it can handle. This is not to say that microprocessor's can't handle decimal arithmetic. However, to do so, they must rely on software.

Decimal arithmetic is also called **floating point arithmetic**. As we shall see, GWBASIC allows you to use floating point arithmetic which is implemented as part of the GWBASIC program.

Programs to perform floating point arithmetic tend to execute much more slowly than circuitry designed to perform the same tasks. And floating point arithmetic is of central importance for programs in science and finance. For these reasons, IBM PC's and compatibles have the ability to make use of a

math coprocessor, an auxiliary microprocessor designed to perform floating point arithmetic and values of trigonometric and other scientific functions.

There are a number of different math coprocessors of varying speeds and sophistication. The Intel 8087 is the lowest level coprocessor and is designed to work with 8088 and 80286 microprocessors. The Intel 80287 is designed to work with 80286 and 80386 microprocessors. The Intel 80387 is designed to work with 80386 microprocessors. Certain 80386-based computers are able to make use of Weitek math coprocessors, which were originally used in scientific workstations. A math coprocessor plugs into a socket on the mother board of your computer.

A program must be designed to take advantage of a math coprocessor. Most compilers can be used to create programs which sense whether or not a coprocessor is present and to use it for floating point arithmetic if it is.

The increase in the floating point arithmetic speed afforded by a coprocessor can be dramatic, ranging from a factor of 10 to 100!

Floppy Diskettes

Your floppy diskette drives are a critical part of your computer system. They allow you to store and retrieve both programs and data. Even on systems with a hard disk, the floppy diskette drive(s) are important for loading new software onto the hard disk and for backing up the contents of the hard disk. Before we proceed any further, let's get acquainted with these remarkable devices.

The Anatomy of a Diskette

There are two broad categories of diskette drives: those that use 5.25-inch diskettes and those which use 3.5-inch diskettes. The 3.5-inch diskettes are floppy diskettes, whereas the 3.5-inch diskettes are made with a rigid plastic jacket.

Within each category, there are low density and high density diskettes. For 5.25-inch diskettes, a **low-density diskette** (also called a **double density diskette**) can hold 360K bytes. A **byte** is a computer term for a single character. One K equals 1,024 bytes. So a low density diskette holds approximately 362,000 bytes. A high-density 5.25-inch diskette holds 1.2 megabytes. A megabyte equals 1024×1024 bytes, or about one million bytes. So a high-density 5.25-inch diskette holds about 1.2 million characters of information. A low-density 3.5-inch diskette holds 720K bytes and a high-density 3.5-inch diskette holds 1.44 megabytes.

Figure 1-5 illustrates the essential parts of a diskette. The diskette itself is a magnetically coated circular piece of mylar plastic that rotates freely within a protective jacket. The labels on the jacket identify the contents of the diskette.

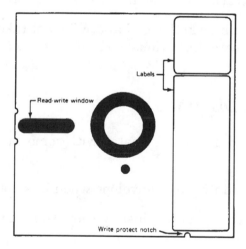

Figure 1-5.
The parts of a diskette.

The diskette drive reads and writes on the diskette through the **read-write window**. On 5.25-inch diskettes, the read-write window is a hole cut into the jacket. On 3.5-inch diskettes, the read-write window is covered by a sliding metal cover, which is pushed aside by the diskette drive when the diskette is inserted into the drive.

Never, under any circumstances, touch the mylar surface of the diskette. The recording surfaces of a diskette are fragile. A small piece of dust or even oil from a fingerprint could damage the diskette and render parts of the information on it totally useless.

A diskette always has a **write-protect** feature that allows you to prevent the diskette from being written on or enhanced in anyway. This allows you to prohibit alterations, additions, or deletions from the data on the diskette. For a 5.25-inch diskette the write-protect feature is a notch in the side of the diskette. When this notch is covered with one of the metallic labels provided with the diskettes, the computer may read the diskette, but it will not write or change any information on the diskette. To write on a diskette, the write-protect notch must be uncovered. On an 3.5-inch diskette the write-protect feature is a small plastic button that slides in a track. When light is visible through the track, then the diskette is write-protected.

You should have a few blank diskettes on hand. Why not take a moment to inspect one of them and locate the various parts of the diskette described above.

Cautions in Handling Diskettes

Diskettes are sensitive and should be treated with some care. Here are some tips in using diskettes:

1. Always keep a diskette in its paper envelope when it is not in use.

2. Store diskettes in a vertical position, just like you would a phonograph record.

3. Never touch the surface of a diskette or try to wipe the surface of a diskette with a rag, handkerchief, or other piece of cloth.

4. Keep diskettes away from extreme heat, such as that produced from radiators or direct sun.

5. Never bend a diskette.

6. When writing on a diskette label already in place on a diskette, use only a felt-tipped pen. Never use any sort of instrument with a sharp point.

7. Keep diskettes away from magnetic fields, such as those generated by electrical motors, radios, televisions, tape recorders, telephones, and other electrical devices. A strong magnetic field may erase data on a diskette.

8. Never remove a diskette while the drive is running. (You can tell if a drive is running by the sound of the motor and the "in use" light on the front of the drive.) Doing so may cause permanent damage to the diskette.

The above list of precautions may seem overwhelming if you are just starting out. However, once you set up a suitable set of procedures for handling and storing diskettes, you will find that they are a reliable, long-lasting storage medium.

Using Diskettes

To insert a diskette into a diskette drive, open the door of the drive. Turn the diskette drive that the label side is facing up and the read-write window is closest to the drive opening. Gently push the diskette into the drive until you hear a click. If the diskette drive has a handle on it, rotate the handle to close the drive door. (This is not necessary with 3.5-inch drives.)

Each diskette drive has a light that is lit when the computer is reading or writing to the diskette in the drive. Never attempt to change diskettes when this light is on. The location of the drive light varies with the computer design, but is most often on the face plate of the drive.

To remove a diskette from a drive, first be sure that the light to the left of the drive door is off. Lift the drive door and gently pull the diskette forward and out of the drive. In the case of a 3.5-inch drive, there is a button on the drive that you must push in order to pop the diskette from the drive.

Organization of a Diskette

Data are recorded on a diskette in circular configurations called **tracks**. Each track is divided into a number of regions called **sectors**. When data is stored, it is given an address in this system of tracks and sectors. When a diskette comes out of the box, the organization of tracks and sectors are not on the diskette. The electronic boundaries of the tracks and sectors must be set up on the diskette in a process called **formatting**. We will discuss formatting diskettes in the next chapter.

The first (innermost) track of a diskette contains information about the data on the diskette. It contains a directory listing the various files on the diskette and information about each file (the date and time the file was last changed, the length of the file, the location of the first sector, and so forth). The initial track of a diskette also contains a table, called the **file allocation table** (or FAT table) which tells which sectors are in use and, for each sector within a file, the location of the next sector of the file.

It is not necessary for the casual user to understand the technical data about diskette organization. However, it is often necessary to consult the directory to determine which files are on a diskette and when they were last written to. We'll learn how to do that shortly.

Hard Disks

A fixed disk (also called a hard disk) is a magnetic storage medium in the form of one or more circular platters (the size varies) that rotate within a sealed enclosure. Not only do fixed disks hold much more data than do diskettes, but they rotate much more rapidly than diskettes, allowing the computer to access their data much more rapidly.

In recent years, the price of fixed disks has plunged and they have become very common equipment on personal computers. For example, in 1984 a moderate- performance 20-megabyte hard disk sold for $2,000–$3,000, while now (in 1989) a higher-performance, physically smaller 20-megabyte hard disk now sells for $200–$300. As programs for personal computers have become more complex, a hard disk has become almost a necessity, unless you are willing to put up with continually swapping diskettes.

Just like a diskette, a hard disk's platters are organized into tracks and cylinders. These are written on the platters in a process called formatting. Usually, hard disks that are sold as part of a computer system are already formatted and you will never need to worry about formatting them unless it becomes necessary to reinitialize the disk (a rare event).

Just like a diskette, a hard disk has a directory and a file allocation table. In fact, as far as the beginning user is concerned, you may think of a hard disk as a large diskette, which provide very rapid access to your programs and data.

Monitors and Video Adapters

The video portion of your computer system consists of two parts: the monitor itself and a circuit board, called a **video adapter**, which sends the appropriate signals from the computer to your monitor. The video adapter is most often inserted into one of the so-called **expansion slots** located within the case of your computer. (A few personal computers have the video adapter built into the main circuit board.) The video capabilities of your system include the resolution (sharpness) of the screen and the colors that the system can display. These capabilities are determined both by your choice of display adapter and monitor.

A monitor that can display a single color is called **monochrome**: one monitor that can display multiple colors is called a **color monitor**. Using some video adapters, you can represent color on a monochrome monitor using different levels (gray tones) of the single color available.

The simplest and oldest video adapters are the **monochrome display adapter** (MDA) and the **color graphics adapter** (CGA). The monochrome display adapter allows you to display a single color on a monochrome monitor and does not allow display of any graphics. The color graphics adapter allows you to display up to four colors simultaneously on a color monitor and allows you to display graphics with a resolution of 320×200 in four colors or 640×200 in two colors (black and white).

Since IBM introduced these video adapters, there have been a large number of additions. In fact, IBM no longer manufacturers the color graphics adapter. With its PS/2 computer series, IBM has created a new graphics standard, the Video Graphics Array (VGA) with a resolution of 640×480 in 16 colors. VGA boards mark a shift in video display from digital to analog technology. The VGA adapter will work, however, with the older digital monitors—both monochrome and color. IBM has even gone beyond its VGA standard with its 8514/A graphics board with a 1024×768 resolution. This option, however, is available only to the high-end PS/2 80386 computers. Finally, Compaq has just introduced its Compaq Advanced Graphics System for all non-PS/2 80386-based computers; this plug-in board too offers a resolution of 1024×768.

The newer and more typical video adapters found on today's PCs include the following:

Hercules—720×348 graphics on a monochrome monitor;

Enhanced Graphics Adapter (EGA)—640×350 graphics in 16 colors on an EGA color monitor or a 640×400 graphics in two colors on a monochrome monitor;

Video Graphics Array (VGA)—up to 640×480 graphics in 16 colors or 320×200 in 256 colors on a VGA monitor.

In addition, there are a number of other graphics configurations supported by various video adapters. So many, in fact, that we can't even begin to survey the variety that exists. Some of the better known graphics board manufacturers are: Paradise Systems, AST Research, etc. Suffice it to say that when you buy a system, you must acquire both a monitor and a video adapter and that the two must be capable of working together. As you might expect, as the resolution of the graphics and the number of colors increases, so does the cost.

Serial and Parallel Adapters

There are hundreds of different devices that can be connected to a personal computer. These range from pointing devices (mice) to printers from scanners to communications devices (eg. modems and fax machines). There are two general-purpose ways of connecting such devices to a computer, namely via either a **serial adapter** or a **parallel adapter**. Each of these adapters has an outlet or a plug, into which you can insert the appropriate cable from your printer or other device. We don't need to go into how these adapters work. Suffice it to say that most modern personal computers come with at least one built-in serial adapter (also called a **serial port**) and one built-in parallel adapter (also called a **parallel port**). Parallel ports are designed primarily for printers. They are so named because data can be transmitted through them in 8-, 16- or 32-bit clusters, that is, in parallel. Serial ports are most often used for printers and modems; serial ports send data one bit at a time, or serially, resulting in slower transmission time. To connect a device to your computer using one of these adapters requires an appropriate cable connecting the device to the adapter. In configurations requiring connection of many devices, it is necessary to equip the computer with multiple parallel and/or serial ports or a switching box to permit different devices used one at a time to be connected to the port.

Speed Considerations

The speed of a computer is regulated by an internal clock generated by the vibrations of a crystal. The "ticks" of the clock specify the "beat" at which the computer performs operations. The speed of the clock is measured in **megahertz**, or millions of cycles per second. A cycle is one "tick" of the clock. The original IBM PC had a clock speed of 4.77 megahertz. Now it is common for 8088-based clones to have clock speeds of 6 or 8 megahertz. PCs based on an 80286 CPU typically have clock speeds of 8, 10, or 12 megahertz. The 80386 machines have clock speeds of 16, 20, or 25 megahertz. The faster the clock speed, the more operations per second the computer will perform.

However, that's not the entire story. The 8088 machines process data one character (or 8-bits) at a time, the 80286 machines up to two characters (or 16-bits) at a time, and the 80386 machines up to four characters (or 32-bits) at a time. In comparing the relative "horsepower" of machines, it is necessary to take into account both the clock speed and the amount of data being processed per operation. It is also necessary to take into account the data access speed, or the time it takes the computer to read from and write to the hard disk.

More About RAM and Memory Board Options

The amount of RAM in a computer is measured in terms of **bytes**, where a byte equals the capacity to store a single character. Most modern PCs come with at least 640K bytes of RAM. At first, the number 640 seems odd. But this is the largest amount of RAM that the MS-DOS operating system allows a program to use. When the IBM PC was first designed, this seemed like a large number. However, many of today's powerful programs that handle large quantities of data are bumping up against this 640K limitation. These powerful programs, as well as the need to run several programs simultaneously has accelerated the development of new techniques that allows the computer to break the 640K barrier.

For this reason, many of today's more powerful computers come equipped with 1000K, 2000K, or even more RAM. In addition, the original 8088 and 80286 PCs can be enhanced with memory boards and supporting software to make use of memory beyond 640K. In 1985 Lotus, Intel, and Microsoft announced Expanded Memory Specification version 3.0 (LIM EMS 3.0). Software programs written for EMS 3.0 could use up to 8 megabytes of RAM, although only 64K of this expanded memory could be active at one time. With EMS 3.0 therefore data had to be clearly divisible into 64K chunks so that it could be easily swapped in and out of active memory. AST Research then came out with an enhanced EMS (or EEMS) standard which provided access to 16 megabytes of RAM and allowed for 1 megabyte of active memory. Finally in 1987 the Lotus/Intel/Microsoft team upgraded their EMS to

IIIBradyLine

You rely on Brady's bestselling computer books for up-to-date information about high technology. Now turn to BradyLine for the details behind the titles.

Find out what new trends in technology spark Brady's authors and editors. Read about what they're working on, and predicting, for the future. Get to know the authors through interviews and profiles, and get to know each other through your questions and comments.

BradyLine keeps you ahead of the trends with the stories behind the latest computer developments. Informative previews of forthcoming books and excerpts from new titles keep you apprised of what's going on in the fields that interest you most.

- Peter Norton on operating systems
- Jim Seymour on business productivity
- Jerry Daniels, Mary Jane Mara, Robert Eckhardt, and Cynthia Harriman on Macintosh development, productivity, and connectivity

Get the Spark. Get BradyLine.

Published quarterly, beginning with the Summer 1988 issue. Free exclusively to our customers. Just fill out and mail this card to begin your subscription.

Name _____

Address _____

City _____ State _____ Zip _____

Name of Book Purchased _____

Date of Purchase _____

Where was this book purchased?   *(circle one)*

    Retail Store   Computer Store   Mail Order

F R E E

Mail this card for your free subscription to BradyLine

Brady Books

One Gulf+Western Plaza
New York, NY 10023

Place
First Class
Postage
Here
Post Office
Will Not
Deliver
Without Postage

version 4.0. EMS 4.0 (or LIM 4.0) allows access to 32 megabytes of RAM. The computer industry continues to improve its ability to make use of more and more RAM.

Printers

Printer technology has progressed rapidly in the last decade. There are literally hundreds of models of printers to choose from with prices ranging from $100 to $30,000. There are two basic types of printers:

1. **Dot-matrix printers.** These printers print letters as a collection of dots created by a set of wires or pins impacting on a ribbon. The most important distinguishing characteristics among these are the printing speed and the number of dots it takes to form a character (resolution).

   The least capable dot-matrix printers produce fair-to-medium print quality. However, many dot-matrix printers have a "near-letter quality" mode in which letters are printed with a very dense array of dots. In this mode, it is very hard to distinguish the individual dots, so that the print quality approximates that of a typewriter.

2. **Laser printers.** These printers, the most expensive, combine high-quality printing with great speed. A laser printer can produce from eight to more than 50 pages a minute. The print quality rivals or equals that of typeset text (depending on the printer's resolution).

   Laser printers have made possible the field of **desktop publishing** in which personal computers are used to design and typeset written material, which formerly was the exclusive domain of publishers.

Your printer must be connected to the system unit. The exact nature of this connection will depend on the printer. Some printers are equipped with a parallel interface and some with a serial interface. For a parallel interface, you must connect the printer to a parallel printer adapter; for a serial interface, you must connect the printer to a serial adapter.

Other Components

Designing a personal computer system is somewhat analogous to designing a component stereo system. You can mix and match components at will. Some components may be added by simply plugging them into serial or parallel ports. Components in this category are joysticks, mice, and voice synthesizers.

Other components require an adapter board inserted into a slot in the system unit. The component connects to the computer via a connector extending from the adapter board. Components of this type include scanners and tape backup systems.

Two

Using Your PC for the First Time

In this chapter, we present the information you need to know to use your computer for the first time. In particular, we:

- Introduce you to certain fundamental fundamental MS-DOS concepts.

- Discuss starting the computer.

- Learn the layout and operation of the keyboard.

- Learn some basic troubleshooting ideas.

- Discuss the need for backing up programs and data.

Fundamental System Concepts

In the preceding chapter, we discussed the common hardware elements of IBM PCs, PS/2s, and PC-compatible computers. However, in using a personal computer, hardware is only part of the story. In order to do anything with your computer, you must run software—that is, programs that instruct the computer to perform useful functions.

The MS-DOS Operating System

The operation of your computer is supervised by a program (actually a collection of programs) called the **operating system**. The operating system provides a variety of functions, including the following:

- A means for giving commands to the computer. (One such command might be: "Run this program.")

- A set of routines that programmers can use within their programs. These include routines for reading and writing diskette drives, hard disks, writing to the screen, and reading the keyboard.

- A set of routines to monitor the equipment of the system. When the operating system detects an equipment abnormality, it informs the current program. If the operating system detects a serious abnormality, it will halt the current program.

- A set of "housekeeping" programs to perform various systems tasks, such as formatting disks, copying files, and displaying directories.

In the case of IBM computers, the operating system is called **PC-DOS** while for PC-compatible computers, the operating system is called **MS-DOS**. Here MS stands for Microsoft, the company that developed the operating system. In order to operate an IBM or IBM PC-compatible computer, it is necessary to learn the fundamentals about PC-DOS or the very similar MS-DOS. We will do this in the remainder of this chapter and in the next two chapters. (For the remainder of this book, we will use MS-DOS as a generic reference to either PC-DOS or MS-DOS.)

System Configuration and Set Up

Before you can use your system, it is necessary to properly configure it. This involves two steps. First, the various system components must be properly assembled and connected to one another. Second, the system must be told about the various components it contains so that it can manage them all properly. This is done in some machines via switches inside the case of the system unit; in others, it is done by running a system set-up program whose results are stored in a region of memory maintained by battery, so that the set-up information is available each time the system is powered up. Since system configuration and set-up vary from model to model, we won't go into further detail here. Instead, we will assume that you (or your dealer) have followed the instructions supplied with your system and have succeeded in performing the system configuration and set up.

Booting the System

The process of powering up your computer and starting MS-DOS is called **booting the system**. Let's describe how to do this.

Drive Names and the Boot Drive

MS-DOS names the drives (diskette and hard disk) using a letter followed by a colon. The first diskette drive is named A:, the second diskette drive is named B:, and the first hard disk drive C:. If you have two diskette drive, here's how to tell which is the drive A:. If the drives are arranged horizontally, then the one on the left is A: and the one on the right is B:. If the drives are arranged vertically, then the drive on top is A: and the one on the bottom is B:.

If there is only one diskette drive, then it is given both names A: and B:. (This dual naming helps DOS instruct you in performing two-diskette operations, such as copying from one diskette to another.)

To boot up the system, it is necessary to load a copy of MS-DOS into RAM. This copy of the operating system comes either from a diskette placed in drive A: or from a copy of MS-DOS recorded on the first hard disk C:. Here's how to start the system in each of the two situations.

System Start-up—Using a Diskette

A diskette used to boot the system must have a copy of the operating system on it. Such a diskette is called a **boot diskette**. The original DOS diskette that came with your computer is a boot diskette and may be used to start your computer for the first time. In the next chapter, we will discuss how you may make copies of this diskette or making other diskettes into boot diskettes.

To boot the system from a diskette, follow these steps:

1. Insert a boot diskette into drive A:.
2. Turn on the power. First turn on the power to the system unit, then the power to the monitor (if controlled by a separate on-off switch), then the power to the printer.
3. You will see various lights on the front of the computer go on. On the screen, you will see information about various diagnostic tests on the system components.
4. The screen displays an MS-DOS copyright notice and the MS-DOS prompt A>, indicating that MS-DOS is ready to accept a command from you. (See Figure 2-1.)

```
Toshiba Personal Computer MS-DOS Version 3.20 /R3B
Copyright (C) Toshiba Corporation 1983, 1987
Copyright (C) Microsoft Corporation 1981, 1986


Current date is Thu 11-17-1988
Enter new date (mm-33-yy):
Current time is 22:08:03.56

COMMAND Version 3.20

A>_
```

Figure 2-1.
**Booting the
system from a
diskette.**

5. Systems that don't have battery storage of set-up information will ask you to input the time and date. Input the date in the format 12-4-90 for December 4, 1990 and the time in the format 14:05 for 2:05 P.M.

System Start-up—From a Hard Disk

To boot the system from a hard disk, the operating system must have been copied to hard disk C:. This is usually done during system configuration and set up. We assume that this has been carried out for your computer.

To boot the system from hard disk C:, follow these steps:

1. Make sure that there is no diskette in drive A: or that the drive door on drive A: is open. (The computer always looks to read from drive A: first—a safety precaution in case there is a hard disk failure.)

2. Turn on the power. First turn on the power to the system unit, then the power to the monitor (if controlled by a separate on-off switch), then the power to the printer.

3. You will see various lights on the front of the computer go on. On the screen, you will see information about various diagnostic tests on the system components.

4. The screen displays an MS-DOS copyright notice and the MS-DOS prompt C>, indicating that MS-DOS is ready to accept a command from you (see Figure 2-2).

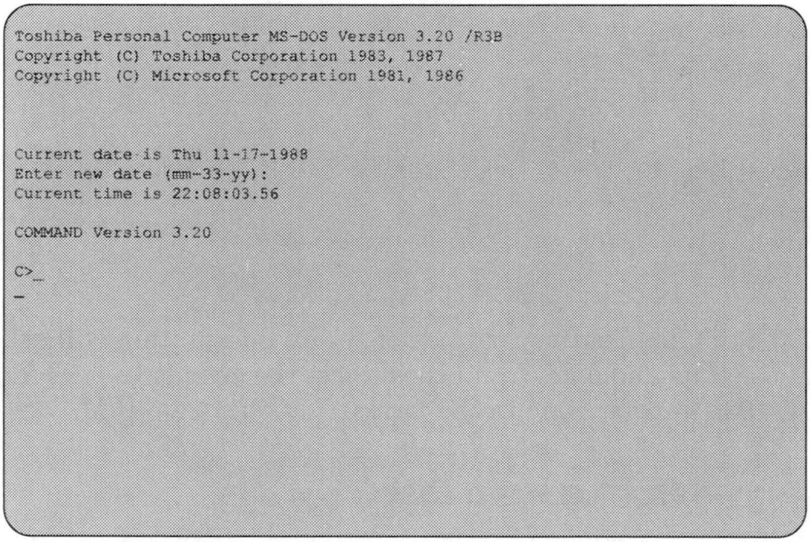

```
Toshiba Personal Computer MS-DOS Version 3.20 /R3B
Copyright (C) Toshiba Corporation 1983, 1987
Copyright (C) Microsoft Corporation 1981, 1986


Current date is Thu 11-17-1988
Enter new date (mm-33-yy):
Current time is 22:08:03.56

COMMAND Version 3.20

C>_
_
```

Figure 2-2.
Booting the system from a hard disk.

5. Systems that don't have battery storage of set up information will ask you to input the time and date. Input the date in the format 12-4-90 for December 4, 1990 and the time in the format 14:05 for 2:05 P.M.

The Keyboard

Basic Keyboard Structure

Let us examine the PC keyboard (see Figure 2-3). This keyboard looks complex, but can be understood if we examine it a section at a time. Let's begin with the central section (see Figure 2-4).

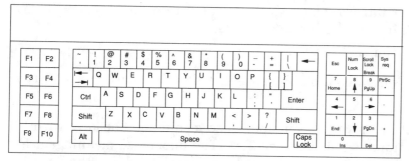

Figure 2-3.
**The IBM
personal
computer
keyboard.**

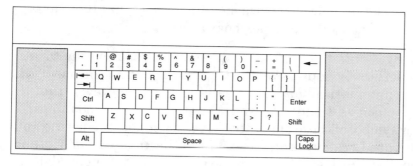

Figure 2-4.
**The central
section of the
keyboard.**

The central section is very much like a typewriter keyboard. There are a few symbols that are not present on a typewriter, such as:

<
>
^
~
[
]
\
{
}

Also, you should note the following important differences from a typewriter keyboard:

1. There are separate keys for 1 (one) and l (el). (Many typewriters use the lowercase l to do double duty as a one.)

2. The number 0 (zero) has a slash through it on screen (0). This is to distinguish it from the capital letter O.

Here are the functions of the other keys in the central portion of the keyboard:

Space bar. Generates a blank space just like the space bar on a typewriter.

Shift key. Shifts keys to their uppercase meanings. For keys with two symbols, the upper symbol takes effect. The uppercase meanings are in effect only as long as the Shift key is held down. Releasing the Shift key causes keys to assume their lowercase meanings. Note that there are two Shift keys, one on each side of the keyboard.

Caps Lock key. Locks the Shift key into all capitals. You may turn off the lowercase letters by depressing the Caps Lock key. In this mode, the letter keys are automatically typed as capitals. Note, however, that the nonletter keys (such as 1 and ! or , and .) or still have two meanings. To type the upper symbol of these non-letter keys, you must still use the Shift key when the Caps Lock key is on. To exit from the uppercase mode, once again depress the Caps Lock key. With the Caps Lock key engaged, if you press the Shift key and a letter key, a lowercase letter is displayed.

Backspace key. Moves the cursor back one space. Erases any letter it backs over.

Enter key. Similar to a carriage return key on a typewriter. Used to end a line and to place the cursor at the beginning of the next line. A line may be corrected with backspaces until the ENTER key is pressed.

Tab key. Works like the tab key on a typewriter. Moves the cursor to the next tab stop.

Ctrl (Control) key. Used in combination with other keys. For example, the key combination Ctrl-A means to simultaneously press Ctrl and A. Such combinations are used to generate control codes for the screen and printer.

Esc (Escape key). Used to indicate that certain sequences of letters are to be interpreted as control codes.

Alt (Alternate) key. Used in combination with other keys in a manner similar to the Ctrl key.

PrtSc key. Use to print the screen. (See the discussion below.)

Turn on your PC and obtain the DOS prompt A> or C>. Strike a few keys to get the feel of the keyboard. Note that as you type, the corresponding characters will appear on the screen. Note also how the cursor travels along the typing line. It always sits at the location where the next typed character will appear.

As you type, you should notice the similarities between the IBM Personal Computer keyboard and that of a typewriter. However, you should also note the differences. At the end of a typewriter line, you return the carriage, either manually or, on an electric typewriter, with a carriage return key. Of course, your screen has no carriage to return. However, you still must tell the computer that you are ready to move on to the next line. This is accomplished by pressing the ENTER key. If you depress the ENTER key, the cursor then returns to the next line and positions itself at the extreme left side of the screen. The ENTER key also has another function. It signals the computer to accept the line just typed. Until you hit the ENTER key, you may add to the line, change portions, or even erase it. (We'll learn to do these editing procedures shortly.)

Keep typing until you are at the bottom of the screen. If you press ENTER, the entire contents of the screen will move up by one line; the line at the top of the screen will disappear to provide new blank space at the bottom of the screen. It is as if everything you type is being recorded on an enormous scroll. Indeed, this movement of lines on and off the screen is called **scrolling**.

As you may have already noticed, the computer will respond to some of your typed lines with error messages. Don't worry about these now. The computer has been taught to respond only to certain typed commands. If it encounters a command that it doesn't recognize, it announces this fact with an error message. It is extremely important for you to realize that these errors in no way harm the computer. In fact, there is little you can do to hurt your computer (except by means of physical abuse, of course). Don't be intimidated by the occasional slaps on the wrist handed out by your computer. Whatever happens, don't let these "slaps" stop you from experimenting. The worst that can happen is that you might have to turn your computer off and start all over!

System Reset

You may restart the computer from the keyboard by pressing the Ctrl, Alt, and Del keys simultaneously. This key sequence returns the computer to the state it was in just after being turned on. Both RAM and the screen will be erased. The process of starting the computer from the keyboard is called a **warm boot**. (A **cold boot** means restarting the computer with the main on/off power switch.)

Printing the Screen

The PC provides several features that allow you to print what appears on the screen. Obtain the DOS prompt A> and press the key combination Ctrl-PrtSc. (Also make sure your printer is turned on.) All subsequent text that appears on your screen will also be printed. This provides you with a written record of a session at the computer. To turn off the printing, press Ctrl-PrtSc again.

You may obtain a printed copy of just the current screen by pressing the key combination Shift-PrtSc. On many of the newest keyboards there is a separate Print Screen key that required no key combination.

Numeric Keypad

Let us now turn our attention to the right side of the keyboard. Note that each of the digits 0–9 appears twice: once in the usual place at the top of the keyboard and a second time at the right-hand side (see Figure 2-5). The numeric keys on the right side are arranged like the keys of a calculator and are designed to make typing numbers easier. It makes no difference which set of numerical keys you use. In fact, you may alternate them in any manner, entering a 1 from the top set, then a 5 from the right set, and so forth. The right set of keys is called the **numeric keypad.**

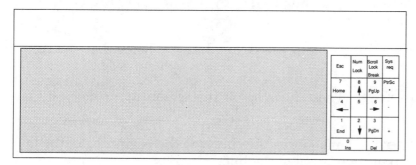

Figure 2-5.
The numeric keypad.

Actually, the keys of the numeric keypad do double duty. They are also used in BASIC as cursor movement key for editing (or altering) text that has already been typed). For now just remember that the Num Lock key controls which function the keys of the numeric keypad assume. When the Num Lock key is engaged (or when a keypad key is pressed in combination with the Shift key), the numeric keypad functions like a calculator keyboard. With the Num Lock key disengaged, the numeric keypad is used for editing. When the computer is first turned on, the keypad is set for editing. So for your first use of the numeric keypad, it will be necessary to disengage the Num Lock key.

The keys of numeric keypad do double duty. With the Num Lock key engaged, the keys may be used for various editing functions. Actually, the meanings of these keys can vary with the program. However, here are the most common uses for them:

Cursor Motion Keys. These four arrow keys are used to move the cursor in the indicated directions on the screen. Note that these keys move the cursor in BASIC and in most applications programs. However, at the DOS prompt, they don't have any function.

Insert Key. When this key is pressed, you may insert text at the current cursor position. As text is inserted, existing text is moved to the right to accommodate the new letters. The effect of the Ins key is cancelled either by pressing Ins again, by pressing Del, or by pressing ENTER, or by using the cursor motion keys.

Delete Key. When this key is pressed, one letter is deleted at the cursor position.

PgUp and PgDn Keys. These keys scroll the screen up or down by one screenful.

Home and End Keys. Home moves the cursor to the beginning of the line. End moves the cursor to the end of the line.

Function Keys. The function keys are the keys labelled F1, F2, ... These keys have functions that vary according to the program being run. As we shall see, these keys have certain predefined meanings within MS-BASIC. But even within that program they may be redefined. We will discuss these facts later.

Alternate Keyboards

We have discussed the structure of the original IBM PC keyboard. There are a number of variations of this keyboard that have appeared in recent years. Some keyboards have 12 function keys rather than 10. And some have separate keys for the doubled-up functions of the numeric keypad. That is, these keyboards have separate cursor motion keys and separate Home, End, PgUp, PgDn, Ins, and Del keys. Moreover, the positions of some keys, such as Ctrl, Esc, and ~ vary with different keyboard models. However, the fundamental purpose and operation of the keyboard remains the same despite various possible configurations.

Part Two

An Introduction to
MS-DOS

Three

Manipulating Files

The Disk Operating System (DOS) intrudes into every aspect of PC use. It is no exaggeration to say that every time you sit down at your computer, you are using DOS. In this chapter, you will learn to use some of the most essential aspects of DOS. In particular, we learn about:

- Files and file-naming rules.

- The directory of a diskette or hard disk.

- Device names and file specifications.

- Executing commands and programs from DOS.

Files and Filenames

The contents of a diskette are broken into units called **files.** For our present purposes, think of a file as a collection of characters. For example, the characters comprising Chapter 3 of this book, when stored on a diskette, might comprise one file. (In fact, as this book was being written, the chapters were stored on a hard disk in exactly that way.)

A diskette may contain many files. (The maximum number depends on which version of DOS you are using, as well as on the type of drives your computer has.) However, diskette files may be classified into two broad categories: **programs** and **data files**.

Programs. A program is a sequence of computer instructions. Throughout this book, we will be discussing programs of one sort or another—programs to compute loan interest, to play tic-tac-toe, and to print form letters, to mention but a few.

Data files. A data file contains data, such as payroll information, personnel data, recipes, train and airline schedules, appointment calendars, and so forth. Programs often make use of data files. This is done by including instructions within the program for reading (or writing) particular data files. In this way you may, for example, look up appointments and let the computer make decisions based on data in the file.

Filenames

Each file is identified by a filename. Here are some examples of valid filenames:

```
BASIC.COM
FORMAT.COM
PAYROLL
GAME.001
```

A filename consists of two parts—the main filename (BASIC, FORMAT, PAYROLL, GAME) and an optional extension (COM, no extension, 001). The main filename may contain as many as eight characters, the extension as many as three. The two parts of the filename are separated by a period.

The following characters are allowed in a filename:

The letters A–Z

The digits 0–9

Any of these characters:

    ! @ # $ % & ( ) - _ { } ' `

Note that a filename cannot include any of the following characters; they are reserved because they have special meanings for DOS:

    | \ < > , / ? " ~ : + = * ^

The only period allowed in a filename is the one separating the two parts of the filename. Moreover, a filename cannot contain any spaces.

A filename may be spelled with either upper- or lowercase letters. However, DOS will convert the filename into uppercase. For example, the filenames:

          JOHN   John

refer to the same file.

Test Your Understanding 1 (Answer on Page 41)

What is wrong with the following filenames?

    ALICE 01
    #2324/1
    alphabetical

A particular diskette can have only one file with a particular name. However, there is nothing to stop you from using the same filename to refer to different files on different diskettes, although this is not a very good idea because you (not the computer) may get confused about where a particular file is located.

When you name a file, choose a name that somehow suggests the contents. For example, if you generate a monthly payroll file, you may name the various monthly files:

    PAYROLL.JAN, PAYROLL.FEB, PAYROLL.MAR, . . .

and so forth.

Wild Cards

The wildcard characters * and ? in a filename have a special meaning for DOS.

The character * may be used as a substitute for any number of characters in this the main filename or the extension. This is useful for finding files whose exact names you do not recall, or for dealing with groups of files at a time. For example, consider this filename:

```
*.COM
```

This filename stands for any file with the extension COM. Similarly, the filename:

```
WS.*
```

stands for any file with the main name WS. The filename:

```
WSP*.*
```

stands for files beginning with the letters WSP.

Finally, the filename:

```
*.*
```

stands for any file.

Such "ambiguous" filenames can shorten various DOS commands. For example, we may copy a file from one diskette to another using the COPY command (see the section on Elementary DOS commands in Chapter 4). To copy all files from the diskette in drive A: to the diskette in drive B:, use the simple command

```
COPY A:*.* B: <ENTER>
```

Similarly, to copy all files on the diskette in drive A: with a COM extension onto the diskette in drive B:, use the command

```
COPY A:*.COM B: <ENTER>
```

The character ? in a filename allows a single character to be ambiguous. For example, consider this filename:

```
EXAMPLE.00?
```

The third letter in the extension may be anything. Similarly, consider this filename:

```
N??.000
```

The main filename has three letters, begins with N, and the last two letters of the main filename may be anything.

Exercises

Which of the following filenames are valid? If invalid, tell why.

1. `SALLY.001`

2. `EXAMPLE.TXT`

3. `E>`

4. `S:001`

5. `#$%&{}`

6. `A.B.C`

7. `ACCOUNT.0123`

8. `DEMONSTRATION.823`

Answer to Test Your Understanding 1

1. Illegal space
   Illegal character (/)
   Too many characters

Paths, Directories, and Subdirectories

Once you begin to apply your computer to handle everyday applications, your files will begin to proliferate. Within a short period of time, you will acumulate hundreds, perhaps even thousands, of files. As you might imagine, organizing such a large number of files can be a great problem. Without any organization scheme, imagine searching for the file containing the report you just completed? To combat this problem, DOS allows you to organize your files into directories like file folders, which in turn are organized into a "tree structure."

Consider a disk, either a diskette or a hard disk. To distinguish it from other disks, you may decide to give the disk a name, its **volume name**. (Up to 11 characters are allowed in the volume name; we'll show you how to do this in the next chapter.) For instance, you might name your hard disk C: with your name (first or last; it doesn't matter). As we shall see in the next chapter, when you perform backups, they will be labeled with the volume name. By using your name for the volume name, your backup is then automatically distinguished from other backups. In our programming shop we use more exotic volume names, such as SPEEDY and NIGHT_RIDER.

A volume can contain files and directories. A directory, in turn, can contain files and other directories or subdirectories. And so on. Figure 3-1 shows a diagram of part of my hard disk C:. The main directory of C: is shown at the left. This directory is called the **root directory**. It contains a number of files (not shown) and a number of subdirectories (listed in the second column). For example, the root directory contains the subdirectories DOS and MANSCRPT. I use the subdirectory DOS for storing various MS-DOS utility programs and other system utilities. Rather than lumping all of these into one place, I have partitioned the DOS directory into a number of subdirectories, shown in the third column. Among these subdirectories are ARCHIVE, NORTON, and SIDEKICK.

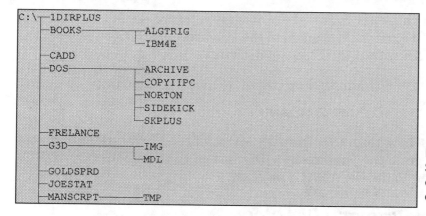

Figure 3-1.
**Subdirectory
organization of
a hard disk.**

It often helps to visualize the directory structure of a disk as a tree. The root directory is at the bottom and represents the main trunk. The files in the main directory are leaves growing from the main trunk. The subdirectories are branches growing from the main trunk. Their leaves are the files they contain. Their subdirectories are the branches growing out from them, and so forth. The analogy of a directory structure to a tree is the reason for saying MS-DOS directories are arranged in a **tree structure**.

Directories are named using the same rules as for file names. A directory name may consist of a main part and an extension, separated by a period. The main name can contain eight or fewer characters, the extension is optional, and so forth.

The location of a file or subdirectory within a directory structure is described using a **path**. For instance, the file BASICA.EXE contained in the directory DOS of Figure 3-1 is described by the path:

```
C:\DOS\BASICA.EXE
```

Note that the path describes how to get to the file starting at the root. The symbol \ is called a backslash. An initial \ before a full path name refers to the root directory. Further backslashes separate each subdirectory down the tree. For instance, the combination of symbols C:\ indicates the root directory of C:. Be careful not to confuse the backslash character with the ordinary slash character /. The above path is interpreted as follows: Start from the root directory C:\; then go to the subdirectory DOS; then go to the file BASICA.EXE within the DOS subdirectory.

Paths may be of any length. For instance, consider the path:

```
C:\DOS\OPTIMIZE\ANALYZE.EXE
```

This describes how to get to the file ANALYZE.EXE: Start at the root directory C:\, go to the subdirectory DOS, then to its subdirectory OPTI-MIZE, and then to the file ANALYZE.EXE.

The Current Drive and Directory

At any given moment, MS-DOS considers one drive to be the **current drive**. This is the drive that MS-DOS looks to for commands and data files (unless you explicitly specify another drive). When the system is first started, the current drive is the one you used to boot the system, either A: or C:.

At any given moment, each disk drive has a directory designated as the **current directory.** Unless you specify a file using a complete path, DOS assumes that the file is located in the current directory. For instance, suppose that a command refers to the file ANALYZE.EXE. If the current directory is C:\DOS\OPTIMIZE, the DOS assumes that you are referring to the file C:\DOS\OPTIMIZE\ANALYZE.EXE.

When DOS is started, the current directory is the root directory for each drive.

Changing the Current Drive and Directory

To change the current drive, just type the drive name and press ENTER. For example, to change the current drive to B:, type:

```
B: <ENTER>
```

The current drive then is B: until you explicitly change it.

You may change the current directory using the command CHDIR or its abbreviated version CD. For instance, to make C:\DOS the current directory, use either of the commands:

```
CHDIR C:\DOS <ENTER>
CD C:\DOS <ENTER>
```

You may abbreviate paths used in commands by taking into account the current directory. For example, suppose that the current directory is C:\DOS and you wish to change the directory to C:\DOS\OPTIMIZE. You may do this by using the command:

```
CD OPTIMIZE <ENTER>
```

This command tells DOS to look for the subdirectory OPTIMIZE of the current directory. (Remember not to include an initial backslash unless you are referring to a directory located in the root.)

The symbol .. may be used in a path to indicate a move one level up the tree, from a subdirectory to its "parent directory." For example, suppose that the current directory is C:\DOS\OPTIMIZE. Then the command

```
cd ..
```

will bring you to the directory C:\DOS. Similarly, if the current directory is the subdirectory C:\DOS\OPTIMIZE, then the command

```
cd ..\..
```

will move you two steps up the tree to the root directory. As yet another example, suppose that we wish to get to the subdirectory C:\MANSCRPT from the subdirectory C:\DOS\OPTIMIZE. We must go down to the root directory and up to MANSCRPT. We would type:

```
cd \MANSCRPT
```

NOTE: MS-DOS limits path lengths to 63 characters.

Keeping Track of the Current Directory

It is possible to create incredibly complicated directory structures. DOS provides a very useful way for you to keep track of the current directory, so you always know where you are. When the DOS prompt is displayed, give the command:

```
PROMPT $P$G <ENTER>
```

From here on, the DOS prompt will be replaced by a path indicating the current directory. For example, Figure 3-2 shows the DOS prompt that is displayed when the current directory is C:\DOS\OPTIMIZE (first line). Then a command is given to change this directory to C:\DOS. Note how the DOS prompt changes.

```
C:\DOS\OPTIMIZE>_
```

Figure 3-2.
Displaying the current directory as part of the DOS prompt.

Creating Subdirectories

You may create subdirectories using the DOS command MKDIR or its abbreviation MD. For example, to create the subdirectory UTILS in the existing directory C:\DOS, use either of the commands:

```
MKDIR C:\DOS\UTILS <ENTER>
MD C:\DOS\UTILS <ENTER>
```

If the current directory is C:\DOS, these commands may be abbreviated to:

```
MKDIR UTILS <ENTER>
MD UTILS <ENTER>
```

Removing Subdirectories

You may remove subdirectories using the DOS command RMDIR or its abbreviation RD. As a precaution, DOS will not allow you to remove a subdirectory that has files in it. To remove a subdirectory, you must first erase all the files in it and then give the RMDIR command. (See the discussion of the ERASE command in the next chapter for erasing files.) For example, to remove the subdirectory C:\DOS\UTILS, use either of the commands:

```
RMDIR C:\DOS\UTILS <ENTER>
RD C:\DOS\UTILS <ENTER>
```

If the current directory is C:\DOS, these commands may be abbreviated to:

```
RMDIR UTILS <ENTER>
RD UTILS <ENTER>
```

Executing Commands and Programs

MS-DOS comes equipped with several dozen commands that you can execute. In addition, you will be using your computer to run an assortment of programs that perform applications ranging from spreadsheets to graphics and word processing.

A file containing either a program to run or a command to be executed has a file name with one of the extensions COM or EXE. Some examples of such file names are:

```
FORMAT.COM
BASICA.EXE
WP.EXE
```

To run a program or execute a command:

1. Obtain the MS-DOS prompt.
2. Type the file name without the extension.
3. Press the ENTER key.
4. MS-DOS will execute the command or run the program. When done, MS-DOS will redisplay the DOS prompt.

For example, to execute the MS-DOS command FORMAT, contained in the file FORMAT.COM, you would type from the DOS prompt as follows:

```
FORMAT <ENTER>
```

As far as MS-DOS is concerned, MS-BASIC is just another program to execute. MS-BASIC is contained in the file BASICA.EXE. To start this program, from the DOS prompt type:

```
BASICA <ENTER>
```

MS-DOS, unless otherwise instructed, will look for the command or program in the current directory of the current drive. You may force DOS to look at another drive by preceding the command name with the drive name. For instance, the command:

```
B:BASICA <ENTER>
```

will look for the program BASICA.EXE on the current directory of drive B:. Note that if the program is in a directory other than the current one of drive B:, then DOS will not be able to locate it. Whenever DOS is unable to locate a program or command file you specify, it displays the error message:

```
Bad Command or File Name
```

DOS then redisplays the DOS prompt to allow you to correct the error by correctly specifying the location of the file. Typically, this involves changing the current directory on the drive containing the file, changing the current directory, or changing the drive name in the command.

Interrupting Commands or Programs

Sometimes you will want to interrupt a program or a DOS command before it is done. In general, this may be done by pressing the key combination Ctrl-Break. To make such a key combination, first press down Ctrl, hold it down and then press Break. This will interrupt the current program and return you to the DOS prompt. There is a catch, however. Ctrl-Break is recognized only when the program or command allows recognition of keystrokes. This is generally true when the program is doing input or output operations, say to the printer or screen. However, some programs do input/output-free operations for long periods of time and are uninterruptible during those periods. The only way to stop a program during such a period is by pressing the key combination Ctrl-Alt-Del to reboot the system.

Four

Topics in MS-DOS

Introduction

In the preceding chapter, we learned to boot the computer and thus start the operating system MS-DOS. Moreover, we learned about file names and the directory structure of a disk. Finally, we learned how to give commands and run programs. In this chapter, we apply what we learned and provide an elementary introduction to MS-DOS.

Elementary DOS Commands

MS-DOS provides commands for performing various functions. These commands are classified into **internal commands** and **external commands**. Internal commands (like the frequently used copy, delete or chdir commands) are always resident in RAM. External commands (like the format or diskcompare commands) first must read in the relevant program into RAM from diskette or hard disk. When external commands are issued, MS-DOS has to look for the appropriate program in either the current directory of the current drive or in the directory specified by previous execution of a PATH command. It then loads the command program into RAM and executes it. When external commands are completed, they are removed from RAM, opening up memory space for other programs or commands. If MS-DOS does not find the program for an external command, it displays the error message:

```
Bad Command or File Name
```

It then redisplays the MS-DOS prompt.

Let's begin by discussing the commands that you will certainly need as soon as you begin to use your computer.

The FORMAT Command

The external command FORMAT allows you to format a disk (hard disk or diskette). Every diskette must be prepared to receive data, or formatted, before it can be used. A hard disk needs to be formatted only once, when you first configure and set up your computer.

The simplest form of this command is:

```
FORMAT <drive name>
```

Here *drive name* is the name of the drive containing the disk to be formatted. Thus, for example, to format a diskette in drive A:, you would give the command:

```
FORMAT A: <ENTER>
```

In response, MS-DOS gives you an opportunity to insert the diskette into drive A:. When you have done so, press ENTER. The disk will then be formatted. This can take as long as several minutes for a diskette and up to an hour or more for a hard disk. When the formatting is complete, MS-DOS asks whether you wish to format another disk (the same drive is assumed).

If so, type Y; otherwise type N. In the former case, you will be directed to insert another diskette and the process of formatting is repeated. The FORMAT command is set up so that you may format any number of diskettes in sequence without giving the command again.

As each disk is formatted, MS-DOS displays a message indicating the number of bytes on the formatted disk, the number of bytes in bad sectors (these bytes can't be used for normal DOS operation and are hidden from subsequent access), and the number of bytes that may be used for programs and data. The number of bytes on the disk will vary with the type of disk drive.

Note that formatting a disk, for all practical purposes, erases its contents. Once formatting has begun, there is no easy way to recover the contents of the disk. Because erasure of a hard disk could lead to a loss of so much data, MS-DOS asks if you are sure you wish to proceed if you give a command to format a hard disk. Unless you know what you are doing, always answer no to this query!

As part of the formatting, you may make the diskette or hard disk a boot disk by using /S at the end of the command line. This causes the necessary MS DOS files for boot-up to be copied onto the disk after formatting is complete. For example to format a diskette in drive A: and then make it a boot diskette, use the command:

```
FORMAT A: /S <ENTER>
```

To format the hard disk C: and to copy the boot files onto it, use the command:

```
FORMAT C: /S <ENTER>
```

WARNING: If you are using DOS Version 2, the command:

```
FORMAT <ENTER>
```

will result in formatting the current drive, possibly C:. That is, the command can result in reformatting your hard disk. Later versions of MS-DOS built in safeguards which ask if you really wish to do that.

The DIR Command

The internal command DIR allows you to display the contents of a directory. The form of this command is:

> **DIR <*Directory*>** <ENTER>

Here <*Directory*> is a description of the directory is to be displayed. Here are some examples of the DIR command:

> **DIR C:\DOS <ENTER>**
> **DIR LETTERS**
> **DIR A:**
> **DIR**

The first command displays the contents of the directory C:\DOS. The second displays the contents of the directory LETTERS of the current directory of the current drive. The third command displays the directory of the current directory of the diskette in drive A:. The fourth command displays the contents of the current directory of the current drive. Figure 4-1 shows the display created by a typical DIR command.

```
 Volume in drive C:  has no label
 Directory of  C:\DOS

 .               <DIR>        4-21-88   11:22a
 ..              <DIR>        4-21-88   11:22a
 NORTON          <DIR>        4-21-88    2:32p
 ARCHIVE         <DIR>        4-21-88    2:34p
 SIDEKICK        <DIR>        4-21-88    2:37p
 OPTIMIZE        <DIR>        4-21-88    2:48p
 SKPLUS          <DIR>        5-25-88    8:53p
 APPEND    COM       1725     5-18-87    8:00a
 CHKDSK    EXE      10272     5-18-87    8:00a
 FORMAT    EXE      14567     7-10-87    8:00a
 GFTABLE   COM       3243     5-18-87    8:00a
 GRAPHICS  EXE      19456     9-25-87    8:00a
 JOIN      EXE       8942     5-18-87    8:00a
 LABEL     EXE       3646     5-18-87    8:00a
 MODE      COM       2377     5-18-87    8:00a
 MORE      \COM       282     5-18-87    8:00a
 PRINT     EXE      11840     5-18-87    8:00a
 BASICA    EXE      66464     4-22-85   12:00p
 MSDOS           <DIR>       11-17-88   11:53p
       19 File(s)  26306560 bytes free

 C:\DOS>_
```

Figure 4-1.
The display generated by a DIR command.

Note that subdirectories are indicated by the notation <DIR>. Files lack this notation. Instead, the entry for a file contains the number of bytes in the file, and the date and time the file was last altered.

Note that some directories contain so many entries (subdirectories and files) that they cannot all be displayed on the screen at one time. You can create abbreviated directory displays by asking only for particular files. For example, a command of the form that uses the DOS wild card character (*):

    DIR *.EXE

displays all files in the current directory of the current drive that have the extension EXE. Figure 4-2 shows the result of such a command.

```
C:\DOS>dir *.exe

 Volume in drive C:  has no label
 Directory of  C:\DOS

CHKDSK   EXE     10272   5-18-87    8:00a
FORMAT   EXE     14567   7-10-87    8:00a
GRAPHICS EXE     19456   9-25-87    8:00a
JOIN     EXE      8942   5-18-87    8:00a
LABEL    EXE      3646   5-18-87    8:00a
PRINT    EXE     11840   5-18-87    8:00a
BASICA   EXE     66464   4-22-85   12:00p
         7 File(s)   26302464 bytes free

C:\DOS>_
```

Figure 4-2.
The display generated by a DIR *.EXE command.

You can create a multiple-column directory display containing abbreviated entries by using the parameter /W (wide display) at the end of the DIR command, as in:

    DIR C: /W

This command creates a display of the type shown in Figure 4-3.

```
C:\DOS>dir /w

 Volume in drive C:  has no label
 Directory of  C:\DOS

 .                    ..                NORTON           ARCHIVE          SIDEKICK
OPTIMIZE             SKPLUS             FIG0401  SCT     FIG0402  SCT     APPEND   COM
CHKDSK    EXE        FORMAT   EXE       GFTABLE  COM     GRAPHICS EXE     JOIN     EXE
LABEL     EXE        MODE     COM       MORE     COM     PRINT    EXE     BASICA   EXE
MSDOS
        21 File(s)   26298368 bytes free

C:\DOS>_
```

Figure 4-3.
**A wide directory
display**.

A disadvantage of the /W form of the DIR command is that it does not display the sizes of files or date and time information. Another variant of the DIR command that does not suffer from this defect is the command:

        DIR /P

This command displays a screenful of directory data and asks you to press any key to continue. In response to a keystroke, the command then displays the next screenful of directory data. In this way you can browse through all the information in all the entries in a directory.

The COPY Command

The internal command COPY allows you to copy a file from one place to another within the system. You can copy a file from one subdirectory to another and even copy from disk to disk. The form of this command is:

        COPY <SourceFile> <TargetFile>

The specifications for both *SourceFile* and *TargetFile* may include paths. If *TargetFile* is omitted, then *SourceFile* is copied to the current directory of the current drive, using the same file name as *SourceFile*. If *TargetFile* is a drive name, then *SourceFile* is copied to the current directory of the designated drive using the same file name as *SourceFile*. Here are some examples of the COPY command.

```
COPY A:FILEA B:FILEB <ENTER>
COPY C:\DOS\BASICA.EXE A: <ENTER>
COPY A:\COMMAND.COM C: <ENTER>
COPY FILEA FILEB <ENTER>
```

The first command copies FILEA on drive A: to FILEB on drive B. The second command copies the file BASICA.EXE in the subdirectory C:\DOS to the file BASICA.EXE on drive A:. The third command copies the file COMMAND.COM on drive A: to the file COMMAND.COM in the current directory of drive C:. The fourth command copies FILEA of the current directory of the current drive to FILEB of the current directory of the current drive.

The COPY command may be used with wild card characters. For example, the command:

```
COPY *.* A: <ENTER>
```

copies all files in the current directory of the current drive to drive A:. The command

```
COPY *.DOC C:\WORD\FILES <ENTER>
```

copies all files with an extension of DOC in the current directory of the current drive to the subdirectory C:\WORD\FILES.

The ERASE Command

The internal command ERASE is used to erase files. The form of the command is:

```
ERASE <File>
```

Here *<File>* is a specification of the file to be erased. Here are some examples of the ERASE command.

```
ERASE C:\DOS\FORMAT.COM <ENTER>
ERASE JAN.ACT <ENTER>
ERASE *.DOC <ENTER>
ERASE *.* <ENTER>
```

The first command erases the file FORMAT.COM in the directory C:\DOS. The second erases the file JAN.ACT in the current directory of the current drive. The third command erases all files with extension DOC in the current directory of the current drive. The fourth command erases all files in the current directory of the current drive.

Using wild cards in connection with the erase command is a powerful and dangerous feature. With a single command, you can erase a large number of files. For this reason, any ERASE command that specifies a file *.* causes MS-DOS to display a query:

```
Are you sure? (Y/N)
```

Don't answer this question Y automatically. Think before you erase! To exit from the command without erasing, type N.

The DISKCOPY Command

The external command DISKCOPY allows you to make a copy of a diskette. The form of this command is:

```
DISKCOPY <SourceDrive> <TargetDrive>
```

Here *<SourceDrive>* is the drive name for the original diskette and *<TargetDrive>* is the drive name for the copy diskette. For instance, the command:

```
DISKCOPY A: B: <ENTER>
```

copies the diskette in drive A: to the diskette in drive B:. After you give the command, you are prompted to insert the source and target diskettes.

Note that the two drives used must be of the same type. For instance, you can't copy a 3 1/2-inch diskette to a 5 1/4-inch diskette.

If you have only a single diskette drive, A:, then the above command causes the single drive to be regarded alternately as A: and B:. The program prompts you to swap diskettes in and out of the single drive.

If the target diskette is not formatted, then DISKCOPY will automatically perform the required formatting. However, in this case, the time for copying will be increased considerably.

You should use the DISKCOPY command to make copies of all your important diskettes. This should certainly include all original program diskettes, including the DOS diskettes you received with your system. You should also make copies of all diskettes containing your programs or data. It is all too simple to damage a diskette, thereby rendering it unreadable. If you have a spare copy of the diskette, no programs or data will be lost. (Note that certain program diskettes may be copy protected by their manufacturers and cannot be copied using DISKCOPY.)

The RENAME Command

The internal command RENAME allows you to rename a file. Its form is:

```
RENAME <File> <NewName>
```

For example, the command

```
RENAME C:\DOS\OPTIMIZE\ANALYZE.EXE X <ENTER>
```

renames the file ANALYZE.EXE in the subdirectory C:\DOS\OPTIMIZE with the new name X.

The MODE Command

MODE command is an external DOS command that performs a number of technical functions. Let's cite only the two that you are likely to require.

First, the MODE command allows you to set the parameters of the serial ports, which DOS calls COM1: and COM2:. A common setting required to connect a laser printer to serial port COM1: is given by the command:

```
MODE COM1:9600,n,8,1 <ENTER>
```

(Don't worry about what the numbers mean. The correct numbers for your printer will be specified in your printer installation information.)

A second application of the MODE command is to redirect the output from one of the parallel ports to one of the serial ports. (Unfortunately, the reverse is not possible.) Normally, printer output is directed to one of the parallel (printer) ports, which DOS called LPT1: and LPT2:. Some printers need to be connected to a serial port. To redirect output from LPT1: to COM1:, say, you may give the command:

```
MODE LPT1: = COM1: <ENTER>
```

For the remainder of the session, all output that programs direct to printer port LPT1: will be output the serial port COM1:.

The PATH Command

When you tell DOS to run a program, DOS will look for the program in the current directory of the current drive. You can direct DOS to look for the program in the current directory of another drive by preceding the program name with the drive name, as in:

```
A:BASICA
```

This command will run the program BASICA found in the current directory of the diskette in drive A:.

You can expand the region DOS will search for the program using the PATH command (internal). This command allows you to specify a sequence of paths to be searched for any program you attempt to run. For instance, suppose you give the command:

```
PATH = C:\DOS;C:\WORD;C:\123 <ENTER>
```

There are three paths specified in the PATH command, namely C:\DOS, C:\WORD, and C:\123. Note that the various paths are separated by semicolons. In attempting to run any subsequent program, DOS will search first the current directory of the current drive and then the paths specified in the PATH command, in the order they are listed. As soon as DOS finds a file with one of the extensions .COM, .EXE, or .BAT with the specified name, it will run it. For example, suppose that the current directory is the root directory of C:, namely C:\, and that you give the command:

WP <ENTER>

DOS will look for a file WP.COM, WP.EXE, or WP.BAT first in the current directory. Not finding such a file, it will then look in the directory C:\DOS. Not finding such a file there, it will then look in the directory C:\WORD. Assuming that WP.EXE is in that directory, DOS will then run the program.

By giving a PATH command at the beginning of a session (say, by using a batch command), you avoid worrying about specifying directories when running programs. DOS will find any program located in one of the specified directories.

Other DOS Commands

In this section we present a brief survey of some other MS-DOS commands.

DATE (internal) allows you to set the date. For example, to set the date to 4-12-83, use the command

DATE 4-12-83

TIME (internal) allows you to set the time. For example, to set the time to 1:04:00 P.M., use the command

TIME 13:04:00

TYPE (internal) allows you to display the contents of a text file (one that consists of ASCII characters). For example, to display the contents of the file A:TEST1, use the command

```
TYPE A:TEST1
```

If you try to display a program, it will usually look like a bunch of gibberish. Program files are designed for the convenience of the computer, not for humans. However, a text file will be displayed in readable form.

COMP (external) allows you to compare two files to determine whether they are identical. For example, suppose that we wish to compare FILE1 on the diskette in drive A: with FILE2 on the diskette in drive B:. Give the command

```
COMP A:FILE1 B:FILE2
```

This command may be used to check on the results of a COPY operation to determine whether the copy is identical to the original. Note that the COMP command does not give you a chance to change diskettes. Therefore, the diskettes with the files needed for comparison must be in the drives prior to giving the COMP command.

DISKCOMP (external) allows you to compare the contents of two diskettes, byte by byte. For example, to compare the diskettes in drives A: and B:, use the command

```
DISKCOMP A: B:
```

If your system has only one drive, you would also use this command for diskette comparison, even though you don't have a drive B:. DOS will prompt you to swap the diskettes in your single drive so that a comparison may be made.

CHKDSK (external) allows you to check the number of bytes remaining on a diskette. It also performs a check to determine if any inconsistencies exist in the way the files are stored. To perform a CHKDSK operation on the diskette in drive C:, use the command

```
CHKDSK C:
```

The result of this command is a display of the form shown in Figure 4-4.

```
C:\DOS>chkdsk c:

 42696704 bytes total disk space
    43008 bytes in 2 hidden files
    59392 bytes in 24 directories
 16300032 bytes in 702 user files
 26294272 bytes available on disk

   655360 bytes total memory
   477936 bytes free

C:\DOS>_
```

Figure 4-4.
Output of the CHKDSK command.

As usual, your numbers may vary, depending on your system, version of DOS, and so forth.

You should execute a CHKDSK every so often for each of your diskettes and hard disks, in order to assure the integrity of your files and to determine the space remaining on the diskette.

Batch Files

In the preceding sections, we learned about the most useful DOS commands. Most often, you will execute DOS commands by typing them directly from the keyboard, as described earlier in the chapter. In many applications, however, it is necessary to execute the same sequence of DOS commands repeatedly. For example, consider the following situation.

Suppose that you have a diskette containing four files named ACCOUNTS.MAY, PROFIT.MAY, PAYABLE.MAY, and SALES.MAY. Your business is computerized and every one of your ten managers has an

IBM PC. Rather than distribute the contents of the files via paper copies, in the traditional manner, you wish to send each manager a copy of the files on diskette.

A simple solution is to use DISKCOPY to make ten copies of the diskette containing the files. Suppose, however, that your diskette also contains some sensitive information that you do not wish to circulate. In this case, you may prepare the duplicate diskettes by copying the files one at a time. This may be done via the COPY command. Here are the DOS commands required to prepare one duplicate diskette, starting from an unformatted diskette:

```
FORMAT B:/S
COPY A:ACCOUNTS.MAY B:
COPY A:PROFIT.MAY B:
COPY A:PAYABLE.MAY B:
COPY A:SALES.MAY B:
```

Assume that your files are contained on the same diskette as FOR-MAT.COM and that this diskette is in drive A:. The duplicate diskette is in drive B:.

It is possible to prepare the ten duplicates by typing these commands in manually. But what a chore! And it is easy to make a mistake in typing, especially as the afternoon draws to a close. There is, fortunately, a much better way to proceed: using a batch file.

A batch file is a diskette file consisting of a list of DOS commands. A batch file must have a filename with the extension BAT. In our case, let's name the batch file C.BAT, and let's store it on the diskette in drive A:. In order to create the batch file, use the COPY command. Type

```
COPY CON A:C.BAT
```

and press ENTER. Now type in the DOS commands exactly as they appear in the above list. At the end of each line, press ENTER. After typing the last line and pressing ENTER, press function key F6 and then ENTER. DOS responds with the message

```
1 file(s) copied
```

The file C.BAT is now on the diskette in drive A:.

To execute the list of DOS commands, we now merely type the letter C and press ENTER. (It is just as if we created a new DOS command with the name C.) DOS then searches the current diskette (A:), finds the batch file, and executes the various commands, in the order specified.

Test Your Understanding 1 (Answer on Page 66)

Modify the above list of DOS commands so that they include a check that the copies of the files are identical to the originals.

Now our copying job is cut down to size:

1. Insert a blank diskette into drive B:.
2. Type C and press ENTER.
3. Wait for the commands to be executed.
4. Repeat operations 1–3 until all ten copies are made.

Parameters

Let's stick with our fictitious company. Suppose that the ten diskettes are to be prepared and sent every month. The filenames are always the same, but the month abbreviations, as given in the filename extensions, vary. You can prepare a new batch file C.BAT every month. However, there is a better way. Designate the month abbreviation by the symbol %1. (% is an abbreviation for parameter and 1 is the number of the parameter.) The commands of the batch file are then written:

```
FORMAT B:
COPY A:ACCOUNTS.%1 B:
COPY A:PROFIT.%1 B:
COPY A:PAYABLE.%1 B:
COPY A:SALES.%1 B:
```

For the month of MAY, give the batch command

```
C MAY
```

For the month of JUNE, give the batch command

```
C JUN
```

and so forth.

You may use up to nine parameters, %1, %2, ... ,%9. You specify the values of these parameters when you give the batch command, with consecutive parameter values separated by spaces. For example, if a batch file D uses the two parameters %1 and %2, then to execute the batch file with %1 = JAN and %2 = FEB, we use the command

```
D JAN FEB
```

Answer to Test Your Understanding 1

1. Add the DOS commands

```
COMP A:ACCOUNTS.MAY B:
COMP A:PROFIT.MAY B:
COMP A:PAYABLE.MAY B:
COMP A:SALES.MAY B:
```

The AUTOEXEC.BAT File

MS-DOS treats a batch file with the name AUTOEXEC.BAT in a special way, provided that the file is contained in the root directory of the boot disk. Such a batch file is automatically executed whenever DOS is started. For example, suppose that you want your PC to start BASIC automatically whenever DOS is started. Just create a diskette file called AUTOEXEC.BAT that includes the command:

```
BASICA
```

The AUTOEXEC.BAT file can contain any number of commands to initialize your system exactly as you find convenient. For example, your AUTOEXEC.BAT file may initialize a desktop manager program that gives you access to a calendar, notepad, and calculator to be used even while a program is running. Or the AUTOEXEC.BAT file may contain commands that set the screen width or directs output so that the printer is properly connected. And so forth. The AUTOEXEC.BAT file can save you from manually executing a large number of commands required on machine start-up.

Note that you may have only one AUTOEXEC.BAT file on a given diskette or hard disk. On the other hand, you may have many ordinary batch files (but these are not executed automatically).

Test Your Understanding 1 (Answer on Page 69)

Modify your DOS diskette so that BASIC is started whenever you start DOS.

The AUTOEXEC.BAT file may be used for some clever purposes. For example, let's return to our company with ten managers. Suppose that you wish to include a covering memo that reads:

```
TO: MANAGERS
HERE ARE THE STATEMENTS FOR MAY.
WE'LL MEET TO DISCUSS THEM ON 6/4
AT 5:30 pm.
JR
```

Here is how the message can be automatically displayed:

1. Create a file on your diskette that contains the text of the message. Call the file MSSG.
2. Create a file AUTOEXEC.BAT containing the DOS command
   ```
   TYPE MSSG
   ```

3. Modify the batch file C.BAT so that it copies MSSG and AUTOEXEC.BAT onto each of the 10 copies.

Each manager will start his or her PC using a duplicate diskette. The AUTOEXEC.BAT file will cause the file MSSG to be displayed on the screen.

Some Typical AUTOEXEC.BAT Commands

The AUTOEXEC.BAT file is designed to allow you to have the computer start up configured the way you would like it to be. Only you can determine what commands should be in your AUTOEXEC.BAT file. However, here are some suggestions.

1. Include a PROMPT pg command so that the DOS prompt will display the current directory. This is handy for telling you where you currently are in the system.

2. Include a PATH statement that states the paths to your most commonly used programs. This will allow you to run programs with the minimum of directory switching.

3. Include whatever MODE statements are required to set up serial ports and redirect output for your printer. By doing these operations at boot time, output to your printer may be obtained without any further set-up during the session.

4. Include commands to load any memory-resident utilities, such as calculators, notepads, outliners, calendars, etc. By including these in your AUTOEXEC.BAT file, the utility programs will be immediately available as soon as you complete booting up.

5. If you will be continually using a single program, say your word processor, you might want to include a command to run it as the last command in your AUTOEXEC.BAT file. In this way, the process of booting the system also starts the application program you will need.

The CONFIG.SYS File

The CONFIG.SYS file is the other file that is read by DOS automatically on system start-up (provided it is present). It allows you to tell DOS to recognize additional devices other than those specified by DOS device names. For example, to include a Microsoft mouse as a device in your system, it is necessary to include a line:

```
device = MOUSE.SYS
```

within the CONFIG.SYS file. Here MOUSE.SYS is the name of a file that tells DOS the characteristics of the mouse device and how to access it. This file is supplied when you purchase the mouse.

There are many different devices that can be added to the list of DOS devices using the CONFIG.SYS file, including mice, joysticks, light pens, additional (extended or expanded) memory, special-purpose monitors, and graphics boards. Once you set up the CONFIG.SYS file, you need do nothing further. Each time the system is started, the devices specified in CON-FIG.SYS are installed. Make sure, however, that the files referenced in CONFIG.SYS are contained on the disk you use to start the computer.

Answer to Test Your Understanding 1

1. Add the file AUTOEXEC.BAT consisting of the single DOS command

```
BASICA
```

More About DOS

In Chapters 3 and 4, we have given only a beginner's sketch of the features of DOS. There are many features that we haven't even mentioned. For example, the external DOS command, ASSIGN, allows you to redirect all input and output for one disk drive to another drive. There are other batch file commands that allow for elaborate decision-making in executing a batch file. And beginning in DOS Version 3.1, there is networking, which allows DOS to control a system consisting of multiple computers and assorted peripheral devices.

To go further into DOS takes us beyond the introductory level of this book. If you would like to learn more, however, there are several books you can go to:

- *Inside the IBM PC, 2nd edition* by Peter Norton, Brady Communications Company, Inc., 1984.

- *Beginner's Guide to MS-DOS* by Peter Norton, Brady Communications Company, Inc., 1983.

Part Three

An Introduction to BASICA Programming

Five

Getting Started in GWBASIC

Programming and GWBASIC

GWBASIC, the version of BASIC produced by Microsoft, Inc., is the "standard" BASIC language interpreter that is supplied with the MS-DOS operating system. It is a versatile, easy-to-use programming language that gives you access to the many features of the IBM PC and compatible computers and is, at the same time, an excellent environment for learning programming. In the remainder of this book (Chapters 5–21) I will provide you with an introduction to the modern science of programming, using GWBASIC as the programming language of instruction.

The BASIC Programming Language

BASIC is an acronym that stands for *Beginners All-purpose Symbolic Instruction Code.* As the name suggests, BASIC was designed as a language for beginners to programming. It was developed by John Kemeny and Kenneth Kurtz, two Dartmouth professors, in the mid 1960s as a computer language to teach college students the rudiments of programming.

The original version of BASIC ran on a large computer (a so-called main frame) that employed time sharing (a system in which many users simultaneously use the same computer, accessing its capabilities via terminals). Because it was easy to learn, BASIC rapidly became extremely popular as a language to write applications programs. It was especially popular with users in noncomputer fields who needed to write computer programs to solve their problems.

The growth in the popularity of BASIC and the personal computer revolution went hand in hand. When the first personal computers were developed in the late 1970s, versions of BASIC were supplied with them. Very quickly, BASIC became the programming language of choice for millions of personal computer enthusiasts.

Each personal computer had its own version of BASIC, tooled to take advantage of the particular features of the computer. The most popular of these versions of BASIC were Applesoft BASIC, designed to run on the Apple II family of computers and GWBASIC (also called BASICA), designed to run on IBM-compatible microcomputers using the MS-DOS operating system.

BASIC Versus Other Programming Languages

There are many programming languages available for any particular personal computer. The IBM-compatible family of computers is particularly blessed with a variety of computer languages, including assembly language, BASIC, Pascal, C, Modula 2, FORTRAN, and FORTH, to mention just a few. And each of these languages is available in a number of different dialects. This virtual babble of languages is hard for a beginner to understand. After all, why not cut through all the different languages and versions and standardize on one language that everyone can use? If only it were possible! But each programmer has his or her own favorite language. Moreover, each language or version of a language has features that make it attractive and most suitable for particular types of programming.

There are two essential features that make GWBASIC a popular language (aside from the fact that it comes free with most IBM compatibles):

1. GWBASIC allows you to write programs quickly and with a minimum of effort. (See below for an explanation of why this is so.)
2. GWBASIC supports all of the machine-specific features of IBM-compatible computers. This allows programs to easily incorporate graphics, sound, and file manipulation, for example.

However, the advantages of GWBASIC must be weighed against three serious disadvantages:

3. GWBASIC and most early versions of BASIC do not allow programs to be designed and implemented according to the dictates of modern programming methodology, so-called **structured programming**.
4. Running a GWBASIC program requires that the user possess a copy of the GWBASIC interpreter. In contrast, programs that have been produced using a compiler can be run stand-alone, without reference to the compiler used to create them.
5. Confusion often results when a user attempts to run a program under a version of BASIC that is different from the one under which the program was originally written. Similarly, attempting to run mismatched versions of GWBASIC and MS-DOS (say GWBASIC Version 3.00 and MS-DOS Version 2.00) sometimes leads to compatability problems.

Interpreters Versus Compilers

A computer language allows you to give instructions to the computer in a form that resembles English. Actually, the computer can execute only instructions in a numerical form that is not readily intelligible to humans. In order to execute a program written in a computer language (such as BASIC or Pascal), it is necessary to translate the instructions into the numerical form that the computer can understand directly. The numerical form of the instructions is called **machine language**. Various language versions use three common methods for accomplishing this translation: **interpretation**, **compilation to memory**, and **compilation to file**.

An interpreter translates computer language instructions into machine language, one instruction at a time, while the program is running. GWBASIC is an example of an interpreter.

With an interpreter, a user can stop the translation process in the middle, examine the values of variables, and restart the translation from any point within the program. This makes testing and debugging easy. However, the interpreter must be present in RAM in order to run the program.

Other programming environments compile instructions to memory. Here the compilation is accomplished by translating the entire program into machine language and storing just the machine language translation in RAM for running later. In such environments, the process of translation or compilation is separated from the process of running the program. But as with interpreters, running the program still requires the programming environment to be present.

Compile-to-memory systems, then, are of two types. In the first type, compilation is done as a separate process *after* the entire program has been entered in source code form. In the second, compilation takes place *as* each line of program source code is entered. The GWBASIC programming environment is of the second type.

The third method of program translation is to compile the program to a file. This method creates a stand-alone program that functions independently of the programming environment. GWBASIC has no option for doing this sort of program translation, although programs written in GWBASIC can be so translated using compilers such as QuickBASIC from Microsoft and Turbo BASIC from Borland International.

Interpreters like GWBASIC, usually run programs very slowly compared to the other two types of programming environments. Factors of 10 to 50 times slower, in fact. The convenient interaction between the programmer and the computer comes only at a price!

Spaghetti Code Versus Structured Code

An interpreter looks at a program one line at a time, usually without making any analysis of the program's structure. Because the interpreter does not impose any discipline as to program structure, it is easy for inexperienced programers to write structureless programs.

A program should be organized so that it is easily deciphered, even (especially) by someone other than its author. Programs written in most early versions of BASIC (including BASICA) were not like this. Instead, they sent the computer from place to place within the program so that if you put arrows on a printout to indicate the logical flow of the program, the paper would look like a plate of spaghetti (see Figure 5-1).

```
10 IF X>5 THEN 40 ELSE 60
20 PRINT "The value of X is "; X
30 END
40 X=X^2+5
50 GOTO 20
60 X=0
70 PRINT "X is too small."
80 GOTO 30
```

Figure 5-1.
Spaghetti code.

Compare the mess in Figure 5-1 with the code shown in Figure 5-2. Note that you can almost guess what the program does without knowing BASIC. Figure 5-2 illustrates structured code, which is written so that the program consists of a series of tasks executed in sequential order.

```
10 IF X>5 THEN 60
20 'Otherwise
30   X=0
40   PRINT "X is too small."
50   GOTO 90
60 'X>5 true
70   X=X^2+5
80   PRINT "The value of X is "; X
90 'End IF
100 END
```

Figure 5-2.
Structured code.

Because BASIC did not lend itself very well to writing structured code, many programmers shunned using it for "serious" programming. However, by working carefully and observing a rigid discipline, you may learn to write BASIC programs that are reasonably structured. Moreover, programs in GWBASIC can be compiled using one of the compilers *QuickBASIC* or *Turbo BASIC,* which support almost all of the features required by structured programming. So GWBASIC, far from being an obsolete language, can be used as a stepping stone in learning the modern discipline of programming.

The Goals of This Book

This part of the book has a number of distinct, but interrelated goals. First and foremost, it is designed as a tutorial on the GWBASIC computer language. In it, we don't assume any knowledge of computer programming and so we develop the details of GWBASIC from the most elementary level.

Many readers will be learning GWBASIC as a second computer language, typically after using BASICA or GWBASIC interpreters. For such readers, we have included an extensive array of "advanced" topics, including memory management, sorting, and graphics.

In learning computer programming, a certain core of essential knowledge pertains, independent of the language being taught. This core includes:

- An organized approach to program development

- Using top-down design methodology

- Using structured coding techniques

- An organized approach to debugging programs

In this book, we will discuss each of these topics. We present GWBASIC as a structured programming language and attempt to foster good programming habits. In accord with its mission as a tutorial, this book includes exercises, both in the form of Test Your Understanding questions within sections and End of Section questions. By considering these questions, you can use this book for a hands-on course in modern programming techniques, with the emphasis on the GWBASIC language.

The GWBASIC Environment

GWBASIC is a computer program itself. Within this program are a number of separate features that, together, comprise what we call the **GWBASIC environment.** This environment consists of the following components:

- A system for accepting commands from the user (in technical jargon, a **user interface**),

- An editor that allows you to enter programs into the computer,

- An interpreter that allows you to execute programs,

- A set of commands for manipulating programs (saving them on disk, recalling them, merging them, and so forth),

- A debugging system for locating errors in programs and tracing the progress of a program while it is running.

With all of these components incorporated into the system, you would think that GWBASIC is complicated to work. Actually, nothing could be further from the truth. In order to see how the system works, let's start up GWBASIC and do some experimentation.

Starting GWBASIC

To start GWBASIC, follow the set-up instruction in the GWBASIC manual to make backup copies of your distribution diskettes and, in case you have a hard disk, to copy the GWBASIC files onto it.

To start GWBASIC:

1. Turn the computer and obtain the DOS prompt.
2. Either insert the GWBASIC diskette in the current drive (in case of a floppy system) or chose as the current directory the one containing the GWBASIC program files. For instance, if these files are in the directory C:\GWBAS, use the command:

```
CD C:\GWBAS <ENTER>
```

3. Give the command:

```
BASICA <ENTER>
```

The GWBASIC Screen

In response to the above sequence of commands, GWBASIC will display the screen shown in Figure 5-3.

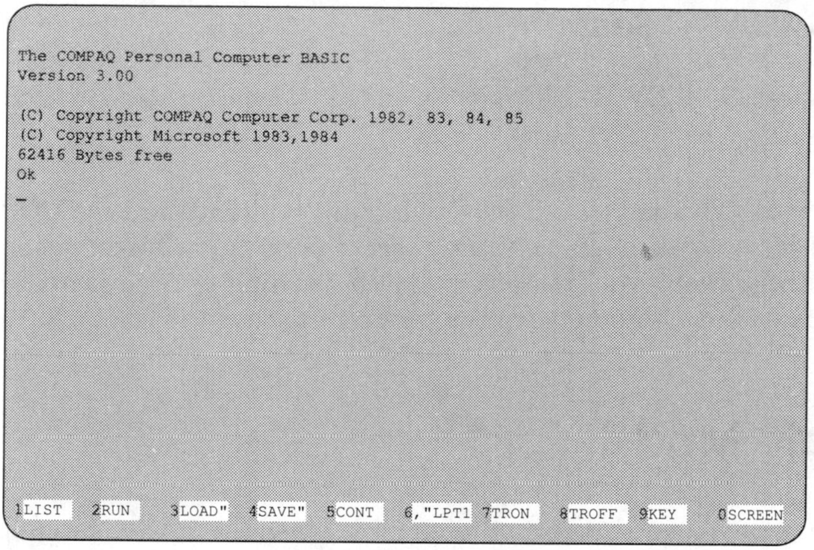

```
The COMPAQ Personal Computer BASIC
Version 3.00

(C) Copyright COMPAQ Computer Corp. 1982, 83, 84, 85
(C) Copyright Microsoft 1983,1984
62416 Bytes free
Ok
_
```

```
1LIST    2RUN    3LOAD"   4SAVE"   5CONT   6,"LPT1 7TRON   8TROFF  9KEY    0SCREEN
```

Figure 5-3.
**The initial
GWBASIC
screen**.

The first few lines give copyright information and the version of the program. The program then tells you the number of bytes free for your programs. This number will vary depending on your version of GWBASIC. The last line contains the **Ok**. This message is called the **BASIC prompt.** It indicates that GWBASIC is not currently performing a task and is ready to accept input from you. This input may consist of a command or the line of a program.

At the bottom of the screen is a list of the various function key assignments. The number 1 stands for function key F1, 2 for function key F2, and so forth. The function keys provide shortcuts for many of the most common commands you will be required to use.

The GWBASIC screen is a general-purpose scratch pad. You use it to enter commands and type in programs. GWBASIC also uses the screen to communicate information back to you, either the results of programs or error messages. One of the important things to learn is to control the screen so that its displays are exactly the way you want them. But more about that later.

Ending a GWBASIC Session

The current session of GWBASIC may be ended by typing the command

    SYSTEM

and pressing the ENTER key. GWBASIC will then terminate and the DOS prompt will be redisplayed. Note that the current program is erased when you end GWBASIC. Moreover, you are given no warning to first save the program. It's up to you to make sure the program is saved if you wish to refer to it later.

Immediate Mode

Assume that you have loaded BASIC and have obtained the BASIC prompt **Ok.** GWBASIC is now waiting for you to type something. You may type either a **program line** or a **command.** A program line always begins with a line number whereas a command does not. In both cases, you end a line by pressing the ENTER key. If you have typed in a command, GWBASIC will execute that command when you press ENTER. When BASIC is executing a command, it is said to be in immediate mode.

For example, type in the command

    PRINT 3+2

and press ENTER. The computer immediately fires back the answer:

    5
    Ok

The Ok prompt indicates that BASIC is awaiting another instruction. Type

    CLS

and press ENTER. The screen is erased and the cursor is positioned in the upper left corner (the so-called home position).

Now try some other BASIC instructions. Here is an interesting instruction to try if you have a monitor attached to a video adapter that supports graphics. Type

    SCREEN 1,0

and press ENTER. This instruction tells BASIC to enter medium-resolution graphics mode (SCREEN 1). The 0 portion of the command enables color. Next, set the background and text colors by typing the statement

    COLOR 1,2 <ENTER>

(From now on, we will write <ENTER> to mean "and press the ENTER key.") Notice that the screen turns blue and the Ok prompt is displayed in yellow. If you try this command and you don't have a video adapter that supports color (or at least shades of a single color), then BASICA will report an illegal command.

Test Your Understanding 1

Try this statement:

    COLOR 2,4 <ENTER>

What does it do?

Test Your Understanding 2

Try this statement:

    COLOR n <ENTER>

and replace n with 0,1,2,3,4,.... How many different background colors are possible?

BASIC is equipped with an incredible array of statements that perform a variety of tasks. As just a hint of things to come, try out a few graphics and music statements.

Type the statement

PLAY "CDEF" <ENTER>

The computer plays four notes. These notes are C, D, E, and F.

Here is another command to try on a system with a video adapter that supports graphs. Type the statement

SCREEN 2: CIRCLE (100,100),75 <ENTER>

BASIC will draw a circle as shown in Figure 5-4.

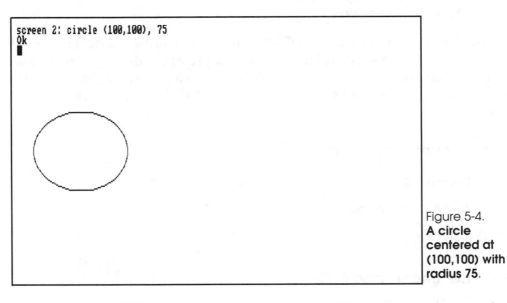

```
screen 2: circle (100,100), 75
Ok
```

Figure 5-4.
A circle centered at (100,100) with radius 75.

Actually, BASIC has an extensive repertoire of graphics statements that you will learn shortly.

The exercises below give you an opportunity to explore a few more of BASIC's instructions.

Exercises

Determine the effect of the following BASIC instructions.

1.   **LOCATE 3,4**

2.   `LOCATE 12,8`

3. Guess what the instruction `LOCATE x,y` does.

4.   `PRINT 3*6`

5.   `PRINT 2*9`

6. Guess what the instruction `PRINT X*Y` does.

7.   `PRINT 5 MOD 3`

8.   `PRINT 6 MOD 2`

9.   `PRINT 7 MOD 5`

10. Guess what the instruction `PRINT X MOD Y` does.

BASIC Programs

Entering A Program

Even though we have not yet discussed the details of programming in GWBASIC, let's develop a feel for the cycle of program creation, entry, running, saving, and reloading. Remember, a line of program code is preceded by a line number. Consider the following very simple program:

```
1 CLS
2 INPUT "What is your first name? ", FIRSTNAME$
3 PRINT "Hello "; FIRSTNAME$
4 PRINT "GWBASIC is a powerful programming language."
5 END
```

This program first clears the screen. Then it asks you for your first name and stores it in the variable FirstName$. Suppose, for example, that you responded that your first name was JOE. The program then prints out the message:

```
Hello JOE
GWBASIC is a powerful programming language.
```

To enter this program, start from the BASIC prompt Ok. Type in the program exactly as it appears above. Be sure to include all the punctuation marks and to include spaces as indicated. You may use the backspace or Del keys to erase characters. If a line is hopelessly messed up, just hit ENTER and retype the line. Examine your finished program by typing the command CLS and pressing ENTER. (This clears the screen.) Then type the command LIST and press ENTER. This causes your program to be displayed on the screen. Your screen should now look like the one shown in Figure 5-5.

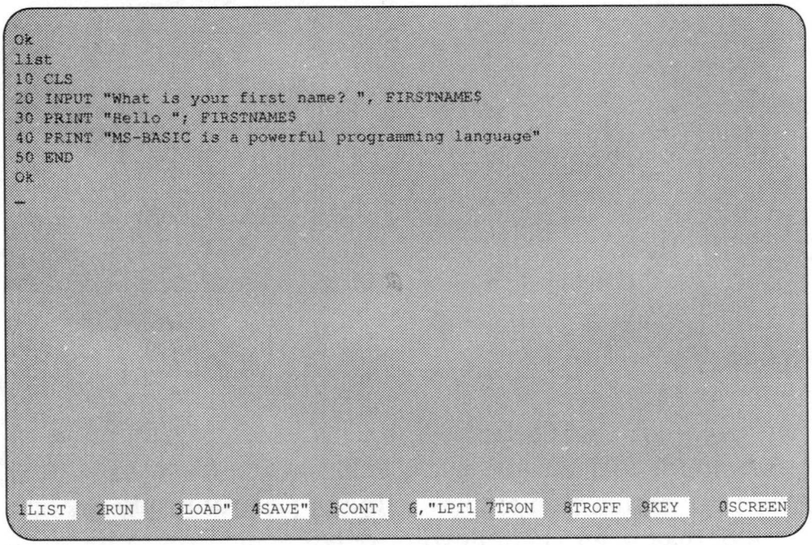

```
Ok
list
10 CLS
20 INPUT "What is your first name? ", FIRSTNAME$
30 PRINT "Hello "; FIRSTNAME$
40 PRINT "MS-BASIC is a powerful programming language"
50 END
Ok
_
```

```
1LIST   2RUN   3LOAD"   4SAVE"   5CONT   6,"LPT1 7TRON   8TROFF   9KEY   0SCREEN
```

Figure 5-5.
**Entering a
program**.

Running a Program

Once your program has been typed in, you may run it by typing the command RUN and pressing ENTER. Figure 5-6 shows the result.

Let's now see the effect of an error in the program. Display the program using the LIST command. Use the arrow keys to move the cursor to the U in INPUT on the second line of the program. Delete the U by pressing the Del key. The word INPUT is now misspelled, so that GWBASIC cannot understand it.

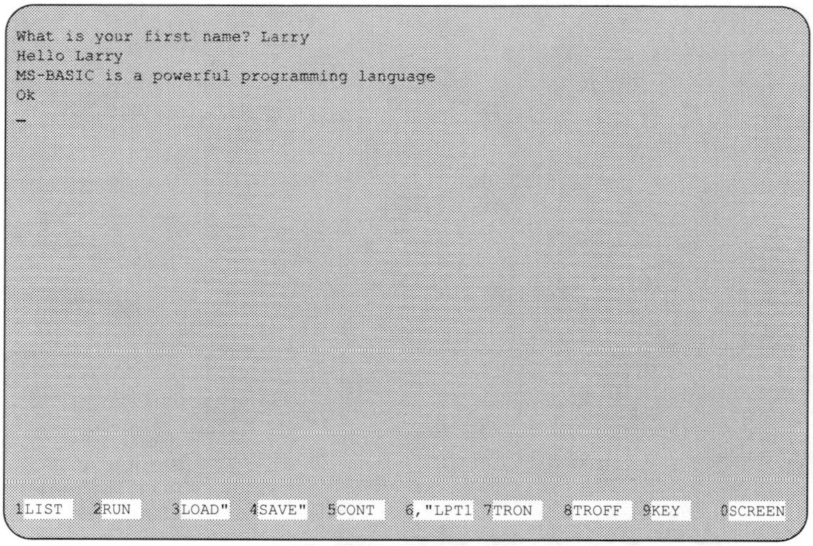

```
What is your first name? Larry
Hello Larry
MS-BASIC is a powerful programming language
Ok
_
```

```
1LIST   2RUN   3LOAD"  4SAVE"  5CONT  6,"LPT1 7TRON  8TROFF  9KEY   0SCREEN
```

Figure 5-6.
Running the Program.

Run the new version of the program by again giving the RUN command. Note the error message displayed (see Figure 5-7). Moreover, the Ok prompt indicates that GWBASIC is finished and is awaiting your command. However, none of the program dialogue was printed. This is because the program was terminated by the error, which occurred before any printing could occur. In addition, note that the line with the error has been displayed and the cursor positioned at the point where BASICA was unable to interpret.

Instead of typing RUN and pressing ENTER, you may just press function key F2.

We'll learn more about GWBASIC's error messages and how to interpret them later.

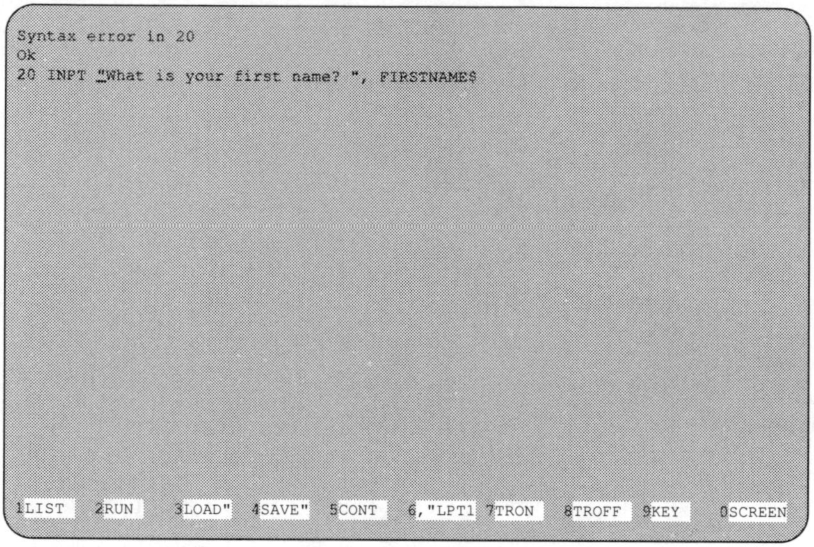

```
Syntax error in 20
Ok
20 INPT "What is your first name? ", FIRSTNAME$
```

| 1LIST | 2RUN | 3LOAD" | 4SAVE" | 5CONT | 6,"LPT1 | 7TRON | 8TROFF | 9KEY | 0SCREEN |

Figure 5-7.
Running a program with an error.

Saving a Program

You may save a program on diskette or hard disk using the SAVE command. The format of this command is:

        SAVE "*programname*"

Here *programname* is the name of the file in which the program will be saved. Any legal DOS file name is acceptable. For example to save the program currently in memory (the one with INPUT misspelled) under the name ERROR, we use the command:

        SAVE "ERROR"

Although we didn't specify an extension to the file name, GWBASIC will supply the default extension .BAS, so the program is saved in the file ERROR.BAS. You may override the default extension by specifying an extension of your own.

You may save some typing by using the function key F4 when saving. Pressing F4 displays SAVE ". All you need to do is fill in the file name and press ENTER. (The final quotation mark is optional.)

When you start GWBASIC, the current directory becomes the current directory of GWBASIC. This is the directory in which files are saved and from which files are recalled. Once in GWBASIC, you may change the current directory using a command of the form:

```
CHDIR "pathname"
```

For example, to change the current directory to C:\DOS, you would give the command:

```
CHDIR "C:\DOS"
```

After giving this command, a SAVE command (such as the one given above) would save the program in the file C:\DOS\ERROR.BAS.

Recalling a Program

You may recall a program from the current directory using the command:

```
LOAD "programname"
```

Here *programname* is the DOS file name under which the program has been saved. Note that if the extension of the file name is .BAS, then it may be omitted from *programname*. For example, to recall the program ERROR.BAS from the current directory, use the command:

```
LOAD "ERROR"
```

Note that RAM can contain only one program at a time. Loading a program erases the program that is currently in RAM. Once erased from RAM, there is no way to retrieve the program.

Function key F3 displays the letters LOAD ", which provides a shortcut in entering LOAD commands.

Starting a New Program

You may erase the program currently in RAM by typing the command NEW followed by pressing ENTER.

Turning Off the Function Key Display

You may turn off the function key display on the last line of the screen by giving the command:

```
KEY OFF <ENTER>
```

Even though the display is off, the function keys functions exactly as described in the function key display. To turn the function key display back on, use the command:

```
KEY ON <ENTER>
```

The GWBASIC Editor

The GWBASIC editor allows you to enter programs in RAM.

To enter a program into RAM, just type the program lines exactly as you see them. As you type, the corresponding characters are displayed on the edit screen. Terminate each program line by pressing ENTER. Don't worry if a program line extends beyond the screen. The GWBASIC editor allows lines to be up to 255 characters long. If you attempt to type any more, then the excess characters will be ignored. When we speak of a program line, we will refer to all characters typed prior to pressing ENTER. In some books, a program line is also called a **logical line**. By way of contrast, a line of text proceeding from left to right on the screen is called a **physical line**.

Correcting Errors

The GWBASIC editor provides a number of methods for correcting errors. For erasing a single character, you may use the backspace key or the Del (= Delete) key.

Pressing the backspace key moves the cursor to the left one space and erases the character in that space. Text to the right of the cursor moves to the left in order to fill the space occupied by the deleted character.

Pressing the Del key deletes the character at the cursor position. Text to the right of the cursor moves to the left to fill the space occupied by the deleted character.

You may replace a program line with another by retyping the line. GWBASIC automatically retains only the most recent version of each line.

You may delete a program line by typing its line number and pressing ENTER.

Moving the Cursor

Typed letters are always inserted at the current cursor position. You may move the cursor within the document using the arrow keys provided on the numeric keypad, usually on the right side of the keyboard. Using these keys, you may move the cursor up, down, right, and left a line or character at a time.

Note, however, that the keys of numeric keypad may be used for cursor movement only when the NumLock key is not engaged (the default state). If the cursor motion keys don't seem to be working, try pressing the NumLock key!

Inserting a Program Line

You may insert a program line anywhere within a program. Just type the line with a line number indicating its correct position within the program. GWBASIC automatically rearranges lines within RAM so that they are in numerical sequence. The order in which the lines are typed doesn't matter.

Overtype Mode Versus Insert Mode

There are two typing mode provided by the GWBASIC editor. In overtype mode, characters you type replace characters already typed. This is similar to typing on a typewriter. In insert mode, characters you type are inserted. Any text to the right of the cursor is moved over to make room for the characters you type.

The default mode is the insert mode.

You may switch between insert and overtype mode by pressing the Insert key.

For beginners, the insert mode may seem clumsy since it violates what may be your expectations from using a typewriter. However, after using it, you will become accustomed to insert mode, which is more useful than overtype mode for most work.

The LIST Command

In order to edit a program line, it is necessary for the line to be displayed on the screen. A display of program lines is called a **listing**. You may create listings using the LIST command. There are a number of variations of this command. The simplest is:

```
LIST <ENTER>
```

This command produces a listing of all program lines. This is fine for programs that fit on a single screen. However, for longer programs, you will want to list only program segments, say from lines 100 through 500. This may be accomplished with a command of the form:

```
LIST 100-500 <ENTER>
```

Similarly, the commands

```
LIST -200 <ENTER>
LIST 500- <ENTER>
```

respectively list the program lines with numbers less than or equal to 200 and greater than or equal to 500.

The AUTO Command

GWBASIC can generate program line numbers automatically for you. Just use the command:

```
AUTO <ENTER>
```

In response, GWBASIC will display a program line numbered 10, as shown in Figure 5-8.

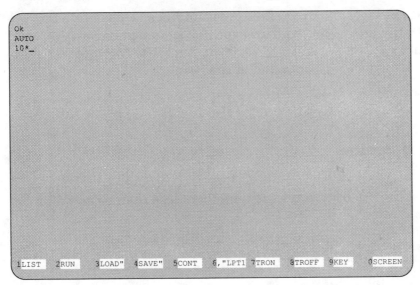

```
Ok
AUTO
10*_
```

```
1LIST   2RUN   3LOAD"   4SAVE"   5CONT   6,"LPT1 7TRON   8TROFF   9KEY   0SCREEN
```

Figure 5-8.
**The AUTO
command.**

When you type program line 10 and press ENTER, GWBASIC then generates a line number 20, and so forth.

To cancel AUTO mode, press the key combination Ctrl-Break. This causes the BASIC prompt to be displayed, but does not affect any program lines already entered.

You may have wondered why line numbers are generated in multiples of 10. Actually they don't need to be. Line numbers can be any integers. However, it is good practice to allow space between program lines so that you may add intermediate lines as you develop your program. What happens if you run out of space between program lines? Just use the RENUM command to renumber the lines in multiples of 10 (see below).

Variations of the AUTO command allow you to control the starting line number and the step between line numbers. the command

        AUTO 100 <ENTER>

generates the sequence of line numbers 100, 110, 120,.... The command

        AUTO 100,5 <ENTER>

generates the sequence of line numbers 100, 105, 110,....

The RENUM Command

The RENUM command allows you to renumber the lines of a program. As with the AUTO command, it has a number of variations. The simplest is the command:

RENUM

This command renumbers the lines with numbers 10, 20, 30,.... (see Figure 5-9).

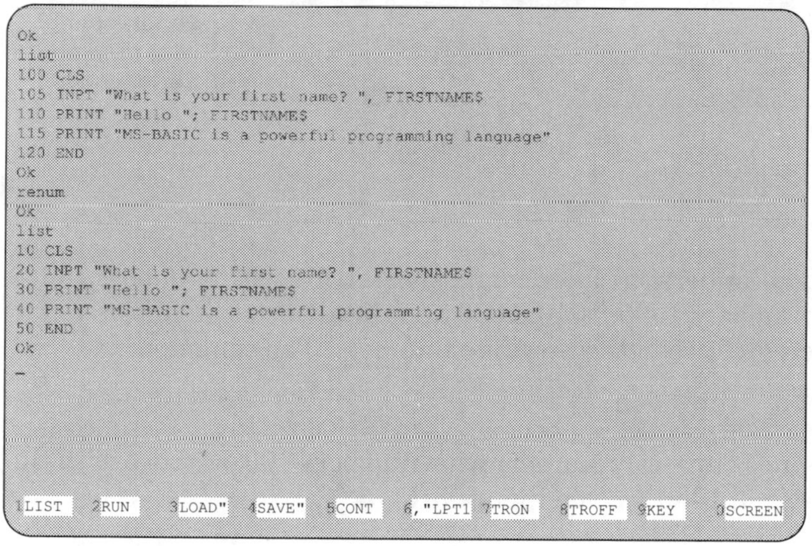

```
Ok
list
100 CLS
105 INPT "What is your first name? ", FIRSTNAMES
110 PRINT "Hello "; FIRSTNAMES
115 PRINT "MS-BASIC is a powerful programming language"
120 END
Ok
renum
Ok
list
10 CLS
20 INPT "What is your first name? ", FIRSTNAMES
30 PRINT "Hello "; FIRSTNAMES
40 PRINT "MS-BASIC is a powerful programming language"
50 END
Ok
_
```

```
1LIST   2RUN   3LOAD"  4SAVE"  5CONT  6,"LPT1 7TRON  8TROFF  9KEY   0SCREEN
```

Figure 5-9.
The RENUM Command.

Another variation is:

RENUM 1000

This command renumbers the lines with numbers 1000, 1010, 1020, 1030,.... (see Figure 5-10).

```
Ok
list
10 CLS
20 INPT "What is your first name? ", FIRSTNAMES
30 PRINT "Hello "; FIRSTNAMES
40 PRINT "MS-BASIC is a powerful programming language"
50 END
Ok
renum 1000
Ok
list
1000 CLS
1010 INPT "What is your first name? ", FIRSTNAMES
1020 PRINT "Hello "; FIRSTNAMES
1030 PRINT "MS-BASIC is a powerful programming language"
1040 END
Ok
_
```

| 1LIST | 2RUN | 3LOAD" | 4SAVE" | 5CONT | 6,"LPT1 | 7TRON | 8TROFF | 9KEY | 0SCREEN |

Figure 5-10.
**Renumbering
lines from a
certain point**.

Yet another variation is:

RENUM 1000, 100

This command numbers the lines currently starting with numbers 100 or above with the numbers 1000, 1010, 1020,.... A final variation allows you to control the spacing between the new line numbers. The command:

RENUM 1000, 100, 200

renumbers the lines currently starting with numbers 100 or above with the numbers 1000, 1200, 1400,.... (see Figure 5-11).

```
Ok
list
1000 CLS
1010 INPT "What is your first name? ", FIRSTNAMES
1020 PRINT "Hello "; FIRSTNAMES
1030 PRINT "MS-BASIC is a powerful programming language"
1040 END
Ok
renum 1000,100,200
Ok
list
1000 CLS
1200 INPT "What is your first name? ", FIRSTNAMES
1400 PRINT "Hello "; FIRSTNAMES
1600 PRINT "MS-BASIC is a powerful programming language"
1800 END
Ok
_
```

```
1LIST   2RUN   3LOAD"   4SAVE"   5CONT   6,"LPT1 7TRON   8TROFF  9KEY   0SCREEN
```

Figure 5-11.
**Renumbering
lines from a
certain point
with a given
spacing
between
numbers**.

The DELETE Command

In developing your programs, you will often need to selecively delete lines
from your program. This may be accomplished with the DELETE command.
This command allows you to delete a single line or a range of lines. Here are
some typical DELETE commands.

```
DELETE  100-300 <ENTER>
DELETE  25730 <ENTER>
DELETE  -200 <ENTER>
```

The first command deletes program lines 100–300 (inclusive). The second
deletes program line 25730. The third deletes program lines from 1 through
200 (inclusive).

If you wish to delete from a certain program line to the end of the program,
use a command of the first sort with a line number larger than the number
of the last line of the program.

Exercises

1. Use the AUTO feature to input the example program in the text with line numbers 10, 20, ...

2. Save the program of 1. in the file PROG1.

3. Erase the program of 1. from RAM.

4. Reload PROG1.

5. List PROG1.

6. Renumber the lines of PROG1 so that the numbers are 5000, 5050, 5100,....

7. Save the renumbered program under the name PROG1.

8. Erase the current program from memory.

9. Reload PROG1 and list it. What can you conclude about saving a program twice?

Six

Elementary Programming in GWBASIC

GWBASIC Programs

Just as humans use language to communicate with one another, programmers use computer languages to communicate sequences of instructions to the computer. Just as natural languages, such as English or French, have a set of grammatical rules for constructing proper sentences, computer languages have rules for constructing statements and programs. These rules constitute the so-called **syntax** of the language.

Humans have a great capacity for understanding sentences that have missing components or faulty grammar. However, compilers, which are assigned the task of interpreting computer languages into machine language, are not so understanding. In order for a compiler to correctly interpret instructions, they must be formed strictly according to the rules. Throughout this book we will be describing rules for using various types of statements in GWBASIC. Pay close attention to them, because unless you write programs according to the rules, the compiler will reject them. On the other hand, don't be intimidated or overwhelmed. If you violate the rules, the worst that can happen is that the compiler will give you an error message. And you can repair an error by editing the program. Within a short period of time, the essential rules for GWBASIC programming will seem quite natural and you won't give them a second thought.

Statements and Lines

A single instruction is called a **statement.** A typical program involves many statements. As we shall see, GWBASIC has statements for accomplishing many different things. Some statements print data on the screen, some perform calculations, some play music, and some send data to be printed on the printer.

Statements involve GWBASIC keywords, which are words that have special meaning within the GWBASIC language. Some examples of GWBASIC keywords are: PRINT, PLAY, USING, IF, THEN, DO, LOOP. You may find a list of all the keywords used in GWBASIC in the reference manual for the program.

In addition to keywords, statements can involve **constants**, **variables,** and **operators.** Constants can be numerical, like 15.87 or -1300, or text, like "HELLO". A variable is a name, which you introduce, to hold a value. Variables can hold numerical or text values. An operator is a symbol that indicates either an operation between values or a relationship between values. For instance, the standard arithmetic operators + and - are used to indicate addition and subtraction among numbers. The operator < (Less than) indicates a relationship between values that is either true or false. For example, we have the true relationship $5 < 10$ (this is a true relationship since 5 is less than 10).

A typical GWBASIC statement incorporates keywords, constants, variables, and operators. For example, consider the following statement:

```
10 IF A < B THEN PRINT "A is less than B by "; B-A
```

This statement will determine whether A is less than B. If so, it will display the message "A is less than B by" followed by the difference $B - A$. In this statement, the keywords are IF, THEN, and PRINT. The variables are A and B. The operators are <, ;, and +.

A GWBASIC program consists of a number of lines, each of which has the format:

```
line# statement [:statement] ... [' Remark]
```

In this notation, the brackets [] indicate an optional element. As the above notation shows, any number of statements can be included on a line, separated by colons. A line can end with an optional remark introduced by an apostrophe.

A GWBASIC program is a sequence of lines written in the GWBASIC language. Unless you specify otherwise, the statements are executed in order. The end of a program is indicated by the statement:

```
END
```

Actually, the END statement is optional. However, in writing structured programs, it is good to get into the habit of including it.

GWBASIC programs have a certain organization to which they must adhere. But we know enough to get started with some elementary programs and return to this topic later.

Uppercase Versus Lowercase and Extra Spaces

The computer is a stern taskmaster! It has a very limited vocabulary (GWBASIC keywords), and this vocabulary must be used according to very specific rules concerning the order of words, punctuation, and so forth. However, GWBASIC allows for some freedom of expression. For example, GWBASIC statements may be typed in uppercase, lowercase, or a mixture of the two. Also, any extra spaces are ignored. Thus, GWBASIC will interpret all of the following instructions as the same:

```
10 PRINT A
10 print a
10 Print A
10 print    A
10                   print A
```

Note, however, that GWBASIC expects spaces in certain places. For example, there must be a space separating PRINT and A in the above command. Otherwise, GWBASIC will read the command as PRINTA, which is not in its vocabulary!

A Word of Warning

Many people think of a computer as an "electronic brain" that somehow has the power of human thought. This is very far from the truth. The electronics of the computer and the rules of the GWBASIC language allow it to recognize a very limited vocabulary, and to take various actions based on the data that are given to it. It is very important to realize that the computer does not have "common sense." The computer attempts to interpret whatever data you input. If what you input is a recognizable command, the computer performs it. It does not matter that the command makes no sense in a particular context. The computer has no way to make such judgments. It can only do what you instruct it to do. Because of the computer's inflexibility in interpreting commands, you must tell the computer exactly what you want it to do. Don't worry about confusing the computer. If you communicate a command in an incorrect form, you won't damage the machine in any way! However, in order to make the machine do our bidding, it is necessary to learn to speak its language precisely.

BASIC Constants and Arithmetic Operators

In learning to use a language, you first must learn the alphabet of the language. Next, you must learn the vocabulary of the language. Finally, you must study the way in which words are put together into sentences. In learning the GWBASIC language, we will follow the progression just described. Next, you'll learn some vocabulary words. The simplest "words" are the so-called constants.

BASIC Constants

BASIC allows you to manipulate numbers and text. In BASIC, we distinguish between these two types of data as follows: a **numeric constant** is a number, and a **string constant** is a sequence of characters that may include letters, numbers, or any other symbols within the GWBASIC character set. For now, let's worry only about string constants consisting of standard keyboard characters. We will come back to discuss the other symbols in the GWBASIC character set later in the book. The following are examples of numeric constants:

```
5
-2
3.145
23456
456.7834
27134000000000
```

It is very important to note that within GWBASIC, numerical constants are specified without the usual formatting characters, such as commas, dollar signs, or percent signs. As we will shortly learn, you may format numbers for display or printing using any of these formatting characters. However, when specifying numbers for input to GWBASIC, you must omit these. Thus, for example, if you wish to input $10,485.45, you must enter it as the number 10485.45. Similarly, 58.2% must be entered as the decimal .582.

The following are examples of string constants:

```
"John",
"Accounts Receivable"
"$234.45 Due"
"Dec. 4,1981"
```

Note that string constants are always enclosed in quotation marks. (When written in this form, a string constant cannot contain a quotation mark. We will later show how to include a quotation mark within a string constant.) Numbers may appear within a string constant, such as "$45.30". However, you cannot use such numbers in arithmetic. Only numbers not enclosed by quotation marks may be used for arithmetic.

In many applications, it is necessary to refer to a string constant that has no characters within its quotation marks, namely the string " ". This string constant is called the **null string.**

In GWBASIC, a string may contain as many as 32,767 characters.

Arithmetic in GWBASIC

GWBASIC allows you to perform all the usual arithmetic operations. You indicate such operations using the various arithmetic operators of GWBASIC. The arithmetic operators indicating addition and subtraction are the usual symbols + and -. For example, you indicate addition of 5 and 4 by the expression:

```
5 + 4
```

You indicate the difference of 9 minus 8 by the expression:

```
9 - 8
```

The operator indicating multiplication is an asterisk (*). As an example, the product of 5 and 3 is indicated by the expression:

```
5*3
```

The operator indicating division is the slash (/). For example, 8.2 divided by 15 is indicated by the expression:

```
8.2/15
```

All elementary arithmetic operations (addition, subtraction, multiplication, and division) are carried out to seven decimal places. The results of arithmetic operations may be displayed on the screen using the PRINT statement. For example, the result of the statement

    PRINT 8.2/15

is the display

    .5466666

Example 1. Write a BASIC statement to calculate the sum of 54.75, 78.83, and 548.

Solution.   The sum is indicated by typing

    54.75 + 78.83 + 548

so the desired display is created by the statement :

    10 PRINT 54.75 + 78.83 + 548

The Order of Operations and Parentheses

GWBASIC carries out arithmetic operations in a special order. Namely, it scans an expression and carries out all multiplication and division, proceeding in left-to-right order. It then returns to the left side of the expression and performs addition and subtraction proceeding left-to-right.

For example, consider this expression:

    2*3 + 4*5 + 3*3

GWBASIC first scans the expression from left to right and performs all multiplications and divisions in the order in which they are encountered. It simplifies the expression to

    6 + 20 + 9

GWBASIC then starts again at the left and performs all addition and subtraction operations in the order encountered. This gives the result:

```
35
```

The order of operations is extremely important. Let's try another example:

```
1 - 3/2*5
```

GWBASIC first performs the division 3/2. This simplifies the expression to:

```
1 - 1.5*5
```

Next, it performs the multiplication 1.5*5 to obtain

```
1 - 7.5
```

Finally, it starts from the left again and performs addition and subtraction to obtain

```
-6.5
```

Knowing the order of operations helps you to correctly translate familiar arithmetic procedures into computer language. For example, consider this fraction:

$$\frac{5+\frac{3}{2}}{5*8}$$

According to the rules of arithmetic, you simplify this fraction by first simplifying the numerator and denominator to obtain:

$$\frac{6.5}{40}$$

Note that you must perform the operations specified in the numerator and denominator before performing the division indicated in the fraction. You may indicate this in BASIC (as in algebra) by using parentheses:

```
(5+3/2)/(5*8)
```

BASIC does all the math inside the parentheses first, following the precedence rules given above. For example, in the above expression, the parentheses (5+3/2) and (5*8) are evaluated first, to give

    6.5/40

BASIC then performs the division.

Test Your Understanding 1 (Answer on Page 114)

Evaluate this expression:

    3*5 - 4*3/2 + 4 - 8/2

What is the result?

In evaluating parentheses, GWBASIC uses the same rules stated above: First perform all multiplications and divisions in left-to-right order. Then perform all additions and subtractions in left-to-right order.

What about parentheses within parentheses? Well, you have enough knowledge to figure out what BASIC does. Work out this example:

    (1+3*(4+5))*(1+4)

GWBASIC looks at the expression and decides it must first evaluate the left-most parenthesis (1+3*(4+5)). When it attempts to evaluate it, however, it encounters a parenthesis within, namely (4+5), which must be evaluated first. So the first simplification is

    (1+3*9)*(1+4)

Now GWBASIC begins all over. It evaluates the left-most parenthesis to get

    28*(1+4)

Next, it evaluates the right parenthesis to get

    28*5

Finally, it performs the multiplication to obtain the answer:

140

Example 2.   What numeric values will BASIC calculate from these expressions?

   a. (5 + 7)/2
   b. 5 + 7/2
   c. 5 + 7*3/2
   d. (5 + 7*3)/2

Solution.   a. The computer first applies its rules for the order of calculation to determine the value in the parentheses, namely 12. It then divides 12 by 2 to obtain 6.

   b. The computer scans the expression from left to right performing all multiplication and division in the order encountered. First it divides 7 by 2 to obtain 3.5. It then rescans the line and performs all additions and subtractions in order. This gives us

```
5 + 3.5 = 8.5
```

   c. The computer first performs all multiplication and division in order:

```
5 + 10.5
```

It then performs addition to obtain 15.5.

   d. The computer calculates the value of all parentheses first. In this case, it computes 5 + 7*3 = 26. (Note that it does the multiplication first!) Next, it rescans the line, which now looks like this:

```
26/2
```

It performs the division to obtain 13.

Test Your Understanding 2 (Answer on Page 114)

Calculate 5+3/2+2 and (5+3)/(2+2). What is the result?

Example 3. Write a GWBASIC statement to calculate the quantity

$$\frac{22 \times 18 + 34 \times 11 - 12.5 \times 8}{27.8 + 42.1}$$

Solution. Here is the instruction:

```
10 PRINT (22*18 + 34*11 - 12.5*8)/(27.8+42.1)
```

The parentheses tell the compiler to calculate the values of the numerator and denominator before doing the division implied by the fraction. First calculate (22*18 + 34*11 - 12.5*8) and (27.8 + 42.1) before performing the division.

Test Your Understanding 3 (Answer on Page 114)

Write BASIC programs to calculate:

a. $((4 \times 3 + 5 \times 8 + 7 \times 9)/(7 \times 9 + 4 \times 3 + 8 \times 7)) \times 48.7$

b. 27.8 percent of $(112 + 38 + 42)$

c. The average of the numbers 88, 78, 84, 49, and 63

Scientific Notation

For certain applications, you may wish to specify your numeric constants in exponential format (also called scientific notation). This is especially helpful in the case of very large and very small numbers. Consider the number 15,300,000,000. You could type this number as:

```
15300000000
```

However, it is very inconvenient to type all the zeros, but it can be written more easily as 1.53E10. The 1.53 indicates the first three digits of the number. E10 means that you move the decimal point in the 1.53 to the right 10 places. Similarly, the number -237,000 may be written in the exponential format as -2.37E5. Exponential format also may be used for very small numbers. For example, the number 0.00000000054 may be written in exponential format as 5.4E-10. The -10 indicates that the decimal point in 5.4 is to be moved 10 places to the left.

Test Your Understanding 4 (Answer on Page 114)

a. Write these numbers in exponential format: .00048 and -1374.5

b. Write these numbers in decimal format: -9.7E3, 9.7E-3 and -9.7E-3

GWBASIC can display at most 18 significant digits of a number. If you ask it to display a number with more than 18 significant digits, GWBASIC will give an error message: Invalid Numerical Format.

For more details about numeric precision and rounding, see the discussion in Chapter 11.

Exponentiation

Suppose that A is a number and N is a positive whole number (this means that N is one of the numbers 1,2,3,4,...). Therefore, A raised to the Nth power is the product of A times itself N times. This quantity usually is denoted A^N, and the process of calculating it is called exponentiation. For example,

```
2³ = 2*2*2 = 8,    5⁷ = 5*5*5*5*5*5*5 = 78125

Aᴺ = A*A*A*...*A  (N times)
```

It is possible to calculate A^N by repeated multiplication. However, if N is large, this can be tiresome to type. BASIC provides a shortcut for typing this function. Exponentiation is denoted by the symbol ^, which is produced by hitting the key with the upward-pointing arrow (this symbol shares the "6" key at the top of the keyboard). For example, 2^3 is denoted 2^3. The operation of exponentiation is done before multiplication and division. This is illustrated in the following example.

Example 4. Determine the value that GWBASIC assigns to this expression:

    20*3 - 5*2^3

Solution. The exponentiation is performed first to yield

        20*3 - 5*8 = 60 - 40

                   = 20

Test Your Understanding 5 (Answer on Page 114)

Evaluate the following, first manually and then using GWBASIC.

   a. 24*33
   b. 22*33 - 122/32*2

Integer Division

Recall the days when you first learned division. Your first problems involved dividing one whole number by another. You were taught to express the answer as a quotient and a remainder. For example, the result of dividing 14 by 5 is the quotient 2 and the remainder 4. This type of division may be performed in BASIC using the operations \ and MOD. For example:

    14\5 = 2

and

    14 MOD 5 = 4

That is, 14\5 equals the (whole number) quotient of 14 divided by 5; 14 MOD 5 equals the remainder. The symbol \ is called a backslash and should not be confused with the ordinary slash (/).

Here is a table showing the order in which \ and MOD are performed in relationship to the other operations. The operations that are higher in the list are performed first.

```
^

*, /

\

MOD

+, -
```

Let's apply this fact to evaluating the expression:

```
5*3\2*2 MOD 2
```

The multiplications are performed first to obtain

```
15\4 MOD 2
```

Next, the \ is performed, to obtain

```
3 MOD 2
```

Finally, this last expression is simplified to obtain

```
1
```

Exercises

Write BASIC programs to calculate the following quantities.

1. `57 + 23 + 48`

2. `57.83 * (48.27 - 12.54)`

3. `127.86/38`

4. `365/.005 + 1.025`

Convert the following numbers to exponential format.

5. `23,000,000`

6. `175.25`

7. `-200,000,000`

8. `.00014`

9. `-.000000000275`

10. `53,420,000,000,000,000`

Convert the following numbers in exponential format to standard format.

11. `1.59E5`

12. `-20.3456E6`

13. `-7.456E-12`

14. `2.39456E-18`

Calculate the following quantities.

15. `18\6`

16. `17 MOD 3`

17. `25 MOD 2*3`

18. `(17\4 MOD 3)^2`

19. `(17\4) MOD 3^2`

Answers to Test Your Understandings 1, 2, 3, 4, and 5

1. `9`

2. `8.5 and 2`

3. a. `10 PRINT ((4*3 + 5*8 + 7*9)/(7*9 + 4*3 + 8*7))*48.7`
    b. `20 PRINT .278*(112+38+42)`
    c. `30 PRINT (88+78+84+49+63)/5`

4. a. `4.8E-4, -1.3745E3`
    b. `-9700, .0097, -.0097`

5. a. `792`
    b. `718.375`

The PRINT Statement

Printing Words

So far, you have used the PRINT statement only to display the answers to numeric problems. However, this statement is very versatile. It also allows you to display string constants. For example, consider this instruction:

```
10 PRINT "Patient History"
```

During program execution, this statement creates the following display:

```
Patient History
```

In order to display several string constants on the same line, separate them by commas in a single PRINT statement. For example, consider the instruction:

```
10 PRINT "AGE", "SEX", "ADDRESS"
```

It will cause three words to be printed as follows:

AGE   **SEX**   **ADDRESS**

Both numeric constants and string constants may be included in a single PRINT statement. The various quantities to be printed are separated by commas. For example:

```
10 PRINT "AGE", 65.43, 65000
```

Here is how the computer determines the spacing when printing multiple data items. Each line is divided into print zones. In 80-character width, the first five print zones each have 14 spaces and the sixth 10 spaces. In 40-character width, there are three print zones, the first two with 14 characters and the third with 12 characters.

By placing a comma in a PRINT statement, you are telling the computer to start the next string of text at the beginning of the next print zone. For example, the four words above begin in columns 1, 15, 29, 44 respectively, assuming an 80-character width (see Figure 6-1). If a PRINT statement requests a print zone beyond the current line, printing will automatically move to the first print zone of the next line.

Henceforth, we will assume that the line width is 80 characters, unless we explicitly say otherwise.

```
1...          14 15...      28 29...      43 44...      57 58...      71 72...     80
┌────────────┬────────────┬────────────┬────────────┬────────────┬────────────┐
│ print zone 1 │ print zone 2 │ print zone 3 │ print zone 4 │ print zone 5 │ print zone 6 │
└────────────┴────────────┴────────────┴────────────┴────────────┴────────────┘
```

Figure 6-1. **Print zones in 80-column mode**.

Test Your Understanding 1 (Answer on Page 117)

Write a program to print the following display.

	NAME		
LAST	FIRST	MIDDLE	GRADE
SMITH	JOHN	DAVID	87

Test Your Understanding 2 (Answer on Page 118)

Write a computer program that creates the following display.

```
                    BUDGET-APRIL

      FOOD          387.50
      CAR           475.00
      GAS           123.71
      UTILITIES      46.00
      ENTERTAINMENT 100.00
                    _____

      TOTAL         (Calculate total)
```

Exercises

1. Make a table of the first, second, third, and fourth powers of the numbers 2, 3, 4, 5, and 6. Put all first powers in a column, all second powers in another column, and so forth.

2. Mrs. Anita Smith went to her doctor with a broken leg. Her bill consists of $45 for removal of the cast, $35 for therapy, and $5 for drugs. Her major medical policy will pay 80 percent directly to the doctor. Use the computer to prepare an invoice for Mrs. Smith.

3. A school board election is held to elect a representative for a district consisting of Wards 1, 2, 3, and 4. There are three candidates: Mr. Thacker, Ms. Hoving, and Mrs. Weatherby. The tallies by candidate and ward are as follows:

	Ward 1	Ward 2	Ward 3	Ward 4
Thacker	698	732	129	487
Hoving	148	928	246	201
Weatherby	379	1087	148	641

Write a BASIC computer program to calculate the total number of votes achieved by each candidate, as well as the total number of votes cast.

Describe the output from each of these programs.

```
4.   10 PRINT 8*2 - 3*(2^4 - 10)
     20 END
```

```
5.   10 PRINT "SILVER","GOLD","COPPER","PLATINUM"
     20 PRINT 327,448,1052,2
     30 END
```

```
6.   10 PRINT ,"GROCERIES","MEATS","DRUGS"
     20 PRINT "MON", "1,245","2,348","2,531"
     30 PRINT "TUE", "  248","3,459","2,148"
     40 END
```

Answers to Test Your Understanding 1, 2, and 3

```
1.   10 PRINT ,"NAME"
     20 PRINT
     30 PRINT "LAST","FIRST","GRADE"
     40 PRINT
     50 PRINT "SMITH","JOHN",87
     60 END
```

```
2.  10 PRINT ,"   BUDGET-APRIL"
    20 PRINT "FOOD",,387.50
    30 PRINT "CAR",, 475.00
    40 PRINT "GAS",, 123.71
    50 PRINT "UTILITIES",, 46.00
    60 PRINT "ENTERTAINMENT",, 100.00
    70 PRINT , "_____"
    80 PRINT "TOTAL", 387.50+475.00+123.71+146.00+100.00
    90 END
```

GWBASIC Variables

A variable is a reserved portion of RAM in which to store a particular piece of data. GWBASIC supports a number of different types of variables and the amount of memory reserved depends on the variable type.

Variable Names

Each variable is assigned a name, which is a sequence of letters and digits, beginning with a letter, and containing as many as 40 characters. Variable names are usually chosen to reflect the data stored in the variable. For example, here are some typical variable names.

```
Payroll
Tax
NextInLine
Cust0513
```

Note, however, that not every sequence of characters is a legal variable name. For one thing, reserved words of GWBASIC may not be used as variable names. Furthermore, a variable name cannot begin with a number. For example, 1A is not a legal variable name. If you attempt to use an illegal sequence of characters as a variable name, GWBASIC provides an error message when you attempt to compile.

To distinguish keywords from variable names, we will adopt the following convention: Keywords will always be written in all capital letters: PRINT, ON, GO, NEXT. Variable names will be written with the initial letters of words capitalized, as in the example variable names given above.

Variable Types

GWBASIC variables are classified according to the type of data that they store. In the course of this text, we will introduce all of GWBASIC's data types. However, to start with, let's consider just two. A numeric variable is a variable that stores a number; a string variable is a variable that stores a string. A string variable is indicated by a variable name ending in the type declaration $. A variable without a type declaration is assumed to be a numeric variable. (Actually, as we shall see later, the numeric variables we are speaking of at this point are single precision real variables. However, this is irrelevant at this point.)

Here are some variable names for string variables:

```
FIRSTNAME$
PATHIN$
A$
```

Here are some variable names for numeric variables:

```
AMOUNT
X
BALANCE
INTEREST
```

Value of a Variable

At any given moment during a program's execution, a variable has a particular value. For example, the variable A might have the value 5 while B might have the value -2.137845. One method for changing the value of a variable is through use of the assignment statement. Either of the statements

```
10 LET A = 7
20 A= 7
```

sets the value of A equal to 7. The statement

```
10    FIRSTNAME$ = "Joe"
```

sets the value of the string variable FirstName$ to the string "Joe".

The precise syntax of an assignment statement is:

```
[LET] variable = value
```

The brackets around the keyword LET indicate that this word is optional.

Assignment of Numerical Expressions

In the above examples of assignment statements, the value assigned to the variable was given as a constant, either a numeric constant or a string constant. However, the value assigned can also be given as an expression formed from variables and operators. Examples of numeric expressions involving the variable A are:

```
A+5
3*A
2*A^2 - A/2
```

Such expressions are familiar from algebra.

At any given moment during program execution, an expression has a value. For instance, if A has the value 7, then the expression

```
A + 5
```

has the value 7 + 5 or 12. The expression

```
3*A - 10
```

is evaluated as $3*7 - 10 = 21 - 10 = 11$. The expression $2*A^2$ is evaluated as

```
2*7^2 = 2*49 = 98
```

Test Your Understanding 1 (Answer on Page 132)

Suppose that A has the value 4 and B has the value 3. What is the value of the expression A^2/2*B^2 ?

Note the following important fact:

GWBASIC initially assigns numeric variables the value 0 and string variables the null string.

If, in particular, you forget to assign a value to a variable and then use it within your program, the variable will have the value initially assigned to it by GWBASIC. It is not considered good programming style to allow GWBASIC to assign your variable values. This practice can too easily lead to errors. Rather, it is best to assign values to all your variables at the beginning of the program. This process is called **initialization of the variables**.

Using the PRINT Statement With Variables

The PRINT statement is used to display values of expressions. For example, the statement

```
10 PRINT A
```

causes the computer to print the current value of A (in the first print zone, of course). The statement

```
10 PRINT A,B,C
```

results in printing the current values of A, B, and C in print zones 1, 2, and 3, respectively.

If the value of a variable is too long for one print zone it will be printed, extended over several print zones.

Test Your Understanding 2 (Answer on Page 132)

Suppose that A has the value 5. What will be the result of the instruction

```
10 PRINT A,A^2,2*A^2
```

Example 1.   Consider the three numbers 5.71, 3.23, and 4.05. Calculate their sum, their product, and the sum of their squares (i.e., the sum of their second powers; such a sum is often used in statistics).

Solution.   Introduce the variables A, B, and C and set them equal, respectively, to the three numbers. Then compute the desired quantities:

```
10 A = 5.71
20 B = 3.23
30 C = 4.05
40 PRINT "THE SUM IS", A+B+C
50 PRINT "THE PRODUCT IS", A*B*C
60 PRINT "THE SUM OF SQUARES IS", A^2+B^2+C^2
70 END
```

Test Your Understanding 3 (Answer on Page 132)

Consider the numbers 101, 102, 103, 104, 105, and 106. Write a program that calculates the product of the first two, the first three, the first four, the first five, and then all six numbers.

More About Assignment

The following mental imagery is often helpful in understanding how BASIC handles variables. When BASIC first encounters a variable, say A, it sets up a box (actually a memory location) that it labels "A" (see Figure 6-2). It stores the current value of A in this box. When you request a change in the value of A, the computer throws out the current contents of the box and inserts the new value.

Let

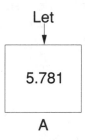

5.781

A

Figure 6-2.
The variable A.

Note that the value of a variable need not remain the same throughout a program. At any point in the program, you may change the value of a variable (with an assignment statement, for example). If a program is called on to evaluate an expression involving a variable, it always uses the current value of the variable, ignoring any previous values the variable may have had at earlier points in the program.

Test Your Understanding 4 (Answer on Page 132)

Suppose that a loan for $5,000 has an interest rate of 1.5 percent on the unpaid balance at the end of each month. Write a program to calculate the interest at the end of the first month. Suppose that at the end of the first month, you make a payment of $150 (after the interest is added). Design your program to calculate the balance after the payment. (Begin by letting B = the loan balance, I = the interest, and P = the payment. After the payment, the new balance is B+I-P.)

Example 2. What will be the output of the following computer program?

```
10 A = 10
20 B = 20
30 A = 5
40 PRINT A + B + C, A*B*C
50 END
```

Solution.   Note that no value for C is specified, so C is equal to zero. Also note that the value of A initially is set to 10. However, in line 20, this value is changed to 5. So in line 30, A, B, and C have the respective values 5, 20, and 0. Therefore, the output will be:

    25   0

To the computer, the statement

    A = value

means the following:

1. Evaluate the expression specifying value.

2. Replace the current value of A by that value.

Therefore, if you write

    10   A = A + 1

you are asking the computer to replace the current value of A with the current value of A + 1. So if the current value of A is 4, the value of A after executing this statement is 4 + 1, or 5.

Test Your Understanding 5 (Answer on Page 132)

What is the output of the following program?

```
10 A = 5.3
20 A = A+1
30 A = 2*A
40 A = A+B
50 PRINT A
60 END
```

The following example provides an interesting application of variable assignment and the arithmetic operations \ and MOD.

Example 3. Write a program to convert Change cents into an equivalent number of quarters, dimes, nickels, and pennies.

Solution. Integer division may be used to compute change in terms of the number of quarters, dimes, nickels, and pennies. Indeed, suppose that change of CHANGE cents is due. The number of quarters in this amount is

```
CHANGE \ 25
```

Moreover, the amount left after subtracting the equivalent of the quarters is

```
CHANGE MOD 25
```

Integer dividing this amount by 10 gives the number of dimes and performing MOD 10 gives the amount left for conversion to smaller coins, and so forth. In order to get the number Change into the program, we use the INPUT statement. The statement:

```
INPUT CHANGE
```

types a question mark and waits for the user to type in an amount. For an amount of change $38.25, you would type in 3825.

Here is the program.

Listing 6-1

```
1 '****************************************
2 'This program computes the change in
3 ' terms of dollar bills and coins due
4 ' if the total is Change cents.
5 '****************************************
10 PRINT "HOW MUCH CHANGE IS DUE?
20 INPUT CHANGE
30 QUARTERS = CHANGE \ 25
40 CHANGE = CHANGE MOD 25
50 DIMES = CHANGE \10
60 CHANGE = CHANGE MOD 10
70 NICKELS = CHANGE \ 5
80 CHANGE = CHANGE MOD 5
90 PENNIES = CHANGE
```

```
100 PRINT CHANGE;"CENTS EQUALS"
110 PRINT QUARTERS;"QUARTERS"
120 PRINT DIMES;"DIMES"
130 PRINT NICKELS;"NICKELS"
140 PRINT PENNIES;"PENNIES"
150 END
```

The variables you have been using are called **single-precision numeric variables**, which are capable of holding up to seven significant digits of information. (Later on, we'll talk about double-precision numeric variables, which can provide more than seven significant digits.)

String Variables

The assignment statement may be used to assign a string constant to a string variable. Just use the statement with the desired value inserted in quotation marks after the equal sign. To set A$ equal to the string "Balance Sheet", use the statement

```
10  A$ = "Balance Sheet"
```

You may print the value of a string variable just as you print the value of a numeric variable. For example, if A$ has the value just assigned, the statement

```
20 PRINT A$
```

results in the following screen output

```
Balance Sheet
```

Example 3. What will be the output of the following program:

```
10 A$ = "MONTHLY RECEIPTS":B$ = "MONTHLY EXPENSES"
20 A = 20373.1: B = 17584.31
```

```
30 PRINT A$,B$
40 PRINT A,,B
50 END
```

Solution. The first line prints the values of the two string variables A$ and B$, namely, "RECEIPTS" and "EXPENSES", at the beginning of two print zones. Line 40 displays the values of A and B. Note the use of two commas in printing the second line of output. These are used to move the second number to the third print field, to align properly with the heading. Here is the output of the program:

```
RECEIPTS          EXPENSES
20373.10          17584.31
```

Note that we have used the variables A and A$ (as well as B and B$) in the same program. The variables A and A$ are considered different by the computer. One further comment about spacing: Note that the numbers do not exactly align with the headings, but are offset by one space. This is because BASIC allows room for a sign (+ or -) in front of a number. In the case of positive numbers, the sign is left out, but the space remains.

GWBASIC maintains a rigid separation between numeric data and string data. In particular, this means that numeric variables may be assigned only numeric values and string variables only string values.

If you attempt to assign a string value to a numeric variable or vice versa, the compiler will give you an error message.

The SWAP Statement

Suppose that your program involves the two variables A and B and that you wish to reassign the values of these variables so that A assumes the value of B, and B the value of A. This may be accomplished using the GWBASIC statement:

```
10 SWAP A, B
```

For example, if A currently has the value 1.8 and B the value 7.5, then after the above statement is executed, A will have the value 7.5 and B the value 1.8.

Note that SWAP also may be used to exchange the values of two string variables, as in the statement

```
20 SWAP A$, B$
```

However, you may never SWAP values between a string variable and a numeric variable. BASIC will report an error if you try this.

Test Your Understanding 6 (Answer on Page 132)

Write a BASIC program to exchange the values of the variables A and B without using the SWAP statement. (It's tricky. That's why BASIC includes the SWAP statement.)

Remarks in Programs

It is very convenient to explain programs using remarks. For one thing, remarks make programs easier to be read by a human being. Remarks also assist in finding errors and making modifications in a program. To insert a remark in a program, you may use the REM statement. For example, consider the line

```
10 REM X DENOTES THE STARSHIP POSITION
```

Since the line starts with REM, it is ignored during program execution. As a substitute for REM, you may use an apostrophe, as in the following example:

```
20 'Y IS THE LASER FORCE
```

To insert a remark on the same line as a program statement, use a colon followed by an apostrophe (or REM), as in this example:

```
30 LET A = PI*R^2 : ' A IS THE AREA, R IS THE RADIUS
```

Note, however, that everything after an apostrophe is ignored. Therefore, you cannot put an instruction after a remark. In the line

```
LET B=A^2: 'B is the area: C=B+8
```

the instruction C=B+8 will be ignored.

The importance of remarks cannot be overemphasized. It is all too easy to write programs that no one (you included) can decipher. You should aim at writing programs that can be read like text. The most significant step in this direction is to include many remarks in your programs. In what follows, we will be generous in our use of remarks, not only to make the programs easier to read, but also to set an example of good programming style.

Test Your Understanding 7 (Answer on Page 132) What is the result of the following program line?

```
10 A=7:B$="COST":C$="TOTAL":PRINT C$,B$,"=",A
```

Using a Printer

In writing programs and analyzing their output, it is often easier to rely on written output, rather than output on the screen. In computer terminology, written output is called **hard copy** and may be provided by a wide variety of printers, ranging from a dot-matrix printer costing only a few hundred dollars to a laser printer costing several thousand dollars. As you begin to make serious use of your computer, you will find it difficult to do without hard copy. Indeed, writing programs is much easier if you can consult a hard copy listing of your program at various stages of program development. (One reason is that in printed output you are not confined to looking at your program in 25-line "snapshots.") Also, you will want to use the printer to produce output of programs, ranging from tables of numeric data to address lists and text files.

You may produce hard copy on your printer by using the BASIC statement LPRINT. For example, the statement

```
10 LPRINT A, A$
```

prints the current values of A and A$ on the printer, in print zones 1 and 2. As is the case with the screen, GWBASIC divides the printer line into print zones that are 14 columns wide. Moreover, the statement

```
10 LPRINT "Customer","Credit Limit","Most Recent Pchs"
```

results in printing three headings in the first three print zones, namely:

```
Customer          Credit Limit     Most Recent Pchs
```

Printing on the printer proceeds very much like printing on the screen. It is important to realize, however, that in order to print on both the screen and the printer, it is necessary to use both statements PRINT and LPRINT. For example, to print the values of A and A$ on both the screen and the printer, we must give two instructions, as follows:

```
10 PRINT A, A$
20 LPRINT A, A$
```

Memory Considerations

GWBASIC allocates 64K bytes of RAM for storage of variable values and another 64K bytes to the storage of strings. It is unlikely that you will exceed these limits in writing elementary programs. However, you should know that these limits exist. If you attempt to use more memory than is allowed for these purposes, GWBASIC will display one of the error messages:

```
Out of variable space
Out of string space
```

Exercises

In Exercises 1–6, determine the output of the given program.

```
1.        10 A = 5:B = 5
          20 PRINT A + B
          30 END

2.        10 LET AA = 5
          20 PRINT AA*B
          30 END

3.        10 LET A1 = 5
          20 PRINT A1^2+5*A1
          30 END

4.        10 A=2: B=7: C=9
          20 PRINT A+B, A-C, A*C
          30 END

5.        10 LET A$ = "JOHN JONES"
          20 LET B$ = "AGE": C = 38
          30 PRINT A$, B$, C
          40 END

6.        10 X=11: Y=19
          20 PRINT 2*X
          30 PRINT 3*Y
          40 END
```

What is wrong with the following BASIC statements?

7. `10 A = "YOUTH"`

8. `10 AA = -12`

9. `10 A$ = 57`

10. `10 ZZ$ = Address`

11. `10 AAA = -9`

12. `10 1A = -2.34567`

13. Consider the numbers 2.3758, 4.58321, and 58.11. Write a program that computes their sum, their product, and the sum of their squares.

14. A company has three divisions: Office Supplies, Computers, and Newsletters. The revenues of these three divisions for the preceding quarter were, respectively, $346,712, $459,321, and $376,872. The expenses for the quarter were $176,894, $584,837, and $402,195,

respectively. Write a program that displays this data on the screen, with appropriate explanatory headings. Your program should also compute and display the net profit (loss) from each division and the net profit (loss) for the company as a whole.

Answers to Test Your Understandings 1, 2, 3, 4, 5, 6, and 7

1. 72

2. It prints the display:
   52550

3.
```
10 LET A=101:B=102:C=103:D=104:E=105:F=106
20 PRINT A*B
30 PRINT A*B*C
40 PRINT A*B*C*D
50 PRINT A*B*C*D*E
60 PRINT A*B*C*D*E*F
70 END
```

4.
```
10 LET B = 5000: I = .015: P = 150.00
20 IN = I*B
30 PRINT "INTEREST EQUALS", IN
40 B = B+IN
50 PRINT " BALANCE WITH INTEREST EQUALS", B
60 B = B - P
70 PRINT "BALANCE AFTER PAYMENT EQUALS", B
80 END
```

5. 12.6

6.
```
10 TEMPORARY=A
20 A=B
30 B=TEMPORARY
```

7. It creates the display:

```
TOTAL COST= 7
```

The INPUT Statement

It is very convenient to have the computer request information from you while the program is actually running. This can be accomplished via the INPUT statement. To see how, consider the statement

```
10 INPUT A
```

When the computer encounters this statement in the course of executing the program, it displays a ? and waits for you to respond by typing the desired value of A (and then pressing the ENTER key). The computer then sets A equal to the numeric value you specified and continues running the program.

You may use an INPUT statement to specify the values of several different variables at one time. These variables may be numeric or string variables. For example, suppose that the computer encounters the statement

```
10 INPUT A,B,C$
```

It will display

```
?
```

You then type in the desired values for A, B, and C$, in the same order as in the program, and separate them by commas. For example, suppose that you type

```
10.5,11.42,BEARINGS
```

followed by an ENTER. The computer then sets

```
A = 10.5,  B = 11.42,  C$ = "BEARINGS"
```

If you respond to the above question mark by typing only a single number, 10.5 for example, the computer responds with

```
? Redo from start
?
```

to indicate that you should repeat the input from the beginning. If you attempt to specify a string constant where you should have a numeric constant, the computer responds with the same message:

```
? Redo from start
?
```

and will wait for you to repeat the INPUT operation.

It is helpful to include a prompting message that describes the input the computer is expecting. To do so, just put the message in quotation marks after the word INPUT and place a semicolon after the message (before the list of variables to be input). For example, consider the statement

```
10 INPUT "ENTER COMPANY, AMOUNT"; A$, B
```

When the computer encounters this program line, the dialog will be as follows:

```
ENTER COMPANY, AMOUNT? AJAX OFFICE SUPPLIES, 2579.48
```

The underlined portion indicates your response to the prompt. The computer will now assign these values:

```
A$ = "AJAX OFFICE SUPPLIES", B = 2579.48
```

Test Your Understanding 1 (Answer on Page 137)

Write a statement that allows you to set variables A and B to any desired values via an INPUT statement. Use the program to set A equal to 12 and B equal to 17.

More About Inputting Data

The INPUT statement, as we have seen, may be used to input one or more constants (string or numeric) to a running program. However, the INPUT statement has a serious defect. To explain this defect, consider this statement:

```
10 INPUT A$,B$
```

Suppose that you wish to set A$ equal to the string

```
"Washington,George"
```

and B$ to the string

```
"Jefferson,Thomas"
```

Suppose that you respond to the INPUT prompt by typing

```
Washington,George, Jefferson,Thomas
```

BASIC will report an error:

```
? Redo from start
?
```

Here is the reason. INPUT looks for commas to separate the data items. The first comma occurs between "Washington" and "George". So INPUT assigns A$ the string "Washington" and B$ the string "George". But this gives excess data so BASIC declares an error. There's a simple way around this. Whenever you wish to INPUT data containing a comma, surround the appropriate strings with quotation marks. In our example, the response

```
"Washington,George","Jefferson,Thomas"
```

will assign A$ and B$ as we wished.

It is something of a bother to surround strings in quotation marks, so BASIC provides another statement that is not sensitive to commas: LINE

INPUT. The LINE INPUT statement may be used to assign only one variable at a time. It reads the input until it encounters ENTER. For example, suppose that we use the statement

```
10 LINE INPUT A$
```

The computer waits for a response. Suppose that we respond with the string

```
Washington, George
```

and press ENTER. LINE INPUT will then assign A$ the string constant "Washington,George". LINE INPUT may be used only to input data to a string variable.

You may use a prompt with LINE INPUT exactly as you do with INPUT. For example, the statement

```
10 LINE INPUT "Type NAME?";A$
```

results in the prompt

```
Type NAME?
```

to which you would respond. Note that LINE INPUT does not automatically display a ? like the INPUT statement. In the above example, the ? came from the prompt.

There is a third statement that you may use to input data from the keyboard, namely INPUT$. This statement allows you to specify an input of only a specified length. For example, consider the statement

```
10 A$=INPUT$(5)
```

This causes the program to wait for five characters from the keyboard and assigns them to A$. For example, if you type ALICE, then A$ will be assigned the string constant "ALICE". INPUT$ is a more specialized statement than either INPUT or LINE INPUT because of the following facts:

1. INPUT$ does not automatically display the input characters on the screen. If you want them displayed, it is your responsibility to display them.

2. INPUT$ accepts all keyboard characters, including Backspace and ENTER. In particular, it does not allow you to correct your input.

If you are a beginning programmer, it's probably wisest to stick to INPUT and LINE INPUT, but we mention INPUT$ mainly for completeness.

Exercises

Suppose that you respond by typing 1<ENTER> to each of the following statements. What output will each of the following programs produce?

1.
```
10 INPUT A
20 PRINT A,A
```

2.
```
10 INPUT A$
20 PRINT A$, A$
```

3.
```
10 LINE INPUT A$
20 PRINT A$,A$
```

4. Write a program that asks a user for a name, address, telephone number, and social security number and stores each of these quantities in appropriate variables.

Answers to Test Your Understanding 1

1.
```
10 INPUT A,B
```

Seven

GWBASIC's Control Structures

Introduction

In this chapter, we discuss the class of GWBASIC statements called **control structures**. These statements are used to perform repetitive tasks and to make decisions within a program, statements which can be used to control the order of statement execution within a GWBASIC program. In addition, we discuss GWBASIC's subprograms and their role in top-down design and structured programming.

FOR...NEXT Loops

Suppose that we wish to solve 50 similar multiplication problems. It is certainly possible to type in the 50 problems one at a time and let the computer solve them. However, this is a very clumsy way to proceed. Suppose that instead of 50 problems there were 500, or even 5,000. Typing the problems one at a time is not practical. If, however, we can describe to the computer the entire class of problems we want solved, then we can instruct the computer to solve them using only a few BASIC statements. Let us consider a concrete problem. Suppose that we wish to calculate the quantities

$$1^2, \ 2^2, \ 3^2, \ \ldots \ , \ 10^2$$

That is, we wish to calculate a table of squares of integers from 1 to 10. This calculation can be described to the computer as calculating N^2, where the variable N is allowed to assume, one at a time, each of the values 1,2,3,...,10. Here is a sequence of GWBASIC statements that accomplishes the calculations:

Listing 7-1

```
1 ' **********************************
2 ' This program lists the squares of
3 '   all the numbers from 1 to 10
4 ' **********************************
10 FOR N=1 TO 10
20    PRINT N^2
30 NEXT N
40 END
```

The sequence of statements FOR...NEXT N is called a **loop**. When the computer encounters the FOR statement, it sets N equal to 1 and continues executing the statements. The PRINT N^2 statement calls for printing N^2. Since N is equal to 1, we have N^2 = 1^2 = 1. So the computer prints a 1. After that, the computer executes the NEXT N statement, which calls for the next N. This instructs the computer to return to the FOR statement in

10, increase N to 2, and to repeat instructions 20 and 30. This time, N^2 = 2^2 = 4. The PRINT statement then prints a 4. The NEXT N directs the program back to line 10 and increases N to 3 and so forth. The three statements FOR...NEXT N are repeated ten times! After the computer executes lines 10, 20, and 30 with N = 10, it will leave the loop and execute line 40.

Type in the above program and give the RUN command. The output will look like this:

```
1
4
9
16
25
36
49
64
81
100
```

Figure 7-1 shows a trace for the above program. This screen gives a sketch of program operation. (We'll learn how to operate the trace function later.) The numbers in brackets denote line numbers. The numbers outside of brackets denote program output generated by the PRINT statement within the loop. Closely examine the way the program operates and make sure that it coincides with your understanding of the way in which the FOR...NEXT statement works.

```
Ok
run
[10][20] 1
[30][20] 4
[30][20] 9
[30][20] 16
[30][20] 25
[30][20] 36
[30][20] 49
[30][20] 64
[30][20] 81
[30][20] 100
[30][40]
Ok
_
```

Figure 7-1.
A trace of a FOR...NEXT loop.

The variable N is called the **loop variable**. It may be used inside the loop just like you would any other variable. For example, it may be used in algebraic calculations and PRINT statements.

Test Your Understanding 1 (Answer on Page 157)

a. Devise a loop allowing N to assume the values 3 to 77.

b. Write a program that calculates N^2 for N = 3 to 77.

Making Loops More Readable. Note that we have indented the statements in the loop that will be repeated. This allows us to clearly see the beginning and end of the loop. It is good programming practice to always indent loops in this way since it increases program readability. The TAB key may be used to indent. You may set GWBASIC at whatever character positions you wish. (See the description of the GWBASIC editor commands in Chapter 1.) These tab stops may be used just like the tab stops on a typewriter. Whenever you press the TAB key, the cursor moves over to the next tab stop.

Let's modify the above program to include on each line of output not only N^2, but also the value of N. To make the table easier to read, let's also add two column headings. The new program reads:

Listing 7-2

```
10 ' *****************************************
20 ' This program prints all the numbers from
30 '    1 to 10 along with their squares
40 ' *****************************************
50 PRINT " N","N^2"
60 FOR N=1 TO 10
70    PRINT N,N^2
80 NEXT N
90 END
```

The output now looks like this:

```
N             N^2
1             1
2             4
3             9
4             16
5             25
6             36
7             49
8             64
9             81
10            100
```

Let us now illustrate some of the many uses loops have by means of some examples.

Example 1. Write a BASIC program to calculate 1+2+3+...+100.

Solution.   Let us use a variable S (for sum) to contain the sum. Let us start S at 0 and use a loop to successively add to S the numbers 1,2,3,...,100. Here is the program.

Listing 7-3

```
 1 '****************************
 2 '  This program calculates the
 3 '  sum of all the integers from
 4 '  1 to 100.
 5 '****************************
10 LET S = 0
20 FOR N = 1 TO 100
30    LET S = S + N
40 NEXT  N
50 PRINT S
60 END
```

When we enter the loop the first time, S = 0 and N = 1. The program then replaces S by S + N, or 0 + 1. The NEXT N statement then sends us back to the beginning of the loop, where the value of N is now set equal to 2. In the next repetition of the loop, S (which is now 0 + 1) is replaced by S + N, or 0 + 1 + 2. NEXT N now sends us back to the beginning of the loop, where N is now set equal to 3. Line 30 then sets S equal to 0 + 1 + 2 + 3. Finally, on the 100th time through the loop, S is replaced by 0 + 1 + 2 + ... + 100, the desired sum. If we run the program, we derive the output

```
5050
```

Test Your Understanding 2 (Answer on Page 157)

Write a BASIC program to calculate 101+102+...+110.

Test Your Understanding 3 (Answer on Page 157)

Write a BASIC program to calculate and display the numbers 2,2^2,2^3,...,2^20.

Example 2.   Write a program to calculate this sum:

$$1*2 + 2*3 + 3*4 + \ldots + 49*50$$

Solution.   We let the sum be contained in the variable S, as we did in the preceding example. The quantities to be added are just the numbers $N*(N+1)$ for $N = 1, 2, 3,..., 49$. Here is our program:

Listing 7-4

```
10 ' *********************************
20 ' This program calculates the sum:
30 '    1x2 + 2x3 + 3x4 + ... + 49x50
40 ' *********************************
50 LET S = 0
60 FOR N = 1 TO 49
70    LET S = S + N*(N+1)
80 NEXT N
90 PRINT S
100 END
```

Some Cautions Concerning Loops

Here are three of the errors you are most likely to make in dealing with loops:

1. Every FOR statement must have a corresponding NEXT and every NEXT must have a FOR. Otherwise, the compiler will display one of the error messages

   ```
   FOR without NEXT
   NEXT without FOR
   ```

2. Be sure that the loop variable is not already used with some other meaning. For example, suppose that the loop variable N is used before the loop begins. Then the loop will destroy the old value of N and there is no way to get that value back after the loop is over.

3. Don't modify the loop variable within the loop. The loop variable is used to count the number of times the loop has been executed. If you change this number within the loop, you are destroying the program's ability to keep track of how many times the loop has been executed and when to stop repeating the loop.

Nested Loops

In many applications, it is necessary to execute a loop within a loop. For example, suppose that we wish to compute the following series of numbers:

```
1^2, 2^2, 3^2,..., 10^2,
101^2, 102^2, 103^2,..., 110^2,
...
...
501^2, 502^2, 503^2,..., 510^2
```

There are 21 groups of ten numbers each. Each line may be computed using a loop. For example, the first line may be computed using

```
100 FOR I=1 TO 10
110 PRINT I^2
120 NEXT I
```

The second line may be computed using

```
100 FOR I=1 TO 10
110 PRINT (100+I)^2
120 NEXT I
```

And the last line may be computed using

```
100 FOR I=1 TO 10
110 PRINT (500+I)^2
120 NEXT I
```

We could compute the desired numbers by repeating essentially the same instructions 21 times. However, it is much easier to do the repetition using a loop. The numbers to be added to I range from 0 (which is 0*100) for the first line, to 100 (which is 1*100) for the second line, to 500 (which is 5*100) for the last line. This suggests that we represent these numbers as J*100, where J is a loop variable that runs from 0 to 5. We may then compute our desired table of numbers using this program:

Listing 7-5

```
10 ' *********************************************
20 ' This program displays the following numbers:
30 '     1^2, 2^2, 3^2, 4^2
40 '     101^2, 102^2, 103^2, 104^2
50 '     ...
60 '     ...
70 '     501^2, 502^2, 503^2, 504^2
80 ' *********************************************
100   FOR J=0 TO 5
110     FOR I=1 TO 4
120     PRINT (100*J+I)^2,
130   NEXT I
140     PRINT
150   NEXT J
160   END
```

The instructions that are indented one level are repeated six times, corresponding to the values J=0 through J=5. On the first repetition, (J=0), lines 100–120 print the numbers in the first line; on the second repetition (J=1), lines 100–120 print the numbers in the second line, and so forth. Note how the indentations help one to read the program. This is an example of good programming style. Figure 7-2 is a trace of the above program.

```
Ok
run
[100] [110] [120]  1          [130] [120]  4  [130] [120]  9  [130] [120]  16
[130] [140]
[150] [110] [120]  10201      [130] [120]  10404          [130] [120]  10609
[130] [120]  10816            [130] [140]
[150] [110] [120]  40401      [130] [120]  40804          [130] [120]  41209
[130] [120]  41616            [130] [140]
[150] [110] [120]  90601      [130] [120]  91204          [130] [120]  91809
[130] [120]  92416            [130] [140]
[150] [110] [120]  160801     [130] [120]  161604         [130] [120]  162409
[130] [120]  163216           [130] [140]
[150] [110] [120]  251001     [130] [120]  252004         [130] [120]  253009
[130] [120]  254016           [130] [140]
[150] [160]
Ok
_
```

Figure 7-2.
**Tracing a
nested loop.**

If a loop is contained within a loop, then we say that the loops are nested. BASIC allows you to have nesting in as many layers as you wish (a loop within a loop within a loop, and so forth).

Test Your Understanding 4 (Answer on Page 157)

Write a BASIC program to print the following table of numbers.

```
1  11  21  31
2  12  22  32
.
.

.
9  19  29  39
```

Warning: Nested loops may not "overlap." That is, the following sequence is not allowed:

```
10 FOR J=1 TO 100
20    FOR K=1 TO 50
.
.
.
80 NEXT J
90    NEXT K
```

Rather, the NEXT K statement must precede the NEXT J, so that the K loop is "completely inside" the J loop.

Applications of Loops

Example 3.   You borrow $7,000 to buy a car. You finance the balance for 36 months at an interest rate of one percent per month. Your monthly payments are $232.50. Write a program to compute the amount of interest each month, the amount of the loan repaid, and the balance owed.

Solution.   Let Balance denote the balance owed. Initially we have Balance equal to 7,000 dollars. At the end of each month let us compute the interest (Interest) owed for that month, namely .01*Balance. For example, at the end of the first month, the interest owed is .01*7000.00 = $70.00. Let Payment = 232.50 to denote the monthly payment, and let Repay denote the amount repaid out of the current payment. Then Repay = Payment - Interest. For example, at the end of the first month, the amount of the loan repaid is 232.50 -70.00 = 162.50. The balance owed may then be calculated as Balance - Repay. At the end of the first month, the balance owed is 7000.00 - 162.50 = 6837.50. Here is a program to perform these calculations:

Listing 7-6

```
' **********************************************
' This program computes the monthly interest,
' amount repaid, and balance owed on a loan.
' **********************************************
10 Balance=7000
```

```
20 Payment =232.50
30 FOR Year = 0 TO 2    :'Year=year number
40    PRINT "MONTH","INTEREST","PAYMENT","BALANCE"
50    FOR Month = 1 TO 36
60       Interest = .01*Balance
70       Repay = Payment - Interest
80       Balance = Balance - Repay
90       PRINT 12*Year+Month,Interest,Repay,Balance
100   NEXT Month
110 NEXT Year
120 END
```

Try to run this program. Notice that most of the output goes flying by before you can read it. Let us now describe a method of adapting the output to our screen size by printing only 12 months of data at one time. This amount of data will fit since the screen contains 24 lines. We will use a second loop to keep track of 12-month periods. The variable for the new loop will be Year (for "years"), and Year will go from 0 to 2. The month variable will be Month as before, but now Month will go only from 1 to 12. The month number will now be 12*Year + Month (12 times the number of years plus the number of months). Here is the revised program.

Listing 7-7

```
' **********************************************
' This program computes the monthly interest,
' amount repaid, and balance owed on a loan.
' The data are displayed 12 months at a time.
' The user presses ENTER to see the next
' year's display.
' **********************************************
10 Balance=7000
20 Payment =232.50
30 FOR Year = 0 TO 2    :'Year=year number
40    PRINT "MONTH","INTEREST","PAYMENT","BALANCE"
50    FOR Month = 1 TO 12
60       Interest = .01*Balance
70       Repay = Payment - Interest
80       Balance = Balance - Repay
```

```
90      PRINT 12*Year+Month,Interest,Repay,Balance
100  NEXT Month
110 'Halt execution
120 PRINT "Press ENTER to continue"
130 'Wait till ENTER key is pressed
140 INPUT A$
150 CLS
160 NEXT Year
170 END
```

Figures 7-3, 7-4,and 7-5 show what the output looks like.

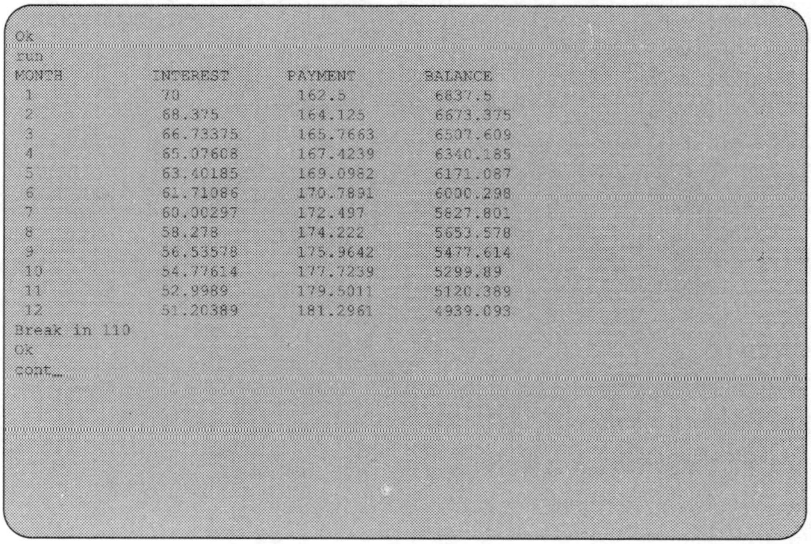

```
Ok
run
MONTH           INTEREST        PAYMENT         BALANCE
 1              70              162.5           6837.5
 2              68.375          164.125         6673.375
 3              66.73375        165.7663        6507.609
 4              65.07608        167.4239        6340.185
 5              63.40185        169.0982        6171.087
 6              61.71086        170.7891        6000.298
 7              60.00297        172.497         5827.801
 8              58.278          174.222         5653.578
 9              56.53578        175.9642        5477.614
10              54.77614        177.7239        5299.89
11              52.9989         179.5011        5120.389
12              51.20389        181.2961        4939.093
Break in 110
Ok
cont_
```

Figure 7-3.
**Paying a loan,
year 1.**

```
MONTH          INTEREST        PAYMENT         BALANCE
13             49.39093        183.1091        4755.984
14             47.55984        184.9402        4571.044
15             45.71044        186.7896        4384.255
16             43.84255        188.6575        4195.597
17             41.95597        190.544         4005.053
18             40.05053        192.4495        3812.603
19             38.12603        194.374         3618.229
20             36.18229        196.3177        3421.912
21             34.21912        198.2809        3223.631
22             32.23631        200.2637        3023.367
23             30.23367        202.2663        2821.101
24             28.21101        204.289         2616.812
Break in 110
Ok
cont_
```

Figure 7-4.
**Paying a loan,
year 2.**

```
MONTH          INTEREST        PAYMENT         BALANCE
25             26.16812        206.3319        2410.48
26             24.1048         208.3952        2202.085
27             22.02085        210.4792        1991.606
28             19.91606        212.584         1779.022
29             17.79022        214.7098        1564.312
30             15.64312        216.8569        1347.455
31             13.47455        219.0255        1128.43
32             11.28429        221.2157        907.2138
33             9.072137        223.4279        683.7859
34             6.837859        225.6622        458.1238
35             4.581238        227.9188        230.205
36             2.30205         230.198         7.034302E-03
Break in 110
Ok
_
```

Figure 7-5.
**Paying a loan,
year 3.**

Note that the data in the output are carried out to seven figures, even though the problem deals with dollars and cents. We will look at the problem of rounding numbers later. Also note the balance listed at the end of month

36. It is in scientific notation. The -03 indicates that the decimal point is to be moved three places to the left. The number listed is .007034302 or about .70 cents (less than one cent)! The computer shifted to scientific notation since the usual notation (.007034302) requires more than seven digits. The computer made the choice of which form of the number to display.

Using Loops to Create Delays

By using a loop we can create a delay inside the computer. Consider the following sequence of instructions:

```
10 FOR N = 1 TO 3000
20 NEXT N
```

This loop doesn't do anything! However, the computer repeats instructions 10 and 20 three thousand times! This may seem like a lot of work. But not for a computer. To obtain a feel for the speed at which the computer works, you should time this sequence of instructions. Such a loop may be used as a delay. For example, when you wish to keep some data on the screen without stopping the program, just build in a delay. Here is a program that prints two screens of text. A delay is imposed to give a person time to read the first screen.

Listing 7-8

```
10 ' ****************************************
20 ' This program demonstrates the use of a
30 '     delay loop between pages of text
40 ' ****************************************
50 PRINT "THIS IS A GRAPHICS PROGRAM TO DISPLAY SALES"
60 PRINT "FOR THE YEAR TO DATE"
70 FOR N = 1 TO 5000
80 NEXT N:'Delay Loop
90 CLS
100 PRINT "YOU MUST SUPPLY THE FOLLOWING PARAMETERS:"
110 PRINT "PRODUCT, TERRITORY, SALESPERSON"
120 END
```

Example 4. Use a loop to produce a blinking display for a security system.

Solution. Suppose that your security system is tied in with your computer and the system detects that an intruder is in your warehouse. Let us print out the message

```
SECURITY SYSTEM DETECTS INTRUDER - ZONE 2
```

For attention, let us blink this message on and off by alternately printing the message and clearing the screen.

```
10 FOR N = 1 TO 2000
20    PRINT "SECURITY SYSTEM DETECTS INTRUDER - ZONE 2"
30 FOR K = 1 TO 50
40 NEXT K
50    CLS
60 NEXT N
70 END
```

The loop in the above program is a delay loop to keep the message on the screen a moment. The first line of the loop turns the message off, except for the PRINT statement. The message will blink 2,000 times.

Test Your Understanding 5 (Answer on Page 157)

Write a program that blinks your name on the screen 500 times, leaving your name on the screen for a loop of length 50 each time.

More About Loops

In all of our loop examples, the loop variable increased by one with each repetition of the loop. However, it is possible to have the loop variable change by any amount. For example, the instructions

```
10  FOR N = 1 TO 5000 STEP 2
```

.
.
```
100 NEXT N
```

define a loop in which N jumps by 2 for each repetition, so N assumes the values

```
1,3,5,7,9,...,4999
```

Similarly, using STEP .5 in the above loop causes N to advance by .5 and assume the values

```
1, 1.5, 2, 2.5, 3, 3.5, 4, 4.5, ... , 5000
```

It is even possible to have a negative step. In this case, the loop variable will run backwards. For example, the instructions

```
10  FOR N = 100 TO 1 STEP -1
```
.
.
.
```
100 NEXT N
```

will "count down" from N = 100 to N = 1 one unit at a time. We will give some applications of such instructions in the Exercises.

Test Your Understanding 6 (Answer on Page 158)

Write instructions allowing N to assume the following sequences of values:

a. 95,96.7,98.4,...,112
b. 200,199.5,199,...,100

Exercises

Write BASIC programs to compute the following quantities.

1. $12+22+32+...+252$

2. $(1/2)^0 + (1/2)^1 + (1/2)^2 + ... + (1/2)^{10}$

3. $13+23+33+...+103$

4. $1 + (1/2) + (1/3) + ... + (1/100)$

5. Write a program to compute N2, N3, and N4 for $N = 1,...,12$. The format of your output should be as follows:

```
    N        N^2       N^3       N^4

    1
    2
    3
    .
    .
    .
   12
```

6. Suppose that you have a car loan whose current balance is $4,000.00. The monthly payment is $125.33 and the interest is one percent per month on the unpaid balance. Make a table of the interest payments and balances for the next 12 months.

7. Suppose you deposit $1,000 on January 1 of each year into a savings account paying 10 percent interest. Suppose that the interest is computed on January 1 of each year, based on the balance for the preceding year. Calculate the balances in the account for each of the next 15 years.

8. A stock market analyst predicts that Tyro Computers, Inc. will achieve a 20 percent growth in sales in each of the next three years, but profits will grow at a 30 percent annual rate. Last year's sales were $35 million and last year's profits were $5.54 million. Project the sales and profits for the next three years, based on the analyst's prediction.

Answers to Test Your Understandings 1, 2, 3, 4, 5, and 6

1.   a.
```
10 FOR N=3 TO 77
   .
   .
100 NEXT N
```

   b.
```
10 FOR N=3 TO 77
20 PRINT N^2
30 NEXT N
40 END
```

2.
```
10 SUM=0
20 FOR N=101 TO 110
30   SUM=SUM+N
40 NEXT N
50 PRINT SUM
60 END
```

3.
```
10 FOR N=1 TO 20
20   PRINT 2^N
30 NEXT N
40 END
```

4.
```
10 FOR J=1 TO 9
20   FOR I=0 TO 3
30     PRINT 10*I+J;
40   NEXT I
50 PRINT
60 NEXT J
70 END
```

5.
```
10 FOR N=1 TO 500
20   PRINT "<YOUR NAME>"
30   FOR K=1 TO 50
40   NEXT K
```

```
50   CLS
60   NEXT N
70 END
```

6.   a. 10 FOR N=95 TO 112 STEP 1.7
      b. 10 FOR N=200 TO 100 STEP -.5

Relational Expressions

In Chapter 2, we discussed numerical expressions that are formed from constants and variables using numeric operators, such as +, - , *, and /. GWBASIC allows you to use another type of expression, the so-called **relational expression**, which is an expression that has a value TRUE or FALSE. As we shall see later in the chapter, relational expressions can be used in constructing loops and in asking questions within a program.

Relational expressions are formed from numeric or string expressions and **relational operators**. Here are some examples of relational expressions:

```
TIME > 30
INTEREST < 10000
LETTER$ = "A"
```

Depending on the value of the variables TIME, Interest, and Letter$, these expressions have a value of TRUE or FALSE. For instance, if TIME has the value 100, then the first expression has the value TRUE, since TIME is greater than 30; if TIME has the value 10, then the first expression is FALSE, since TIME is not greater than 30. On the other hand, if LETTER$ has the value "B", then the third expression is false, whereas if LETTER$ has the value "A", then the third expression is TRUE. In these examples, the relational operators are, respectively > (greater than), < (less than) and = (equal to).

Three other relational operators that are useful are:

```
<= (less than or equal to)
>= (greater than or equal to)
<> (not equal to)
```

The relational expression

```
A <= B
```

is TRUE provided that A is less than B or A is equal to B; the expression is FALSE otherwise.

Similarly, the relational expression

```
A >= B
```

is TRUE provided that either A is greater than B or A is equal to B; the expression is FALSE otherwise.

The relational expression

```
A <> B
```

is TRUE provided that A is not equal to B ; the expression is FALSE otherwise.

Expressions that involve a single relational operator are called simple relational expressions. Expressions involving several relational operators are called complex. Typically, complex relational expressions are formed by joining several simple relational expressions using the relational operators AND, OR, XOR, and NOT.

For example, consider the simple relational expressions A > 1 and B < 3. the complex relational expression

```
(A > 1) AND (B < 3)
```

is TRUE provided that both of the expressions A > 1 and B < 3 are TRUE; the expression is false otherwise.

Similarly, the complex relational expression

```
(A > 1) OR (B < 3)
```

is TRUE provided that at least one of the expressions A < 1 and B > 3 is TRUE; the expression is FALSE otherwise.

The complex relational expression

```
(A > 1)  OR  (B < 3)
```

is TRUE provided that precisely one or the other of the two expressions A > 1 and B < 3 is TRUE; the expression is FALSE otherwise.

The complex relational expression

```
NOT  (A > 1)
```

is TRUE provided that the expression A > 1 is FALSE; it is FALSE provided that the expression A > 1 is TRUE. That is, the NOT operator forms the logical opposite of a relational expression.

Using the various relational operators described above, we can build relational expressions of arbitrary complexity, such as:

```
(NOT  (A > 1))  AND  ((A > 2)  OR  (B = 3))
```

We use parentheses to clarify the meaning of such expressions. In evaluating such expressions, proceed just as if they were numerical expressions. Evaluate parentheses from the innermost pair out. In expressions not involving parentheses, expressions are evaluated by taking the relational operators from left to right, according to the following table of precedence. (The top of the list are the operators of highest precedence)

```
NOT

AND,  OR,  XOR

>, <, = , >=, <=
```

TRUE and FALSE

GWBASIC evaluates the value of a relational expression using a numerical value. A TRUE relational expression is assigned the value -1 and a FALSE relational expression is assigned the value 0. Accordingly, it is convenient to create constants TRUE and FALSE with the values:

```
TRUE  =  -1
FALSE  =  0
```

You can then write relational expressions like:

```
(A < 1)  =  TRUE
```

Logically, this expression is the same as the expression:

```
A < 1
```

However, it is very intuitive and appealing to use the expanded form within a program since it makes the code more readable.

Exercises

Suppose that A has the value 5 and B the value 2.1. Determine the values of the following relational expressions.

1. `A > 1`

2. `A = 5`

3. `A <= B`

4. `A-1 > B+3`

5. `NOT (A = 0)`

6. `NOT (A <> 0)`

7. `(A < 0) OR (B = 2.1)`

8. `(A*B < 3) OR (A*B > 5)`

9. `(A-B > 0) AND (A > 1)`

10. `(A < -1) XOR (B > 2)`

WHILE and DO Loops

The FOR...NEXT statement provides a very explicit type of loop, namely a loop for a given number of repetitions specified by bounds for the loop counter. However, in many repetitive situations, you wish to repeat a loop until a specific condition holds. GWBASIC provides two statements for implementing such loops, the WHILE...WEND statement and the DO...LOOP statement. Let's now explore these looping structures.

WHILE...WEND Loops

The syntax of a WHILE...WEND loop is as follows:

```
WHILE relational expression
   statements
WEND
```

The **relational expression** is tested before each repetition of the loop. If the value of the expression is TRUE, then the statements are executed. They can consist of one or more statements of any type.

For example, consider the loop:

```
10 J=0
20 WHILE J <= 10
30  PRINT J
40  J=J+1
50 WEND
```

Initially, J is set equal to 0. Then the loop begins. It begins by testing to determine whether J is less than or equal to 10. Since J is 0, the expression J <= 0 is TRUE and the two following statements are executed. That is, 0 is displayed and J is replaced by J+1 or 0+1 or 1. The WEND tells GWBASIC to repeat the loop. So the condition J <= 10 is checked again. Since J is now 1, the condition is still true, so the two statements of the loop are executed. That is, J (or 1) is displayed and J is replaced by 2, and so forth until J has the value 11. In this case, the condition is FALSE and the loop ends. The program goes to the statement after WEND. The output of the loop is:

```
0
1
2
3
4
5
6
7
8
9
10
```

Note that in using a WHILE...WEND loop, there is no need to specify in advance the number of repetitions of the loop. Rather, the number of repetitions of the loop is determined by the value of a relational expression. For this reason, a WHILE...WEND loop is sometimes called an **indefinite loop**.

Example 1. Write a loop that keeps reading characters from the keyboard until one of the letters "Y", "N", "y", or "n" is input.

Solution.   Let's use A$ to store the character being read. Initially, set A$ equal to the null string. Let's use a WHILE...WEND loop with the testing condition

```
(A$="Y") OR (A$="N") OR (A$="y") OR (A$="n")
```

Here is the loop:

```
10 A$=""
20 WHILE (A$="Y") OR (A$="N") OR (A$="y") OR (A$="n")
30   INPUT A$
40 WEND
```

Infinite Loops and Ctrl-Break

As we saw above, it is very convenient to be able to execute a loop without knowing in advance how many times the loop will be executed. However, with this convenience comes a danger. It is perfectly possible to create a loop that will be repeated an infinite number of times! For example, consider this program:

```
10 N = 1
20 WHILE N > 0
30    PRINT N
40    N = N+1
50 WEND
60 END
```

The variable N starts off at 1. We print it and then increase N by 1 (to 2), print it, increase N by 1 (to 3), print it, and so forth. This program will go on forever! Such a loop is called an infinite loop and should clearly be avoided. However, even experienced programmers occasionally create infinite loops. When this happens, there is no need to panic. There is a way to stop the computer. At the very worst, you can turn off the power.

However, there is a much more satisfactory way of ending an infinite loop, in particular, or of interrupting a program generally. Just use the key combination Ctrl-Break. This will stop the program in progress and return you to the Main Menu. The current program is undisturbed.

Exercises

Write a WHILE...WEND loop that displays the following:

1. The squares of the integers from 1 to 10.
2. The integers starting with 1 whose square are less than 2,000.
3. The question "Do you wish to continue" until the letter "N" is pressed.
4. Write the loops in 1–3 using DO loops.
5. Write the following loop using WHILE...WEND

```
10 FOR J=1 TO 5 STEP .5
20    PRINT J
30    PRINT J^2
40 NEXT J
```

Conditional Statements

One of the principal features that makes computers useful as problem-solving tools is their ability to make decisions. GWBASIC contains statements, called conditional statements, that allow you to ask a question and to make a response within the program based on the answer to the question.

Simple IF...THEN...ELSE Statement

GWBASIC's conditional statement is the IF...THEN...ELSE statement, which has the following syntax:

```
IF relational expression THEN statement [ELSE statement]
```

This statement consists of a single logical line and works as follows: The relational expression is tested. If it is TRUE, then the statement after THEN is executed; the program then proceeds with the statement on the next line. If the relational expression is FALSE, the statements after ELSE are executed. If the optional ELSE clause is not used and the relational expression is FALSE, then the program proceeds to the next line of the program. Note that there can be any number of statements after THEN or ELSE, with the statements separated by colons.

For example, consider the following statement:

```
IF A$="Y" THEN PRINT MSG1$ ELSE CLS: PRINT "Goodbye"
```

If A$ equals "Y", then the program prints the string MSG1$. If A$ is not equal to "Y", then the program clears the screen and then prints "Goodbye".

An alternate version of the IF...THEN...ELSE statement allows you to replace one or both of the statements with line numbers. For instance, the statement

```
10 IF Z=0 THEN 100 ELSE 200
```

works like this: If Z is equal to 0, then GWBASIC goes to line 100 for its next line; otherwise, it goes to line 200. This form of the conditional statement is highly nonstructured and should be avoided if at all possible. However, if a large number of statements follow THEN or ELSE, it may be impossible to fit them on a single logical line (at most 255 characters). In this case, you may use GOTO after THEN, or else to branch to the appropriate sequence of instructions in each case.

Example 1.   At $20 per square yard, a family can afford up to 500 square feet of carpet for their dining room. They wish to install the carpet in a circular shape. It has been decided that the radius of the carpet is to be a whole number of feet. What is the radius of the largest carpet they can afford? (The area of a circle of radius R is Pi times R^2, where Pi equals approximately 3.14159.)

Solution.   Let us compute the area of the circle of radius 1,2,3,4,... and determine which of the areas are less than 500.

```
10 ' ****************************************
20 ' This program lists the affordable sizes
30 '    of carpet for a certain family
40 ' ****************************************
50  PI = 3.14159
60  R = 1 :               ' R=radius
70  A = PI*R^2 :          ' A=area
80 'Is A>=500 ?  If so, END. Otherwise, PRINT R .
90  IF A >=  500 THEN 120 ELSE PRINT R
100 LET R = R + 1 :       ' Go to next radius
110 GOTO 70 :             ' Repeat
120 END
```

Exercises

1. Write a program to calculate all perfect squares that are less than 45,000. (Perfect squares are the numbers 1,4,9,16,25,36,49,....)

2. Write a program to determine all of the circles of integer radius and area less than or equal to 5,000 square feet. (The area of a circle of radius R is PI*R^2, where PI = 3.14159, approximately.)

3. Write a program to determine the sizes of all those boxes that are perfect cubes, have integer dimensions, and have volumes of less than 175,000 cubic feet. (That is, find all integers X for which X3 is less than 175,000.)

4. Modify the arithmetic testing program of Example 7 so that the operation tested is multiplication instead of addition.

5. Modify the arithmetic testing program of Example 7 so that it allows you to choose, at the beginning of each group of ten problems, from among these operations: addition, subtraction, or multiplication.

6. Write a program that accepts three numbers via an INPUT statement and determines the largest of the three.

7. Write a program that accepts three numbers via an INPUT statement and determines the smallest of the three.

8. Write a program that accepts a set of numbers via INPUT statements and determines the largest among them.

9. Write a program that accepts a set of numbers via INPUT statements and determines the smallest among them.

10. The following data were collected by a sociologist. Six cities experienced the following numbers of burglaries in 1980 and 1981:

City	Burglaries 1980	Burglaries 1981
A	5,782	6,548
B	4,811	6,129
C	3,865	4,270
D	7,950	8,137
E	4,781	4,248
F	6,598	7,048

For each city, calculate the increase (decrease) in the number of burglaries. Determine which had an increase of more than 500 burglaries.

11. Write a program that does the arithmetic of a cash register. That is, let the program accept purchases via INPUT statements, then total the purchases, figure out the sales tax (assume five percent), and compute the total purchase. Let the program ask for the amount of payment given and then let it compute the change due.

12. Write a program that analyzes cash flow. Let the program ask for cash on hand as well as accounts expected to be   received in the next month, and let it compute the total anticipated accounts receivable for the month. Let the program ask for the bills due in the next month, and let it compute the total accounts payable during the month. By comparing the amounts to be received and to be paid out, let the program compute the net cash flow for the month.

Eight

Working With Data

Introduction

In this chapter, we discuss ways to organize and format data, including:

- Use of arrays, including the DIM and CLEAR statements.

- Inputting data using the READ, DATA, and RESTORE statements.

- Using semicolons in PRINT statements.

- Formatting output using TAB and SPC.

- Formatted output with PRINT USING.

- Using random numbers to simulate random events within programs, and applications to games of chance.

Working With Tabular Data—Arrays

In Chapter 5 we introduced the notion of a variable and used variable names like:

    TAX, BALANCE, A1, TOTAL

Unfortunately, the supply of variables available to us is not sufficient for many programs. Indeed, as we shall see in this chapter, there are relatively innocent programs requiring hundreds or even thousands of variables. To meet the needs of such programs, BASIC allows for the use of so-called subscripted variables. Such variables are used constantly by mathematicians and are identified by numbered subscripts attached to a letter. For instance, here is a list of 1,000 variables as they might appear in a mathematical work:

    A1, A2, A3,..., A1000

The numbers used to distinguish the variables are called subscripts. Likewise, the BASIC language allows definition of variables to be distinguished by subscripts. However, since the computer has difficulty placing the numbers in the traditional position, they are placed in parentheses on the same line as the letter. For example, the above list of 1,000 different variables is written in BASIC as

    A(1),A(2),A(3),...,A(1000)

Please note that the variable A(1) is not the same as the variable A1. You may use both of them in the same program and BASIC will interpret them as being different.

A subscripted variable is really a group of variables with a common letter identification distinguished by different integer "subscripts." For instance, the above group of variables constitute the subscripted variable A( ). It is often useful to view a subscripted variable as a table or array. For example, the subscripted variable A( ) considered above can be viewed as providing the following table of information:

```
A(1)
A(2)
A(3)
   .
   .
   .
A(1000)
```

As shown here, the subscripted variable defines a table consisting of 1,000 rows. Suppose that J is an integer between 1 and 1,000. Then row number J contains a single entry, namely, the value of the variable A(J): the first row contains the value of A(1), the second the value of A(2), and so forth. Since a subscripted variable can be thought of as a table (or array), subscripted variables are often called arrays.

The array shown above is a table consisting of 1,000 rows and a single column. GWBASIC allows you to consider more general arrays. For example, consider the following financial table, which records the daily income for three days from each of a chain of four computer stores:

	Store #1	Store #2	Store #3	Store #4
Day 1	1258.38	2437.46	4831.90	987.12
Day 2	1107.83	2045.68	3671.86	1129.47
Day 3	1298.00	2136.88	4016.73	1206.34

This table has three rows and four columns. Its entries may be stored in the computer as a set of 12 variables:

```
A(1,1)   A(1,2)   A(1,3)   A(1,4)

A(2,1)   A(2,2)   A(2,3)   A(2,4)

A(3,1)   A(3,2)   A(3,3)   A(3,4)
```

This array of variables is very similar to a subscripted variable, except that there are now two subscripts. The first subscript indicates the row number and the second subscript indicates the column number. For example, the variable A(3,2) is in the third row, second column. A collection of variables such as that given above is called a **two-dimensional array** or a **doubly-subscripted variable**. Each setting of the variables in such an array defines a tabular array. For example, if we assign the values

```
A(1,1) =   1258.38, A(1,2) = 2437.46,

A(1,3) =   4831.90,
```

and so forth, then we will have the table of earnings from the computer store chain.

So far, we have only considered numeric arrays—arrays whose variables can assume only numerical values. However, it is possible to have arrays with variables that assume string values. (Recall that a string is a sequence of characters: letter, numeral, punctuation mark, or other printable keyboard symbol.) For example, here is an array that can contain string data:

```
A$(1)
A$(2)
A$(3)
A$(4)
```

The dollar signs indicate that each of the variables of the array is a string variable. If we assign the values

```
A$(1) = "SLOW"
A$(2) = "FAST"
A$(3) = "FAST"
A$(4) = "STOP"
```

then the array is this table of words:

```
SLOW
FAST
FAST
STOP
```

Similarly, the employee record table

Soc Sec #	Age	Sex	Marital Status
178654775	38	M	S
345861023	29	F	M
789257958	34	F	D
375486595	42	M	M
457696064	21	F	S

may be stored in an array of the form B$(I,J), where I assumes any one of the values 1, 2, 3, 4, 5 (I is the row), and J assumes any one of the values 1, 2, 3, 4 (J = the column). For example, B$(1,1) has the value "178654775", B$(1,2) has the value "38", B$(1,3) has the value "M", and so forth.

GWBASIC allows you to have arrays that have three, four, or even more subscripts. For example, consider the computer store chain array introduced above. Suppose that we had one such array for each of ten consecutive three-day periods. This collection of data can be stored in a three-dimensional array of the form C(I,J,K), where I and J represent the row and column, just as before, and K represents the year. (K can assume the values 1,2,3,...,10.)

An array may involve any number of dimensions up to 255. The subscripts corresponding to each dimension may assume values from 0 to 32,767. For all practical applications, any size array is permissible. However, you should note that arrays can take up large amounts of memory. For example, an array A(I,J,K), where each of I, J, and K can assume the values 1 through 1,000 consists of 1,000*1,000*1,000 = 1,000,000,000 entries, which will not fit into any PC's memory.

You must inform the computer of the sizes of the arrays you plan to use in a program. This allows the computer to allocate memory space to house all the values. To specify the size of an array, use a DIM (dimension) statement. For example, to define the size of the subscripted variable A(J), J=1,...,1,000, we insert the statement

```
DIM A(1000)
```

in the program. This statement informs the computer to expect variables A(0), A(1), ..., A(1,000) in the program and that it should set aside memory space for 1,001 variables.

In many applications, it is convenient to have subscripts be integers from a particular range, say the integers 5, 6, ..., 15 inclusive. You may define a numerical array called, say ALPHA, having these subscripts using a DIM statement of the form

```
DIM ALPHA(5 TO 12)
```

To define the size of a two-dimensional array A(), use a DIM statement of the form

```
DIM A(5,4)
```

This statement defines an array A(I,J), where I can assume the values 0, 1, 2, 3, 4, 5, and J can assume the values 0, 1, 2, 3, 4. Arrays with three or more subscripts are defined similarly. You may define each subscript to run over a different interval. For example, to define an array A(I,J) in which I runs over the integers 5, 6, ..., 12, and J runs over the integers 10, 11, ..., 20, use a DIM statement of the form:

```
DIM A(5 TO 12, 10 TO 20)
```

Note: A DIM statement is optional. If your program does not have a DIM statement corresponding to a particular array, then GWBASIC assumes a DIM statement in which the subscripts range from 0 to 10. However, allowing the compiler to dimension your arrays is considered bad programming style. It is much better programming practice to explicitly dimension each array that you use.

Test Your Understanding 1 (Answers on Page 180)

Here is an array.

```
12   645.80
148  489.75
589  12.89
487  14.50
```

a. Define an appropriate subscripted variable to store this data.

b. Define an appropriate DIM statement.

It is possible to dimension several arrays with one DIM statement. For example, the dimension statement

```
DIM A(1000), B$(5), A(5,4)
```

defines the array A(0), ..., A(1000), the string array B$(0), ..., B$(5) and the two-dimensional array A(I,J), I=0, ..., 5; J=0, ..., 4.

Subscript Out of Range Errors

In defining an array, make sure that it is large enough to include all subscripts that occur in your program. For example, in the case of the array defined above, a reference to either of the variables ALPHA(1), ALPHA(13) is illegal. If the compiler encounters such a reference in compiling the program, it will provide an error message:

```
Subscript out of range
```

In a program, you may refer to a subscript by specifying an integer constant (as in A(3)) or an integer expression (as in A(2*I+1)). In using a subscript specified by an expression, it is very possible to produce an illegal subscript value (e.g., if I equals -3 in A(2*I+1)). It is not possible to detect such illegal subscript values during compilation. However, for debugging purposes, you may have GWBASIC check for subscript out-of-range errors during program operation. This may be done by selecting the Debug command from the main menu and selecting the Bounds option. In this case, subsequent compilations generate code to check array bounds before they are used. This code adds to program length and will slow down execution.

So it is probably a good strategy to use it only during debugging. Once you are sure that you are using only legal subscripts, you may turn off the Bounds option and recompile the program.

Using Arrays

We now know how to set aside memory space for the variables of an array. We must next take up the problem of assigning values to these variables. We can use individual assignment statements, but with 1,000 variables in an array, this can lead to an unmanageable number of statements. There are more convenient methods that make use of loops. The next two examples illustrate two of these methods.

Example 1. Define an array $A(J)$, $J=1, 2,..., 1,000$ and assign the following values to the variables of the array:

        A(1)=2, A(2)=4, A(3)=6, A(4)=8, . . .

Solution. We wish to assign each variable a value equal to twice its subscript. That is, we wish to assign $A(J)$ the value $2*J$. To do this we use a loop:

```
10 DIM A(1000)
20 FOR J = 1 TO 1000
30   A(J) = 2*J
40 NEXT J
50 END
```

Note that the program ignores the variable $A(0)$. Like any variable that has not been assigned a value, it has the value zero.

Test Your Understanding 2 (Answer on Page 180)

Write a program that assigns the variables $A(0),..., A(30)$ the values $A(0)=0$, $A(1)=1$, $A(2)=4$, $A(3)=9$, ...

Example 2.   Define an array corresponding to the employee record table above. Input the values given and print the table on the screen.

Solution. Our program will print the headings of the columns and then ask for the table entries, one row at a time. We will store the entries in the array B$(I,J), where I is one of 1, 2, 3, 4, 5 and J is one of 1, 2, 3, 4. We dimension the array as B$(5,4).

```
10 ' *********************************************
20 ' This program sets up an array to hold four
30 ' pieces of data for each of five employees,
40 ' accepting values from the user and
50 ' displaying them in a table
60 ' *********************************************
100  DIM B$(5,4):          ' Set up array
110  FOR I=1 TO 5:         ' Input the data
120    INPUT "SS #,Age,Sex,Mar.St.";
       B$(I,1),B$(I,2),B$(I,3),B$(I,4)
130  NEXT I
140  CLS:                  ' Print the table
150  PRINT "Soc. Sec. #", "Age", "Sex","Marital Status"
160  FOR I=1 TO 5
170    PRINT B$(I,1),B$(I,2),B$(I,3),B$(I,4)
180  NEXT I
190  END
```

Test Your Understanding 3 (Answer on Page 179)

Suppose that your program uses a 9×2 array A$(I,J), a 9×1 array B$(I,J), and a 9×1 array C(I,J). Write an appropriate DIM statement.

If you plan to dimension an array, always insert the DIM statement before the variable first appears in your program. Otherwise, the first time BASIC comes across the array, it assumes that the subscripts go from 0 to 10. If it subsequently comes across a DIM statement, it will think you are changing the size of the array in the midst of the program, something that is not allowed. If you try to change the size of an array in the middle of a program, you will get this error message:

```
Duplicate Definition
```

Memory Considerations for Arrays

An array (numeric or string) requires four bytes of RAM per variable. (See Chapter 17 for a discussion of double precision, single-precision, and integer arrays.) The variables for numeric arrays are located in a special 64K section of RAM reserved specifically for them. The variables for a string array also occupy space in this section of RAM. However, the string data stored in these variables are stored with the other string variable data, in its own 64K section of RAM.

Thus, for example, a numeric array with 1,000 variables takes up 4*1,000 = 4,000 bytes of array variable space. A string array with 1,000 variables also takes up 4,000 bytes of array variable space. Moreover, if its variables store strings totaling 12,000 bytes, then the array also occupies 12,000 bytes of string memory.

Deleting Arrays

Arrays can take up large amounts of memory. In order to handle large amounts of data, it is often necessary to delete one array from memory in order to manipulate another. You may do this using the ERASE statement. For example, to delete the array A, we can use the statement

```
ERASE A
```

Once you execute ERASE, all the values of array A( ) are lost and the DIM statement dimensioning A( ) is canceled. In particular, you may redimension an array after an ERASE statement.

The ERASE statement may be used to delete several arrays at once, as in this statement:

```
ERASE B,C,D
```

Exercises

For each of the following tables, define an appropriate array and determine
the appropriate DIM statement.

1.	5	2.	1.1	2.0	3.5
	2		1.7	2.4	6.2
	1.7				
	4.9				
	11				

3.   MARY
     JOHN
     SIDNEY

4.   1   2   3

5.   RENT   575.00
     UTILITIES   249.78
     CLOTHES   174.98
     CAR   348.70

6. Display the following array on the screen:

	Receipts		
	Store #1	Store #2	Store #3
1/1–1/10	57,385.48	89,485.45	38,456.90
1/11–1/20	39,485.98	76,485.49	40,387.86
1/21–1/31	45,467.21	71,494.25	37,983.38

7. Write a program that displays the array of Exercise 6 along with totals
   of the receipts from each store.

8. Expand the program in Exercise 7 so that it calculates and displays the
   totals of ten-day periods. (Your screen will not be wide enough to display
   the ten-day totals in a fifth column, so display them in a separate array.)

9. Devise a program that keeps track of the inventory of an appliance store chain. Store the current inventory in an array of the form

```
            Store #1    Store #2    Store #3    Store #4
Refrig.
Stove
Air Cond.
Vacuum
Disposal
```

Your program should (1) input the inventory corresponding to the beginning of the day, (2) continually ask for the next transaction—the store number and the number of appliances of each item sold, and (3) in response to each transaction, update the inventory array and redisplay it on the screen.

Answers to Test Your Understandings 1, 2, and 3

1. a. `A(I,J), I=1,2,3,4; J=1,2`
    b. `DIM A(4,2)`

2. `DIM A(30)`
    `FOR J=0 TO 30`
    `   A(J)=J^2`
    `NEXT J`
    `END`

3. `DIM A$(9,2),B$(9,1),C(9,5)`

Inputting Data

In Chapter 4, we introduced arrays and discussed several methods for assigning values to the variables of an array. The most flexible method was via the INPUT statement. However, this can be a tedious method for large arrays. Fortunately, BASIC provides us with an alternate method for inputting data.

A given program may need many different numbers and strings. You may store the data needed in one or more DATA statements. A typical DATA statement has the form

```
DATA 3.457, 2.588, 11234, "WINGSPAN"
```

Note that this DATA statement consists of four data items, three numeric and one string. The data items are separated by commas. You may include as many data items in a single DATA statement as the line allows. Moreover, you may include any number of DATA statements in a program and they may be placed anywhere in the program, although a common placement is at the end of the program (just before the END statement). Note that we enclosed the string constant "WINGSPAN" in quotation marks. Actually, this is not necessary. A string constant in a DATA statement does not need quotes, as long as it does not contain a comma or colon, or start with a blank.

The DATA statements may be used to assign values to variables and, in particular, to variables in arrays. Here's how to do this. In conjunction with the DATA statements, you use one or more READ statements. For example, suppose that the above DATA statement appears in a program. Further, suppose that you wish to assign these values:

```
A = 3.457, B = 2.588, C = 11234, Z$ = "WINGSPAN"
```

This can be accomplished via the READ statement:

```
READ A,B,C,Z$
```

Here is how the READ statement works. On encountering a READ statement, the computer looks for a DATA statement. It then assigns values to the variables in the READ statement by taking the values, in order, from the DATA statement. If there is insufficient data in the first DATA statement, the computer continues to assign values using the data in the next DATA statement. If necessary, the computer proceeds to the third DATA statement, and so forth.

Test Your Understanding 1 (Answer on Page 189)

Assign the following values:

A(1)=5.1, A(2)=4.7, A(3)=5.8, A(4)=3.2, A(5)=7.9, A(6)=6.9

The computer maintains an internal pointer that points to the next DATA item to be used. If the computer encounters a second READ statement, it will start reading where it left off. For example, suppose that instead of the above READ statement, we use the two READ statements

```
READ A,B
READ C,Z$
```

Upon encountering the first statement, the computer looks for the location of the pointer. Initially, it points to the first item in the first DATA statement. The computer assigns the values A=3.457 and B=2.588. Moreover, the position of the pointer is advanced to the third item in the DATA statement. Upon encountering the next READ statement, the computer assigns values beginning with the one designated by the pointer, namely C=11,234 and Z$="WINGSPAN".

Test Your Understanding 2 (Answer on Page 189)

What values are assigned to A and B$ by the following program?

```
10 DATA 10,30,"ENGINE","TACH"
20 READ A,B
30 READ C$,B$
40 END
```

The following example illustrates the use of DATA statements in assigning values to an array.

Example 1. Suppose that the monthly electricity costs of a certain family are as follows:

Jan.	$89.74	Feb.	$95.84	March	$79.42
Apr.	78.93	May	72.11	June	115.94
July	158.92	Aug.	164.38	Sep.	105.98
Oct.	90.44	Nov.	89.15	Dec.	93.97

Write a program calculating the average monthly cost of electricity.

Solution. Let us unceremoniously dump all of the numbers shown above into DATA statements at the end of the program. Arbitrarily, let's start the DATA statements at line 1000, with END at 2000. This allows us plenty of room. To calculate the average, we must add up the numbers and divide by 12. To do this, let us first create an array A(J), J=1, 2, ..., 12 and set A(J) equal to the cost of electricity in the Jth month. We do this via a loop and the READ statement. We then use a loop to add all the A(J)s. Finally, we divide by 12 and PRINT the answer. Here is the program.

```
10 ' **************************************************
20 ' This program finds the average of twelve monthly
30 '    costs read into an array from DATA statements
40 ' **************************************************
100 DIM A(12):          ' Set up the array
110 FOR J=1 TO 12:      ' Read in the data
120    READ A(J)
130 NEXT J
140 C=0
150 FOR J=1 TO 12
160    C=C+A(J):        ' C accumulates the sum
170 NEXT J
180 C=C/12:             ' Divide sum by 12 to find avg
190 PRINT "THE AVERAGE MONTHLY COST OF ELECTRICITY IS",C
1000 DATA 89.74, 95.84, 79.42, 78.93, 72.11, 115.94
1010 DATA 158.92, 164.38, 105.98, 90.44, 89.15, 93.97
2000 END
```

The following program can be helpful in preparing the payroll of a small business.

Example 2. A small business has five employees. Here are their names and hourly wages.

Name	Hourly Wage
Joe Polanski	7.75
Susan Greer	8.50
Allan Cole	8.50
Betsy Palm	6.00
Herman Axler	6.00

Write a program that accepts as input hours worked for the current week, and calculates the current gross pay and the amount of Social Security tax to be withheld from their pay. (Assume that the Social Security tax amounts to 7.05 percent of gross pay.)

Solution. Let us keep the hourly wage rates and names in two arrays, called A(J) and B$(J), respectively, where J = 1, 2, 3, 4, 5. Note that we can't use a single two-dimensional array for this data since the names are string data, and the hourly wage rates are numerical. (Recall that BASIC does not allow us to mix the two kinds of data in an array.) The first part of the program will be to assign the values to the variables in the two arrays. Next, the program will, one by one, print out the names of the employees and ask for the number of hours worked during the current week. These data will be stored in the array C(J), J = 1, 2, 3, 4, 5. The program will then compute the gross wages as A(J)*C(J) (that is, <wage rate> times <number of hours worked>). This piece of datum will be stored in the array D(J), J=1, 2, 3, 4, 5. Next, the program will compute the amount of Social Security tax to be withheld as .0705*D(J). This piece of datum will be stored in the array E(J), J=1, 2, 3, 4, 5. Finally, all the computed data will be printed on the screen. Here is the program:

```
10 ' ********************************************
20 ' This program determines the social security
30 '    tax due from five employees whose salary
40 '    rates are read into an array and whose
50 '    hours are typed in by the user
60 ' ********************************************
100  DIM A(5),B$(5),C(5),D(5),E(5)
110  FOR J=1 TO 5:            ' Read in the data
120    READ B$(J),A(J)
130  NEXT J
```

```
140   FOR J=1 TO 5:          ' Input hours worked
150     PRINT "TYPE CURRENT HOURS OF", B$(J)
160     INPUT C(J)
170     D(J)=A(J)*C(J)
180     E(J)=.067*D(J)
190   NEXT J
200 'Print in a table the employee names, wages and tax
210   PRINT "EMPLOYEE","GROSS WAGES","SOC.SEC.TAX"
220   FOR J=1 TO 5
230     PRINT B$(J),D(J),E(J)
240   NEXT J
300   DATA JOE POLANSKI, 7.75, SUSAN GREER, 8.50
310   DATA ALLAN COLE, 8.50, BETSY PALM, 6.00
320   DATA HERMAN AXLER, 6.00
400 END
```

In certain applications, you may wish to read the same DATA statements more than once. To do this you must reset the pointer via the RESTORE statement. For example, consider the following program.

```
10 DATA 2.3, 5.7, 4.5, 7.3
20 READ A,B
30 RESTORE
40 READ C,D
50 END
```

Line 20 sets A equal to 2.3 and B equal to 5.7. The RESTORE statement of line 30 moves the pointer back to the first item of data, 2.3. The READ statement of line 40 then sets C equal to 2.3 and D equal to 5.7. Note that without the RESTORE in line 30, the READ statement in line 40 would set C equal to 4.5 and D equal to 7.3.

There are two common errors in using READ and DATA statements. First, you may instruct the program to READ more data than are present in the DATA statements. For example, consider the following program.

```
10 DATA 1,2,3,4
20 FOR J=1 TO 5
30    READ A(J)
40 NEXT J
50 END
```

This program attempts to read five pieces of data, but the DATA statement only has four. In this case, you will receive an error message:

```
Out of data
```

A second common error is attempting to assign a string value to a numeric variable or vice versa. Such an attempt leads to an error message:

```
Type mismatch
```

Exercises

Each of the following programs assigns values to the variables of an array. Determine which values are assigned.

1.
```
10   DIM A(10)
20   FOR J=1 TO 10
30      READ A(J)
40   NEXT J
50   DATA 2,4,6,8,10,12,14,16,18,20
60   END
```

2.
```
10   DIM A(3),B(3)
20   FOR J=0 TO 3
30      READ A(J), B(J)
40   NEXT J
50   DATA 1.1,2.2,3.3,4.4,5.5,6.6,7.7,8.8,9.9
60   END
```

3.
```
10   DIM A(3),B$(3)
20   FOR J=0 TO 3
30      READ A(J)
40   NEXT J
```

```
50   FOR J=0 TO 3
60      READ B$(J)
70   NEXT J
80   DATA 1,2,3,4,A,B,C,D
90   END
```

4.
```
10   DIM A(3), B(3)
20   READ A(0),B(0)
30   READ A(1),B(1)
40   RESTORE
50   READ A(2),B(2)
60   READ A(3),B(3)
70   DATA 1,2,3,4,5,6,7,8
80   END
```

5.
```
10   DIM A(3,4)
20   FOR J=1 TO 4
30      FOR I=1 TO 3
40         READ A(I,J)
50      NEXT I
60   NEXT J
70   DATA 1,2,3,4,5,6,7,8,9,10,11,12
80   END
```

The following programs contain errors. Find them.

6.
```
10   DIM A(5)
20   FOR J=1 TO 5
30      READ A(J)
40   NEXT J
50   DATA 1,2,3,4
60   END
```

7.
```
10   DIM A(5)
20   FOR J=1 TO 5
30      READ A(J)
```

```
40   NEXT J
50   DATA 1,A,2,3
60   END
```

8. Here is a table of Federal Income Tax withholding of weekly wages for an individual claiming one exemption. Assume that each of the employees in the business discussed in Example 2 claims a single exemption. Modify the program given so that it correctly computes Federal withholding and the net amount of wages. (That is, the total after Federal withholding and Social Security are deducted.)

Wages at Least	But Less Than	Tax Withheld
200	210	29.10
210	220	31.20
220	230	33.80
230	240	36.40
240	250	39.00
250	260	41.60
260	270	44.20
270	280	46.80
280	290	49.40
290	300	52.10
300	310	55.10
310	320	58.10
320	330	61.10
330	340	64.10
340	–	67.10

9. Here is a set of 24 hourly temperature reports as compiled by the National Weather Service. Write a program to compute the average temperature for the last 24 hours. Let your program respond to a query concerning the temperature at a particular hour. (For example, what was the temperature at 2:00 P.M.?)

	AM	PM
12:00	10	38
1:00	10	39

2:00	9	40
3:00	9	40
4:00	8	42
5:00	11	38
6:00	15	33
7:00	18	27
8:00	20	22
9:00	25	18
10:00	31	15
11:00	35	12

Answers to Test Your Understandings 1 and 2

1.
```
10  DATA 5.1,4.7,5.8,3.2,7.9,6.9
20  FOR J=1 TO 6
30    READ A(J)
40  NEXT J
50  END
```

2. A = 10, B$ = "TACH"

Formatting Your Output

In this section, we will discuss the various ways in which you can format output on the screen and on the printer. IBM PC BASIC is quite flexible in the form in which you can cast output. You have control over the size of the letters on the screen, placement of output on the line, degree of accuracy to which calculations are displayed, and so forth. Let us begin by reviewing what we have already learned about printing.

Semicolons in PRINT Statements

The BASIC screen may be set for 40- or 80-character lines using the WIDTH statement. This gives 40 or 80 print positions in each line. These are divided into print zones of 14 characters each[1]. To start printing at the beginning of the next print zone, insert a comma between the items to be printed.

In many applications, it is necessary to print more columns than there are print zones. Or, output may look better if the columns are less than a full print zone wide. To avoid any space between consecutive print items, separate them in the PRINT statement by a semicolon. Consider this instruction:

```
10 PRINT "PERSON";"NAL COMPUTER"
```

It results in the output shown in Figure 8-1.

---

1 For an 80-column width, the last print zone has only ten characters. For a 40-column width, the last print zone has only 12 characters.

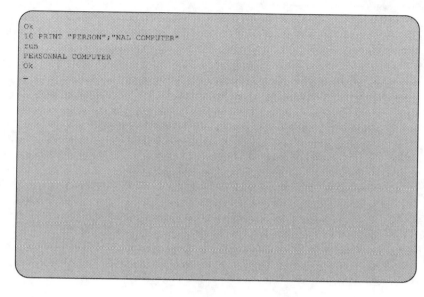

```
Ok
10 PRINT "PERSON";"NAL COMPUTER"
run
PERSONNAL COMPUTER
Ok
_
```

Figure 8-1.
Use of a semi-colon in a print statement.

The semicolon suppresses any space between the display of PERSON and NAL COMPUTER.

In displaying numbers, remember that all positive numbers begin with a blank space, which is in place of the understood plus (+) sign. Negative numbers, however, have a displayed minus (-) sign and do not begin with a blank space. For example, the statement

```
10 PRINT "THE VALUE OF A IS";2.35
```

results in the first display shown in Figure 8-2.

```
Ok
10 PRINT "THE VALUE OF A IS";2.35
20 PRINT "THE VALUE OF A IS";-2.35
30 PRINT "THE VALUE OF A IS ";-2.35
run
THE VALUE OF A IS 2.35
THE VALUE OF A IS-2.35
THE VALUE OF A IS -2.35
Ok
_
```

Figure 8-2.
Using a semi-colon with numeric data.

The space between the S and the 2 comes from the blank, which is considered part of the number 2.35. On the other hand, the statement

```
20 PRINT "THE VALUE OF A IS";-2.35
```

results in the second display of Figure 8-2.

To obtain a space between the S and the - , we must include a space in the string constant:

```
30 PRINT "THE VALUE OF A IS ";-2.35
```

Test Your Understanding 1 (Answer on Page 204)

Write a program that allows you to input two numbers. The program should then display them as an addition problem in the form 5 + 7 = 12.

At the completion of a PRINT statement, BASIC automatically supplies an ENTER so that the cursor moves to the beginning of the next line. You may suppress this ENTER by ending the PRINT statement with a semicolon. For example, the statements

```
10 PRINT "THE VALUE OF A IS";
20 PRINT 2.35
```

results in the display

```
THE VALUE OF A IS 2.35
```

Test Your Understanding 2 (Answer on Page 204)

Describe the output from this program.

```
10   A=5:B=3:C=8
20   PRINT "THE VALUE OF A IS",A
30   PRINT "THE VALUE OF B";
40   PRINT " IS";B
50   PRINT "THE VALUE OF C IS";-C
60   END
```

Our discussion so far has been oriented to the display of data on the screen. However, you may also use semicolons in LPRINT statements to control spacing of output on the printer.

Horizontal Tabbing

You may begin a print item in any print position. To do this, use the TAB command. The print positions are numbered from 1 to 255, going from left to right. (Note that a line may be up to 255 characters long. On the screen, an oversized line wraps around to the next line. However, the line prints correctly on a printer having a wide enough print line.) For example, the command TAB(7) means to move to column 7. TAB is always used in conjunction with a PRINT statement. For example, the PRINT statement

```
10 PRINT TAB(7) A
```

prints the value of the variable A, beginning in print position 7. It is possible
to use more than one TAB per PRINT statement. For example, the statement

```
20 PRINT TAB(5) A; TAB(15) B
```

prints the value of A beginning in print position 5, and the value of B
beginning in print position 15. Note the semicolon between the two TAB
instructions. (see Figure 8-3).

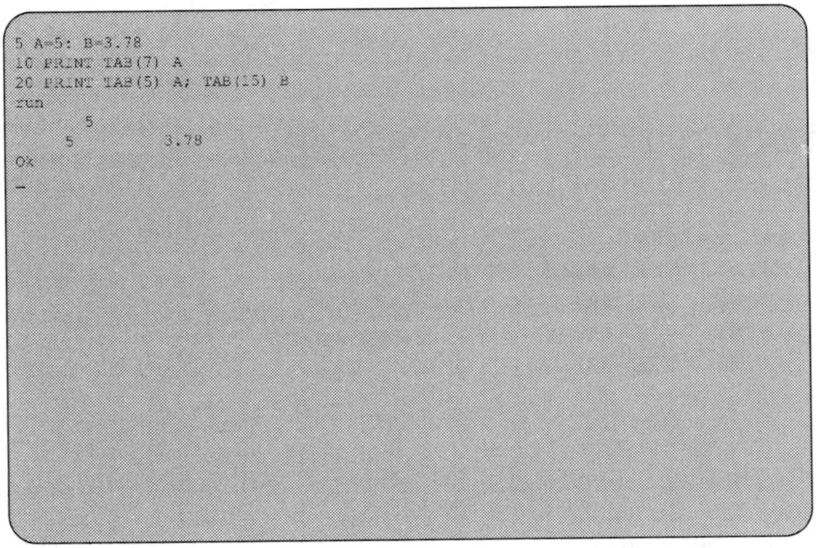

```
5 A=5: B=3.78
10 PRINT TAB(7) A
20 PRINT TAB(5) A; TAB(15) B
run
        5
    5           3.78
Ok
_
```

Figure 8-3.
**Use of the TAB
clause.**

Test Your Understanding 3 (Answer on Page 204)

Write an instruction printing the value of A in column 25 and the value of
B seven columns further to the right.

In some applications, you may wish to add a certain number of spaces
between output items (as opposed to TABing where the next item appears
in a specified column). This may be accomplished using the SPC (=space)
function, which works very much like TAB. For example, to print the values
of A and B with 5 blank spaces between them, we may use the statement

```
10 PRINT A; SPC(5) B
```

See Figure 8-4.

```
5 A=5: B=3.78
10 PRINT A; SPC(5) B
run
 5        3.78
Ok
_
```

Figure 8-4.
Use of the SPC clause.

Formatting Numbers

GWBASIC has rather extensive provisions for formatting numerical output. Here are some of the things you may specify with regard to printing a number:

- Number of digits of accuracy
- Alignment of columns (one's column, ten's column, hundred's column, and so forth)
- Display and positioning of the initial dollar sign
- Display of commas in large numbers (as in 1,000,000)
- Display and positioning of + and - signs.

All of these formatting options may be requested with the PRINT USING statement. Roughly speaking, you tell the computer what you wish your number to look like by specifying a "prototype." For example, suppose you wish to print the value of the variable A with four digits to the left of the decimal point and two digits to the right. This can be done via the instruction

```
PRINT USING "####.##"; A
```

Here, each # stands for a digit and the period stands for the decimal point. If, for example, A was equal to 5,432.381, this instruction would round the value of A to the specified two decimal places and would print the value of A as

```
5432.38
```

On the other hand, if the value of A is 932.547, then the computer prints the value as

```
932.55
```

In this case, the value is printed with a leading blank space, since the format specified four digits to the left of the decimal point. This sort of printing is especially useful in aligning columns of figures like this:

```
  367.1
 1567.2
29573.3
    2.4
```

The above list of numbers can be printed using this program:

```
10 ' ******************************************
20 ' This program lists four numbers read into
30 '    an array, with decimal points lined up
40 ' ******************************************
50 DATA 367.1, 1567.2, 29573.3, 2.4
60 FOR J=1 TO 4
70    READ A(J)
80    PRINT USING "#####.#";A(J)
90 NEXT J
100 END
```

Test Your Understanding 4 (Answer on Page 204)

Write an instruction that prints the number 456.75387 rounded to two decimal places.

You may use a single PRINT USING statement to print several numbers on the same line. For example, the statement

```
10 PRINT USING "##.##"; A,B,C
```

prints the values of A, B, and C on the same line, all in the format ##.##. Only one space is allowed between each of the numbers. Additional spaces may be added by using extra #s. If you wish to print numbers on one line in two different formats, then you must use two different PRINT USING statements, with the first ending in a semicolon (;) to indicate a continuation on the same line.

If you try to display a number larger than the prototype, the number will be displayed preceded by a percent (%) symbol. For example, consider the statement

```
20 PRINT USING "###"; A
```

If the value of A is 5,000, then the display will look like this:

```
%5000
```

Test Your Understanding 5 (Answer on Page 204)

Write a program to calculate and display the numbers 2^J, J=1,2,3,...,15. The columns of numbers should be properly aligned on the right.

You may have the computer insert a dollar sign on a displayed number. These two statements illustrate the procedure:

```
10 PRINT USING "$####.##"; A
20 PRINT USING "$$####.##";A
```

Suppose that the value of A is 34.78. The results of lines 10 and 20 will then be displayed as

```
$   34.78
$34.78
```

Note the difference between the displays produced by lines 10 and 20. The single $ produces a dollar sign in the fifth position to the left of the decimal point. This is just to the left of the four digits specified in the prototype ####.##. However, the $$ in line 20 indicates a "floating dollar sign." The dollar sign is printed in the first position to the left of the number without leaving any space.

Various formatting options for integers are illustrated in Figure 8-5.

```
Ok
list
10 PRINT USING "###.##"; 138.1
20 PRINT USING "$###.##"; 12.9
30 PRINT USING "$$####.##"; 15.8
40 PRINT USING "+####"; 35.11
50 PRINT USING "####-"; -50.9
60 PRINT USING "**#####"; 154
70 PRINT USING "#######,"; 87124!
80 PRINT USING "##.###^^^^"; 18.1
90 PRINT USING "_X##.#_Y"; 15
Ok
run
138.10
$ 12.90
   $15.80
   +35
   51-
****154
 87,124
 1.810E+01
X15.0Y
Ok
-
```

Figure 8-5.
Formatting numbers with PRINT USING.

Example 1. Here is a list of checks written by a family during the month of March.

$15.32, $387.00, $57.98, $3.47, $15.88

Print the list of checks on the screen with the columns properly aligned and the total displayed below the list of check amounts, in the form of an addition problem.

Solution. We first read the check amounts into an array A(J), J = 1, 2, 3, 4, 5. While we read the amounts, we accumulate the total in the variable B. We use a second loop to print the display in the desired format.

```
10 ' *********************************************
20 ' This program displays several monetary amounts
30 '   and their total, aligned by decimal points
40 ' *********************************************
100 DATA 15.32, 387.00, 57.98, 3.47, 15.88
110 FOR J=1 TO 5
120    READ A(J):           ' Read a data item
130    B=B+A(J):            ' Add it to the total
140    PRINT USING "$###.##"; A(J):  ' Display the item
150 NEXT J
160 PRINT "_____"
170 PRINT USING "$###.##"; B
180 END
```

Here is what the output will look like:

```
$ 15.32
$387.00
$ 57.98
$  3.47
$ 15.88
_____
$479.65
```

Note that line 160 is used to print the line under the column of figures.

The PRINT USING statement has several other variations. To print commas in large numbers, insert a comma anywhere to the left of the decimal point. For example, consider the statement

```
10 PRINT USING ###,###; A
```

If the value of A is 123456, it will be displayed as

```
123,456
```

The PRINT USING statement may also be used to position plus and minus signs in connection with displayed numbers. A plus sign at the beginning or the end of a prototype causes the appropriate sign to be printed in the position indicated. For example, consider the statement

```
10 PRINT USING "+####.###"; A
```

Suppose that the value of A is -458.73. It will be displayed as

```
-  458.730.
```

Note the four spaces between the minus sign and the decimal point and the three places to the right of the decimal point.

Similarly, consider the statement

```
10 PRINT USING "+###.##"; A
```

Suppose that A has the value .05873. Then A will be displayed as

```
+    .06
```

Important Note   In the above discussion, we have only mentioned output on the screen. However, all of the features mentioned may be used on a printer via the LPRINT USING instruction. Note, however, that the wider line of the printer allows you to display more data than the screen. In particular, there are more 14-character print fields (just how many depends on which printer you own), and you may TAB to a higher-numbered column than on the screen.

Recall that BASIC uses two different representations for numbers—the usual decimal representation and scientific (or exponential notation). You may use ^^^^ to format numbers into scientific notation. For example, to display a number in scientific notation with two digits to the left of the decimal point and two to the right, use the format string

```
"##.##^^^^"
```

In this format, the number 100 is displayed as

```
10.00E+01
```

Other Variants of PRINT USING

There are several further things you can do with the PRINT USING statement. They are especially useful to accountants and others concerned with preparing financial documents.

If you precede the prototype with **, this causes all unused digit positions in a number to be filled with asterisks. For example, consider the statement

```
10 PRINT USING "**####.#";A
```

If A has the value 34.86, the value is displayed as

```
****34.9
```

Note that four asterisks are displayed since six digits to the left of the decimal point are specified in the prototype, the asterisks count, but the value of A uses only two. The remaining four are filled with asterisks.

You may combine the action of ** and $. You should experiment with this combination. It is especially useful for printing dollar amounts of the form

```
$*******387.98
```

Such a format is especially useful in printing amounts on checks to prevent modification.

By using a minus sign immediately after a prototype, you will print the appropriate number with a trailing minus sign if it is negative and with no sign if it is positive. For example, the statement

```
10 PRINT USING "####.##-"; A
```

with A equal to -57.88 results in the display

```
57.88-
```

On the other hand, if A is equal to 57.88, the display is

    57.88

This format for numbers is often used in preparing accounting reports.

The various format strings we have discussed are summarized in Figure 8-6.

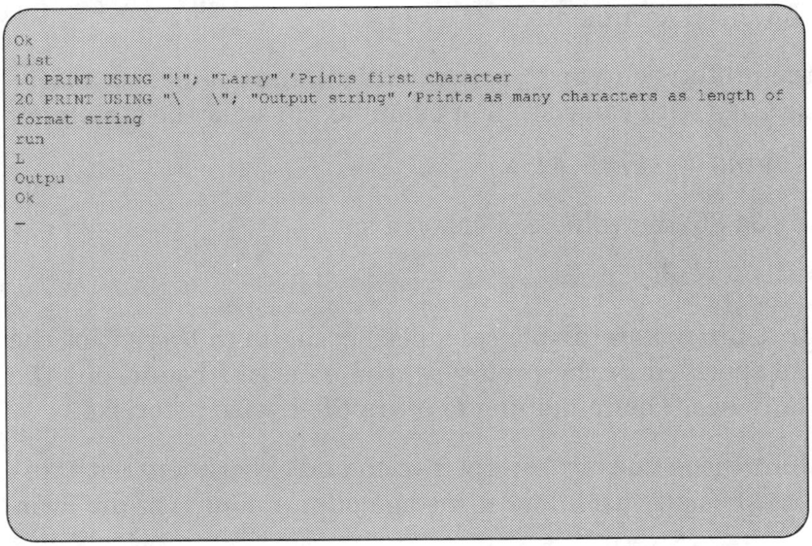

```
Ok
list
10 PRINT USING "!"; "Larry" 'Prints first character
20 PRINT USING "\   \"; "Output string" 'Prints as many characters as length of
format string
run
L
Outpu
Ok
_
```

Figure 8-6.
**Additional for-
mat strings for
PRINT USING.**

Exercises

Write programs to generate the following displays.

1. **THE VALUE OF X IS 5.378**

2. **THE VALUE OF X IS5.378**

3. **DATE   QTY   @   COST   DISCOUNT   NET COST**

4.

6.753	$ 12.82
15.111	$117.58
111.850	$ 5.87
6.702	$ .99
	$ .99
_____	
Calculate	_____
Sum	Calculate
	Sum

5.

Date   3/18/85

Pay to the Order of   Wildcatters, Inc.

The Sum of   ********$89,385.00

6.

```
   5,787
     387
 127,486
  38,531

 _____
Calculate
Sum
```

7.

```
   $385.41
  -$17.85

 _____
Calculate
Difference
```

8. Write a program that prints a number rounded to the nearest integer. For example, if the input is 11.7, the output is 12. If the input is 158.2, the output is 158. Your program should accept the number to be rounded via an INPUT statement.

9. Write a program that allows your computer to function as a cash register. Let the program accept purchase amounts via INPUT statements. Let the user tell the program when the list of INPUTs is complete. The program should then print out the purchase amounts,

with dollar signs and columns aligned, compute the total purchase, add 5 percent sales tax, compute the total amount due, ask for the amount paid, and compute the change due.

10. Prepare the display of Exercise 4 using 40 characters per line.

Answers to Test Your Understandings 1, 2, 3, 4, and 5

1.
```
10  INPUT A,B
20  PRINT A;" +";B;" =";A+B
30  END
```

2.
```
10  THE VALUE OF A IS   5
20  THE VALUE OF B IS 3
30  THE VALUE OF C IS-8
```

3.
```
10  PRINT TAB(25) A;TAB(32) B
```

4.
```
10  PRINT USING "###.##"; 456.75387
```

5.
```
10  FOR J=1 TO 15
20     PRINT USING "#####"; 2^J
30  NEXT J
40  END
```

Gambling With Your Computer

One of the most interesting features of your computer is its ability to generate events whose outcomes are "random." For example, you may instruct the computer to "throw a pair of dice" and produce a random pair of integers between 1 and 6. You may instruct the computer to "pick a card at random from a deck of 52 cards." You may also program the computer to choose a two-digit number "at random," and so forth. The source of all such random choices is the BASIC function RND. To explain how this function works, let us consider this program:

```
10 ' ****************************************
20 ' This program prints 500 random numbers
30 ' between 0.0000000 and 1.0000000
40 ' ****************************************
50 FOR X=1 TO 500
60    PRINT RND
70 NEXT X
80 END
```

This program consists of a loop that prints 500 numbers, each called RND. Each of these numbers lies between 0.000000 (inclusive) and 1.000000 (exclusive). Each time the program refers to RND (as in line 20 here), the computer makes a "random" choice from among the numbers in the indicated range. This is the number that is printed.

To obtain a better idea of what we are talking about, generate some random numbers using a program like the one above. Unless you have a printer, 500 numbers will be too many for you to look at in one viewing. You should print four random numbers on one line (one per print zone) and limit yourself to 25 displayed lines at one time. Here is a partial printout of such a program:

.245121	.305003	.311866	.515163
.984546	.901159	.727313	6.83401E-03
.896609	.660212	.554489	.818675
.583931	.448163	.86774	.0331043
.137119	.226544	.215274	.876763

What makes these numbers "random" is that the procedure the computer uses to select them is "unbiased," with all numbers having an equal likelihood of selection. Moreover, if you generate a large collection of random numbers, then numbers between 0 and .1 will comprise approximately ten percent of those chosen, those between .5 and 1.0 will comprise 50 percent of those chosen, and so forth. In some sense, the random number generator provides a uniform sample of the numbers between 0 and 1.

Test Your Understanding 1 (Answer on Page 220)

Assume that RND is used to generate 1,000 numbers. Approximately how many of these numbers would you expect to lie between .6 and .9?

The random number generator is controlled by a so-called "seed" number, which controls the sequence of numbers generated. Once a particular seed number has been chosen, the sequence of random numbers is fixed. This would make computer games of chance rather uninteresting since they would always generate the same sequence of play. This may be prevented by changing the seed number using the RANDOMIZE command. A command of the form

```
10 RANDOMIZE
```

causes the computer to print out the display

```
Random Number Seed (-32768 to 32767)?
```

You then respond with a number in the indicated interval. Suppose, for example, you choose 129. The computer will then reseed the random number generator with the seed 129 and generate the sequence of random numbers corresponding to this seed. Another method of choosing a seed number is with a command of this form:

```
20 RANDOMIZE 129
```

This command sets the seed number to 129 without asking you. Later in this section, we will show you how to use the computer's internal clock to provide a seed number. This is a method of generating a seed over which no one has any control.

The function RND generates random numbers lying between 0 and 1. However, in many applications, we will require randomly chosen integers lying in a certain range. For example, suppose that we wish to generate random integers chosen from among 1, 2, 3, 4, 5, 6. Let us multiply RND by 6, to obtain 6*RND. This is a random number between 0.00000 and 5.99999. Next, let us add 1 to this number. Then 6*RND+1 is a random number between 1.00000 and 6.99999. To obtain integers from among 1, 2, 3, 4, 5, 6, we must "chop off" the decimal portion of the number 6*RND+1. To do this, we use the INT function. If X is any number, then INT(X) is the largest integer less than or equal to X. For example,

```
INT(5.23)=5,  INT(7.99)=7,  INT(100.001)=100
```

Be careful in using INT with negative X. The definition we gave is correct, but unless you think things through, it is easy to make an error. For example,

```
INT(-7.4)=-8
```

since the largest integer less than or equal to -7.4 is equal to -8. (Draw -7.4 and -8 on a number line to see the point!)

Let us get back to our random numbers. To chop off the decimal portion of 6*RND+1, we compute INT(6*RND+1). This last expression is a random number from among 1, 2, 3, 4, 5, 6. Similarly, the expression

```
INT(100*RND+1)
```

may be used to generate random numbers from among the integers 1, 2, 3,..., 100.

Test Your Understanding 2 (Answer on Page 220)

Generate random integers from 0 to 1. (This is the computer analog of flipping a coin: 0=heads, 1=tail.) Run this program to generate 50 coin tosses. How many heads and how many tails occur?

Example 1.   Write a program that turns the computer into a pair of dice. Your program should report the number rolled on each, as well as the total.

Solution.   We will hold the value of die #1 in the variable X and the value of die #2 in variable Y. The program will compute values for X and Y, print out the values, and the total X+Y.

```
10 ' **********************************
20 ' This program simulates the roll of
30 '   two dice, displaying the value of
40 '   each roll and their total
50 ' **********************************
100 RANDOMIZE
110 CLS
120 X=INT(6*RND + 1)
130 Y=INT(6*RND + 1)
140 PRINT "LADIES AND GENTLEMEN, BETS PLEASE!"
150 INPUT "ARE ALL BETS DOWN(Y/N)"; A$
160 IF A$ = "Y" THEN 170 ELSE 140
170 PRINT "THE ROLL IS",X,Y
180 PRINT "THE WINNING TOTAL IS " ; X+Y
190 INPUT "PLAY AGAIN(Y/N)"; B$
200 IF B$="Y" THEN 110
210 PRINT "THE CASINO IS CLOSING. SORRY!"
220 END
```

Note the use of computer-generated conversation on the screen. Note also, how the program uses lines 190–200 to allow the player to control how many times the game will be played. Finally, note the use of the command RAN-DOMIZE in line 100. This will generate a question to allow you to choose a seed number.

Figure 8-7 illustrates a typical run of the above program.

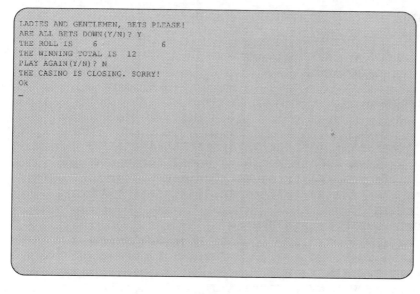

```
LADIES AND GENTLEMEN, BETS PLEASE!
ARE ALL BETS DOWN(Y/N)? Y
THE ROLL IS    6              6
THE WINNING TOTAL IS   12
PLAY AGAIN(Y/N)? N
THE CASINO IS CLOSING. SORRY!
Ok
_
```

Figure 8-7.
Sample run of the program dice.

Test Your Understanding 3 (Answer on Page 220)

Write a program that flips a "biased coin." Let it report "heads" one-third of the time and "tails" two-thirds of the time.

You may enhance the realism of a gambling program by letting the computer keep track of bets as in the following example.

Example 2. Write a program that turns the computer into a roulette wheel. Let the computer keep track of bets and winnings for up to five players. For simplicity, assume that the only bets are on single numbers. (In the next example, we will let you remove this restriction!)

Solution. A roulette wheel has 38 positions: 1–36, 0, and 00. In our program, we will represent these as the numbers 1–38, with 37 corresponding to 0 and 38 corresponding to 00. A spin of the wheel will consist of choosing a random integer between 1 and 38. The program will start by asking the number of players. For a typical spin of the wheel, the program will ask for bets by each player. A bet will consist of a number (1–38) and an amount bet. The wheel will then spin. The program will determine the winners and losers. A payoff for a win is 32 times the amount bet. Each player has an account, stored in an array A(J), J = 1, 2, 3, 4, 5. At the end of each spin, the accounts are adjusted and displayed. Just as in Example 1, the program asks if another play is desired.

Here is the program:

```
1  ' ********************************************
2  ' This program runs a roulette wheel for up to
3  '    five people, allowing bets on any number
4  ' ********************************************
5    RANDOMIZE
10   INPUT "NUMBER OF PLAYERS";N
20   DIM A(5),B(5),C(5):        'At Most 5 Players
30   FOR J= 1 TO N :            'Initial Purchase of Chips
40     PRINT "PLAYER "; J
50     INPUT "HOW MANY CHIPS"; A(J)
60   NEXT J
100  PRINT "LADIES AND GENTLEMEN! PLACE YOUR BETS PLEASE!"
110  FOR J=1 TO N :             'Place Bets
120    PRINT "PLAYER "; J
130    INPUT "NUMBER, AMOUNT"; B(J),C(J):'INPUT BET
140  NEXT J
200  X=INT(38*RND + 1):         'Spin the wheel
220  PRINT "THE WINNER IS NUMBER"; X
300  'Compute winnings and losses
310  FOR J=1 TO N
320    IF X=B(J) THEN 400
330    A(J)=A(J)-C(J):          'Player J loses
340    PRINT "PLAYER ";J;"LOSES"
350    GOTO 420
400    A(J)=A(J)+32*C(J):       'Player J wins
410    PRINT "PLAYER ";J;"WINS "; 32*C(J); "DOLLARS"
420  NEXT J
430  PRINT "PLAYER BANKROLLS": 'Display game status
440  PRINT
450  PRINT "PLAYER", "CHIPS"
460  FOR J=1 TO N
470    PRINT J,A(J)
```

```
480 NEXT J
500 INPUT "DO YOU WISH TO PLAY ANOTHER ROLL (Y/N)";R$
510 CLS
520 IF R$ = "Y" THEN 100:       'Repeat game
530 PRINT "THE CASINO IS CLOSED. SORRY!"
600 END
```

Try a few spins of the wheel. The program is fun as well as instructive. Note that the program allows you to bet more chips than you have. We will leave it to the exercises to add in a test that there are enough chips to cover the bet. You can also build lines of credit into the game! In the next example, we will illustrate how the roulette program may be extended to incorporate the bets even and odd.

Figure 8-8 illustrates a typical run of the above program.

```
Ok
run
Random number seed (-32768 to 32767)? 12
NUMBER OF PLAYERS? 2
PLAYER  1
HOW MANY CHIPS? 100
PLAYER  2
HOW MANY CHIPS? 300
LADIES AND GENTLEMEN! PLACE YOUR BETS PLEASE!
PLAYER  1
NUMBER, AMOUNT? 12, 50
PLAYER  2
NUMBER, AMOUNT? 30, 100
THE WINNER IS NUMBER 34
PLAYER  1 LOSES
PLAYER  2 LOSES
PLAYER BANKROLLS

PLAYER        CHIPS
  1             50
  2            200
DO YOU WISH TO PLAY ANOTHER ROLL (Y/N)? _
```

Figure 8-8.
Sample run of the roulette program.

Before we proceed to the next example, however, let's discuss one further defect of the program in Example 2. Note that line 5 contains a RANDOMIZE statement. The program will then ask for a random number seed. The person who selects the random number seed has control over the random number sequence and hence over the game. This is most unsatisfactory. However, there is a simple way around this difficulty.

IBM PCs and compatibles have an internal clock that is set each time you sign on to the computer. This clock keeps track of time in hours, minutes, and seconds. The value of the clock is accessed via the function TIME$. We will discuss use of the clock in detail in Chapter 16. For the moment however, let's borrow a fact from that discussion. The current reading of the seconds portion of the clock is equal to:

```
VAL(RIGHT$(TIME$,2))
```

Let's use this number as our random number seed. (It is unlikely that anyone can control the precise second at which the game begins.)

Example 3. Modify the Roulette program of Example 2, so that it allows bets on even and odd. A one-dollar bet on either of these pays one dollar in winnings.

Solution. Our program will now allow three different bets: on a number and on even or odd. Let us design subprograms, corresponding to each of these bets, which determine whether player J wins or loses. For each subprogram, let X be the number (1–38) that results from spinning the wheel. In the preceding program, a bet by player J was described by two numbers: B(J) equals the number bet and C(J) equals the amount bet. Now let us add a third number to describe a bet. Let D(J) equal 1 if J bets on a number, 2 if J bets on even, and 3 if J bets on odd. In case D(J) is 2 or 3, we will again let C(J) equal the amount bet, but B(J) will be ignored. The subprogram for determining the winners of bets on numbers can be obtained by making small modifications to the corresponding portion of our previous program, as follows:

```
1000  'Bet=NUMBER
1010      IF B(J)=X THEN 1050 ELSE 1020
1020      PRINT "PLAYER ";J; " LOSES"
1030      A(J)=A(J)-C(J)
1040      GOTO 1070
```

```
1050        PRINT "PLAYER ";J; " WINS"; 32*C(J); "DOLLARS"
1060        A(J)=A(J)+32*C(J)
1070 RETURN
```

Here is the subprogram corresponding to the bet even. In line 2010, we use the test $INT(X/2) = X/2$ to determine whether or not X is even. The function INT throws away the fraction part of the number $X/2$. For even numbers X, then, $INT(X/2)$ is the same as $X/2$, whereas for odd X, the two are different.

```
2000 'Bet=EVEN
2010        IF INT(X/2) = X/2 THEN 2050
2020        PRINT "PLAYER ";J;" LOSES"
2030        A(J)=A(J)-C(J)
2040        GOTO 2070
2050        PRINT "PLAYER " ;J;" WINS ";C(J);" DOLLARS"
2060        A(J)=A(J)+C(J)
2070 RETURN
```

Finally, here is the subprogram corresponding to the bet odd.

```
3000 'Bet=ODD
3010        IF INT(X/2) < X/2 THEN 3050
3020        PRINT "PLAYER ";J;" LOSES"
3030        A(J)=A(J)-C(J)
3040        GOTO 3070
3050        PRINT "PLAYER ";J;" WINS ";C(J);" DOLLARS"
3060        A(J)=A(J)+C(J)
3070 RETURN
3080 END
```

Now we are ready to assemble the subprograms together with the main portion of the program, which is almost the same as before. The only essential alteration is that we must now determine, for each player, which bet was placed.

```
1 ' ***************************************
2 ' This program runs a roulette wheel for
3 '   up to five people, allowing bets on
4 '   any number, or EVEN or ODD
5 ' ***************************************
```

```
10 CLS
20 RANDOMIZE VAL(RIGHT$(TIME$,2))
30 INPUT "NUMBER OF PLAYERS";N
40 DIM A(5),B(5),C(5)
50 FOR J=1 TO N
60    PRINT "PLAYER ";J
70    INPUT "HOW MANY CHIPS";A(J)
80 NEXT J
90 PRINT "LADIES AND GENTLEMEN! PLACE YOUR BETS PLEASE!"
100 FOR J=1 TO N:            'Place bets
110    PRINT "PLAYER" ;J
120    PRINT "BET TYPE:1=NUMBER BET, 2=EVEN, 3=ODD"
130    INPUT "BET TYPE (1,2, OR 3)";D(J)
140    IF D(J)=1 THEN 170
150    INPUT "AMOUNT";C(J)
160    GOTO 180
170    INPUT "NUMBER, AMOUNT BET";B(J),C(J)
180 NEXT J
190 X=INT(38*RND+1):    'Spin Wheel
200 CLS
210 PRINT "THE WINNER IS NUMBER";X
220 FOR J=1 TO N:            'Determine winnings and losses
230   ON D(J) GOSUB 1000,2000,3000
240 NEXT J
250 PRINT "PLAYER BANKROLLS"
260 PRINT "PLAYER", "CHIPS"
270 FOR J=1 TO N
280   PRINT J,A(J)
290 NEXT J
300 INPUT "DO YOU WISH TO PLAY ANOTHER ROLL(Y/N)";R$
310 CLS
320 IF R$="Y" OR R$="y" THEN 90
330 PRINT "THE CASINO IS CLOSED. SORRY!"
340 END
1000 'Bet=NUMBER
1010      IF B(J)=X THEN 1050 ELSE 1020
1020      PRINT "PLAYER ";J; " LOSES"
1030      A(J)=A(J)-C(J)
1040      GOTO 1070
1050      PRINT "PLAYER ";J; " WINS"; 32*C(J); "DOLLARS"
```

```
1060          A(J)=A(J)+32*C(J)
1070 RETURN
2000 'Bet=EVEN
2010          IF INT(X/2) = X/2 THEN 2050
2020          PRINT "PLAYER ";J;" LOSES"
2030          A(J)=A(J)-C(J)
2040          GOTO 2070
2050          PRINT "PLAYER " ;J;" WINS ";C(J);" DOLLARS"
2060          A(J)=A(J)+C(J)
2070 RETURN
3000 'Bet=ODD
3010          IF INT(X/2) < X/2 THEN 3050
3020          PRINT "PLAYER ";J;" LOSES"
3030          A(J)=A(J)-C(J)
3040          GOTO 3070
3050          PRINT "PLAYER ";J;" WINS ";C(J);" DOLLARS"
3060          A(J)=A(J)+C(J)
3070 RETURN
3080 END
```

Figure 8-9 (a and b) illustrates a typical run of the above program.

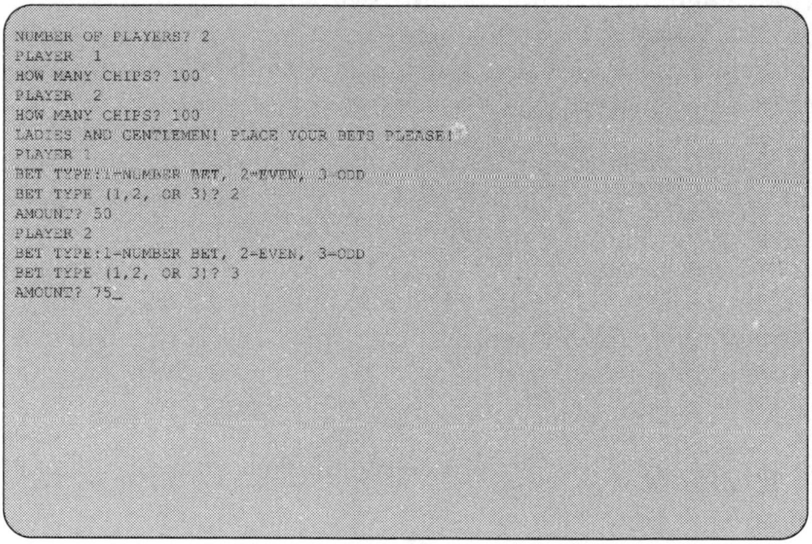

```
NUMBER OF PLAYERS? 2
PLAYER  1
HOW MANY CHIPS? 100
PLAYER  2
HOW MANY CHIPS? 100
LADIES AND GENTLEMEN! PLACE YOUR BETS PLEASE!
PLAYER 1
BET TYPE:1-NUMBER BET, 2-EVEN, 3-ODD
BET TYPE (1,2, OR 3)? 2
AMOUNT? 50
PLAYER 2
BET TYPE:1-NUMBER BET, 2-EVEN, 3-ODD
BET TYPE (1,2, OR 3)? 3
AMOUNT? 75_
```

Figure 8-9a.
Sample run of the modified roulette program.

```
THE WINNER IS NUMBER 18
PLAYER  1  WINS  50  DOLLARS
PLAYER  2  LOSES
PLAYER BANKROLLS
PLAYER          CHIPS
   1            150
   2             25
DO YOU WISH TO PLAY ANOTHER ROLL(Y/N)? _
```

Figure 8-9b.
Sample run of the modified roulette program *(continued).*

Note how the subroutines help to organize our programming. Each subroutine is easy to write and each is a small task, and you will have less to think about than when considering the entire program. It is advisable to break a long program into a number of subroutines. Not only is it easier to write in terms of subroutines, but it is much easier to check the program and to locate errors since subroutines may be individually tested.

You may treat the output of the random number generator as you would any other number. In particular, you may perform arithmetic operations on the random numbers generated. For example, 5*RND multiplies the output of the random number generator by 5, and RND+2 adds 2 to the output of the random number generator. Such arithmetic operations are useful in producing random numbers from intervals other than 0 to 1. For example, to generate random numbers between 2 and 3, we may use RND+2.

Example 4.   Write a program that generates ten random numbers lying in the interval from 5 to 8.

Solution. Let us build up the desired function in two steps. We start from the function RND, which generates numbers from 0 to 1. First, we adjust for the length of the desired interval. From 5 to 8 is 3 units, so we multiply RND by 3. The function 3*RND generates numbers from 0 to 3. Now we adjust for the starting point of the desired interval, namely 5. By adding 5 to 3*RND, we obtain numbers lying between 0+5 and 3+5, that is between 5 and 8. Thus, 3*RND+5 generates random numbers between 5 and 8. Here is the program required.

```
10 FOR J=1 TO 10
20    PRINT 3*RND+5
30 NEXT J
40 END
```

Figure 8-10 illustrates a typical run of the above program.

Figure 8-10.
Random numbers lying within a given interval.

Example 5. Write a function to generate random integers from among 5, 6, 7, 8, ..., 12.

Solution.   There are eight consecutive integers possible. Let us start with the function 8*RND, which generates random numbers between 0 and 8. Since we wish our random number to begin with 5, let us add 5 to get 8*RND+5. This produces random numbers between 5.00000 and 12.9999. We now use the INT function to chop off the decimal part. This yields the desired function:

    INT(8*RND+5)

Figure 8-11 show several sample values of this function.

Figure 8-11.
Generating random integers.

Exercises

Write BASIC functions that generate random numbers of the following sorts.

1. Numbers from 0 to 100.

2. Numbers from 100 to 101.

3. Integers from 1 to 50.

4. Integers from 4 to 80.

5. Even integers from 2 to 50.

6. Numbers from 50 to 100.

7. Integers divisible by 3 from 3 to 27.

8. Integers from among 4, 7, 10, 13, 16, 19, and 22.

9. Modify the dice program so that it keeps track of payoffs and bankrolls, much like the roulette program in Example 2. Here are the payoffs on a bet of one dollar for the various bets:

outcome	payoff
2	35
3	17
4	11
5	8
6	6.20
7	5
8	6.20
9	8
10	11
11	17
12	3

10. Modify the roulette program of Example 2 to check that a player has enough chips to cover the bet.

11. Modify the roulette program of Example 2 to allow for a $100 line of credit for each player.

12. Construct a program that tests one-digit arithmetic facts with the problems randomly chosen by the computer.

13. Make up a list of ten names. Write a program that will pick four of the names at random. (This is a way of impartially assigning a nasty task!)

Answers to Test Your Understanding 1, 2, and 3

1. about 300

2.
```
10 FOR J=1 TO 50
20 PRINT INT(2*RND)
30 NEXT J
40 END
```

3.
```
10 X=INT(3*RND)
20 IF X=0 THEN PRINT "HEADS" ELSE PRINT "TAILS"
30 END
```

Nine

Program Planning, Testing, and Debugging

In the preceding chapters, we covered the elementary statements used to build programs in GWBASIC. However, we haven't said much about how to go about actually building a program. Of course, we have given a number of examples, and made some isolated comments about good programming style. But we haven't discussed the problem of program design and development in an organized fashion. Actually, to do justice to these subjects would take an entire book. We can't give that extensive a discussion in this book. However, in this chapter we give a survey of the most important facts a beginner needs to know about program design and development.

The Program Development Process

In order to construct a house, you must follow an organized sequence of steps: design, permits, excavation, foundation, framing, and so forth. Each step in the building process prepares the way for the next. Moreover, by pursuing an organized approach to building, you minimize the amount of time it takes and cut down on the number of errors.

Constructing a program is very similar to building a house. In order to carry out a programming task in the minimum amount of time and with the fewest possible errors, you must follow an organized program development process that should consist of all of the following steps:

1. *Program Planning*—Decide what the program is to do.
2. *Program Design*—Plan how the program will work.
3. *Coding*—Write the program code in an appropriate computer language.
4. *Debugging*—Correct any errors in the program.
5. *Documentation*—Write a detailed description of how the program works and how it may be used.
6. *Maintenance*—Correct errors as users point them out. Modify the program in response to user suggestions and needs.

Let's discuss in further detail what is involved in each of these steps.

Program Planning. One of the principal defects of the classic BASIC programming language is that it allows you to sit down and start writing a program without much thought or planning. (And I'll bet many of you thought that was an advantage!) You may be able to get away without planning if you are writing a small program. But as soon as the program becomes the slightest bit complex, program planning becomes a necessity. Your planning must include the following:

- A clear statement of what the program is supposed to accomplish. Unless you are clear about the goals of the program, it is highly unlikely that you will be able to successfully write a program to accomplish those goals.

- A list of the inputs to the program. This list must include all data the program requires to accomplish its goals and the sources for these data. Potential sources include user input from the keyboard, data files on disk, communications input, as well as input from a mouse, a digitizer, or any of the many other devices that can be connected to a PC.

- A list of the outputs from the program. This list must contain all data that result from running the program and the form in which the data is output: screen, printer, disk file, plotter, and so forth.

- An analysis of the data manipulation that must be accomplished within the program. That is, what operations must the program perform on the data in order to transform inputs into the required outputs?

- A plan for the user interface to the program. That is, you just decide on how the user will interact with the program and how this interaction will take place so as to make it as "user-friendly" as possible.

Program Design. The second step in program development is transforming your program plan into a design, which can be used as the basis for coding and debugging. In this step, you describe the operation of your program using either flow charts or pseudocode. Flow charts are useful in providing a visual description of a program's parts and how they interrelate to one another. On the other hand, pseudocode consists of a description of a program in English-like shorthand. Flow charts are useful for visualizing the inter-relationship of the various sections of a program and the corresponding necessary divisions of labor if several programmers are required to simultaneously to work on it. On the other hand, the pseudocode resembles the actual program code. If you do a careful job of describing the program in pseudocode, the coding process can be significantly shortened.

Both flow charts and pseudocode are in common use. In fact, for some complex programming tasks, you may want to describe the program using both of them. We will discuss pseudocode and flow charts further in the next section.

Your program design should include a description of any data organization that the program requires. Some data may be stored in individual variables, whereas other data may be organized into arrays of one or more dimensions.

Furthermore, the program design should include a description of any required algorithms for manipulating the data. (An algorithm is a sequence of computer instructions that accomplishes a specific task.) That is, the program design should include a detailed description of how you expect the program to handle the required calculations, data searching, data sorting, data input, and data output.

Finally, the program design should incorporate a description of the user interface. That is, it should include the design of any required input and output screens, and the technique to be used for user interaction with the program.

Coding.   The third step in developing a program consists of writing the program code. (This is the step that novices like to jump right into.) In this step, you write computer instructions that carry out the tasks described in the program design. The computer instructions are written in a computer language that allows you to describe the program in a language close to English. For the purposes of this book, we assume that the computer language is GWBASIC. However, there are hundreds of languages available. The language you use could just as well be assembly language, Pascal, C, FORTRAN, or Ada.

Although you describe a program in terms of a computer language, in order to run a program it must at some point be translated into machine code, the internal language of the computer. As we described in Chapter 5, this translation process is handled in GWBASIC by interpretation.

Testing and Debugging.   Testing is the process of checking that a program actually does what you planned it to do. Debugging is the process of correcting programming errors. Testing and debugging are related operations carried out at various stages during coding (to test sections of a program) and after coding is complete (to test the operation of the entire program). Throughout the book, we will give tips on testing and debugging procedures.

Documentation.   Documentation is written material used to describe a program. Generally speaking, documentation is divided into two categories: user documentation and technical documentation.

User documentation is a description, in nontechnical terms, of how to use the program. This description tells the user what the program does, how to install it for a particular installation, how to respond to the various requests for user interaction, and how to interpret output and error messages provided by the program.

Technical documentation describes, in technical terms, how the program is organized and operates. This documentation is principally addressed to programmers who may be called on later to correct bugs and to modify the program. The technical documentation consists of two parts: documented source code and a reference manual. The documented source code consists of the program code with remarks that describe how each section of the program functions and the reasons for the various design decisions made by the original programmer. The reference manual consists of a detailed description of the action of the program in response to each of its user commands.

Maintenance.   Maintenance involves repairing bugs that are spotted by program users and making alterations of the program, often in response to user requests for improved operation or additional program features. Program maintenance often must be carried out by a programmer other than the one who did the original programming. Accordingly, it is vitally dependent on the quality of the documentation created in the original program development.

Even if the original programmer must do the maintenance, good documentation is still the key. Imagine trying to remember how a program works several years after you wrote it! Moral: Create detailed documentation. The best idea is to generate your document as you proceed with the program development process. Write your documentation as you develop the code. In that way the rationale for the code will be fresh in your mind and you won't need to remember just why you handled coding in a particular fashion.

The program development process is summarized in Figure 9-1.

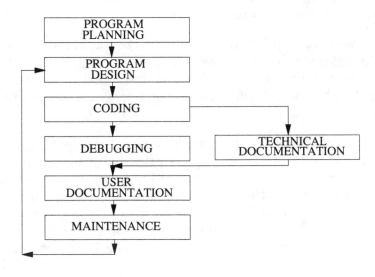

Figure 9-1.
The program development process.

Top-down Design

Complex problems typically have solutions composed of a number of parts. In order to solve the problem, it is therefore useful to break it down into smaller problems and solve each of the component problems. A similar approach works in planning complex programs: Break the program down into a sequence of subprograms. Plan each of the subprograms as if it were a program in its own right. In planning each of the subprograms, it may be necessary to break them down further into subprograms. And so on, using as many levels of refinement as proves necessary to completely plan all details of the program.

The process we have just described is called **top-down design**, since it proceeds from the "top" (the main program) "down" (toward a more detailed description of program components). This process is the one used by most professional programmers in designing their programs. It is a good idea for you to learn how to apply it in designing your programs.

To illustrate the process of top-down design, it is best to give a particular example. Let's keep the programming simple and use top-down design to create a program to test addition of two digit numbers. This program, which we will call Addition, consists of several parts, which can be described by the following outline:

Program Addition

> Tell the user the purpose of program
> Choose two 2-digit numbers at random
> Display the numbers
> Ask user for the sum
> Determine whether the answer is correct
> Does user wish to ask for another problem?

The above outline uses English phrases to describe the steps the program requires. Such a description of a program is called pseudocode. Note that each descriptive phrase corresponds to a section of program code, which may consist of one or many instructions. The details describing each phrase are not given. Rather, the outline describes the logical structure of the program. Of course, in order to code the program, further details are necessary. Each of the steps that are not completely detailed must be fleshed out. For example, consider the second step:

Choose two 2-digit numbers at random

```
Number1 = INT(100*RND(1))
Number2 = INT(100*RND(1))
```

This last description gives the details for choosing two integers between 0 and 99 in a random fashion.

In a similar fashion, you can give the details for each of the main steps in the program. In giving the second-level details, it may be useful not to give complete details but to give summaries similar to those we used at the first level. In this case, specifying the program completely would require a third level of detail, expanding the steps given at the second level.

A program developed in this fashion very closely resembles an outline. The main steps of the program provide the first level of detail, the next level of detail corresponds to the second level of the outline, the next level of detail to the third level, and so forth. The idea of writing a program in such an outline form is to make clear the logical structure of the program. At each level of program design (i.e., at each outline level), you are worrying only about program details of a particular level of specificity. This allows you to plan a program and develop it in a sequence of orderly steps, progressively pinning down details as you address higher levels of the outline.

The final outline of the program should allow you to write the code with little additional thought.

An English-language outline for a program, as illustrated above, is called **pseudocode**. Use of pseudocode is a common technique for implementing top-down design in preparation for coding in a program language.

Structured Programming

In the preceding section, we described the top-down procedure for designing programs. This procedure allows you to design programs that have a structure to them. This structure is conferred by the outline you use to organize the program. Actually, in your design and implementation of a program, there is much you can do to make the program structure work for you in making the program easier to design, debug, and maintain. There are a few rules you should follow in designing your program structure:

1. The program design should be stated (in pseudocode) so that you may easily trace the sequence of tasks to be performed.
2. Each task should correspond to a subprogram (also called a module).

3. Carefully plan the exchange of data between sections of a program. Specifically, state the input data that each section receives and the output data that it must supply.

4. Each module should perform its task independently of the other modules. That is, given the appropriate input data, a module should carry out its task and supply the required data to the main program without interfering with the other modules. In particular, the only variables of the main program a module should change are those that represent data the module is asked to supply.

If you don't adhere to rule 4, you can create what are known as **side effects**. A side effect of a module is a program statement that has an unintended effect in the main program. For example, suppose that the main program uses the variable J. Within a module, you use J as a variable in a FOR...NEXT loop. On exiting the module, J has the final value it achieved within the loop. In particular, the original value of J in the main program has been lost. This loss of J's value is a side effect of the module. Side effects create bugs that are often very difficult to track down. One of the fundamental goals of structured programming is to avoid side effects.

Traditionally, structured programming in BASIC has not been as easy as structured programming in other languages (e.g., Pascal or C). However, in recent years, new versions of BASIC, such as GWBASIC, have incorporated features that make it much easier to write structured programs. Later in the book, we will describe how these features work. In any case, throughout the book, we will point out some of the traps to avoid if you want to structure your programs, no matter which version of BASIC you are using.

Flowcharting

The old saying "A picture is worth a thousand words" is true for computer programming. In designing a program, especially a long one, it is helpful to draw a picture depicting the instructions of the program and their interrelationships. Such a picture is called a **flowchart**.

A flowchart is a series of boxes connected by arrows. Within each box is a series of one of more computer instructions. The arrows indicate the logical flow of the instructions. Let's illustrate the use of a flowchart to plan a program to convert feet to inches. One foot contains 12 inches, so we convert feet to inches using the formula

```
number-of-inches = 12 x number-of-feet
```

This formula is a general one. It may be used to convert any value for number-of-feet into the corresponding number-of-inches. When we create our program to carry out this calculation, we want it to work in the same way. It should ask the user for the number-of-feet. Then it should calculate the number-of-inches and display the value on the screen. Let's call the program FEET_TO_INCHES. Here is the pseudocode for the program.

```
PROGRAM: FEET_TO_INCHES
    Ask user for the value of number-of-feet;
    Calculate number-of-inches;
    Print number-of-inches;
```

Our program can be represented in a flowchart, as shown in Figure 9-2.

The flowchart indicates the procedures the program carries out. A flowchart is read from the top, starting at the box marked START. Each box in the flowchart indicates a single procedure. Each box has an arrow leaving it. This arrow points to the box containing the next procedure. By following the arrows, you can trace the order in which the various procedures are carried out. The program ends when it reaches the box marked STOP.

Flowcharts are used to design most programs, especially large programs involving many procedures with complex interrelationships. They help in the planning and writing of a program, and serve as a handy reference to explain the code long after it is written.

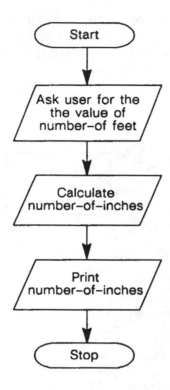

Figure 9-2.
Flowchart for conversion of feet to inches.

Flowcharting and Top-down Design

Some programs involve thousands of procedures and hundreds of thousands of lines of code. The way to write such programs (and all but the most trivial programs) is to use top-down design to break the program into modules, each of the modules into submodules, and so on, continually refining the level of detail of the program plan.

The initial breaking of the plan into modules leads to an initial flowchart called the **main-control** or **macro flowchart** or **hierarchy chart**. This flowchart indicates the overall logical flow of the program. The creation of submodules breaks each of the boxes in the initial flowchart into a flowchart of its own. Each level of breaking of the plan leads to a new level of flowcharts in the initial flowchart. As the plan becomes more and more specific, the flowchart also becomes more and more specific. In Figure 9-3, we show the top-down design of a program for entering orders and preparing bills for a telephone sales firm. The figure shows how boxes in the initial flowchart are expanded into whole flowcharts at the next level.

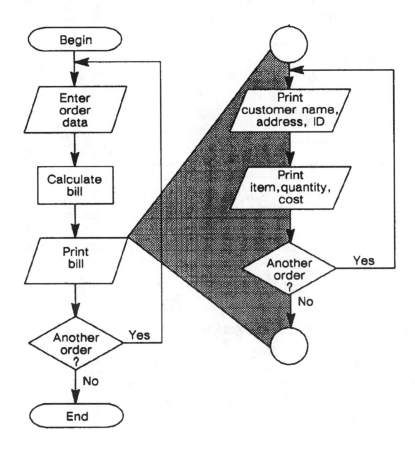

Figure 9-3.
Top-down design of program for entering orders and preparing bills for telephone sales.

Flowchart Symbols

Flowcharts contain symbols with specific meanings. The symbols are standardized through the American National Standards Institute (ANSI), so they have the same meanings in all flowcharts. Here are the main symbols used in flowcharts.

Terminal. The terminal symbol is used to indicate either a beginning, end, or interruption point of a program.

Processing Function. The processing function symbol indicates a function for numerical or text processing. An example of a numerical processing function is calculating payroll deductions for state and local taxes; a text processing function is deleting all spaces in front of a word or phrase.

Input/Output. The input/output symbol indicates action by an input/output device. These actions include reading the keyboard, printing on the screen, printing on the printer, reading a diskette, writing on a hard disk, and so on.

Decision. The decision symbol indicates that a decision has to be made. A question is asked within the box. The box has two exit arrows. The path taken by the program depends on the answer to the question.

Connector. The connector symbol is used to indicate a connection to another part of the flowchart without drawing a continuous line. For example, if the connector symbol contains the letters A3, it connects to a similarly labeled connector symbol elsewhere on the flowchart.

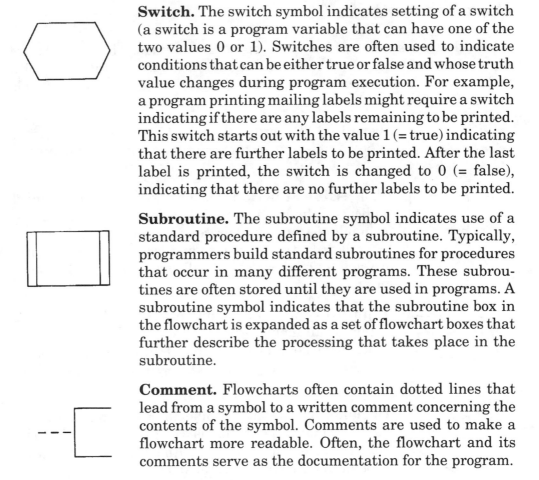

Switch. The switch symbol indicates setting of a switch (a switch is a program variable that can have one of the two values 0 or 1). Switches are often used to indicate conditions that can be either true or false and whose truth value changes during program execution. For example, a program printing mailing labels might require a switch indicating if there are any labels remaining to be printed. This switch starts out with the value 1 (= true) indicating that there are further labels to be printed. After the last label is printed, the switch is changed to 0 (= false), indicating that there are no further labels to be printed.

Subroutine. The subroutine symbol indicates use of a standard procedure defined by a subroutine. Typically, programmers build standard subroutines for procedures that occur in many different programs. These subroutines are often stored until they are used in programs. A subroutine symbol indicates that the subroutine box in the flowchart is expanded as a set of flowchart boxes that further describe the processing that takes place in the subroutine.

Comment. Flowcharts often contain dotted lines that lead from a symbol to a written comment concerning the contents of the symbol. Comments are used to make a flowchart more readable. Often, the flowchart and its comments serve as the documentation for the program.

We will see how the various flowchart symbols are used in the next section, where we will discuss some practical examples of program planning.

Exercises

1. What is a flowchart?

2. Why are flowcharts used in specifying programs?

3. What is top-down program design?

4. What do you think bottom-up design means?

5. What are the advantages of using top-down design to specify a program?

6. What is a program module?

7. Suppose that two programmers are working on two different modules for the same program. What information must they share?

8. What is the flowchart symbol for a terminal?

9. What is the flowchart symbol for a processing function?

10. What is the flowchart symbol for an input/output function?

11. Write a flowchart symbol for the decision IS PROCESSING COMPLETE?.

12. What is the flowchart symbol for a connector?

13. Give an example of a switch.

14. What is a subroutine? Why are subroutines important?

15. True or false: Comments only clutter up a flowchart. For clarity, they should be used sparingly. Explain your answer.

Some Flowcharting Examples

The best way to become familiar with flowcharts is to see how they are prepared for a number of typical problems. That's what we will do in this section. The problems we pose are typical (but simple) ones that arise when managing a small business. The problems are arranged roughly in order of increasing difficulty.

Problem 1. Kreativ Komputers is a company with a single product, a tutorial program in reading for elementary school students. How does the company construct a flowchart for a program that prints bills? The data for the customer's name and address and the number of copies of the program are entered via the keyboard. The price of the program is included within the program and is not given as part of the input.

The program consists of three main procedures:

1. Inputting the customer data and the number of copies (N).
2. Computing the amount owed (A) from the formula $A = N \times P$, where P is the price per program.
3. Printing out the bill.

The flowchart incorporating these three procedures is shown in Figure 9-4.

Each of the boxes in the flowchart must be expanded to give more detail. The first box can be expanded to the flowchart in Figure 9-5(a). This flowchart has the user input the customer data in response to a series of questions.

Similarly, the box calling for printing out the bill can be expanded to the flowchart in Figure 9-5(b). The latter flowchart details exactly what gets printed on the bill.

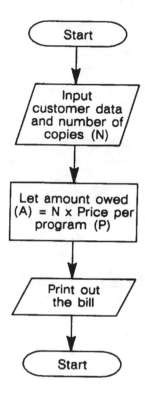

Figure 9-4.
Flowchart for a program that prints bills.

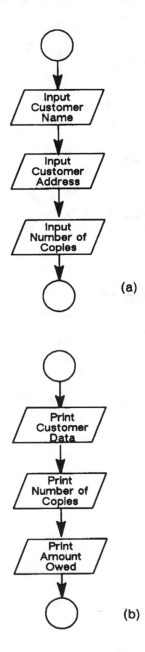

(a)

(b)

Figure 9-5.
(a) User inputs customer data in response to questions.
(b) Box calls for printing out bill.

Problem 2.   Kreativ Komputers expands its product line to include more than 100 different tutorial programs and various computer accessories. How does the company construct a flowchart for a program that will let it print out its bills? The prices of the items are stored in a table within the program and are not supplied as part of the input data.

The difference between Problem 1 and Problem 2 is that Problem 2 requires the program to allow for many different items on the bill. This is easily solved by having the program repeatedly ask for an item name and the quantity ordered.

The principal new difficulty is how to tell the computer that there are no more items. There are many ways to do this. Perhaps the simplest is to agree ahead of time that when the user types the character "@" in response to the name of an item, there are no more items to be included on the bill. This means that the program used to solve Problem 2 has to make a decision. After the name of an item is given, the program must ask: Is the item name "@"? If so, then the program prints out the bill. If not, the program computes the billable amount for the named item. The flowchart describing the program is shown in Figure 9-6.

We won't attempt to expand the boxes of this flowchart, since we are mainly interested in demonstrating the use of the decision box at this point.

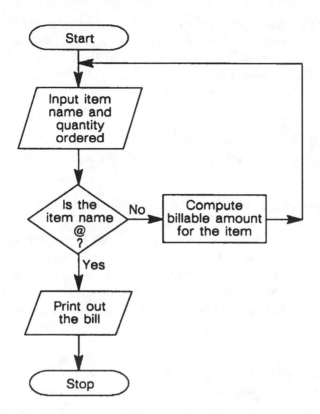

Figure 9-6.
Flowchart to tell the computer that there are no more items.

Problem 3.   The customer list of Kreativ Komputers is contained in a data file on a disk. How does the company construct a flowchart for a program that prints out the customer list on peel-off labels? The labels are on continuous form paper. Six lines of printing are required to space from the top of one label to the top of the next. A customer's name and address take up three lines.

An address label may be printed by first printing the three lines of customer data (1. Name, 2. Street Address, 3. City, State, and Zip Code), followed by three blank lines.

The main problem is to read the list of customers from the data file on the disk. We won't go into detail on how this is done. It is enough to say that the program can start at the beginning of the data file and read the customer data, one customer at a time. The program can also determine whether there is any more customer data to be read. The flowchart uses a decision box to determine whether there are any more data to be read. If so, it reads one customer's address data and prints the corresponding label. Then it repeats the procedure. If there is no more customer data to be read, the program ends.

The flowchart appears in Figure 9-7.

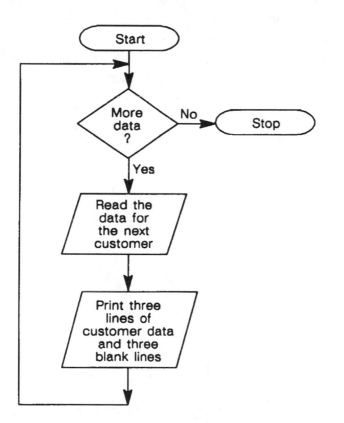

Figure 9-7.
Flowchart describing reading list of customers and ending of program.

Problem 4.   Kreativ Komputers keeps a data file of all its customers and the year-to-date total of their orders. How does the company construct a flowchart for a program that prints out a list of all customers who have ordered more than $500.00 and less than $1,000.00 for the year to date?

This problem is similar to Problem 3, except that not all of the customer data are to be printed out. After reading the customer data from the file, the program must check that the year-to-date total of sales is more than $500.00 (> $500.00) and less than $1,000.00 (< $1,000.00). If so, the customer data are printed out. If not, the customer data are ignored. Note that two new decisions are required, one to see if the total is more than $500.00 and one to see if the total is less than $1,000.00. As in Problem 3, we require a decision to determine when the last customer data have been processed.

The flowchart appears in Figure 9-8.

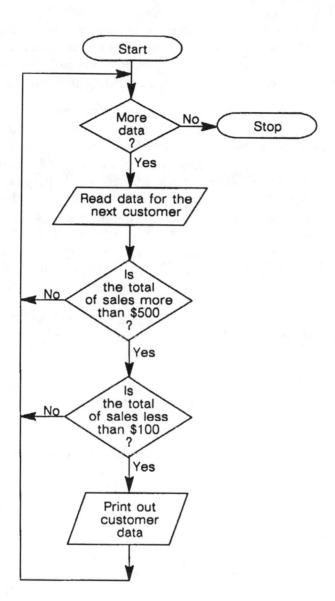

Figure 9-8.
Flowchart to print out list of customers who order > $500 and <$1,000 worth of merchandise.

Problem 5. Kreativ Komputers wants to include three separate procedures in a single program. The user must be able to select from a menu which of the three procedures is to be run. After the procedure is run, the user must be able to run another procedure (or perhaps the same procedure again).

This problem asks us to construct a menu that allows the user to choose from among three programs. Such menus are commonly used to help a program user choose from a list of options. For simplicity, let's call the procedures Procedure 1, Procedure 2, and Procedure 3, and assume that they have already been defined. The program begins by displaying a menu that asks the user to type 1 for Procedure 1, 2 for Procedure 2, 3 for Procedure 3, or 4 to end the program. The program inputs the user's response and determines if the response is a 1, 2, 3, or 4. If the response is anything else, the program redisplays the menu and asks the user to try again. Checking for a valid response requires several decisions, as shown in the flowchart in Figure 9-9.

Problems 2, 3, 4, and 5 illustrate the use of decisions in flowcharting. Let's now look at flowcharts involving loops.

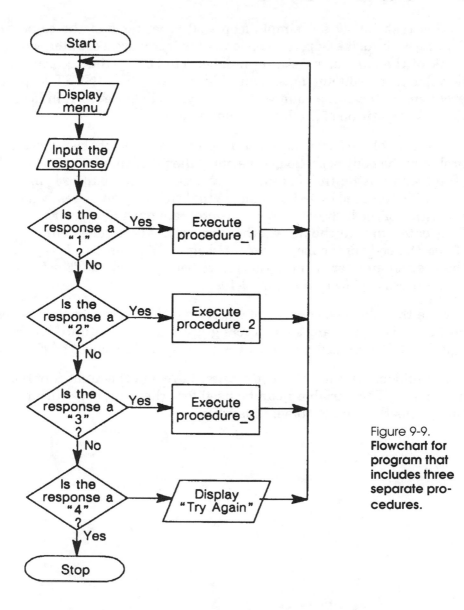

Figure 9-9. **Flowchart for program that includes three separate procedures.**

Problem 6. Kreativ Komputers must print 50 copies of a sales report. How can the company construct a flowchart for a program that accomplishes this task?

This task involves a simple loop—50 repetitions of the same task. In dealing with such a loop, it is convenient to introduce a counter, which keeps track of the current repetition number. (In coding the program from the flowchart, the counter is the variable in the FOR ... NEXT loop.) In this problem, we'll call the counter I. Initially, I will be set to 1, indicating that the first repetition of the loop is beginning.

The body of the loop consists of the program section to be repeated. In this problem, the body of the loop consists of the procedure for printing one copy of the report. After the procedure is carried out, the counter is increased by 1, and I is replaced by I+1 to indicate that the program is ready for the next repetition of the body of the loop. The program must now determine whether I is greater than 50; that is, whether the loop has been repeated often enough. If not, the body of the loop is executed again. This process is repeated until the desired number of repetitions have been carried out. The flowchart for this process is shown in Figure 9-10.

Note that the loop consists of a section of the flowchart that cycles back on itself. The program keeps cycling around the loop until the counter I equals 50. The program then leaves the loop and reaches the END box.

In Problem 6, we use the loop counter I to count the number of repetitions of the loop. The variable I can be used for other purposes within the loop, though, as the next Problem illustrates.

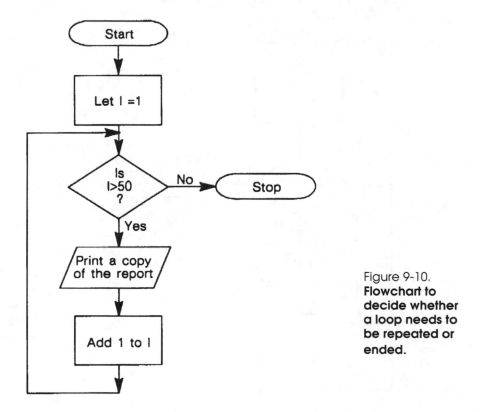

Figure 9-10.
Flowchart to decide whether a loop needs to be repeated or ended.

Problem 7. How can Kreativ Komputers construct a flowchart for a program that prints the numbers 1 through 1,000?

Let us use a loop to control printing consecutive numbers. Let I be the loop counter, starting from 1. Suppose that the Ith repetition of the loop prints the number I. Then the first repetition prints out 1, the second 2, the third 3, and so forth. This simple loop is illustrated in the flowchart in Figure 9-11.

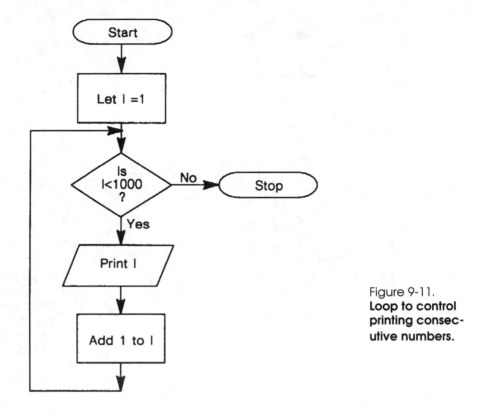

Figure 9-11.
Loop to control printing consecutive numbers.

Problem 8. How can Kreativ Komputers construct a flowchart that calculates the sum of the numbers 1 through 1,000?

This problem introduces another new idea—the accumulator, which we introduced without comment in our earlier discussion of loops. Solving the problem involves having the program accumulate the sum using the variable S. Initially, S will be set equal to 0. The sum is computed by adding the numbers from 1 to 1,000, to the number S one at a time. The program uses a loop with 1,000 repetitions. The first repetition of the loop adds 1 to S, the second repetition 2, and so on. In general, the Ith repetition adds the number I to S. At the end of the last loop, the accumulator S is equal to the desired sum.

The flowchart for this problem is shown in Figure 9-12.

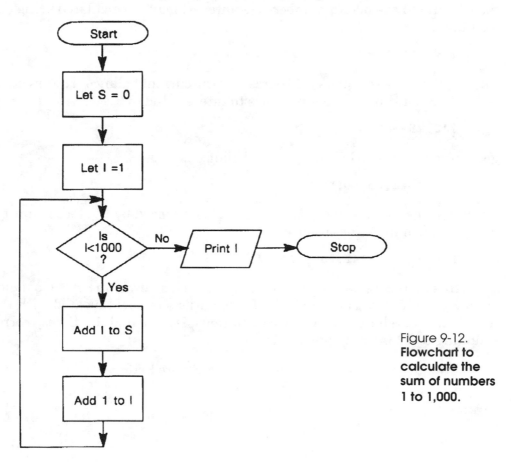

Figure 9-12.
Flowchart to calculate the sum of numbers 1 to 1,000.

Problem 9. Kreativ Komputers took out a car loan to buy a truck to deliver its products. The loan charges 1.25 percent interest per month. The beginning balance is $7,000 and the monthly payment is $242.25. How can the company construct a flowchart for a program that prints a chart displaying the balance at the end of each month for the next 12 months?

Let B equal the balance at any particular time, I the interest for the current month, and M the month number. The interest may be calculated using the formula

```
I = .0125 x B
```

That is, the interest equals 1.25 percent of the current balance. The payment is $242.25. Of this, an amount I goes to interest and

```
242.25 - I
```

goes to reduce the balance. The new balance is

```
B - (242.25 - I)
```

That is, after the payment, the value of B is replaced by the last quantity. This is shown in the notation

```
B --> B - (242.25 - I)
```

Read this as B is replaced by B - (242.25 - I). This new value of the balance is now printed out. The same set of calculations is now repeated with the new balance. The sequence of calculations is repeated 12 times, corresponding to 12 monthly payments.

A flowchart for this problem is shown in Figure 9-13.

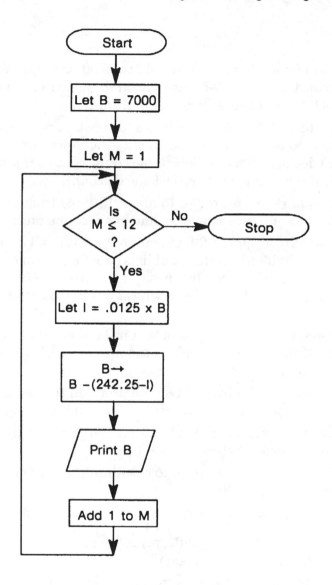

Figure 9-13.
Flowchart for displaying balance of a loan at the end of each month.

Exercises

1. Kreativ Komputers starts to sell a second tutorial program. Working from the flowchart in Figure 9-5, construct a flowchart for a program that computes bills for orders for both programs.

2. Kreativ Komputers sells to both dealers and consumers. The dealers are entitled to a 40 percent discount. Modify the flowchart in Figure 9-7 to include a decision box that determines if the customer is a dealer and, if so, calculates the price to reflect the discount.

3. Modify the flowchart in Figure 9-8 to allow 10 lines from the top of one label to the top of the next and to double-space the address.

4. Modify the flowchart in Figure 9-9 to print out a list of all customers. The list should be divided into three sublists, one for customers whose orders total less than $500, one for those whose orders total between $500 and $1,000, and one for those whose orders total more than $1,000.

5. Modify the flowchart in Figure 9-10 so that if the user hits a key other than 1, 2, 3, or 4, the program displays the message ILLEGAL KEY. PLEASE TRY AGAIN.

6. Modify the flowchart in Figure 9-11 so the program first asks for the number of copies to print and then prints that number of copies.

7. Modify the flowchart in Figure 9-12 so that the program prints out every third number from 1 through 1,000.

8. Construct a flowchart for a program to calculate the sum of the even numbers from 2 through 1,000.

Draw flowcharts planning computer programs to do the following.

9. Calculate the sum $12 + 22 + ... + 1,002$, print the result, and determine whether the result is larger than, smaller than, or equal to 4,873.

10. Calculate the time elapsed since the computer was turned on.

11. The roulette program on page.

12. The payroll program in Example 2 on page.

Debugging, Part I

An error is sometimes called a "bug" in computer jargon. The process of finding these errors or "bugs" in a program is called **debugging**. This can often be a ticklish task. Manufacturers of commercial software must regularly repair bugs they discover in their own programs! GWBASIC is equipped with a number of features to help detect bugs in your programs.

Detecting Errors by Running the Program

When you give the RUN command, GWBASIC begins to interpret the current program. In the course of interpretation, there are a number of errors that can be detected. One category of error is the structural error that reports an error in the way your program is stated. Some examples of such errors are:

Syntax error. There is an unclear instruction (misspelled?), mismatched parentheses, incorrect punctuation, illegal character, or illegal variable name in the program. For example, the line

```
10 Y= 2*(X+1
```

will generate a syntax error since it contains an unmatched parenthesis.

Undefined line number. The program uses a line number that does not correspond to an instruction. This can easily arise if you delete lines that are mentioned elsewhere. It can also occur when testing a portion of a program that refers to a line not yet written.

Duplicate definition. Attempting to DIMension an array that has already been dimensioned. Note that once you refer to an array within a program, even if you don't specify the dimensions, the computer will regard it as being dimensioned at 10. A subsequent DIM statement will generate an error.

NEXT without FOR. A NEXT statement that does not correspond to a FOR statement.

FOR without NEXT. A FOR statement that does not correspond to a NEXT statement.

RETURN without GOSUB. A RETURN statement is encountered while not performing a subroutine.

GOSUB without RETURN. A GOSUB statement does not have a matching RETURN.

When a structural error is encountered, the program is halted and an error message is displayed describing the error and the line in which it occurred.

Run-time Errors

A **run-time error** is an error condition that is created during program operation. As soon as a run-time error is detected, the program is halted and an error message describing the error condition and the line number is displayed. Here are some examples of run-time errors.

Overflow. The program uses a number too large for GWBASIC.

Division by zero. Attempting to divide by zero. This may be a hard error to spot. The computer will round to zero any number smaller than the minimum allowed. Use of such a number in subsequent calculations can result in division by zero. It can also occur in a division operation in which the denominator is a variable whose value has not previously been assigned. (Recall that such variables are assigned the value 0.)

Illegal function call. Attempting to evaluate a function outside of its mathematically defined range. For example, the square root function is defined only for non-negative numbers, the logarithm function only for positive numbers, and the arctangent only for numbers between -1 and 1. Any attempt to evaluate a function at a value outside these respective ranges will result in an illegal function call error.

Missing operand. Attempting to execute an instruction missing required data.

Subscript out of range. Attempting to use an array with one or more subscripts outside the range allowed by the appropriate DIM statement.

String too long. Attempting to specify a string containing more than 255 characters.

Out of memory. Your program will not fit into the computer's memory. This could result from large arrays or too many program steps or a combination of the two.

String formula too complex. Due to the internal processing of your formula, your string formula resulted in a string expression that was too long or complex. This error can be corrected by breaking the string expression into a series of simpler expressions.

Type mismatch. Attempting to assign a string constant as the value of a numeric variable, or a numeric constant value to a string variable.

Out of data. Attempting to read data that aren't there. This can occur in reading data from DATA statements, or diskettes.

Can't continue. Attempting to give a CONT command after the program has ENDed, or before the program has been RUN (such as after an EDIT session).

Error Messages

Figure 9-14 gives a list of all error messages recognized by GWBASIC and their corresponding error codes. (We will discuss the use of error codes later in the text, when we discuss error trapping routines.)

The Trace

Often your first try at running a program results in failure, while giving you no indication as to why the program is not running correctly. For example, your program might just run indefinitely, without giving you a clue as to what it is actually doing. How can you figure out what's wrong? One method is to use the **trace feature**.

Let us illustrate use of the trace, by debugging the following program designed to calculate the sum 1+2+...+100. The variable S is to contain the sum. The program uses a loop to add each of the numbers 1, 2, 3, ..., 100 to S, which is initially 0.

```
10   S=0
20   J=0
30   S=S + J
40   IF J=100 THEN 100 ELSE 200
100 J=J+1
110 GOTO 20
200 PRINT S
300 END
```

This program has two errors in it. (Can you spot them right off?) All you know initially is that the program is not functioning normally. The program

NUMBER	ERROR
1	NEXT without FOR
2	Syntax Error
3	RETURN without GOSUB
4	Out of Data
5	Illegal Function Call
6	Overflow
7	Out of memory
8	Undefined line number
9	Subscript out of range
10	Duplicate definition
11	Division by zero
12	Illegal direct
13	Type mismatch
14	Out of string space
15	String too long
16	String formula too complex
17	Can't continue
18	Undefined user function
19	No RESUME
20	RESUME without error
22	Missing operand
23	Line buffer overflow
24	Device timeout
25	Device fault
26	FOR without NEXT
27	Out of paper
29	WHILE without WEND
30	WEND without WHILE
50	Field overflow
51	Internal error
52	Bad file number
53	File not found
54	Bad file mode
55	File already open
57	Device I/O Error
58	File already exists
61	Disk full
62	Input past end
63	Bad record number
64	Bad file name
66	Direct statement in file
67	Too many files
68	Device unavailable
69	Communication buffer overflow
70	Disk write protect
71	Disk not ready
72	Disk media error
73	Advanced feature

Figure 9-14.
GWBASIC error statements.

runs, but prints out the answer 0, which we recognize as nonsense. How can we locate the errors? Let's turn on the trace function by typing TRON (TRace 300 ON) and pressing ENTER. The computer responds with Ok. Now type RUN. The computer will run our program and print out the line numbers of all executed instructions. The display is as shown in Figure 9-15.

```
Ok
run
[10] [20] [30] [40] [200]  0
[300]
Ok
_
```

Figure 9-15.
Using the trace.

The numbers in brackets indicate the line numbers executed. That is, the computer executes, in order, lines 10, 20, 30, 40, 200, and 300. The zero not in brackets is the program output resulting from the execution of line 200. The list of line numbers is not what we were expecting. Our program was designed (or so we thought) to execute line 100 after line 40. No looping is taking place. How did we get to line 200 after line 40? This suggests that we examine line 40. Lo and behold! There is an error. The line numbers 100 and 200 appearing in line 40 have been interchanged (an easy enough mistake to make). Let's correct this error by retyping the line:

```
40 IF J=100 THEN 200 ELSE 100
```

In triumph, we run our program again. The output is shown in Figure 9-16.

```
0] [40] [100] [110] [20] [30] [40] [100] [110] [20] [30] [40] [100] [110] [20] [30] [40] [100] [11
0] [20] [30] [40] [100] [110] [20] [30] [40] [100] [110] [20] [30] [40] [100] [110] [20] [30] [40]
[100] [110] [20] [30] [40] [100] [110] [20] [30] [40] [100] [110] [20] [30] [40] [100] [110] [20]
[30] [40] [100] [110] [20] [30] [40] [100] [110] [20] [30] [40] [100] [110] [20] [30] [40] [100] [
110] [20] [30] [40] [100] [110] [20] [30] [40] [100] [110] [20] [30] [40] [100] [110] [20] [30] [4
0] [100] [110] [20] [30] [40] [100] [110] [20] [30] [40] [100] [110] [20] [30] [40] [100] [110] [2
0] [30] [40] [100] [110] [20] [30] [40] [100] [110] [20] [30] [40] [100] [110] [20] [30] [40] [100
] [110] [20] [30] [40] [100] [110] [20] [30] [40] [100] [110] [20] [30] [40] [100] [110] [20] [30]
[40] [100] [110] [20] [30] [40] [100] [110] [20] [30] [40] [100] [110] [20] [30] [40] [100] [110]
[20] [30] [40] [100] [110] [20] [30] [40] [100] [110] [20] [30] [40] [100] [110] [20] [30] [40] [1
00] [110] [20] [30] [40] [100] [110] [20] [30] [40] [100] [110] [20] [30] [40] [100] [110] [20] [3
0] [40] [100] [110] [20] [30] [40] [100] [110] [20] [30] [40] [100] [110] [20] [30] [40] [100] [11
0] [20] [30] [40] [100] [110] [20] [30] [40] [100] [110] [20] [30] [40] [100] [110] [20] [30] [40]
[100] [110] [20] [30] [40] [100] [110] [20] [30] [40] [100] [110] [20] [30] [40] [100] [110] [20]
[30] [40] [100] [110] [20] [30] [40] [100] [110] [20] [30] [40] [100] [110] [20] [30] [40] [100] [
110] [20] [30] [40] [100] [110] [20] [30] [40] [100] [110] [20] [30] [40] [100] [110] [20] [30] [4
0] [100] [110] [20] [30] [40] [100] [110] [20] [30] [40] [100] [110] [20] [30] [40] [100] [110] [2
0] [30] [40] [100] [110] [20] [30] [40] [100] [110] [20] [30] [40] [100] [110] [20] [30] [40] [100
] [110] [20] [30] [40] [100] [110] [20] [30] [40] [100] [110] [20] [30] [40] [100] [110] [20] [30]
[40] [100] [110]
^C
Break in 110
Ok
_
```

Figure 9-16.
Tracing the corrected program.

Actually, the above output goes whizzing by us as the computer races madly on executing the instructions. After about 30 seconds, we sense that something is indeed wrong since it is unlikely that our program could take this long. We stop execution by means of the Ctrl-Break key combination. The last line indicates that we interrupted the computer while it was executing line 110. Actually, your screen will be filled with output resembling the above. You will notice that the computer is in a loop. Each time it reaches line 110, the loop goes back to line 20. Why doesn't the loop ever end? In order for the loop to terminate, J must equal 100. Well, can J ever equal 100? Of course not! Every time the computer executes line 20, the value of J is reset to 0. Thus, J is never equal to 100 and line 40 always sends us back to line 20. We clearly don't want to reset J to 0 all the time. After increasing J by 1 (line 100), we wish to add the new J to S. We want to go to 30, not 20. We correct line 110 to read

```
110 GOTO 30
```

We run our program again. There will be a rush of line numbers on the screen followed by the output 5050, which appears to be correct. Our program is now running properly. We turn off the trace by typing TROFF (TRace

OFF) and pressing ENTER. Finally, we run our program once more for good measure. The above sequence of operations is summarized in the following display of Figure 9-17.

```
Ok
run
 5050
Ok
_
```

Figure 9-17.
**Tracing the cor-
rected program.**

In our example above, we displayed all the line numbers executed. For a long program, this may lead to a huge list of line numbers. You may be selective by using TRON and TROFF within your program. Just use them with line numbers, just like any other BASIC instruction. When BASIC encounters a TRON, it begins to display the line numbers executed. When BASIC encounters a TROFF, it stops displaying line numbers. To debug a program, you may temporarily add TRON and TROFF instructions at selected places. As you locate the bugs, remove the corresponding trace instructions.

Exercises

1. Use the error messages to debug the following program to calculate $(1^2+2^2+...+50^2)(1^3+2^3+...+20^3)$.

```
10 S="0"
20 FOR J=1 TO 50
30    S=S + J(2
40 NEXT K
50 T=0
60 FOR J=1 TO 20
70    T=T +J^3
80 NXT T
90 NEXT T
100 A=ST
110 PRINT THE ANSWER IS, A
120 END
```

2. Use the trace function to debug the following program to determine the smallest integer N, for which N^2 is larger than 175263.

```
10 N=0
20 IF N^2 <= 175263 THEN 100
30 PRINT "THE FIRST N EQUALS"
100 N=N+1
110 GOTO 10
200 END
```

Debugging, Part II

Tracking down program bugs can be a very tricky business, and to be good at it you must be a good detective. In the preceding section, we listed some of the clues BASIC automatically supplies, namely the error messages. Sometimes, however, these clues are not enough to diagnose a bug. (For example, your program may run without errors. It may just not do what it is supposed to. In this case, no error messages will be triggered.) In such circumstances you must be prepared to supply your own clues. Here are some techniques.

Insert Extra Print Statements

You may temporarily insert extra PRINT statements into your program to print out the values of key variables at various points in the program. This technique allows you to keep track of a variable as your program is executed.

Insert Stop Commands

It is possible that your program planning may contain a logical flaw. In this case, it is possible to write a program that runs without error messages, but that does not perform as you expect it to. You may temporarily insert a STOP command to force a halt after a specified portion of the program.

This debugging technique may be used in several ways.

1. When the program encounters a STOP instruction, it halts execution and prints out the line number at which the program was stopped. If the program does stop, you will know that the instructions just before the STOP were executed. On the other hand, suppose that the program continues on its merry way. This tells you that the program is avoiding the instructions immediately preceding the STOP. If you determine the reason for this behavior, then you will likely correct a bug.

2. When the program is halted, the values of the variables are preserved. You may examine them to determine the behavior of your program. (See below for more information.)

3. You may insert several STOP instructions. After each halt, you may note the behavior of the program (line number, values of key variables, and so forth). You may continue execution by typing CONT and pressing ENTER. Note that if you change a program line during a halt, then you may not continue execution, but must restart the program by typing RUN and pressing ENTER.

Examine Variables in the Immediate Mode

When BASIC stops executing your program, the current values of the program variables are not destroyed. Rather, they are still in memory and may be examined as an indication of program behavior. This is true even if the program is halted by means of a STOP instruction or by hitting Ctrl-Break.

Suppose that a program is halted and that the BASIC prompt Ok is displayed. For example, to determine the current values of the program variables INVOICE and FILENAME$, type

```
PRINT INVOICE, FILENAME$
```

and press ENTER. Note that there is no line number. This instruction is in immediate mode. BASIC will display the current values of the two variables, just as if the PRINT statement was contained in a program:

```
145.83       ACCTPAY.MAR
```

Warning: As soon as you make any alteration in your program (correct a line, add a line), BASIC resets all the variables. The numeric variables will be reset to zero and the string variables will be set to null. Therefore, if you wish to have an accurate reading of the variable values as they emerge from your program, be sure to request them before making any program changes.

Execute Only a Portion of Your Program

Sometimes it helps to run only a portion of your program. You may start execution at any line using a variation of the RUN command. For example, to begin execution at line 500, type

```
RUN 500
```

and press ENTER. Note, however, that the RUN command causes all variables to be reset. If some earlier portion of your program sets some variables, then starting the program in the middle may not give an accurate picture of program operation. To get around this problem, you may set variables in immediate mode and start the program using the GOSUB instruction. For example, suppose that the earlier portion of your program set INVOICE equal to 145.83 and FILENAME$ equal to ACCTPAY.MAR. To accurately run a portion of the program depending on these variable values, first type

```
INVOICE=145.83:FILENAME$="ACCTPAY.MAR"
```

and press ENTER. (These instructions can be entered on separate lines, each followed by ENTER.) To start the program at line 500, you type

```
GOSUB 500
```

and press ENTER. Note that it is not sufficient to use the command

```
RUN 500
```

The RUN command automatically resets the variables.

Ten

String Manipulation

Introduction

In this chapter, we discuss some of the fine points about strings. In particular, we discuss:

- ASCII codes.

- Control characters.

- Dealing with strings containing quotation marks.

- Operations on strings, including string concatenation, taking the length of a string, forming substrings using LEFT$, RIGHT$, and MID$, translating strings of digits into their numerical equivalents and vice versa, and searching for substrings using INSTR.

- Using ASCII codes to deal with cursor movement.

- Application of everything learned in the chapter to build a game of blackjack.

ASCII Character Codes

Each keyboard character is assigned a number between 1 and 255. The code number assigned is called the ASCII code of the character. For example, the letter "A" has ASCII code 65, while the letter "a" has ASCII code 97. Also included in this correspondence are the punctuation marks and other keyboard characters. As examples, 40 is the ASCII code of the open parenthesis "(" and 62 is the ASCII code of the greater-than symbol ">".

Even the keys corresponding to nonprintable characters have ASCII codes. For example, the space bar has ASCII code 32, and the backspace key ASCII code 8. The printable characters have ASCII codes between 32 and 127. Table 10-1 lists all these characters and their corresponding ASCII codes.

ASCII value	Character	ASCII value	Character	ASCII value	Character
032	(space)	064	@	096	'
033	!	065	A	097	a
034	"	066	B	098	b
035	#	067	C	099	c
036	$	068	D	100	d
037	%	069	E	101	e
038	&	070	F	102	f
039	'	071	G	103	g
040	(	072	H	104	h
041	)	073	I	105	i
042	*	074	J	106	j
043	+	075	K	107	k
044	,	076	L	108	l
045	-	077	M	109	m
046	.	078	N	110	n
047	/	079	O	111	o
048	0	080	P	112	p
049	1	081	Q	113	q
050	2	082	R	114	r
051	3	083	S	115	s
052	4	084	T	116	t
053	5	085	U	117	u
054	6	086	V	118	v
055	7	087	W	119	w
056	8	088	X	120	x
057	9	089	Y	121	y
058	:	090	Z	122	z
059	;	091	[	123	{
060	<	092	\	124	|
061	=	093	]	125	}
062	<	094	^	126	~
063	?	095	_	127	

Table 10-1. **ASCII character codes for printable characters.**

We will discuss the ASCII control codes 0–31 later in this chapter. For now, however, let's call attention to just two:

ASCII Code	Name	Action
10	Line Feed	Moves cursor down one line
13	Carriage Return	Moves cursor to the leftmost position on the current line

Table 10-2. **Control codes 10 and 13.**

Pushing the ENTER key generates a carriage return and a line feed. That is, ENTER generates the two ASCII codes 13 and 10.

The computer uses ASCII codes to refer to letters and control operations. Any file, whether it is a program or data, may be reduced to a sequence of ASCII codes. Consider the following address:

```
John  Jones
2 S.  Broadway
```

As a sequence of ASCII codes, it is be stored as

```
74,111,104,110,32,74,111,110,101,115,13,
50,32,83,46,32,66,114,111,97,100,119,97,121,13
```

Note that the spaces are included (number 32), as are the carriage returns (ASCII code 13). A carriage return is input to GWBASIC when you press the ENTER key. The effect of this ASCII code is to move the cursor to the leftmost position of the next line.

ASCII codes allow us to represent any text generated by the keyboard as a sequence of numbers. This includes all formatting instructions like spaces, carriage returns, upper and lowercase letters, and so forth. Moreover, once a piece of text has been reduced to a sequence of ASCII codes, it also may be faithfully reproduced on the screen or on a printer.

Test Your Understanding 1 (Answer on Page 271)

Write a sequence of ASCII codes to reproduce this ad:

```
FOR SALE: Beagle puppies. Pedigreed.
8 weeks. $125.
```

You may refer to characters by their ASCII codes by using the function CHR$. For example, CHR$(74) is the character corresponding to ASCII code 74 (uppercase J); CHR$(32) is the character corresponding to ASCII code 32 (space). The PRINT and LPRINT instructions may be used in connection with CHR$. For example, the instruction

```
10 PRINT CHR$(74)
```

will display an uppercase J in the first position of the first print field.

Test Your Understanding 2 (Answer on Page 271)

Write a program to print the ad of Test Your Understanding 1 from its ASCII codes.

To obtain the ASCII code of a character, use the command ASC. For example, the command

```
10 PRINT ASC("B")
```

prints the ASCII code of the character "B", namely 66. In place of "B", you may use any string. The computer will return the ASCII code of the first character of the string. For example, the instruction

```
10 PRINT ASC(A$)
```

prints the ASCII code of the first character of the string A$.

Test Your Understanding 3 (Answer on Page 271)

Determine the ASCII codes of the characters $, g, X, and + without looking at the chart.

ASCII codes have many uses in writing even the most simple programs. For example, suppose that you wish to print out a quotation mark on the screen. To do so, you must create a string consisting of a quotation mark. The usual way to define a string is to enclose it in quotation marks. However, if you attempt to do that in this case, you arrive at """". Unfortunately, here is how GWBASIC looks at that string. The first quotation mark tells GWBASIC that a string is about to begin. The second quotation mark tells GWBASIC that the string just ended. The third quotation mark is ignored! For example, the command

```
10 PRINT """
```

prints nothing on the screen!

The ASCII codes provide a way out of this dilemma. The ASCII code of " is 34, and CHR$(34) is a string consisting of a single quotation mark. So we may print " on the screen with the statement

```
10 PRINT CHR$(34);
```

In a similar fashion, ASCII codes may be used to include carriage returns and line feeds within a string. Note that you cannot type a string that includes carriage returns or line feeds from the keyboard. Hitting ENTER is a signal for GWBASIC to accept the line just typed. However, it will not include the carriage return and line feed as part of the string. This must be done using ASCII codes. (More about how this is done is on page 282)

Exercises

1. Determine the ASCII codes of the following characters without looking at the table:

    A, a, B, b, C, c, D, d.

2. Generalize from Exercise 1 to state a relationship between the ASCII code of an uppercase letter and the ASCII code of the corresponding lowercase letter (that is, between A and a).

3. Display the sequence of ASCII codes corresponding to the following sentence.

```
He said to me, "The IBM is an excellent computer."
```

Answers to Test Your Understandings 1, 2, and 3

1. ```
70,79,82,32,83,65,76,69,58,32,66,101,97,103,108,101,32,
112,117,112,112,105,101,115,46,32,80,101,100,105,103,114,
101,13,100,46,13,10,56,32,119,101,101,107,115,46,32,36,
49,50,53,46,13
```

2. ```
10 DATA 70,79,.........(insert data from 1)
20 DATA ........
30 DATA ........
40 FOR J=1 TO 54
50    READ A
60    PRINT CHR$(A);
70 NEXT J
80 END
```

3. ```
10 DATA $,g,X,+
20 FOR J=1 TO 4
30   READ A$
40   B=ASC(A$)
50   PRINT A$, B
60 NEXT J
70 END
```

## Operations on Strings

In earlier chapters, our strings contained only printable characters. Let us now extend that definition to allow characters corresponding to any ASCII
```

code. So, for example, a string may now include line feeds, carriage returns, and any of the other control characters we soon will define. The control characters in a string are treated just like any of the other characters.

Concatenation

GWBASIC lets you perform a number of different operations on strings. The most fundamental operation is string addition (or, in computer jargon, string concatenation). Suppose that A$ and B$ are strings, with A$="word" and B$="processor". Then the sum of A$ and B$, denoted A$+B$, is the string obtained by adjoining A$ and B$, namely

```
"wordprocessor"
```

Note that no space is left between the two strings. To include a space, suppose that C$=" ". C$ is the string consisting of a single space. Thus A$+C$+B$ is the string

```
"word processor"
```

Test Your Understanding 1 (Answer on Page 278)
If A$="4" and B$="7", what is A$+B$?

Test Your Understanding 2 (Answer on Page 278)
Set A$ equal to the string

```
He said, "No."<carriage return>
```

The Length of a String

You may compute the length of a string by using the LEN function. For example,

```
LEN("BOUGHT")
```

is equal to six, since the string "BOUGHT" has six letters. Similarly, if A$ is equal to the string

```
"Family Income"
```

then LEN(A$) is equal to 13. (The space between the words counts!) Note that carriage returns, line feeds, and other control characters count in the length.

Here is an application of the LEN instruction.

Example 1. Write a program that inputs the string A$ and then centers it on a line of the display. (Assume an 80-character line.)

Solution. A line is 80 characters long, with the spaces numbered from 1 to 80. The string A$ takes up LEN(A$) of these spaces, so there are 80-LEN(A$) spaces to be distributed on either side of A$. The line should begin with half of the 80-LEN(A$) spaces, or with (80-LEN(A$))/2 spaces. So we should tab to column (80-LEN(A$))/2+1. Here is our program.

Listing 6-1

```
1 ' ******************************
2 ' This program centers a string
3 '   given by the user
4 ' ******************************
10 INPUT "String to be centered"; A$
20 CLS
30 PRINT TAB((80-LEN(A$))/2+1); A$
40 END
```

Test Your Understanding 3 (Answer on Page 278)

Use the program of Example 1 to center the string "The IBM Personal Computer".

Substrings

It is possible to dissect strings using the three commands LEFT$, RIGHT$, and MID$. These commands allow you to construct a string consisting of a specified number of characters taken from the left, right, or middle of a designated string. Consider the command

```
A$=LEFT$("LOVE",2)
```

The string A$ consists of the two leftmost characters of the string "LOVE". That is, A$="LO". Similarly, the commands

```
B$="tennis"
C$=RIGHT$(B$,3)
```

set C$ equal to the string consisting of the three rightmost letters of the string B$, namely C$="nis". Similarly, if A$= "Republican", then the command

```
D$=MID$(A$,5,3)
```

sets D$ equal to the string consisting of the three characters starting with the fifth character of A$, which is D$="bli".

Test Your Understanding 4 (Answer on Page 278)

Determine the string constant

```
RIGHT$(LEFT$("computer",4),3)
```

Example 2. Write a program that accepts as input a seven-digit telephone number and prints on the screen the first three and the last four digits separated by a hyphen.

Solution.   We input the seven digits of the telephone number as a string. We then use RIGHT$ and LEFT$ to extract the desired strings from this string.

Listing 6-2

```
1 '**********************************
2 'This program accepts a seven-digit
3 'telephone number and reformats it
4 'so that the first three digits and
5 'the last four are separated by a
6 'hyphen.
7 '**********************************
10 INPUT "TELEPHONE NUMBER"; T$
20 PRINT LEFT$(T$,3);
30 PRINT "-";
40 PRINT RIGHT$(T$,4)
50 END
```

Example 3.   Write a program that accepts as input a name consisting of a first name followed by a last name separated by a space. The program should determine the last name and display it on the screen.

Solution.   Our program searches for the first space and then extracts the leftmost portion of the string, starting from the character after the space.

Listing 6-3

```
1 '************************************
2 'This program determines the last name
3 'from a first name-last name combination,
4 'where the two names are separated by
5 'a space.
6 '************************************
10 INPUT "NAME(FIRST LAST);NME$
20 S=INSTR(NME$,' '): 'Search for space between names
30 LAST$ = RIGHT$(NME$,S+1)
40 PRINT LAST$
50 END
```

Strings Representing Numbers

In manipulating strings, it is important to recognize the difference between numerical data and string data. The number 14 is denoted by 14;

the string consisting of the two characters 14 is denoted "14". The first is a numerical constant and the second a string constant. We can perform arithmetic using the numerical constants. However, we cannot perform any of the character manipulation supplied by the instructions RIGHT$, MID$, and LEFT$. Such manipulation may only be performed on strings. How may we perform character manipulation on numerical constants? GWBASIC provides a simple method. We first convert the numerical constants to string constants by using STR$. For example, the number 14 may be converted into the string

```
" 14"
```

using the command

```
A$=STR$(14)
```

As a result of this command, A$ has the value " 14". Note the blank in front of the 14. This occurs because GWBASIC automatically leaves a space for the sign of a number. If the number is positive, then the sign prints out as a space. If the number is negative, then the sign prints out as a minus (-).

As another example, suppose that the variable B has the value 1.457. STR$(B) is then equal to the string

```
" 1.457"
```

To convert strings consisting of numbers into numerical constants, use VAL. Consider this command:

```
B=VAL("3.78")
```

This sets B equal to 3.78. You may even use VAL for strings consisting of a number followed by other characters. VAL picks off the initial number portion and throws away the part of the string beginning with the first non-numerical character. For example,

```
VAL("12.5 inches")
```

is equal to 12.5.

Test Your Understanding 5 (Answer on Page 279)

Suppose that A$ equals "5 percent" and B$ equals "758.45 dollars". Write a program that starts from A$ and B$ and computes five percent of $758.45.

The INSTR Statement

In some applications, it is necessary to search a string for a particular pattern. Here are some examples of such searches:

Find the location of the first "A" in the string A$.

Find the location of the first period in the string B$.

Find the location of the first "1" in A$ occurring after the eighth character.

Does the sequence of characters "ABS" occur anywhere in the string A$?

All such searches are greatly simplified using the INSTR (=INSTRing) function. This function may be used in either of two formats. The simplest is

```
P=INSTR(A$,B$)
```

In response to this statement, P is set equal to the location of the first occurrence of B$ in A$. For example, suppose that

```
A$="This is a test of the INSTR statement."
```

```
B$="te"
```

In this case, the first occurrence of B$ in A$ is at the beginning of the word "test". The location of the initial t is the eleventh character. So INSTR(A$,B$) has the value 11.

If B$ does not occur in A$, then INSTR has the value zero. Therefore, to determine whether the string "ABS" occurs in A$, we can use the program

```
10 P=INSTR(A$,"ABS")
20 IF P=0 THEN PRINT "ABS DOES NOT OCCUR"
30 IF P>0 THEN PRINT "ABS OCCURS"
```

The second format of the INSTR statement allows you to begin the search for B$ beginning with a designated location m. In this format the statement has the form

```
P=INSTR(m,A$,B$)
```

For example, if we wish the search for B$ to begin with the eighth character of A$, we can use the instruction

```
P=INSTR(8,A$,B$)
```

Exercises

1. Write a program to rewrite the addition problem 15+48+97 = 160 in the form

   15
   48
   97
   ___
   160

2. Write a program to input the string constants "$6718.49" and "$4801.96" and calculate the sum of the given dollar amounts.

3. Write a program to list all three-, four-, and five-character substrings contained in the word ANESTHESIA.

4. Write a program to capitalize all the letters in a string input by the user.

Answers to Test Your Understandings 1, 2, 3, 4, and 5

1. "47"

2. ```
   A$ = "He said,"+CHR$(34)+"No"_
         +CHR$(34)+"."+CHR$(13)+CHR$(10)
   ```

3. Type RUN and press ENTER. When prompted, type in the given string.

4. "omp"
   ```

5.  ```
    10 A$="5 percent":B$="758.45 dollars"
    20 A=VAL(A$):B=VAL(B$)
    30 PRINT A$," of ",B$," is"
    40 PRINT A*B*.01
    50 END
    ```

Control Characters

Table 10-3 contains a list of the control characters corresponding to ASCII codes 0–31. Some comments on the functions of the various codes are in order.

Code 000 (null) is exactly what its name suggests. It is a character that does nothing. It often is used in communications, where a message will be started with a string of nulls.

Codes 001–006 are graphics characters. You use them for games.

Code 7 (beep) beeps the speaker of the computer.

Code 8 (backspace) backspaces the cursor one space.

Code 9 (tab) moves the cursor to the next tab stop. GWBASIC automatically places tab stops every five characters across the line.

Code 10 (line feed) advances the cursor one line down.

Code 11 (home) positions the cursor at the upper left corner of the screen.

Code 12 (form feed) advances the paper on the printer to the top of the next page.

Code 13 (carriage return) returns the cursor to the leftmost position on the current line.
    ```

Codes 14–27 are further graphics characters for use in displays.

Code 28 (cursor right) moves the cursor to the right one space.

Code 29 (cursor left) moves the cursor to the left one space.

Code 30 (cursor up) moves the cursor up one space.

Code 31 (cursor down) moves the cursor down one space.

ASCII value	Character	Control character
000	(null)	NUL
001	☺	SOH
002	●	STX
003	♥	ETX
004	♦	EOT
005	♣	ENQ
006	♠	ACK
007	(beep)	BEL
008	▫	BS
009	(tab)	HT
010	(line feed)	LF
011	(home)	VT
012	(form feed)	FF
013	(carriage return)	CR
014	♫	SO
015	☼	SI
016	►	DLE
017	◄	DC1
018	↕	DC2
019	‼	DC3
020	¶	DC4
021	§	NAK
022	▬	SYN
023	↨	ETB
024	↑	CAN
025	↓	EM
026	→	SUB
027	←	ESC
028	(cursor right)	FS
029	(cursor left)	GS
030	(cursor up)	RS
031	(cursor down)	US

Table 10-3.
ASCII codes for control characters.

To use the ASCII control codes, you PRINT them as if they were printable characters. For example, to move the cursor one space up, use the statement

```
10 PRINT CHR$(30);
```

Note that the statement ends with a semicolon (;). This prevents GWBASIC from issuing a carriage return and line feed following the PRINT statement. Otherwise, they would ruin the cursor positioning accomplished by control character 30.

More on the Cursor

The ASCII codes controlling cursor motion allow you to position the cursor relative to its current position. You may move the cursor to a specific position on the screen using the LOCATE statement. The format of this statement is

```
LOCATE row, column
```

For example, to position the cursor in column 5 of row 20, use the statement

```
10 LOCATE 20,5
```

We can determine the column in which the cursor is currently located by using the GWBASIC function POS(0). For example, if the cursor currently is located in column 37, then POS(0) is equal to 37. The variable CSRLIN always equals the number of the line in which the cursor is currently located. For example, if the cursor currently is located in line 5, then CSRLIN is equal to 5. You may use POS(0) and CSRLIN exactly as you would any other variables in GWBASICS.

Test Your Understanding 1 (Answer on Page 283)

Write a program to move the cursor two spaces to the right and two spaces down.

Exercises

1. Print the string "HELLO" and then move the cursor to the H.

2. Write a program that asks the user for some input. In response to an S, it moves the cursor to the left; in response to a D, it moves the cursor to the right; in response to an E, it moves the cursor up; in response to an X, it moves the cursor down. In response to any other input, the program should do nothing.

3. Modify the program of Exercise 2 so that it accepts a series of cursor moves of the type "SSDDXEEEESSSSDDD".

4. Practice moving the cursor to various positions on the screen.

5. Write an instruction to move the cursor to the bottom of the column in which it currently resides.

6. Write an instruction to move the cursor to the left of the screen in the row it is now on.

Answer to Test Your Understanding 1

1. `PRINT CHR$(28);CHR$(28);CHR$(31);CHR$(31);`
   `END`

A Friendly Game of Blackjack

In this section, we present a version of the popular card game Blackjack. In this game, the player (we will allow only one at a time) vies with the dealer. The player makes a bet. The player and dealer are then dealt two cards each. The dealer's first card is face down and the others are face up. The object is to get a hand that totals as closely as possible to 21 without going over. Numbered cards have their usual values; jacks, queens, and kings all have value 10; and aces have a value of either 1 or 11 at the player's (or dealer's) discretion. The player goes first, deciding, one card at a time, whether to be hit (given another card) or to stand (decline further cards). If the player's total goes over 21, the player busts and loses the amount bet. If the player hits 21 exactly, he automatically wins the amount bet.

If the player stops before busting or achieving 21, the dealer plays. First he turns over his first card. As long as the dealer's total is less than 16, he must draw a card. The dealer continues until he either busts, gets 21, or gets at least 16. If the dealer busts, the player wins. Otherwise, the player with the highest total wins. In case of ties, the dealer wins.

Our program to implement this game employs most of what we have learned about string manipulation. The deck of cards is represented as a string:

"AHADACAS2H2D2C2S......"

Here AH stands for the ace of hearts, 2D for the two of diamonds, and so forth. Picking a card then involves choosing a random odd position in the string. The card chosen is then determined by extracting the two-character substring that stands for the character. (See lines 6000 and on in the listing below.)

The program uses the various graphics characters in the IBM PC's character set (see Table 10-3) to draw the cards on the screen (see lines 5000 and on in the listing below). These are characters with ASCII codes from 0 to 31 and from 128 to 255. In this program we use characters to form rectangles (ASCII codes 187, 188, 200, 201, 205) and the characters for the various card suits (ASCII codes 3, 4, 5, and 6). (IBM wisely chose to include these in its character set.)

Here is the listing of the program. It is highly structured and liberally commented so that it is more or less self-explanatory.

```
1000 '***************************************************
1010 'This program plays the traditional game of black-
1020 'jack. You play against the dealer (the computer).
1030 ' Program designed by Jonathan Goldstein.
1040 '***************************************************
```

```
1050 GOSUB 2030: 'Initialize program
1060 LOCATE 23,1
1070 INPUT "HOW MANY CHIPS($1 DOLLAR PER CHIP)";MONEY
1080 WHILE GAMEEND=FALSE
1090   CLS
1100   GOSUB 3000: 'Initialization
1110   GOSUB 4000: 'Place bet
1120   LOCATE 5,50: PRINT "DEALER'S HAND"
1130   LOCATE 20,50: PRINT "PLAYER'S HAND"
1140   GOSUB 4040: 'Deal initial cards
1150   GOSUB 4100: 'Test for blackjack
1160   WHILE BUST=FALSE AND BLACKJACK = FALSE AND
       HIT=TRUE
1170     LOCATE 10,1
1180     INPUT "HIT(H) OR STAND(S)",HIT$
1190     LOCATE 10,1:PRINT SPACE$(80);
1200     IF HIT$="S" OR HIT$="s" THEN HIT=FALSE:GOTO 1220
1210     CARD=PLAYER:GOSUB 6000: 'Deal player's card
1220     GOSUB 4100: 'Test for blackjack or bust
1230   WEND
1240   IF BLACKJACK = TRUE OR BUST = TRUE THEN 1380
1250   GOSUB 7000: 'Turn over dealer's 1st card
1260   WHILE TOTAL(DEALER) < 16  AND BLACKJACK=FALSE
1270     CARD=DEALER:GOSUB 6000: 'Deal dealer's card
1280     GOSUB 4100: 'Test for blackjack or bust
1290   WEND
1300   'Announce results
1310   IF BLACKJACK = TRUE OR BUST = TRUE THEN 1380
1320   FOR J=1 TO 2
1330     IF TOTAL(J) <= 11 AND ACE(J) = TRUE THEN
         TOTAL(J)=TOTAL(J)+10
1340   NEXT J
1350   LOCATE 10,1:PRINT SPACE$(80)
1360   IF TOTAL(DEALER) >= TOTAL(PLAYER) THEN PRINT
       "Dealer Wins!" :WINNER=DEALER
1370   IF TOTAL(DEALER) < TOTAL(PLAYER) THEN PRINT
       "Player Wins!" :WINNER=PLAYER
1380   BEEP:BEEP:BEEP:BEEP:BEEP:BEEP
1390   IF WINNER = PLAYER THEN MONEY = MONEY+BET ELSE
       MONEY = MONEY-BET
```

```
1400    PRINT "PLAYER BALANCE $";MONEY
1410    FOR J=1 TO 10000:NEXT J
1420    CLS: INPUT "PLAY AGAIN(Y/N)";RESPONSE$
1430    IF RESPONSE$ <> "Y" AND RESPONSE$ <> "y" THEN
        GAMEEND=TRUE
1440 WEND
1450 END
2000 '*********************************************
2010 '                   Subroutines
2020 '*********************************************
2030 'Initialization of program
2040    TRUE=1:FALSE=0
2050    GAMEEND = FALSE
2060    CLS:SCREEN 0:WIDTH 80:RANDOMIZE TIMER:KEY OFF
2070    FULLDECK$="2S2H2C2D3S3H3C3D4S4H4C4D5S5H5C5D6S
        6H6C6D7S77C7D8S8H8C8D9S9H9C9D0S0H0C0DJSJHJCJD
        QSQHQCQDKSKHKCKDASAHACAD"
2080    TOP$=CHR$(201)+CHR$(205)+CHR$(205)+CHR$(205)+
        CHR$(205)+CHR$(205)+CHR$(205)+CHR$(205)+CHR$
        (205)+CHR$(187)2090SIDE$= CHR$(186)+""+CHR$(186)
2100    BOTTOM$=CHR$(200)+CHR$(205)+CHR$(205)+CHR$(205)+
        CHR$(205)+CHR$(205)+CHR$(205)+CHR$(205)+CHR$(205)
        +CHR$(188)3000
3000 'Initialization of hand
3010    REMAININGCARDS=52
3020    REMAININGDECK$ = FULLDECK$
3030    PLAYER=0:DEALER=1
3040    PLAYERCARDS = 0:DEALERCARDS=0
3050    ACE(PLAYER)=FALSE:ACE(DEALER)=FALSE
3060    BLACKJACK=FALSE
3070    BUST=FALSE
3080    HIT = TRUE
3090    TOTAL(DEALER)=0:TOTAL(PLAYER)=0
3100    FOR J=1 TO 10
3110       DEALER$(J)=""
3120       PLAYER$(J)=""
3130    NEXT J
3140 RETURN
4000 'Place bet
4010    CLS: LOCATE 23,1:PRINT "PLAYER BALANCE: $";MONEY
```

```
4020    LOCATE 21,1:INPUT "Enter bet:",BET
4030 RETURN
4040 'Deal Initial Cards
4050 CARD=DEALER: GOSUB 6000: 'Deal 1st card
     for Dealer
4060 CARD=PLAYER:GOSUB 6000: 'Deal 1st card for Player
4070 CARD=DEALER:GOSUB 6000: 'Deal 2nd card for Dealer
4080 CARD=PLAYER:GOSUB 6000: 'Deal 2nd card for Player
4090 RETURN
4100 'Test for blackjack or bust
4110    TOTAL(CARD)=0:ACE=FALSE:BLACKJACK=FALSE
4120    IF CARD=DEALER THEN NUMCARDS=DEALERCARDS ELSE
        NUMCARDS=PLAYERCARDS
4130    FOR J=1 TO NUMCARDS : 'Compute total of hand
4140      IF CARD=DEALER THEN CARD$=DEALER$(J) ELSE CARD$
          = PLAYER$(J)
4150      A$=LEFT$(CARD$,1)
4160      IF A$="0" OR A$="J" OR A$="Q" OR A$="K"
          THEN COUNT=10 ELSE IF A$= "A" THEN COUNT =
          1 ELSE COUNT = VAL(A$)
4170      IF A$="A" THEN ACE(CARD)=TRUE
4180      TOTAL(CARD) = TOTAL(CARD)+COUNT
4190    NEXT J
4200    IF TOTAL(CARD)<=21 THEN GOTO 4260
4210 '  Bust
4220    BUST=TRUE
4230    LOCATE 10,1:PRINT SPACE$(80)
4240    IF CARD = PLAYER THEN PRINT "Player Busted!" ELSE
        PRINT "Dealer Busted!"
4250    WINNER=1-CARD
4260 '  Blackjack
4270    IF (TOTAL(CARD)=21) OR (TOTAL(CARD)=11 AND
        ACE(CARD)=TRUE) THEN BLACKJACK=TRUE
4280    IF BLACKJACK = FALSE THEN 4320
4290    LOCATE 10,1:PRINT SPACE$(80)
4300    IF CARD=PLAYER THEN PRINT "Blackjack. Player
wins!"
        ELSE PRINT "Blackjack. Dealer Wins"
4310    WINNER=CARD
4320 RETURN
```

```
5000 'Display current card
5010    IF CARD=PLAYER THEN XLOC=11*PLAYERCARDS-10 ELSE
        XLOC = 11*DEALERCARDS-10
5020    IF CARD=PLAYER THEN YLOC=14 ELSE YLOC=1
5030    LOCATE YLOC,XLOC
5040    PRINT TOP$
5050    FOR J=1 TO 5
5060      LOCATE YLOC+J,XLOC:PRINT SIDE$
5070    NEXT J
5080    LOCATE YLOC+6,XLOC:PRINT BOTTOM$
5090    A$=RIGHT$(C$,1)
5100    B$=LEFT$(C$,1)
5110    IF B$="0" THEN B$="10"
5120    IF A$="H" THEN A$=CHR$(3)
5130    IF A$="D" THEN A$=CHR$(4)
5140    IF A$="C" THEN A$=CHR$(5)
5150    IF A$="S" THEN A$=CHR$(6)
5160    BA$=B$+A$
5170    LOCATE YLOC+3,XLOC+4
5180    IF CARD=PLAYER OR DEALERCARDS>=2 THEN PRINT BA$
5190 RETURN
6000 'Deal card to the hand specified by CARD
6010    'If deck is empty start new deck
6020        IF REMAININGCARDS>0 THEN 6050
6030        REMAININGCARDS=52
6040        REMAININGDECK$=FULLDECK$
6050    'Select card and adjust deck
6060        POSITION=(INT(REMAININGCARDS*RND(1))+1)*2-1
6070        C$ = MID$(REMAININGDECK$,POSITION,2)
6080        FIRSTHALF$=LEFT$(REMAININGDECK$,POSITION-1)
6090        SECONDHALF$ = RIGHT$(REMAININGDECK$,
        2*REMAININGCARDS-POSITION-1)
6100        REMAININGDECK$=FIRSTHALF$+SECONDHALF$
6110        REMAININGCARDS=REMAININGCARDS-1
6120    'Assign card to dealer or player
6130        IF CARD = DEALER THEN 6170
6140        PLAYERCARDS=PLAYERCARDS+1
6150        PLAYER$(PLAYERCARDS)=C$
6160        GOTO 6190
6170        DEALERCARDS=DEALERCARDS+1
```

```
6180        DEALER$(DEALERCARDS)=C$
6190    'Display card
6200        GOSUB 5000
6210 RETURN
7000 'Turn over dealer's first card
7010    C$=DEALER$(1)
7020    A$=RIGHT$(C$,1)
7030    B$=LEFT$(C$,1)
7040    IF B$="0" THEN B$="10"
7050    IF A$="H" THEN A$=CHR$(3)
7060    IF A$="D" THEN A$=CHR$(4)
7070    IF A$="C" THEN A$=CHR$(5)
7080    IF A$="S" THEN A$=CHR$(6)
7090    BA$=B$+A$
7100    LOCATE 4,5
7110    PRINT BA$
7120 RETURN
```

Eleven

Variable Types and Functions

Introduction

In this chapter, we discuss the various types of numbers used by GWBASIC, including:

- Single-precision constants and variables.

- Double-precision constants and variables.

- Integer constants and variables.

- Long integer constants and variables.

- User-defined data types

In addition, we survey the various types of built-in and user-defined functions that GWBASIC incorporates.

Types of Numeric Constants

Up to this point, we have used the computer to perform arithmetic without giving much thought to the level of accuracy of the numbers involved. However, when doing scientific programming, it is absolutely essential to know the number of decimal places of accuracy of the computations. Let's begin this chapter by discussing the form in which GWBASIC stores and uses numbers.

Actually, GWBASIC recognizes four different types of numeric constants: integer, long integer, single-precision, and double-precision.

An integer constant is an ordinary integer (positive or negative) in the range from -32,768 to +32,767. (32,768 is two raised to the 15th power. This number is significant to the internal workings of the computer.) Here are some examples of integer numeric constants:

```
7, 58, 3712, -15, -598
```

Integer constants may be stored very efficiently in RAM. Moreover, arithmetic with integer constants takes the least time. Therefore, in order to realize these efficiencies, GWBASIC handles integer constants in a special way. To store an integer requires two bytes of RAM.

A single-precision constant is a number with six or fewer digits that contains a decimal point. Some examples of single-precision constants are

```
5.135, -63.5785, 123456, -1.46765E12
```

Note that a single-precision constant may be expressed in "scientific" or "floating-point" notation, as in the final example shown here. In such an expression, however, you are limited to seven or fewer digits. In GWBASIC, single-precision constants must lie within these ranges:

$$*1x10^{38} \text{ and } *1x10^{-38}; \qquad 1x10^{-38} \text{ and } 1x10^{38}.$$

This limitation seldom is much of a limitation in practice. After all, $1 \times s10^{-38}$ equals

.000000000000000000000000000000000000001

(37 zeros followed by a 1), which is about as small a number as you are ever likely to encounter! Similarly, 1×10^{38} equals

100,000,000,000,000,000,000,000,000,000,000,000,000

(a 1 followed by 38 zeros), which is large enough for most practical calculations. To store a single-precision constant requires 4 bytes of RAM.

A double-precision constant is a number containing more than seven significant figures and a decimal point. Here are some examples of double-precision numbers:

2.0000000000, 3578930497594, -3946.635475495

A double-precision constant can contain as many as 17 significant digits.

Scientific notation also may be used to represent double-precision numbers. Use the letter D to precede the exponent. For example, the number

2.7575757575D-4

equals the double-precision constant

.00027575757575

The number

1.3145926535D15

equals the double-precision constant

1,314,159,265,350,000

A double-precision constant may have up to 16 significant digits. Double-precision constants are subject to the same range limitations as single-precision constants. To store a double precision constant requires eight bytes of RAM.

Single-precision constants occupy more RAM than integer constants. Moreover, arithmetic with single-precision constants proceeds slower than integer arithmetic (either standard or long). Similarly, double-precision constants occupy even more memory, and arithmetic proceeds even slower than with single-precision constants. GWBASIC recognizes each of the three types of numerical constants and uses only as much arithmetic power as is necessary.

Here are the rules for determining the type of a numerical constant:

1. Any whole number in the range -32,768 and 32,767 is an integer constant.

2. Any number with seven or fewer digits having a decimal point is a single-precision constant. Any number in scientific notation using E before the exponent is assumed to be a single-precision constant. If a number has more than seven digits in scientific notation but uses an E, it is interpreted as a double-precision constant. For example, the number

    `1.23456789E+15`

   is interpreted as the double-precision constant

    `1.23456789D+15`

3. A number with more than seven significant digits is interpreted as a double-precision constant. If more than 17 digits are specified, then the number is truncated after the 16th digit and written in scientific notation. For example, the number

    `123456789123456789`

   is interpreted as the double-precision constant

    `1.234567891234567D+16`

The above rules for specifying the type of a number can be overridden by means of a type declaration tag. For instance, a numeric constant followed by % is interpreted as an integer constant. For example, 1% is interpreted as the integer constant 1. An integer tag in a number containing a decimal or on a number outside the integer range will be ignored. For example,

```
1.85% = 1.85
35000% = 3.5E+4
```

will result in error messages.

A numeric constant followed by ! is interpreted as a single-precision constant and rounded to seven significant digits. For example, the constant

```
1.23456789!
```

is interpreted as

```
1.234568
```

The constant

```
123456789!
```

is rounded to seven significant digits and written in scientific notation as:

```
1.234568E8
```

A # serves as a type declaration tag to indicate a double-precision constant. For example, the constant

```
1.2#
```

is interpreted as the 17-digit double-precision constant

```
1.20000000000000000
```

If more than 17 digits of a decimal number are given, GWBASIC rounds the number to 17 significant digits.

In scientific notation, the letter D serves as a type declaration tag.

Let's discuss the way GWBASIC performs arithmetic with the various constant types. The variable type resulting from an arithmetic operation is determined by the variable types of the data entering into the operation. For example, the sum of two integer constants will be an integer constant, provided that the answer is within the range of an integer constant. If not, the sum will be a single-precision constant. Arithmetic operations among single-precision constants will always yield single-precision constants. Arithmetic constants among double-precision constants yields a double-precision result. Here are some examples of arithmetic:

```
5% + 7%
```

The computer adds the two integer constants 5 and 7 to obtain the integer constant 12.

```
4.21! + 5.2!
```

The computer adds the two single-precision constants 4.21 and 5.2 to obtain the single-precision result 9.41.

```
3/2
```

Here the two constants 3 and 2 are integers. However, since the result, 1.5, is not an integer, it is assumed to be a single-precision type.

The result of

```
1!/3!
```

is the single-precision constant .3333333. Similarly, the result of the double-precision calculation

```
1#/3#
```

is the double-precision constant .33333333333333333.

Exercises

For each of the constants below, determine the number stored by the computer.

1. 3

2. 2.37

3. 5.78E5

4. 2#

5. 3!

6. -4.1!

7. -4.1%

8. 3500.6847586958658!

9. 2.176D2

10. -5.94E12

11. 3.5869504003837265374

12. -234542383746.21

13. -2.367D20

14. 457000000000000000!

For each of the arithmetic problems below, determine the number as stored by the computer.

15. 1 + 45

16. 2/4

17. 3#/5#

18. 3!/5! + 1

19. 2#/3#

20. 2#/3# + .53#

21. 2/3

22. 2/3 + .53

23. .5E4 - .37E2

24. 1.75D3 - 1.0D-5

25. For each of Exercises 15 through 24, determine how the computer will display the result.

26. Calculate 1/3 + 1/3 + 1/3 + ... + 1/3 (1000 1/3s) using single-precision constants. What answer is displayed? Is this answer accurate to seven digits? If not, explain why.

27. Answer the same question as Exercise 26, but use double-precision constants and 17 digits.

Variable Types in GWBASIC

In most programming languages, each variable has a **type,** which defines the nature of the values that it can assume. GWBASIC is no exception. It supports variables of the following type:

1. INTEGER—Variable value is an integer

2. SINGLE—Variable value is a single-precision integer

3. DOUBLE—Variable value is a double-precision integer

4. STRING—Variable value is a string

Each variable must be defined and assigned a type. This process is called **variable declaration.** In the most elementary BASIC programming, it is not necessary for you to worry about declaration, since BASIC takes care of most of the work for you. When a variable is first used in a program, BASIC defines the variable and assigns it a type. In the programs we have constructed thus far, there have been two types of variables used: SINGLE and STRING. A variable whose name ends with a tag $ is declared as type STRING. A variable whose name does not end in a tag character (i.e., contains only letters and digits) is declared as type SINGLE. Letting BASIC declare your variables for you is called **implicit declaration.**

In more advanced programming it is necessary to take the task of variable declaration into your own hands, both to control variable storage requirements and to improved execution speed. GWBASIC provides two methods for declaring variable types: type declaration tags and DEF statements. Let's discuss each of these methods:

Type Declaration Tags.   You may declare the type of a variable other than a fixed length string by appending a variable name with a type declaration tag. The tags used are:

    % - INTEGER (e.g., Count%)
    ! - SINGLE (e.g., Width!)
    # - DOUBLE (e.g. Force#)
    $ - STRING (E.g., FirstName$)

Type declaration tags cause BASIC to assign the variable the type corresponding to the tag. Note, however, that the tag becomes part of the variable name. Thus, for example, the variables A%, A&, A!, A#, and A$ are all **distinct** variables and could be used in a single program (although it would be unwise to do so).

Omitted type declaration tags can lead to nasty errors that are difficult to track down. This is because a forgotten tag can lead BASIC to declare a new variable, so that your program might have two variables, say A& and A. At various points in the program, these variables may not have the values you expect, since A may have been assigned the value meant for A&.

DEF Statements.   You may use the DEF*type* statements to declare the type of a group of variables, where *type* is one of INT, LNG, SNG, DBL, or STR. For instance, the statement:

    DEFINT A-F, M

declares all variables that begin with the letters A through F and M to be of type integer.

A DEF*type* statement can be used anywhere within a program. However, good programming style dictates that it be placed at the beginning of the program, before any executable statements occur. (Definitions should precede actions!)

Within a program, a DEF*type* statement may be overridden by using a type declaration tag. For instance, suppose that a program contained the above DEFINT statement. Then you could still use the string variable Alpha$.

Type Conversions

A variable of a given type is used to store data of a specified type. However, in assigning values to variables, GWBASIC makes certain automatic type conversions, as follows:

a. In assignment of single and double precision values to variables of type INTEGER, GWBASIC rounds the value to the nearest integer. Thus, for example, the assignment:

```
A% = 1.5
```

A% is assigned the value 2.

b. In assigning single-precision constants to double-precision variables, additional zeros are added on the right as significant digits, to make a total of 17 digits.

c. In assigning a double-precision to a single-precision variable, GWBASIC rounds the value to seven significant digits.

Internal Round-Off of SINGLE and DOUBLE Values

Here is a mistake that is easy to make. Consider this program:

```
10 A# = 1.7
20 PRINT A#
30 END
```

This program seems harmless enough. We set the double-precision variable A# to the value 1.7 and then display the result. You probably expect to see the display

```
1.700000000000000
```

If you actually try it, the display will read

```
1.700000047683716
```

What went wrong? Well, it has to do with the way the internal logic of the computer works and the way in which numbers are represented in binary notation. Without going into details, let us merely observe that the computer interprets 1.7 as a single-precision constant. When this single-precision constant is converted into a double-precision constant (an operation that makes use of the binary representation of 1.7), the result coincides in its first 16 digits with the number given above. Does this mean that we must worry about such craziness? Of course not! What we really should have done in the first place is to write

```
A# = 1.7#
```

The display is then 1.7, exactly as expected.

Exercises

Use the computer to calculate the following quantities in single-precision arithmetic.

1. (5.87 + 3.85 - 12.07)/11.98

2. (15.1 + 11.9)^4/12.88

3. (32485 + 9826)/(321.5 - 87.6^2)

4. Rework Exercise 1 using double-precision arithmetic.

5. Rework Exercise 2 using double-precision arithmetic.

6. Rework Exercise 3 using double-precision arithmetic.

7. Write a program to determine the largest integer less than or equal to X, where the value of X is supplied in an INPUT statement.

Determine the value assigned to the variable in each of the following exercises.

8. A% = -5

9. A% = 4.8

10. A% = -11.2

11. A! = 1.78

12. A# = 1.78#

13. A! = 32.653426278374645237

14. A! = 4.25234544321E21

15. A! = -1.23456789E-32

16. A# = 3.283646493029273646434

17. A# = -5.74#

Mathematical Functions in GWBASIC

In performing scientific computations, it is often necessary to use a wide variety of mathematical functions, including the natural logarithm and the exponential and trigonometric functions. GWBASIC has a wide range of these functions "built-in." In this section we describe these functions and their use.

All mathematical functions in GWBASIC work in a similar fashion. Each function is identified by a sequence of letters (SIN for sine, LOG for natural logarithm, and so forth). To evaluate a function at a number X, we write X in parentheses after the function name. For example, the natural logarithm of X is written LOG(X). The program uses the current value of the variable X and calculates the natural logarithm of that value. For example, if X is currently 2, then the computer will calculate LOG(2).

Instead of the variable X, we may use any type of variable: integer, singleprecision, or double-precision. We also may use numerical constants of any type. For example, SIN(.435678889658595) asks for the sine of a double-precision numerical constant. Note that by default GWBASIC returns a single-precision value for its built-in functions. To obtain double-precision values for the various built-in functions, you must start BASIC using the /D option. That is, use a command line of the form:

```
BASICA /D
```

GWBASIC lets you calculate a function for a value specified by an expression. Consider the expression X^2 + Y^2 -3*X. It is perfectly acceptable to call for calculations such as

```
SIN(X^2 + Y^2 - 3*X)
```

The computer will first evaluate the expression X^2 + Y^2 - 3*X using the current values of the variables X and Y. For example, if X = 1 and Y = 4, then X^2 + Y^2 -3*X = 12 + 42 - 3*1 = 14. The above sine function will be calculated as

```
SIN(14) = .9906073556948703
```

Trigonometric Functions

GWBASIC has the following trigonometric functions available:

```
SIN(X) = the sine of the angle X
COS(X) = the cosine of the angle X
TAN(X) = the tangent of the angle X
```

Here the angle X is expressed in terms of radian measure. In this measurement system, 360 degrees equal two times Pi radians. Or one degree equals .017453 radians, and one radian equals 57.29578 degrees. If you want to calculate trigonometric functions with the angle X expressed in degrees, use these functions:

```
SIN(.017453*X)
COS(.017453*X)
TAN(.017453*X)
```

The three other trigonometric functions, SEC(X) (secant), CSC(X) (cosecant), and COT(X) (cotangent), may be computed from the formulas

```
SEC(X)  =  1/COS(X)
CSC(X)  =  1/SIN(X)
COT(X)  =  SIN(X)/COS(X)
```

Here, as above, the angle X is in radians. To compute these trigonometric functions with the angle in degrees, replace X with

```
.017453*X
```

GWBASIC only has one of the inverse trigonometric functions, namely the arctangent, denoted ATN(X). This function returns the angle whose tangent is X. The angle returned is expressed in radians. To compute the arctangent with the angle expressed in degrees, use the function:

```
57.29578*ATN(X)
```

Test Your Understanding 1 (Answer on Page 309)

Write a program that calculates sin 45°, cos 45°, and tan 45°.

Logarithmic and Exponential Functions

GWBASIC allows you to compute X using the exponential function

```
EXP(X)
```

Furthermore, you may compute the natural logarithm of X via the function

```
LOG(X)
```

You may calculate logarithms to base b using the formula:

LOGb(X) = LOG(X)/LOG(b)

Example 1. Prepare a table of values of the natural logarithm function for values X = .01, .02, .03, ..., 100.00. Output the table on the printer.

Solution. Here is the desired program. Note that our table has two columns with a heading over each column.

```
LPRINT "X",  "LOG(X)"
   FOR J=.01 TO 100.00 STEP .01
   LPRINT J, LOG(J)
NEXT J
END
```

Test Your Understanding 2 (Answer on Page 309)

Write a program that evaluates the function

```
f(x)  =  (sin x) / (log x + eˣ)
```

for x = .45 and x = .7.

Example 2. Carbon dating is a technique for calculating the age of ancient artifacts by measuring the amount of radioactive carbon-14 remaining in the artifact, as compared with the amount present if the artifact were manufactured today. If r denotes the proportion of carbon-14 remaining, then the age A of the object is calculated from the formula

```
A = -(1/.00012)*LOG(r)
```

Suppose that a papyrus scroll contains 47 percent of the carbon-14 of a piece of papyrus just manufactured. Calculate the age of the scroll.

Solution.   Here r = .47 so we use the above formula.

```
10 R = .47
20 A = -(1/.00012)*LOG(R)
30 PRINT "THE AGE OF THE PAPYRUS IS", A, "YEARS"
40 END
```

Powers

GWBASIC has a square root function, denoted SQR(X). As with all the functions considered so far, this function accepts any type of input and outputs a double-precision value. For example, the instruction

```
Y = SQR(2.00000000000000000)
```

sets Y equal to 1.414213562373095.

Actually, the exponentiation procedure we learned in Chapter 2 works equally well for fractional and decimal exponents, and, therefore, provides an alternate method for extracting square roots. Here is how to use it. Taking the square root of a number corresponds to raising the number to the 1/2 power. We may calculate the square root of X as

```
X^(1/2)
```

Note that the square root function, SQR(X), operates with greater speed so it is preferred. The alternate method is more flexible, however. For instance, we may extract the cube root of X as

```
X^(1/3)
```

or we may raise X to the 5.389 power, as follows:

```
X^5.389
```

Greatest Integer, Absolute Value, and Related Functions

Here are several extremely helpful functions. The greatest integer less than or equal to X is denoted INT(X). For example, the largest integer less than or equal to 5.46789 is 5, so

```
INT(5.46789) = 5
```

Similarly, the largest integer less than or equal to -3.4 is -4 (on the number line, -4 is the first integer to the left of -3.4). Therefore:

```
INT(-3.4) = -4
```

Note that for positive numbers, the INT function throws away the decimal part. For negative numbers, however, INT works a little differently. To throw away the decimal part of a number (positive or negative), we use the function FIX(X). For example:

```
FIX(5.46789) = 5
FIX(-3.4) = -3
```

The absolute value of X is denoted ABS(X). Recall that the absolute value of X is X itself if X is positive or 0, and is -X if X is negative. Thus:

```
ABS(9.23) = 9.23
ABS(0) = 0
ABS(-4.1) = 4.1
```

Just as the absolute value of X "removes the sign" of X, the function SGN(X) throws away the number and leaves only the sign. For example:

```
SGN(3.4) = +1
SGN(-5.62) = -1
```

Conversion Functions

GWBASIC includes functions for converting a number from one type to another. For example, to convert X to integer type, use the function CINT(X). This function rounds the decimal part of X. Note that the resulting constant must be in the integer range of -32,768 to 32,767 or an error will result.*

To convert X to single-precision, use the function CSNG(X). If X is of integer type, then CSNG(X) causes the appropriate number of zeros to be appended to the right of the decimal point to convert X to a single-precision number. If X is double-precision, then X is rounded to seven digits.

To convert X to double-precision, use the function CDBL(X). This function appends the appropriate number of zeros to X to convert it to a double-precision number.

Exercises

Calculate the following quantities.

1. e^1.54

2. e^-2.376

3. log (58)

4. log (.0000975)

5. sin (3.7)

6. cos (45o)

7. arctan (1)

8. tan (.682)

9. arctan (2) (expressed in degrees)

10. $LOG^{10}(18.9)$

11. Make a table of values of the exponential function EXP(X) for X = -5.0, -4.9,..., 0 , .1,..., 5.0.

12. Evaluate the function

```
3X¹/⁴log(5X) + exp(-1.8X)tan X
```

for X = 1.7, 3.1, 5.9, 7.8, 8.4, and 10.1.

Answers to Test Your Understandings 1 and 2

1.
```
10 A = .017453
20 PRINT SIN(45*A), COS(45*A), TAN(45*A)
30 END
```

2.
```
10 DATA .45, .7
20 FOR J=1 TO 2
30 READ A
40 PRINT SIN(A)/(LOG(A)+EXP(A))
50 NEXT J
60 END
```

Defining Your Own Functions

In mathematics, functions are usually defined by specifying one or more formulas. For instance, here are formulas to define the functions f(x), g(x), and h(x):

$$f(x) = (x^2-1)^{1/2}$$

$$g(x) = 3x^2 - 5x - 15$$

$$h(x) = 1/(x-1)$$

Note that each function is named by a letter, namely f, g, and h, respectively. GWBASIC allows you to define functions like these and to use them by name throughout your program. To define a function, we use the DEF

FN instruction. This instruction is used before the first use of the function in the program. For example, to define the function f(x) above, we use the instruction:

```
DEF FNF(X) = (X^2 - 1)^t
(1/2)
```

To define the function g(x) above, we use the instruction:

```
20 DEF FNG(X) = 3*X^2 - 5*X - 15
```

Note that in each case, we use a letter (F or G) to identify the function. Suppose that we wish to calculate the value of the function G for X = 12.5. Once the function has been defined, this calculation may be described to the computer as FNF(12.5). Such calculations may be used throughout the program and save the effort of retyping the formula for the function in each instance.

You may use any valid variable name as a function name. For example, you may define a function INTEREST by the statement:

```
DEF   FNINTEREST(X) = ...
```

Moreover, in defining a function, you may use other functions. For example, if FNF(X) and FNG(X) are as defined above, then we may define their product by the instruction

```
30 DEF FNC(X) = FNF(X)*FNG(X)
```

All of the functions above are functions of a single variable. However, GWBASIC allows functions of several variables as well. They are defined using the same procedure as above. To define the function

```
A(X,Y,Z) = X^2 + Y^2 + Z^2
```

use the instruction

```
DEF FNA(X,Y,Z) = X^2 + Y^2 + Z^2
```

You may even let one of the variables be a string variable. Consider this function:

```
DEF FNB(A$) = LEN(A$)
```

This function computes the length of the string A$.

Finally, functions may produce a string as a function value. The name for such a function must end in $. Consider this function:

```
DEF FND$(A$,J) = LEFT(A$,J)
```

This function of the two variables A$ and J computes the string consisting of the J leftmost characters of the string A$. For example, suppose that A$ = "computer" and J = 3. Then:

```
FND$(A$,J) = "com"
```

Type Declaration Tags on Functions

A function returns a value. You may declare the type of this value by using a type declaration tag in the function name. For example, the function FNA%(X) is a function that returns an integer. Similarly, the function FNDelta#(X,Y,Z) is a function that returns a double-precision number.

Exercises

Write instructions to define the following functions.

1. $x^2 - 5x$
2. $1/x - 3x$
3. $5\exp(-2x)$
4. $x \log(x/2)$
5. $(\tan x) / x$
6. $\cos(2x) + 1$
7. The string consisting of the right two characters of C$.

8. The string consisting of the four middle characters of A$ beginning with the Jth character.

9. The middle letter of the string B$. (Assume that B$ has an odd number of characters.)

10. Write a program to tabulate the value of the function in Exercise 3 for x = 0, .1, .2, .3, .4, ... , 10.0.

Twelve

Your Computer As a File Cabinet

Introduction

In this chapter, we introduce the techniques for dealing with files on diskette or hard disk. Specifically, we:

- Define sequential files.

- Study the BASIC statements for OPENing, CLOSEing, WRITEing and reading sequential files.

- Study the way BASIC writes sequential files on diskette or hard disk.

- Study the BASIC statements for dealing with random access files.

- Give a short introduction to the subject of sorting.

- Survey the BASIC commands for manipulating files.

What Are Files?

A file is a collection of information stored on a mass storage device (diskette, cassette, or hard disk). There are two common types of files: program files and data files.

Program Files.   When a program is stored on diskette, it is stored as a program file. You already have created some program files by saving BASIC programs on diskette. In addition to the programs you create, your DOS diskette contains program files that are necessary to run your computer, such as DOS and the BASIC language.

Data Files.   Computer programs used in business and industry usually refer to files of information that are kept in mass storage. For example, a personnel department will keep a file of data on each employee: name, age, address, social security number, date employed, position, salary, and so forth. A warehouse will maintain an inventory for each product with the following information: product name, supplier, current inventory, units sold in the last reporting period, date of the last shipment, size of the last shipment, and units sold in the last 12 months. These files are called data files.

In this chapter, we discuss the procedures for handling files in general and data files in particular.

Consider the following example. Suppose that a teacher stores grades in a data file. For each student in the class, there are four exam grades. A typical entry in the data file contains the following data items:

```
student name, exam grade #1, exam grade #2,
exam grade #3, exam grade #4
```

In a data file, the data items are organized in sequence. So the beginning of the above data file might look like this:

```
"John Smith", 98, 87, 93, 76, "Mary Young",
99, 78, 87, 91, "Sally Ronson", 48, 63, 72,
80, ...
```

The data file consists of a sequence of string constants (the names) and numeric constants (the grades), with the various data items arranged in a particular pattern (name followed by four grades). This particular arrangement is designed so the file may be read and understood. For instance, if we read the data items above, we know in advance that the data items are in groups of five with the first one a name and the next four the corresponding grades.

In this chapter, we will learn to create data files containing information such as the data in the above example. As we shall see, data may be stored in either of two types of data files—sequential and random access. For each type of file we will learn to perform the following operations:

1. Create a data file.

2. Write data items to a file.

3. Read data items from a file.

4. Alter data items in a file.

5. Search a file for particular data items.

Sequential Files

A sequential file is a data file in which the data items are accessed in order. That is, the data items are written in consecutive order into the file, and are read in the order in which they were written. You may add data items only to the end of a sequential file. If you wish to add a data item somewhere in the middle of the file, it is necessary to rewrite the entire file. Similarly, if you wish to read a data item at the end of a sequential file, it is necessary to read all the data items in order and to ignore those that you don't want.

OPENing and CLOSEing Sequential Files

Before you perform any operations on a sequential file, you must first open the file. You should think of the file as being contained in a file cabinet drawer (the diskette). In order to read the file, you must first open the file drawer. This is accomplished using the BASIC instruction OPEN. When OPENing a file, you must specify the file and indicate whether you will be reading from the file or writing into the file. For example, to OPEN the file B:PAYROLL for input (for reading the file), we use a statement of the form

```
10 OPEN "B:PAYROLL" FOR INPUT AS #1
```

The #1 is a reference number we assign to the file when opening it. As long as the file remains open, you refer to it by its reference number rather than the more cumbersome file specification B:PAYROLL. The reference number is quite arbitrary. You may assign any positive integer you wish. Just make sure that you don't assign two files that are to be open simultaneously to the same reference number. (If you try this, BASIC will give you an error message.)

Here is an instruction for opening the file "GAMES" on B: for input:

```
20 OPEN "B:GAMES" FOR INPUT AS #1
```

Here is an alternate form of the instruction for opening a file for input:

```
30 OPEN "I",#1,"B:PAYROLL"
```

Here the letter "I" stands for "Input."

To OPEN the file B:GRADES.AUG for output (that is, to write in the file), we use an instruction of the form

```
40 OPEN "B:GRADES.AUG" FOR OUTPUT AS #2
```

Here is an alternate way to write the same instruction:

```
50 OPEN "O",#2,"B:GRADES.AUG"
```

The letter "O" stands for "Output."

BASIC initially allows you to work with three open diskette files at a time. Only one cassette file may be open at a time. This number may be increased by giving the appropriate command when you start BASIC. For example, to allow use of as many as five files at once, start BASIC with the command:

```
BASICA /F:5
```

The "switch" /F:5 is what tells BASIC to set aside memory for simultaneous manipulation of up to five files.

In maintaining any filing system, it is necessary to be neat and organized. The same is true of computer files. A sequential file may be opened for input or for output, but not both simultaneously. As long as the file remains open, it accepts instructions (input or output) of the same sort designated when it was opened. To change operations, it is necessary to first close the file. For example, to close the file B:PAYROLL from line 10 above, we use the instruction

```
60 CLOSE #1
```

After giving this instruction, we may reopen the file for output using an instruction similar to that given in line 20 above. It is possible to close several files at a time. For example, the statement

```
70 CLOSE #5,#6
```

closes the files with reference numbers 5 and 6. We may close all currently open files with the instruction

```
80 CLOSE
```

In an OPEN or CLOSE statement, the # is optional. Thus, it is perfectly acceptable to use

```
90 OPEN 1,2
```

```
100 CLOSE 5,6
```

Good programming practice dictates that all files be closed after use. In any case, the BASIC commands NEW, RUN, and SYSTEM automatically close any files that might have been left open by a preceding program.

WRITEing Data Items Into a Sequential File

Suppose that we wish to create a sequential file called INVOICE.001, which contains the following data items:

```
DJ SALES    50357 4  $358.79    4/5/81
```

That is, we want to write into the file the string constant DJ SALES followed by the two numeric constants 50357 and 4, followed by the two string constants $358.79 and 4/5/81. Here is a program that does exactly that:

```
10 ' This program writes five data items to a file
100 OPEN "B:INVOICE.001" FOR OUTPUT AS #1
110 WRITE#1, "DJ SALES", 50357!,4,"$358.79", "4/5/81"
120 CLOSE #1
130 END
```

The #1 portion of line 110 refers to the identification number given to the file in the OPEN instruction in line 100, namely 1. In a WRITE# statement, a comma must follow the file number.

Note that the WRITE instruction works very much like a PRINT statement, except that the data items are "printed" in the file instead of on the screen.

While a file is open, you may execute any number of WRITE instructions to insert data. Moreover, you may WRITE data items that are values of variables, as in the statement

```
10 WRITE #1, A, A$
```

This instruction will write current values of A and A$ into the file.

Example 1.   Write a program to create a file whose data items are the numbers 1, 1^2, 2, 2^2, 3, 3^2, ..., 100, 100^2.

Solution.   Let's call the file SQUARES and store it on the diskette in drive A:.

```
10 ' *********************************************
20 ' This program makes a file of the all integers
30 '    from 1 to 100, each followed by its square
40 ' *********************************************
50 OPEN "A:SQUARES" FOR OUTPUT AS #1
60 FOR J=1 TO 100
70    WRITE#1, J,J^2
80    NEXT J
90 CLOSE #1
100 END
```

Example 2. Create a data file consisting of names, addresses, and telephone numbers from your personal telephone directory. Assume that you will type the addresses into the computer and will tell the computer when the last address has been typed.

Solution. We use INPUT statements to enter the various data. Let NME$ denote the name of the current person, ADDRESS$ the street address, CITY$ the city , STATE$ the state, ZIPCODE$ the zip code, and TELE-PHONE$ the telephone number. For each entry, there is an INPUT statement corresponding to each of these variables. The program then writes the data to the diskette. Here is the program:

```
10 ' ************************************
20 ' This program creates a file holding
30 '    entries from a telephone directory
40 '    which are entered by the user
50 ' ************************************
100 OPEN "TELEPHON" FOR OUTPUT AS #1
110 INPUT "NAME"; A$
120 INPUT "STREET ADDRESS"; B$
130 INPUT "CITY"; C$
140 INPUT "STATE"; D$
150 INPUT "ZIP CODE"; E$
160 INPUT "TELEPHONE"; F$
170 WRITE#1, A$, B$, C$, D$, E$, F$
200 ' Check whether there is more data
210 INPUT "ANOTHER ENTRY (Y/N)"; G$
```

```
220 IF G$="Y" THEN 110
230 CLOSE #1
240 END
```

Note the unusual spelling of NAME (NME). We are forced into this queer spelling since NAME is a BASIC reserved word. You should use the above program to set up a computerized telephone directory of your own. It is very instructive. Moreover, when coupled with the search program given below, it will allow you to look up addresses and phone numbers using your computer.

Test Your Understanding 1

Use the above program to enter the following addresses into the file:

```
John Jones
1 South Main St. Apt. 308
Phila. Pa. 19107
527-1211

Mary Bell
2510 9th St.
Phila. Pa. 19138
937-4896
```

Reading Data Items

To read items from a data file, it is first necessary to open the file for INPUT (that is, for INPUT from the diskette.) Consider the telephone file in Example 2. We may open it for input, via the instruction

```
10 OPEN "TELEPHON" FOR INPUT AS #2
```

Once the file is open, it may read via the instruction

```
20 INPUT #2, NME$,ADDRESS$,CITY$,STATE$,ZIP$,PHONE$
```

This instruction reads six data items from the file (corresponding to one telephone-address entry), assigns NME$ the value of the first data item, ADDRESS$ the second, and so forth.

In order to read a file, it is necessary to know the precise format of the data in the file. For example, the form of the above INPUT statement was dictated by the fact that each telephone-address entry was entered into the file as six consecutive string constants. The file INPUT statement works like any other INPUT statement: faced with a list of variables separated by commas, it assigns values to the indicated variables in the order in which the data items are presented. However, if you attempt to assign a string constant to a numeric variable or vice versa, BASIC reports an error.

As long as a file is open for INPUT, you may continue to INPUT from it, using as many INPUT statements as you like. These may, in turn, be intermingled with statements that have nothing to do with the file you are reading. Each INPUT statement begins reading the file where the preceding INPUT statement left off.

Here's how to determine if you have read all data items in a file. BASIC maintains the functions EOF(1), EOF(2),..., one for each open file. These functions may be used like logical variables; that is, they assume the possible values true or false. You may test for the end of the file using an IF...THEN statement. For example, consider the statement

```
10 IF EOF(1) THEN 2000 ELSE 10
```

This statement causes BASIC to determine if you are currently at the end of file #1. If so, the program will go to line 2000. Otherwise, the program will go to line 10. Note that you are not at the end of the file until after you read the last data item.

If you attempt to read past the end of a file, BASIC will report an Input Past End error. Therefore, before reading a file, it is a good idea to determine whether you are currently at the end of the file.

Example 3. A data file, called NUMBERS, consists of numerical entries. Write a program to determine the number of entries in the file.

Solution. Let us keep a count of the current number we are reading in the variable COUNT. Our procedure will be to read a number, increase the count, then test for the end of the file.

```
10 ' ******************************
20 ' This program counts the number
30 '    of entries in a file
40 ' ******************************
100 COUNT = 0:              ' Initialize COUNT
110 OPEN "NUMBERS" FOR INPUT AS #1
120 IF EOF(1) THEN 200:  ' Out of data?
130 INPUT #1,A            ' Read an item
140 COUNT=COUNT+1          ' Increment COUNT
150 GOTO 120
200 PRINT "THE NUMBER OF NUMBERS IN THE FILE IS",COUNT
210 CLOSE
220 END
```

Example 4. Write a program that searches for a particular entry of the telephone directory file created in Example 2.

Solution. We will INPUT the name corresponding to the desired entry. The program then reads the file entries until a match of names occurs. Here is the program:

```
10 ' **********************************
20 ' This program searches a file of
30 '    telephone listings for the entry
40 '    of a name given by the user
50 ' **********************************
100 OPEN "TELEPHON" FOR INPUT AS #1
110 INPUT "NAME TO SEARCH FOR"; Z$
120 INPUT #1, A$,B$,C$,D$,E$,F$
130 IF A$ = Z$ THEN 200:   'Matching item?
140 IF EOF(1)  THEN 300:   'Out of data?
150 GOTO 120:   'On to the next item
200 CLS:         'Print the entry
```

```
210 PRINT A$
220 PRINT B$
230 PRINT C$,D$, E$
240 PRINT F$
250 GOTO 400
300 CLS:            'No match
310 PRINT "THE NAME IS NOT ON FILE"
400 CLOSE 1
410 END
```

Test Your Understanding 2

Use the above program to locate Mary Bell's number in the telephone file created in Test Your Understanding 1.

Example 5. (Mailing List Application)   Suppose that you have created your computerized telephone directory, using the program in Example 2. Assume that the completed file is called TELEPHON and it is on the diskette in drive A:. Write a program that reads the file and prints out the names and addresses onto mailing labels.

Solution.   Let's assume that your mailing labels are of the "peel-off" variety, which can be printed continuously on your printer. Further, let's assume that the labels are six printer lines high, so that each label has room for five lines of print with one line space between labels. (These are actual dimensions of labels you can buy.) We will print the name on line 1, the address on line 2, and the city, state, and zip codes all on line 3, with the city and state separated by a comma:

```
10 ' **********************************
20 ' This program prints a mailing label
30 '    for each entry in a directory
40 '    of telephone book listings
50 ' **********************************
100 OPEN "TELEPHON" FOR INPUT AS #1
110 IF EOF(1) THEN 1000
120 INPUT #1, A$, B$, C$, D$, E$, F$
130 LPRINT A$                :'PRINT NAME
```

```
140 LPRINT B$                 :'PRINT ADDRESS
150 LPRINT C$;                :'PRINT CITY
160 LPRINT ",";               :'PRINT COMMA
170 LPRINT TAB(10) D$;        :'PRINT STATE
180 LPRINT TAB(20) E$         :'PRINT ZIP CODE
190 LPRINT:LPRINT:LPRINT      :'NEXT LABEL
200 GOTO 110
1000 CLOSE 1
1010 END
```

Adding to a Data File

Here is an important fact about writing data files: Writing a file destroys any previous contents of the file. (In contrast, you may read a file any number of times without destroying its contents.) Consider the file TELEPHON created in Example 2 above. Suppose we write a program that opens the file for output and writes what we suppose are additional entries in our telephone directory. After this write operation, the file TELEPHON will contain only the added entries. All of the original entries will have been lost! How, then, may we add items to a file that already exists? Easy. IBM PC BASIC has a special instruction to do this. Rather than OPEN the file for OUTPUT, we OPEN the file for APPEND, using the instruction

```
10 OPEN "TELEPHON" FOR APPEND AS #1
```

The computer locates the current end of the file. Any additional entries to the file will be written beginning at that point. However, the previous entries in the file will be unchanged.

Example 6. Write a program that adds entries to the file TELEPHON. The additions should be typed via INPUT statements. The program may assume that the file is on the diskette in drive A:.

Solution. To add items to the file, we first OPEN the file for APPEND. We then ask for the new entry via an INPUT statement and write the new entry into TELEPHON. Here is the program.

```
10 ' ******************************
20 ' This program adds entries to a
30 '    file of telephone listings
40 ' ******************************
100 OPEN "TELEPHON" FOR APPEND AS #1
110 PRINT "TYPE ENTRY:NAME,STREET ADDRESS,CITY, STATE,"
120 PRINT "ZIP CODE, TELEPHONE NO."
130 INPUT A$,B$,C$,D$,E$,F$
140 WRITE#1, A$, B$, C$, D$, E$, F$
150 INPUT "ANOTHER ENTRY  (Y/N)"; Z$
160 IF Z$ <> "Y" THEN 200
170 CLS
180 GOTO 110     :'Add another entry
200 CLOSE 1
210 END
```

Test Your Understanding 3

Use the above program to add your name, address, and telephone number to the telephone directory created in Test Your Understanding 1.

Exercises

1. Write a program creating a diskette data file containing the numbers 5.7, -11.4, 123, 485, and 49.

2. Write a program that reads the data file created in Exercise 1 and displays the data items on the screen.

3. Write a program that adds to the data file of Exercise 1 the data items 5, 78, 4.79, and -1.27.

4. Write a program that reads the expanded file of Exercise 3 and displays all the data items on the screen.

5. Write a program that records the contents of checkbook stubs in a data file. The data items of the file should be as follows:

   ```
   check #, date, payee, amount, explanation
   ```

   Use this program to create a data file corresponding to your previous month's checks.

6.Write a program that reads the data file of Exercise 5 and totals the amounts of all the checks listed in the file.

7.Write a program that keeps track of inventory in a retail store. The inventory should be described by a data file whose entries contain the following information:

   `item, current price, units in stock`

   The program should allow for three different operations: display the data file entry corresponding to a given item, record receipt of a shipment of a given item, and record the sale of a certain number of units of a given item.

8.Write a program that creates a recipe file to contain your favorite recipes.

9.(For Teachers) Write a program that maintains a student file containing your class roll, attendance, and grades.

10.Write a program maintaining a file of your credit card numbers and the party to notify in case of loss or theft.

More About Sequential Files

When you WRITE a data item to a sequential file, BASIC automatically includes certain "punctuation" that allows the data to be read:

1. Strings are surrounded by quotation marks.

2. Data items are separated by commas.

3. The last data item in the WRITE# statement is followed by carriage return (CHR$(13)). In what follows, we denote this character by <CR>.

4. Positive numbers are inserted in the file without a leading blank.

For example, suppose that A$="JOHN", B$="SMITH", C=1234, and D=-14. Consider the following WRITE# statement:

```
10 WRITE#1, A$,B$,C,D
```

Here is how this statement WRITEs the data into file #1:

```
"JOHN","SMITH",1234,-14<CR>
```

When the above data are read by an INPUT# statement, the quotation marks, commas, and ENTER enable BASIC to separate the various data items from one another. For this reason, the punctuation marks are called delimiters. In using the WRITE# statement, you need not worry about delimiters. However, in other sequential file statements, you are not so lucky.

Consider, for instance, the PRINT# statement. This statement may be used to PRINT data to a file exactly as if the data were being printed on the screen. All of the usual features of PRINT, such as TAB, SPC, and semicolons, are active. However, the PRINT# statement does not include any delimiters. Consider the above variables A$, B$, C, and D. The statement

```
10 PRINT#1, A$;B$;C;D
```

writes the following image to file #1:

```
JOHNSMITH 1234-14<CR>
```

Note that:

1. The space before the positive number 1234 is included in the file.

2. There are no separations between the data items.

3. There are no quotation marks around the strings.

In order to correctly read the individual data items, you must supply delimiters in your PRINT# statement. Here's how. First, put commas as strings in PRINT#:

```
20 PRINT#1, A$;",";B$;",";C;",";D
```

Here's how the image in the file will now look:

```
JOHN,SMITH, 1234,-14<CR>
```

The individual data items now may be read.

This is not quite the end of the story, however! Notice that the strings still do not have quotation marks around them. In this example, no harm will be done. To understand why, let's discuss the operation of the INPUT# statement.

INPUT recognizes as delimiters both commas and ENTER. When faced with a stream of data in a file, here is what INPUT# does:

1. INPUT# scans the characters and peels off characters until it finds a delimiter. This indicates the end of the current data item. (The delimiter is not included as part of the data item.)

2. If a numeric data item has been requested, INPUT# checks that the data item is a number (no illegal characters such as A, $, or ;). If illegal characters are detected, a Type Mismatch error occurs.

3. If a string data item has been requested, INPUT# checks to see whether the data item is surrounded by quotation marks. If so, it removes them.

Understanding the above sequence can prevent embarrassing errors. One such error can occur if you wish to include a comma within a data item. For example, suppose that A$="SMITH,JOHN", B$="CARPENTER". The PRINT# statement

```
30 PRINT#1, A$;",";B$
```

writes the following image to the file:

```
SMITH,JOHN,CARPENTER<CR>
```

A subsequent INPUT# statement

```
40 INPUT#1, A$,B$
```

results in A$="SMITH" and B$="JOHN". To get around this problem, you must explicitly include quotation marks around strings that include a comma. A string that consists of a quotation mark is just CHR$(34). (34 is the ASCII code for a quotation mark.) To include the quotation marks around the string A$="SMITH,JOHN", you may use the statement

```
50 PRINT#1, CHR$(34);A$;CHR$(34);",";B$
```

The file image is now

```
"SMITH,JOHN",CARPENTER<CR>
```

Quotation marks must enclose strings containing commas, semicolons, beginning or ending blanks, or ENTER.

As you can see, the PRINT# statement is much less convenient than WRITE#. In most cases, it is much simpler to use WRITE#. However, PRINT# has its advantages. With a PRINT#, you may include the USING option to format your data. For example, to write the value of the variable A to the file in the format ##.#, use the statement

```
60 PRINT#1, USING "##.#";A
```

The INPUT# statement reads a single data item at a time. However, in some applications you may wish to read an entire line from a file. That is, you wish to read data until you encounter an ENTER. This may be done with the LINE INPUT# statement. For example, suppose that the following data is contained in file #1:

```
SMITH,JOHN,CARPENTER<CR>
```

The statement

```
70 LINE INPUT#1, A$
```

sets A$="SMITH,JOHN,CARPENTER". Note the following curious twist, however. If you saved your string data with quotation marks around it, those quotation marks are included as part of the string read by LINE INPUT#. If you plan to read data lines via a LINE INPUT# statement, it is usually wise to save the data using PRINT# so that no extraneous quotation marks are generated.

File Buffers

You may have noticed that the drive light does not always turn on when you are writing to a file. For example, try this experiment: OPEN a data file and write a single numerical data item to the file, but don't CLOSE the file. The disk drive does nothing. However, if you run this program a second time, the drive light will go on. This may seem strange. However, it has to do with the way BASIC writes (and reads) diskette files.

Diskette drives are very slow when compared with the speed at which BASIC executes nondiskette operations. In order to speed up diskette operations, BASIC writes to the diskette using file buffers. A file buffer (or "buffer" for short) is an area of RAM where BASIC temporarily stores data to be written to a file. There is one buffer corresponding to each open file. BASIC reserves the space for a buffer as part of the OPEN operation. When you use any file writing operation, BASIC writes the corresponding information into the file's buffer. When the buffer is full, BASIC writes the data to the file.

The CLOSE operation forces all buffers (full or not) to be written to their corresponding files. When you don't close a file (as in our above experiment), the buffer may be sitting with some data that have not yet been written to diskette. In this case, a RUN or END command will also cause the buffers to be written to diskette. Also, as soon as you modify the program in RAM, the buffers will be written to diskette. In our experiment, it was the RUN statement that caused the drive lights to go on, to write the final results of the previous run.

Exercises

Suppose that A$ = "MY", B$="DOG", C$="SAM", D=1234. What is the format of the data written to file #1 by the following statements?

1. WRITE#1, A$,B$,C$,D

2. PRINT#1, A$,B$,C$,D

3. PRINT#1, A$;",";B$;",";C$;",";D

4. PRINT#1, CHR$(34);A$;" ";B$;", ";CHR$(34);",";C$;",";D

Consider the file as written by Exercise 1. What will be displayed by the following statements?

5. INPUT#1, E$:PRINT E$

6. LINE INPUT#1, E$:PRINT E$

7. Consider the files as written by Exercises 2–4. What will be displayed by the following statement?b

```
INPUT#1, E$:PRINT E$
```

8. Consider the file as written by Exercise 4. Write a program to display

```
MY DOG, SAM
1234
```

Random Access Files

The files considered so far in this chapter are all examples of sequential files. That is, the files are all written sequentially, from beginning to end. These files are very easy to create, but are cumbersome in many applications, since they must be read sequentially. In order to read a piece of data from the end of the file, it is necessary to read all data items from the beginning of the file. Random access files do not suffer from this difficulty. Using a random access file, it is possible to access the precise piece of data you want. Of course, there is a price to be paid for this convenience. (No free lunches!) You must work a little harder to learn how to use random access files.

A random access file is divided into segments of fixed length called **records** (see Figure 12-1.) The length of a record is measured in terms of bytes. For a string constant, each character, including spaces and punctuation marks, counts as a single byte. For example, the record consisting of the string

        ACCOUNTING-5

is of length 12.

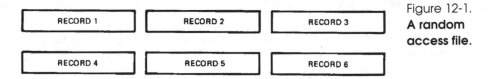

Figure 12-1.
A random access file.

To store a data item in a random access file, all data must be converted into string form. This applies to numeric constants and values of numeric variables. (See below for the special instructions for performing this conversion.) A number (more precisely, a single-precision number) is converted into a string of length 4, no matter how many digits this number has. A record may contain the four data items: ACCOUNTING, 5000, .235, and 7886. These pieces of data are stored in order, with no separations between them. The length of this particular record is 22 bytes (10 for ACCOUNTING and four each for the numerical data items). (See Figure 12-2.)

Field 1										Field 2				Field 3				Field 4			
1	2	3	4	5	6	7	8	9	10	11	12	13	14	15	16	17	18	19	20	21	22
A	C	C	O	U	N	T	I	N	G	5000 in coded form				0.235 in coded form				7886 in coded form			

Figure 12-2.
A typical record.

To write data to a random access file, it is necessary to first open it. To open a file named DEPTS as a random access file with a record length of 22, use the instruction

```
10 OPEN "DEPTS" AS #1 LEN=22
```

Next, we must describe the structure of the records of the file. For example, suppose that each record of file #1 is to start with a 10-character string followed by three numbers (converted to string form). Further, suppose that the string represents a department name, the first number the current department income, the second number the department's efficiency rating, and the third number the current department's overhead. We indicate this situation with the instruction

```
20 FIELD #1, 10 AS DEPT$, 4 AS INCOME$, 4
   AS EFFICIENCY$, 4 AS OVERHEAD$
```

This instruction identifies the file with the number used when the file was opened. Each section of the record is called a **field**. Each field is identified by a string variable and the number of bytes reserved for that variable.

Writing to a Random Access File

To write a record to a random access file, it is first necessary to assemble the data corresponding to the various fields. This is done using the LSET and RSET instructions. For example, to set the DEPT$ field to the string "ACCOUNTING", we use the instruction

```
30 LSET DEPT$="ACCOUNTING"
```

To set the DEPT$ field to the value of the string variable N$, we use

```
40 LSET DEPT$=N$
```

If N$ contains fewer than 10 characters, the rightmost portion of the field is filled with blanks. This is called left justification. If N$ contains more than 10 characters, the field is filled with the leftmost 10 characters.

The instruction RSET works exactly the same as LSET, except that the unused spaces appear on the left side of the field. (The strings are right justified.)

To convert numbers to strings for inclusion in random access files, we use the MKS$ (or MKI$ or MKD$) function. For example, to include .753 in the EFFICIENCY$ field, we first replace it by the string MKS$(.753). To include the value of the variable INC in the INCOME$ field, we first replace it by MKS$(INC). After the conversion, we use the LSET (or RSET) commands to insert the string in the field. In the case of the two examples cited, the sequence is carried out by the respective instructions:

```
50 LSET EFFICIENCY$=MKS$(.753)

60 LSET INCOME$=MKS$(INC)
```

Once the fields of a particular record have been set (using LSET or RSET), you may write the record to the file using the PUT instruction. Records are numbered within the file, starting from one. The significant feature of a random access file is that you may record or retrieve information from any particular record. For example, to write the current data into record 38 of file #1, we use the instruction

```
70 PUT #1, 38
```

Test Your Understanding 1 (Answer on Page 339)

Write a program to create a file containing the following records:

```
ACCOUNTING     5000    .235     7886
ENGINEERING    3500    .872     2200
MAINTENANCE    4338    .381     5130
ADVERTISING   10832    .951    12500
```

Reading a Random Access File

To read a random access file, you must first open it using an instruction of the form

```
10 OPEN "DEPTS" AS #1 LEN=23
```

Note: This is the same as the instruction for opening a random access file for writing. Random access files differ from sequential files in this respect. By opening a random access file you prepare it for both reading and writing. Before closing the file, you may read some records and write others.

The next step in reading a random access file is to define the record structure using a FIELD statement, such as

```
20 FIELD #1, 10 AS DEPT$, 4 AS INCOME$, 4 AS
      EFFICIENCY$, 4 AS OVERHEAD$
```

This is the same instruction we used for writing to the file. Until the FIELD instruction is overridden by another, it applies to all reading and writing for file #1.

To perform the actual reading operation, we use the GET statement. For example, to read record 4 of the file, we use the statement

```
30 GET #1, 4
```

The variables DEPT\$, INCOME\$, EFFICIENCY\$, and OVERHEAD\$ are now set equal to the appropriate values specified in record 4 of file #1. We can, for example, print the value of DEPT\$ using the statement

```
40 PRINT DEPT$
```

If we wish to use the value of EFFICIENCY\$ (in a numerical calculation or in a PRINT statement, for instance), it is necessary first to convert it back into numerical form. This is accomplished using the CVS function. The statement

```
50 PRINT CVS(EFFICIENCY$)
```

prints out the current value of EFFICIENCY\$; the statement

```
LET N=100*CVS(EFFICIENCY$)
```

sets the value of N equal to 100 times the numerical value of EFFICIENCY\$.

It is important to note that field variables such as DEPT$ and EFFI-CIENCY$ contain the values assigned in the most recent GET statement. In order to manipulate data from more than one GET statement, it is essential to assign the values from one GET statement to some other variables before issuing the next GET statement.

Test Your Understanding 2 (Answer on Page 340)

Consider the random access file of Test Your Understanding 1. Write a program to read record 3 of that file and print the corresponding four pieces of data on the screen.

Random access files use no delimiters to separate data items within the file. Rather, the data items are sandwiched together, using the number of characters specified for each field. In order to peel those data items back apart, you must divide the file into records of the correct length and each record into fields of the proper numbers of bytes.

In our discussion above, we used the instructions MKS$ and CVS to convert numerical data to string format and back to numerical format. These functions apply to single-precision numbers. In addition to single-precision numbers, there are double-precision numbers (up to 17 digits) and integers (whole numbers between -32,768 and +32,767). To convert a double-precision number to a string, we use the function MKD$; to convert back to numerical form, CVD. To convert an integer to a string, use the function MKI$; to convert back to numerical form, use CVI.

In either numerical form or string form an integer is represented by two bytes, a single-precision number by four bytes and a double-precision number by eight bytes. In particular, this means that MKI$ produces a two-byte string, MKS$ a four-byte string, and MKD$ an eight-byte string.

The Length of File Function

BASIC provides several functions that help you keep track of random access files. The LOF (=Length Of File) function gives the actual number of bytes in the file. For example, suppose that file #2 contains 140 bytes. Then LOF(#2) is equal to 140.

The LOF function may be used to determine the number of records currently in the file, according to the formula:

```
<number of records> = LOF(<file number>)/<record length>
```

Note that random access files cannot have any "holes." That is, if you write record 150, BASIC sets aside space for records 1 through 149, even if you write nothing in these records.

The LOC (LOCation) function gives the number of the last record read or written to the file. For example, if the last record written or read to file #1 was record 58, then LOC(#1) is equal to 58.

Here is an example that illustrates most of the procedures for using random access files.

Example 1. Write a program to create an address/telephone directory using a random access file. The program should allow for updating the directory and for directory search corresponding to a given name.

Solution. The program first opens the random access file TELEPHON, used to store the various directory entries. Note that the record length is set equal to 128. This allows us to use LOF to calculate the number of records in the file using either BASIC 1.1 or 2.0. The program then displays a menu allowing you to choose from among the various options: Add an entry to the directory, Search the directory, Exit from the program. After an option is completed, the program redisplays the menu allowing you to make another choice. The code corresponding to the three options begins at program lines 1000, 2000, and 3000, respectively. Here is the program:

```
10 '****************************************
20 ' This program incorporates all of the
30 ' routines needed to create and manage
40 ' a telephone directory file using
50 ' random access file techniques.
60 '****************************************
1000 'Main Program
1010 'Open File For Random Access
1020  OPEN "TELEPHON" AS #1 LEN=128
1030  FIELD#1, 20 AS NME$, 20 AS ADDRESS$,20  AS CITY$,
      20 AS STATE$, 5 AS ZIPCODE$, 20 AS TELEPHONE$, 23
      AS BLANK$
1040  LSET BLANK$=""
1050 'Option Menu
1060  CLS:PRINT "OPTIONS"
1070  PRINT "1. MAKE ENTRY IN DIRECTORY"
1080  PRINT "2. SEARCH DIRECTORY"
1090  PRINT "3. EXIT PROGRAM"
1100  INPUT "CHOOSE OPTION (1/2/3)";OPT
1110  ON OPT GOSUB 2000,3010,4010
1120  GOTO 1060
2000 'Add to file
2010  CLS
2020  INPUT "NAME";N$
2030  LSET NME$=N$
2040  INPUT "ADDRESS";N$
2050  LSET ADDRESS$=N$
2060  INPUT "CITY";N$
2070  LSET CITY$=N$
2080  INPUT "STATE";N$
2090  LSET STATE$=N$
2100  INPUT "ZIPCODE";N$
2110  LSET ZIPCODE$=N$
2120  INPUT "TELEPHONE NUMBER";N$
2130  LSET TELEPHONE$ = N$
2140  PUT #1
3000  RETURN
3010 'Search for a name
3020  NREC=LOF(1)/128
3030  INPUT "NAME TO SEARCH FOR";N$
```

```
3040   R=1
3050   GET #1, R
3060   GOSUB 5000: IF M$=N$ THEN 3100
3070   R=R+1
3080   IF R>NREC THEN PRINT "NAME IS NOT ON FILE":   GOTO
4000
3090   GOTO 3050
3100   PRINT NME$
3110   PRINT ADDRESS$
3120   PRINT CITY$
3130   PRINT STATE$
3140   PRINT ZIPCODE$
3150   PRINT TELEPHONE$
4000   RETURN
4010   'Exit from program
4020   CLOSE
4030 END
5000   'Strip trailing blanks
5010   M$=NME$
5020   IF RIGHT$(M$,1) <> CHR$(32) THEN 5050
5030   M$ = LEFT$(M$,LEN(M$)-1)
5040   GOTO 5020
5050   RETURN
```

Exercises

1. Write a program that writes records to an inventory file. Each record should contain 10 bytes for the item ID number, 30 bytes for the item description, four bytes for the quantity of the item, and four bytes for the minimum inventory required.

2. Here is a record from a personnel file. For ease in reading this record, we have replaced all blanks with @.

   JONES@@@@@@@JOHN@@@@@@FILECLERK@@@04/15/82HOURLY$5.85

   Write a field statement that correctly separates the fields of the record.

3. Suppose that a file named SALES consists of 20 records, each containing four numbers. Write a program that reads the file and prints the numbers in four columns on the screen.

4. Write a program that allows you to specify a name in the file TELE-PHON. The program locates the file entry and prints out an address label corresponding to the name.

Answers to Test Your Understandings 1 and 2

1.
```
10 OPEN "DEPTS" AS #1, LEN=23
20 FIELD #1, 11 AS DEPT$, 4 AS INCOME$, 4 AS
   EFFICIENCY$, 4 AS OVERHEAD$
30 FOR J=1 TO 4
40    READ A$,B,C,D
50    LSET DEPT$=A$
60    LSET INCOME$=MKS$(B)
70    LSET EFFICIENCY$=MKS$(C)
80    LSET OVERHEAD$=MKS$(D)
90    PUT #1,J
100 NEXT J
110 DATA "ACCOUNTING",5000,.235,7886
120 DATA "ENGINEERING",3500,.872,2200
130 DATA "MAINTENANCE",4338,.381,5130
140 DATA "ADVERTISING",10832,.951,12500
150 CLOSE #1
160 END
```

2.
```
10 OPEN "DEPTS" AS #1, LEN=23
20 FIELD #1, 10 AS DEPT$, 4 AS INCOME$, 4 AS
   EFFICIENCY$,4 AS OVERHEAD$
30 GET #1, 3
40 PRINT "DEPARTMENT","INCOME","EFFICIENCY","OVERHEAD"
50 PRINT DEPT$,CVS(INCOME$),CVS(EFFICIENCY$),
```

```
      CVS (OVERHEAD$)
60  CLOSE #1
70  END
```

An Application of Ramdom Access Files

In this section, we work out a detailed example illustrating the application of random access files. We will design and build a "list manager" program, which allows you to manipulate a list. A program of this sort is sometimes called a database management program.

Our program will manipulate typical lists. A typical list is structured into a series of entries, with each entry divided into a series of data items. We have allowed each entry of our list to contain as many as five string items and five numerical items. The string items are listed first. A typical list entry has the following form:

```
ITEM #1  (STRING)
ITEM #2  (STRING)
ITEM #3  (STRING)
ITEM #4  (STRING)
ITEM #5  (STRING)
ITEM #6  (NUMBER)
ITEM #7  (NUMBER)
ITEM #8  (NUMBER)
ITEM #9  (NUMBER)
ITEM #10 (NUMBER)
```

It is not necessary to use all ten items. The entries of a particular list might consist of three strings followed by two numbers, for example. The program asks for the structure of the list entries (number of strings and number of numbers). The program then assumes that all entries of the list contain the specified numbers of data items of each type.

The list manager allows you to perform the following activities:

1. Give a name to a list and create a corresponding random access file to contain the list.

2. Give titles to the various items ("NAME", "ADDRESS", "SALARY", and "TELEPHONE #"). An item title may be up to 12 characters long.

3. Enter list items. The program displays the various item names and allows you to type in the various items for the list entry. You may repeat the entry operation as many times as you wish, thereby compiling lists of any length.

4. Change list entries. You may change a list entry by re-entering its data items.

5. Display list entries. You may display a single list entry or an entire set of consecutive list entries.

6. Search the list. You may search the list for entries in which a particular item (say ZIPCODE) has a particular value (say 20001). The program will inform you of a match and give the entry number. It will then ask you if you wish to see the corresponding list entry. If so, it will display the entry for you. After you are done examining the entry, you press ENTER, and the program will continue to search for further matches.

The following program is highly structured (major tasks correspond to subroutines) and the listing is reasonably self-explanatory. However, you should note the following:

1. The titles of the list are stored in record 1.

2. The actual list entries are stored beginning in record 2. The entry number (list entry 5) is always one less than the corresponding record (record 6).

3. There are two menus. The main menu allows you to choose among the following activities:

```
Specify Titles
Specify List Entry
Search and Display
Exit
```

The second menu is displayed if you choose the Search and Display option on the main menu. The various options in this second menu are:

```
Display Single List Entry
Display Consecutive List Entries
Search
```

4. Entry items are numbered from 1 to 10, with the strings 1 to 5 and the numbers 6 to 10. This numbering holds even if some items are not used. That is, the first numerical item is always 6.

Here is a listing of the program:

```
10      '**************
20      ' List Manager
30      '**************
100     'Main Program
110       GOSUB 4200:'Obtain file name and open file
120       GOSUB 1010:'Display Main Menu
130       ON REPLY GOSUB 2000,3000,4100,4140
140       GOTO 120
1000    'Display main menu
1010       CLS
1020       PRINT "THE LIST MANAGER"
1030       PRINT:PRINT
1040       PRINT "PROGRAM ACTIVITIES"
1050       PRINT
1060       PRINT "1. ASSIGN DATA ITEM TITLES"
1070       PRINT "2. SPECIFY LIST ENTRY"
1080       PRINT "3. SEARCH AND DISPLAY LIST"
1090       PRINT "4. EXIT FROM LIST MANAGER"
1100       PRINT
1110       INPUT   "DESIRED ACTIVITY(1-4)";REPLY
1120    RETURN
2000    'Assign Data Item Titles
2010       CLS
2020       IF LOF(1)=1 THEN 2040:'New File ?
2030       GOSUB 4400:'Get old titles
```

```
2040      FOR ITEMNUMBER=1 TO 10
2050        PRINT "DATA ITEM #";ITEMNUMBER;TAB(20)
             "CURRENT DEF'N: ";
2060        PRINT A$(ITEMNUMBER)
2070        INPUT "NEW DEF'N: ";TITLE$(ITEMNUMBER)
2080        LSET A$(ITEMNUMBER)=TITLE$(ITEMNUMBER)
2090      NEXT ITEMNUMBER
2100      PUT #1,1:'Record new titles
2110    RETURN
3000 'Specify list entry
3010      CLS
3020      INPUT "LIST ENTRY NUMBER (0=NEW ENTRY)";
             ENTRYNUMBER
3030      IF ENTRYNUMBER=0 THEN ENTRYNUMBER=LOC(1)+1
             ELSE ENTRYNUMBER=ENTRYNUMBER+1
3040      GOSUB 4400:'Obtain titles
3050      PRINT "LIST ENTRY #";ENTRYNUMBER-1;TAB(20)
             "SPECIFY ENTRY ITEMS"
3060      FOR ITEMNUMBER=1 TO STRINGFIELDS
3070        PRINT "Data Item Title: ";TITLE$(ITEMNUMBER)
3080        INPUT "ENTRY (STRING)";ENTRY$
3090        LSET A$(ITEMNUMBER)=ENTRY$
3100      NEXT ITEMNUMBER
3110      FOR ITEMNUMBER=6 TO 5+NUMERICFIELDS
3120        IF TITLE$(ITEMNUMBER)="" THEN 3160
3130        PRINT "Data Item Title: ";TITLE$(ITEMNUMBER)
3140        INPUT "ENTRY (NUMBER)";ENTRY
3150        LSET A$(ITEMNUMBER)=MKS$(ENTRY)
3160      NEXT ITEMNUMBER
3170      PUT #1,ENTRYNUMBER
3180    RETURN
4000 'Various Subroutines
4100 'Search and Display List
4110      GOSUB 4700:'Search and Display Menu
4120      ON REPLY GOSUB 4800,4900,5100
4130    RETURN
4140 'Exit
4150    CLS
4160    CLOSE #1
4170    END
```

```
4180 RETURN
4200 'Obtain file name and open file
4210    CLS
4220    CLOSE
4230    PRINT "THE LIST MANAGER"
4240    INPUT "NAME OF FILE";FILENAME$
4250    INPUT "NUMBER OF STRING FIELDS (1-5)";STRINGFIELDS
4260    INPUT "NUMBER OF NUMERIC FIELDS (1-5)";
        NUMERICFIELDS
4270    OPEN FILENAME$ AS #1
4280    FIELD 1, 12 AS A$(1), 12 AS A$(2), 12 AS A$(3), 12
        AS A$(4),12 AS A$(5), 12 AS A$(6), 12 AS A$(7), 12
        AS A$(8), 12 AS A$(9), 12 AS A$(10)
4290    GOSUB 4400:'Read Old titles
4300  RETURN
4400 'Read old titles
4410    GET #1,1
4420    FOR J=1 TO 10
4430      TITLE$(J)=A$(J)
4440    NEXT J
4450  RETURN
4500 'Display entry
4510    CLS
4520    PRINT:'Advance to 2nd line
4530    GOSUB 4400:'Read titles
4540    IF DISPLAYENTRY > LOF(1)/128 THEN 4680:
        'Non-existant record
4550    GET #1, DISPLAYENTRY
4560    FOR ITEMNUMBER=1 TO STRINGFIELDS
4570      ENTRY$(ITEMNUMBER)=A$(ITEMNUMBER)
4580      PRINT TITLE$(ITEMNUMBER);TAB(21) ENTRY$
          (ITEMNUMBER)
4590    NEXT ITEMNUMBER
4600    FOR ITEMNUMBER=6 TO 5+NUMERICFIELDS
4610      IF A$(ITEMNUMBER)="" THEN 4620 ELSE 4640
4620      PRINT TITLE$(ITEMNUMBER)
4630      GOTO 4660
4640      ENTRY(ITEMNUMBER)=CVS(A$(ITEMNUMBER))
4650      PRINT TITLE$(ITEMNUMBER);TAB(21) ENTRY
          (ITEMNUMBER)
```

```
4660      NEXT ITEMNUMBER
4670      LOCATE 1,1
4680    RETURN
4700 'Display and Search Menu
4710      CLS
4720      PRINT "DISPLAY AND SEARCH MENU"
4730      PRINT : PRINT
4740      PRINT "1. DISPLAY ENTRY WITH GIVEN NUMBER"
4750      PRINT "2. DISPLAY CONSECUTIVE ENTRIES"
4760      PRINT "3. SEARCH"
4770      PRINT
4780      INPUT "ACTIVITY(1-3)";REPLY
4790    RETURN
4800 'Display entry with given number
4810      CLS
4820      PRINT:'Advance to 2nd line
4830      INPUT "Number of entry to display";DISPLAYENTRY
4840      DISPLAYENTRY=DISPLAYENTRY+1
4850      IF DISPLAYENTRY > LOF(1)/128 THEN 4890
4860      GOSUB 4500
4870      INPUT "TO CONTINUE, HIT ENTER KEY";REPLY$
4880      IF REPLY$="" THEN 4790 ELSE 4670
4890    RETURN
4900 'Display consecutive entries
4910      CLS
4920      PRINT:'Advance to 2nd line
4930      INPUT "NUMBER OF FIRST ENTRY TO DISPLAY";
          DISPLAYENTRY
4940      DISPLAYENTRY=DISPLAYENTRY+1
4950      IF DISPLAYENTRY > LOF(1)/128 THEN 5020
4960      GOSUB 4500
4970      LOCATE 1,1
4980      INPUT "DISPLAY NEXT ENTRY=0,RETURN TO MAIN
          MENU=1";REPLY
4990      IF REPLY=1 THEN 5020
5000      DISPLAYENTRY=DISPLAYENTRY+1
5010      GOTO 4950
5020    RETURN
5100 'Search
5110      CLS
```

```
5120      INPUT "ITEM NUMBER TO SCAN";ITM
5130      PRINT "LOOK FOR ITEM NUMBER";ITM;" EQUAL TO";
5140      IF ITM<6 THEN INPUT MATCHSTRING$
5150      IF ITM>5 THEN INPUT MATCHNUMBER
5160      L=LEN(MATCHSTRING$):'L=length of the match
          string
5170      MATCHSTRING$=MATCHSTRING$+SPACE$(12-L):'Add
          blanks
5180      LNGTH=LOF(1)/128
5190      FOR J=2 TO LNGTH
5200        GET #1, J
5210        IF ITM > 5 THEN A=CVS(A$(ITM)) ELSE
            A$=A$(ITM)
5220        IF ITM < 6 AND A$=MATCHSTRING$  THEN GOSUB 5300
5230        IF ITM > 5 AND A=MATCHNUMBER THEN GOSUB 5300
5240      NEXT J
5250    RETURN
5300 'Response to a match
5310      CLS
5320      LOCATE 1,1
5330      PRINT "MATCH IN ENTRY";J-1
5340      INPUT "Do You Wish to Display Entry(1=Yes,0=No)";
          REPLY
5350      IF REPLY=1 THEN 5360 ELSE 5400
5360      DISPLAYENTRY=J
5370      GOSUB 4500
5380      INPUT "TO CONTINUE, HIT ENTER KEY";REPLY$
5390      IF REPLY$="" THEN 5400 ELSE 5380
5400    RETURN
```

Note that the fields of the file records are all 12 characters wide. This is to accommodate the titles in record 1. Because we do not specify a record length, BASIC assumes that the records are 128 characters long. We are using 120 (12 characters per field × 10 fields) of these characters. If you wish, you may redesign this program to accommodate more data items and longer string items and titles. However, if you use more than 128 characters per record, it is necessary to initialize BASIC to allow for a sufficiently large random access file buffer.

Exercises

1. Type in the list manager program.

2. Use the list manager program to create a Christmas card list.

3. Practice using the search feature to locate particular data items.

Thirteen

Sorting Techniques

The Elements of Sorting

In the preceding sections, we have discussed the mechanisms to create, read, and write data files. In this section, we discuss the organization of data within such files.

If a data file is to be of much use, we must be able to easily access its data. At first this might seem like a simple requirement. After all, we can always search through a data file, examining records until we find the one we want. Unfortunately, this is just not always possible. Until now, we have been working with rather short data files. However, many applications require dealing with data files containing thousands or even tens of thousands of records. When a data file is large, even the great speed of the computer is insufficient to guarantee a speedy search. Indeed, if we are required to search through an entire file for a piece of data, we might be required to wait for hours! For this reason (as well as for others), we usually organize the contents of a file in some way, so that access to its data is improved. Here are some examples of common file organizations:

1. A file of data on customers may be arranged in alphabetical order, according to the customer name.

2. A mailing list may be arranged according to zip code.

3. An inventory list might be arranged according to part number.

4. A credit card company most likely arranges its customer account files according to their credit card number.

In each example, the records in the data file are arranged in a certain order, based on the value of a particular field in the record (name field, zip code field, part number field, card number field). In maintaining such files, it is essential to be able to arrange the records in the desired order. The process of arranging a set of data items is called **sorting**. Actually, sorting is an extremely important topic to computer programmers and has been the subject of many research papers and books. In this section, we will give an introduction to sorting by describing one of the more elementary sorting techniques—the bubble sort.

Let's begin by stating our problem in simple terms. Let's suppose that we wish to arrange the records of a file according to a particular field, say field 1.

Problem: Arrange the records so that the values in field 1 are in ascending order.

For the sake of our initial discussion, let's suppose that the field values are numbers. (Later, we will deal with fields containing strings.)

Let's set up arrays A() and B() as follows: Read the various values of field 1 into the array A().

A(1) = the value of field 1 for record 1,

A(2) = the value of field 1 for record 2,

A(3) = the value of field 1 for record 3,

and so forth. We wish to rearrange the records according to certain rules. Because the actual records may be quite long, we will deal only with the contents of field 1. In order to keep track of the record to which a particular field value belongs, we will use the array B(). That is,

B(1) = the record number for the field value A(1),

B(2) = the record number for the field value A(2),

B(3) = the record number for the field value A(3),

and so forth. Assume that we initially read the values into array A() according to increasing record number. Then we initially have

```
B(1)=1,  B(2)=2,  B(3)=3,  ...
```

The Bubble Sort Procedure

The bubble sort procedure allows you to arrange a set of numbers in increasing order. It involves repeatedly executing a simple reordering process that involves reordering consecutive items. Each repetition of the process is called a **pass**. Let's illustrate the procedure to arrange the following list of numbers in increasing order:

90, 38, 15, 48 , 80, 1

Pass 1. Start from the right end of the list. Compare the adjacent numbers. If they are out of order, switch them. Otherwise leave them alone. Continue this procedure with each pair of adjacent numbers, proceeding from right to left. Here are the results:

90, 38, 15, 48, 1, 80 (1 < 80 so the pair 80,1 is reversed)

90, 38, 15, 1, 48, 80 (1 < 48 so the pair 48,1 is reversed)

90, 38, 1, 15, 48, 80 (1 < 15 so the pair 15,1 is reversed)

90, 1, 38, 15, 48, 80   (1 < 38 so the pair 38,1 is reversed)

1, 90, 38, 15, 48, 80   (1 < 90 so the pair 90,1 is reversed)

This is the end of Pass 1. Note that the number 1 has assumed its correct place in the list.

Pass 2. Apply the procedure of Pass 1 to the rightmost five numbers of the current list.

1, 90, 38, 15, 48, 80   (48 < 80 so no exchange)

1, 90, 38, 15, 48, 80

1, 90, 15, 38, 48, 80

1, 15, 90, 38, 48, 80

Note that the number 15 has now been moved to its proper position on the list.

Pass 3. Apply the procedure of Pass 1 to the rightmost four numbers of the current list.

1, 15, 90, 38, 48, 80

1, 15, 90, 38, 48, 80

1, 15, 38, 90, 48, 80

Pass 4. Apply the procedure of Pass 1 to the rightmost three numbers of the current list.

1, 15, 38, 90, 48, 80

1, 15, 38, 48, 90, 80

Pass 5. Apply the procedure of Pass 1 to the rightmost two numbers of the current list.

1, 15, 38, 48, 80, 90

The list is now in order.

Note the following characteristic of the bubble sort procedure. At each step, the smallest remaining number is moved to its proper position in the list. Suppose that we view the original list as written vertically:

90
38
15
48
 1
80

Then at each step, the least number in the remaining list moves to its proper level in the list. Think of each number as a bubble under water, whose buoyancy is determined by the value of the number. Then at each step, a bubble moves up as far as it can toward the surface. This is the reason for the name **bubble sort**.

We have carried out the manipulations in the above example in excruciating detail to aid us in writing a correct program to implement the bubble sort procedure. Let's suppose that the items to be ordered are stored in the array A() of size N. Here is a program that carries out the bubble sort procedure:

```
1000 'Bubble Sort Subroutine
1010 FOR I=2 TO N
1020    FOR J=N TO I STEP -1
1030       IF A(J-1) > A(J) THEN SWAP A(J-1), A(J)
1040    NEXT J
1050 NEXT I
1060 RETURN
```

Note that we have written this program as a subroutine to be included in a larger program. Note that the DIM statement for the array A() as well as the number N of numbers to be sorted must be set in the larger program. You may test this program with the sequence of numbers 100, 99, 98, 97, 96, ..., 1 by inserting the lines of code 10–190 as follows:

```
10 ' ****************************************
20 ' This program incorporates a subroutine
30 '    to bubble sort 100 numbers
40 ' ****************************************
100 DIM A(100)
110 N=100
120 FOR J=1 TO N
130    A(J)=101-J
140 NEXT J
150 GOSUB 1000
160 FOR J=1 TO 100
170    PRINT J, A(J)
180 NEXT J
190 END
1000 'Bubble Sort Subroutine
1010 FOR I=2 TO N
1020    FOR J=N TO I STEP -1
1030       IF A(J-1) > A(J) THEN SWAP A(J-1), A(J)
1040    NEXT J
1050 NEXT I
1060 RETURN
```

We may use this routine to infer some interesting characteristics of sort routines. Here is a set of run times for various values of N, using the sequence N, N-1, N-2,..., 1. (This is the worst case because interchanges are required at each step.)

Value of Run Time for Bubble Sort (IBM PC at 4.77 MHz)

    N=100 67 seconds
    N=50   17 seconds
    N=20   4 seconds
    N=10   1 second

First note that, with only 100 items to be sorted, the run time is already substantial. Second, note the way that the run time increases as the number of items increases. It appears that if the number of items is doubled then the run time increases by a factor of four. Similarly, multiplying the number of items by 3 increases the run time by 9. Generally, in this worst-case scenario, multiplying the number of items by k multiplies the run time by k^2. On average, the run times are not this bad. However, we have chosen a particularly bad case to illustrate the manner in which sorting times quickly become unmanageable.

Modified Bubble Sort

The bubble sort procedure performs particularly poorly for data that are almost in order and are sorted into the correct order by one of the early passes. The procedure, as stated above, has no way of knowing that that data are already in order and that no further sorting is necessary. Now, let's improve the bubble sort algorithm by building a test into each pass to determine whether any further sorting is necessary.

Our test is based on the value of a variable SORTFLAG. Initially, we set SORTFLAG equal to zero. During each pass, we set SORTFLAG equal to 1 when an interchange takes place. At the end of the pass, we examine the value of SORTFLAG. If SORTFLAG is 0, then no interchange took place and the algorithm is terminated. Otherwise, SORTFLAG is set equal to 0, and the algorithm goes on to the next pass. Here is the code for the modified bubble sort routine:

```
200 'Modified Bubble Sort Subroutine
210 SORTFLAG=0
220 FOR I=2 TO N
230   FOR J=N TO I STEP -1
240     IF A(J-1) > A(J) THEN SWAP A(J-1), A(J):SORTFLAG=1
250   NEXT J
260   IF SORTFLAG=0 THEN I=N ELSE SORTFLAG=0
270 NEXT I
280 RETURN
```

Note the logic in the third line from the end. If SORTFLAG is equal to zero, then the loop variable I is set equal to N. In this case, the NEXT I in line 270 causes the I loop to terminate. Otherwise, SORTFLAG is set equal to 0 and the next value of I is considered.

Test Your Understanding 1

Compare the times required by both the original and modified bubble sort routines in sorting the following list of numbers into ascending order:

5, 4, 3, 2, 1, 6, 7, 8, 9,..., 98, 99, 100

Exercises

1. Write a program to create an array of N random numbers, where N is given in an INPUT statement. The program should arrange the array in increasing order and should use the clock to time the operation. Make a table of sort times for various values of N. (Be sure to use RANDOMIZE to create nonrepetitive arrays.)

2. Write a program to determine the smallest element in a file consisting of real numbers.

3. Use the bubble sort algorithm to sort the following list into ascending numerical order:

   ```
   10091, 7891, 4444, 21248, 30762, 911, 3890, 4579, 1124
   ```

4. Use the bubble sort algorithm to sort the following lists into ascending numerical order:

   ```
   100, 99, 98, ..., 2, 1
   300, 299, 298, ..., 2, 1
   500, 499, 498, ..., 2, 1
   1000, 999, 998, ..., 2, 1
   ```

   Time the execution of each sorting problem. Can you make a guess about how the sorting time grows as the number of elements in the list grows?

5. Perform the sorting problems of Exercise 2, but using the Modified Bubble Sort algorithm. How much of an improvement in sorting time do you observe? Can you explain your observation?

6. Perform Exercises 2 and 3, except use the following lists, each containing 100 numbers:

```
1, 2, ..., 99, 100
1, 2, ..., 299, 300
1, 2, ..., 499, 500
1, 2, ..., 999, 1000
```

7. Perform Exercises 2 and 3, except use the following list of 100 numbers:

   1, 100, 2, 99, 3, 98, ..., 50

8. On the basis of your observations in Exercises 2–5 what sort of lists are hardest for the bubble sort algorithm to sort? What kind of lists will show the largest improvement by replacing BubbleSort with BubbleSort2?

9. In a list with an odd number 2N+1 of entries, the median is the N+1 entry when the entries are arranged in numerical order. That is, the median is the "middle entry." In a list with an even number 2N of entries, the median is the average of the two middle entries, the Nth and N+1. Write a procedure for determining the median of a list.

10. Write a program that counts the number of interchanges made in sorting an array using the bubble sort, the modified bubble sort, and the selection sort. Compare these counts for arrays containing the following lists:

    ```
    100 99 98 ... 1
    100 1 99 2 98 3 ...
    1 2 3 4 ... 100
    100 99 98 ... 51 1 2 3 ... 50
    ```

Sorting Strings

In the preceding section, we discussed sorting via the bubble sort algorithm for arrays of numbers. Now let's turn our attention to sorting arrays of strings into alphabetical order.

Order Relations Among Strings

We arrange single characters in order by their respective ASCII codes. We say that a character A\$ is less than the character B\$ provided that A\$ comes before B\$ in the ASCII table. If A\$ is less than B\$, we write

```
A$ < B$
```

For example, the following are valid inequalities among characters:

```
"A" < "B"  ("A" has ASCII code 65,
            "B" has ASCII code 66)

"a" < "b"  ("a" has ASCII code 97,
            "b" has ASCII code 98)
```

Note that this ordering scheme amounts to arranging the capital letters in alphabetical order, followed by lowercase letters in alphabetical order. However, the following comparisons are valid and are not usually considered in alphabetic arrangements:

```
"A" < "a"
"0" < "a"  ("0" has ASCII code 48)
"*" > "#"  ("*" has ASCII code 42,
            "#" has ASCII code 35)
" " < "0"  (" " has ASCII code 32)
```

Strings having more than a single letter are compared as follows: First compare first letters. If they are the same, compare second letters. If the first two letters are the same, compare third letters. And so forth. For example, consider the two strings "Smith" and "SMITH". Their first letters are the same, so we compare their second letters "m" and "M", respectively. According to their ASCII codes "M" comes before "m", so:

```
"SMith" < "Smith"
```

If the compared strings consist of only uppercase or only lowercase letters, then this comparison procedure arranges the strings in the usual alphabetic order. However, the procedure may be used to compare any strings. For example:

```
"**#" < "**0"
```

Here is a bit of useful notation for strings. The notation

```
A$ >= B$
```

means that either

```
A$ > B$ or A$ = B$
```

Simply, this means that A$ either succeeds B$ in alphabetical order, or A$ and B$ are the same. The notation A$ <= B$ has a similar meaning.

The Bubble Sort for Arrays of Strings

Using the above string order relation, we may design a modified bubble sort procedure for sorting a string array A$() into increasing order. Here is the subroutine:

```
300 'Modified Bubble Sort Subroutine for Strings
310 SORTFLAG=0
320 FOR I=2 TO N
330   FOR J=N TO I STEP -1
340     IF A$(J-1) > A$(J) THEN SWAP A$(J-1), A$(J):SORT-
FLAG=1
350   NEXT J
360     IF SORTFLAG=0 THEN I=N ELSE SORTFLAG=0
370 NEXT I
380 RETURN
```

When this routine is used to sort an array consisting only of uppercase or only of lowercase letters, it sorts the array into alphabetical order. Here is an example of this procedure:

Example 1. Write a program to alphabetize the following list of words: egg, celery, ball, bag, glove, coat, pants, suit, clover, weed, grass, cow, and chicken.

Solution.   We set up a string array A$(J), which contains these 13 words, and apply the bubble sort subroutine.

```
10 ' ********************************
20 ' This program alphabetizes a list
30 '    of words provided as data
40 ' ********************************
100 DIM A$(13)
110 DATA egg,celery,ball,bag,glove,coat
120 DATA pants, suit, clover, weed, grass
130 DATA cow, chicken
140 'Set up array A$
150 FOR J=1 TO 13
160    READ A$(J):N=N+1
170 NEXT J
180 'Sort array A$()
190 GOSUB 300
200 'Print Sorted Array
210 FOR J=1 TO 13
220   PRINT A$(J)
230 NEXT J
240 END
300 'Modified Bubble Sort Subroutine for Strings
310 SORTFLAG=0
320 FOR I=2 TO N
330    FOR J=N TO I STEP -1
340       IF A$(J-1) > A$(J) THEN SWAP A$(J-
1),A$(J):SORTFLAG=1
350    NEXT J
360    IF SORTFLAG=0 THEN I=N ELSE SORTFLAG=0
370 NEXT I
380 RETURN
```

This program can be modified to make a program alphabetizing any collection of strings. We will leave the details to the exercises.

Exercises

1. Write a program to sort an arbitrary array of strings.

2. Write a program to sort a file of strings. The program should write the sorted data back to the file.

Other Sorting Algorithms

There are many different algorithms used for sorting. To give you some idea of the variety, let's discuss a second method of sorting an array of numbers, the so-called **selection sort**. As in the bubble sort algorithm, the selection sort operates as a sequence of passes. Each pass involves a number of interchanges. The selection sort will generally involve fewer interchanges but more passes than the bubble sort.

The Nth Pass of the Selection Sort Algorithm

Determine the smallest entry among the last N entries. Interchange the largest entry with the Nth entry. To sort a list of M entries into increasing order requires M-1 passes.

Here is a concrete example of the selection sort applied to the list:

```
90 38 15 48 1 80
```

Pass 1. Consider the entries beginning with the first. The smallest is 1. So we interchange the 1 with the first entry to obtain the modified list:

```
1 38 15 48 90 80
```

Pass 2. Consider the entries beginning with the second. The smallest is 15. So we interchange 15 with the second entry 38 to obtain:

```
1 15 38 48 90 80
```

Pass 3. Consider the entries beginning with the third. The smallest is 38. It is already in the third position, so no interchange need take place. The list remains the same:

```
1 15 38 48 90 80
```

Pass 4. Consider the entries beginning with the fourth. The smallest is 48. Again no interchange takes place.

    1 15 38 48 90 80

Pass 5. Consider the entries beginning with the fifth. The smallest is 80. Interchange 80 with the fifth entry to obtain:

    1 15 38 48 80 90

The original list had 6 elements and after 6-1 = 5 passes, the list is now sorted into ascending order.

As with the bubble sort, we can describe the selection sort for sorting the elements of an integer array Arr of size ArraySize. Here is a subroutine for carrying out the selection sort on such an array A().

```
10  'Selection Sort of the array A()
20  'PASSNUM is the pass number
30  'POS is the position of the entry being compared
40  'TEMP temporarily holds an array value during an
50  'interchange
60  'The subscripts of A() go from 1 to N
70   FOR PASSNUM=1 TO N-1
80     FOR POS=PASSNUM+1 TO N
90       IF A(PASSNUM) > A(POS) THEN SWAP(A(PASSNUM),
         A(POS))
100    NEXT POS
110 NEXT PASSNUM
```

Sorting is an immense field within computer science, one within which research is still going on. Indeed, sorting is an extremely important operation for applications. However, it is one that can take up large amounts of computer time, even on the fastest machines. Accordingly, the search goes on for ever more efficient sorting algorithms.

Exercises

1. Repeat all of the exercises of Section 1 using the selection sort instead of the bubble sort.

Searching Algorithms

In the preceding sections, we discussed the problem of sorting an array into ascending or descending order. One of the motivations for sorting an array is so that it will be simpler to search through the array elements and determine whether a specified entry is contained in the array and, if so, where it is. This latter problem is called **searching**. In this section, we will take up the problem of searching and present several algorithms for solving it.

Let's begin by stating the searching problem precisely. Suppose that we are given an array A(), which may or may not be sorted. Further, suppose that we are given a number X. We wish to determine for which array indices I do we have A(I) = X.

Although we have stated the problem in terms of single-precision numeric arrays, we could just as well have stated it for arrays of any type, including string arrays.

A Simple Matching Search

The simplest solution to the searching problem is to simply test every element of the array. That is, for each possible value of I, determine whether A(I) = X is true. This solution is called a **matching search**. It is very simple to implement and does not require the array to be sorted, but it is usually very inefficient, in the sense that the length of the average search is about N/2, where N is the size of the array.

A Binary Search

A useful alternative to a matching search is a **binary search**, which operates by the method of "divide and conquer." The binary search applies only to sorted arrays, so let's assume for the sake of explicitness that A() is sorted in ascending order and that the array indices are 1, 2,..., N. Here is how the binary search works. Divide the indices into two groups:

```
1, 2,..., INT(N/2)
```

and

```
INT(N/2)+1, INT(N/2)+2,N
```

The first group is the "lower half" of the indices and the second group is the "upper half" of the indices. We now examine the index at the midpoint, namely J=INT(N/2). If A(J) is less than the desired match X, then any possible match must come from the upper half of the indices. If A(J) is greater than the desired match X, then any possible match must come from the lower half of the indices. Of course, if A(J) is equal to X, then we have a solution to the search. If either of the first two cases prevail, we examine the interval that must contain any desired match and repeat the procedure just described. That is, we divide the interval into two equal intervals and compare the array element at the middle index with X. We keep repeating this process until either a match is achieved or the length of the subintervals is 1.

Here is a subroutine that carries out the above-described search. If a match is achieved, the variable MATCH is set equal to TRUE (=-1).

```
1000 'Binary search routine
1010 'This subroutine does a binary search of the
        sorted array A()
1020 'for the given number TARGET. SIZE is the size of A()
1030 'If TARGET is contained in the array, the index
        containing
1040 'it is returned in the variable TINDEX and SUCCESS
        is set
1050 'equal to TRUE.
1060 'Within the search the variable STARTINT denotes the
        index
1070 'of the first entry in the search interval and ENDINT
1080 'denotes the index of the last entry in the search
        interval.
1090 SUCCESS = 0 ' Success equal to FALSE.
1100 STARTINT = 1: ENDINT = SIZE
1110 IF A(ENDINT) = TARGET THEN SUCCESS=-1: TINDEX=ENDINT:
        GOTO 1170
```

```
1120 WHILE (ENDINT-STARTINT>=0) AND (SUCCESS=0)
1130   MIDPT = INT((ENDINT+STARTINT)/2)
1140   IF A(MIDPT) > TARGET THEN ENDINT = MIDPT-1 ELSE
       STARTINT = MIDPT+1
1150   IF A(MIDPT)= TARGET THEN SUCCESS=-1: TINDEX=MIDPT
1160 WEND
1170 RETURN
```

Figure 13-1 illustrates the use of this searching subroutine to determine if user-specified entries are contained in the array with A(1) = 5, A(2) = 12, A(3) = 15, A(4) = 25, A(5) = 26.

```
Ok
run
INPUT A NUMBER TO SEARCH FOR? 12
 12  IS IN THE ARRAY IN POSITION  2
SEARCH FOR ANOTHER NUMBER(Y/N)? Y
INPUT A NUMBER TO SEARCH FOR? 26
 26  IS IN THE ARRAY IN POSITION  5
SEARCH FOR ANOTHER NUMBER(Y/N)? Y
INPUT A NUMBER TO SEARCH FOR? 0
 0  IS NOT IN THE ARRAY
SEARCH FOR ANOTHER NUMBER(Y/N)? Y
INPUT A NUMBER TO SEARCH FOR? -5
-5  IS NOT IN THE ARRAY
SEARCH FOR ANOTHER NUMBER(Y/N)? N
Ok
_
```

Figure 13-1. **Application of the binary search technique.**

For sorted arrays, the binary search method is far more efficient than a matching search. There are many other search methods that have been developed by computer scientists. However, a further discussion is beyond the scope of this book.

Fourteen

An Introduction to Graphics and Sound

Introduction

GWBASIC is capable of using the graphics and sound capabilities of the IBM PC and its compatibles. This chapter is an introduction to these capabilities and includes:

- Line graphics in text mode.
- Setting colors and graphics modes.
- Relative and absolute coordinates in graphics mode.
- Drawing lines, rectangles, and circles.
- Drawing bar charts and pie charts.
- Painting regions of the screen.
- The Graphics Macro Language.

- Saving and recalling graphics images.
- Setting user-defined coordinates in graphics mode.
- Writing programs to produce sound and music.

Graphics in Text Mode

When you first start BASIC, the screen is in text mode, in which the video display can display only characters from the standard IBM character set. (More about that below.) In text mode, the display contains 25 rows of either 40 or 80 characters each. You may change from 80-character to 40-character width using the WIDTH statement. The various character positions divide the screen into small rectangles. Figure 14-1 shows the subdivision of the screen corresponding to an 80-character line width.

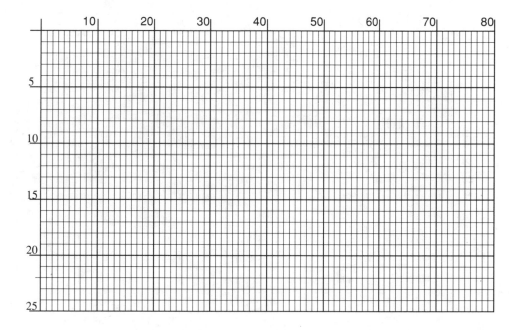

Figure 14-1. **Screen layout for text mode (80-character width)**.

The rectangles into which we have divided the screen are arranged in rows and columns. The rows are numbered from 1 to 25, with row 1 at the top of the screen and row 25 at the bottom. The columns are numbered from 1 to 80, with column 1 at the extreme left and column 80 at the extreme right. Each rectangle on the screen is identified by a pair of numbers, indicating the row and column. For example, the rectangle in the 12th row and 16th column is shown in Figure 14-2.

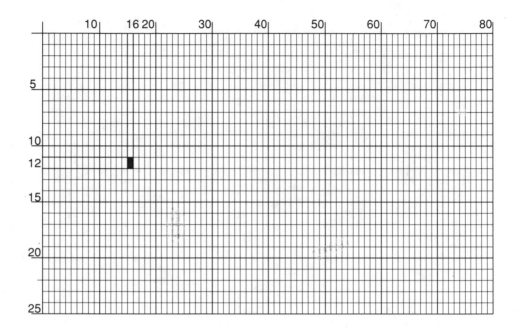

Figure 14-2. **Rectangle in the 12th row and 16th column**.

We may print characters on the screen using the PRINT and PRINT USING instructions. For graphics purposes, it is important to be able to precisely position characters on the screen. This may be done using the LOCATE instruction.

Remember that printing always occurs at the current cursor location. To locate the cursor at row x and column y, we use the instruction:

```
10 LOCATE x,y
```

Example 1. Write a set of BASIC instructions to print the words "IBM Personal Computer" beginning at row 20, column 10.

Solution.

```
10 LOCATE 20,10
20 PRINT "IBM Personal Computer"
```

Until now, we have printed only characters such as those found on a typewriter keyboard (letters, numbers, and punctuation marks). Actually, the IBM PC has a very extensive set of characters, including a collection of graphics characters, as shown in Figure 14-3. Note that each character (including graphics characters) is identified by an ASCII code. In Chapter 10, we introduced the characters corresponding to ASCII codes 0–127. In Figure 14-3 we list the characters corresponding to ASCII codes 128–255. For example, the character with ASCII code 179 is a vertical line (|). To place this character at the current cursor position, we use the instruction:

```
10 PRINT CHR$(179);
```

Note the semicolon that prevents the PRINT statement from sending an unwanted carriage return and line feed. (In most printing involving graphics, you will want to use the semicolon.)

You may insert a graphics character into a program line by holding down the ALT key and entering the character number on the numeric keypad (the calculator-like set of numbers on the right side of the keyboard). This has the advantage that in a PRINT statement, you can see the character to be printed. For example, the above statement line appears on the screen as

```
10 PRINT (|) ;
```

where the symbol is entered from the keyboard by holding down ALT and typing "179". In what follows we will use the CHR$ notation to make clear the code numbers of the various characters. In your own work, however, use the ALT key to indicate graphics characters.

Test Your Understanding 1 (Answer on Page 378)

Write a set of instructions to print graphics character 179 in row 18, column 22.

Test Your Understanding 2 (Answer on Page 378)

Write a program to display all 128 graphics characters on the screen.

ASCII value	Character	ASCII value	Character	ASCII value	Character	ASCII value	Character
128	Ç	166	ª	204	╠	242	≥
129	ü	167	º	205	═	243	≤
130	é	168	¿	206	╬	244	⌠
131	â	169	⌐	207	╧	245	⌡
132	ä	170	¬	208	╨	246	÷
133	à	171	½	209	╤	247	≈
134	å	172	¼	210	╥	248	°
135	ç	173	¡	211	╙	249	•
136	ê	174	«	212	╘	250	·
137	ë	175	»	213	╒	251	√
138	è	176	░	214	╓	252	ⁿ
139	ï	177	▒	215	╫	253	²
140	î	178	▓	216	╪	254	■
141	ì	179	│	217	┘	255	(blank 'FF')
142	Ä	180	┤	218	┌		
143	Å	181	╡	219	█		
144	É	182	╢	220	▄		
145	æ	183	╖	221	▌		
146	Æ	184	╕	222	▐		
147	ô	185	╣	223	▀		
148	ö	186	║	224	α		
149	ò	187	╗	225	β		
150	û	188	╝	226	Γ		
151	ù	189	╜	227	π		
152	ÿ	190	╛	228	Σ		
153	Ö	191	┐	229	σ		
154	Ü	192	└	230	µ		
155	¢	193	┴	231	τ		
156	£	194	┬	232	Φ		
157	¥	195	├	233	Θ		
158	Pts	196	─	234	Ω		
159	ƒ	197	┼	235	δ		
160	á	198	╞	236	∞		
161	í	199	╟	237	Ø		
162	ó	200	╚	238	ε		
163	ú	201	╔	239	∩		
164	ñ	202	╩	240	≡		
165	Ñ	203	╦	241	±		

Figure 14-3.
IBM graphics and special characters.

We may use the graphics characters to build up various images on the screen, as the next example shows.

Example 2. Write a program that draws a horizontal line across row 10 of the screen. (Assume that you have a 80-column screen.)

Solution. Just in case the screen contains some unrelated characters, begin by clearing the screen using the CLS instruction. Then print character 196 (a horizontal line) across row 10 of the screen. Here is the program:

```
10 ' **********************************
20 ' This program prints a horizontal
30 '    line across row 10 of the screen
40 ' **********************************
50 CLS
60 FOR J=1 TO 80
70 LOCATE 10,J
80    PRINT CHR$(196);
90 NEXT J
100 END
```

Note that the semicolon in the PRINT statement causes the characters to be printed in consecutive positions. Lines 30–60 may be abbreviated using the STRING$ function. The function value STRING$(80,196) equals a string consisting of 80 copies of character 196. So lines 30–60 can be written more simply as

```
30 PRINT STRING$(80,196);
```

Example 3. Write a program that draws a vertical line in column 25 from row 5 to row 15. The program should blink the line 50 times.

Solution. The blinking effect may be achieved by repeatedly clearing the screen. Here is our program:

```
10 ' **********************************
20 ' This program draws a vertical line
30 ' in column 25 from row 5 to row 15,
40 ' blinking 50 times before stopping
50 ' **********************************
100 CLS
110 FOR K=1 TO 50:'K CONTROLS BLINKING
```

```
120    FOR J=5 TO 15
130       LOCATE J,25
140       PRINT CHR$(179);
150    NEXT J
160    CLS
170 NEXT K
180 END
```

Test Your Understanding 3 (Answer on Page 378)

Write a program to draw a vertical line from row 2 to row 20 in column 8.

Example 4.   Draw a pair of x- and y-axes as shown in Figure 14-4. Label the vertical axis with the word Profit and the horizontal axis with the word Month. (Assume that you have a 40-column screen.)

Figure 14-4 *X*-axis = Month and *Y*-axis = Profit.

Solution.   The program must draw two lines and print two words. The only real problem is to determine the positioning. The word Profit has six letters. Let's start the vertical line in the position corresponding to the seventh character column. We'll run the vertical line from the top of the screen (row 1) to within two character rows from the bottom. On the next-to-last row, we will place the word month. The layout of the screen is shown in Figure 14-5. Here is our program to generate the display:

```
10 ' *********************************
20 ' This program draws a pair of axes
30 ' labeled "Profit" and "Month"
40 ' *********************************
100   CLS
110 'Print Labels
120   LOCATE 1,1
130   PRINT  "Profit"
140   LOCATE 23,75
150   PRINT  "Month"
160 'Print the vertical axis
170   FOR J=1 TO 22
180     LOCATE J,7: PRINT CHR$(179);
190   NEXT J
200 'Print the corner
210   LOCATE 22,7: PRINT CHR$(192);
220 'Print the horizontal axis
230   FOR J=8  TO 80
240     LOCATE 22,J: PRINT CHR$(196);
250   NEXT J
260   GOTO 260     :'Pause until user hits Ctrl-BREAK
270   END
```

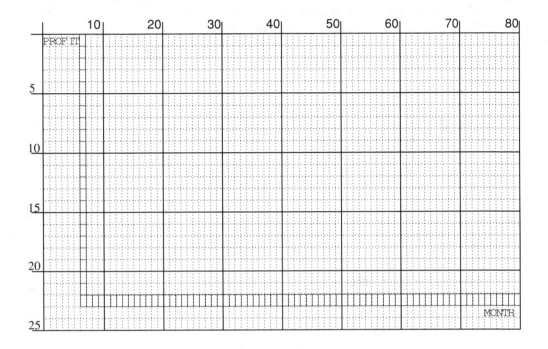

Figure 14-5. **Display layout for chart of Figure 14-4.**

Exercises

Draw the following straight lines. (Assume an 80-column screen width.)

1. A horizontal line completely across the screen in row 18.

2. A vertical line completely up and down the screen in column 17.

3. A pair of straight lines that divide the screen into four equal squares.

4. Horizontal and vertical lines that convert the screen into a tic-tac-toe board.

5. A vertical line of double thickness from rows 1 to 24 in column 30.

6. A diagonal line going through the character positions (1,1),(2,2),..., (24,24).

7. A horizontal line with "tick marks" as follows:

(Hint: Look for a graphics character that will form the tick marks.)

8. A vertical line with tick marks as follows:

9. Display your name in a box formed with asterisks:

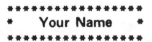

10. Display a number axis as follows:

11. Write a program to display a graphics character that you specify in an INPUT statement.

12. Create a display of the following form:

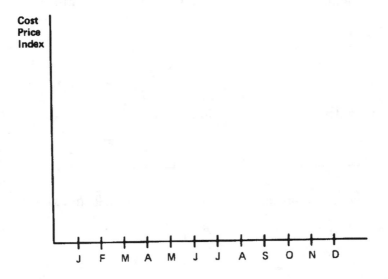

Answers to Test Your Understandings 1, 2, and 3

1.
```
10 LOCATE 18,22
20 PRINT CHR$(179)
```

2.
```
10 FOR J=128 TO 255
20  PRINT CHR$(J); " "; :'One space between characters
30 NEXT J
40 END
```

3.
```
10 CLS
20 FOR J=2 TO 20
30   LOCATE J,8: PRINT CHR$(179);
40 NEXT J
50 END
```

Colors and Graphics Modes

There are ten screen modes in GWBASIC, accessed by the SCREEN statement. Just which of these modes you may use will depend on which video adapter you have. The video adapters that are available are the following: monochrome display adapter (MDA), color graphics adapter (CGA), enhanced color graphics adapter (EGA), video graphics array (VGA), and multicolor graphics array (MCGA).

Screen modes are divided into **text modes** and **graphics modes**. In a text mode, you can control the screen only at the level of individual characters. In a graphics mode, you can control individual dots on the screen. Both text and graphics modes can differ in the number of colors provided.

The screen modes are numbered: 0, 1, 2, and 7–13. Screen 0 is text mode and is available with all graphics adapters. Screens 1 and 2 require a graphics adapter (a video adapter other than the MDA). Screens 7–13 require either an EGA, VGA, or MCGA adapter.

All screen modes work similarly. The difference among the various graphics modes is in the resolution of the screen and the number of simultaneous colors. For purposes of exposition, we will restrict ourselves to the graphics screen modes available with all graphics adapters, namely screens 1–2.

Medium-Resolution Graphics.   In this mode, the screen is divided into 200 rows of 320 rectangles each. You may display four colors.

High-Resolution Graphics.   In this mode, the screen is divided into 200 rows of 640 rectangles each. You may display two colors, namely black and white.

You may select between the various display modes by using the SCREEN command. This command has the form

```
SCREEN <mode>
```

For example, to choose high-resolution, 2-color mode, give the command

```
SCREEN  2
```

You may use the SCREEN command to switch from one display mode to another, either within a program or by using a keyboard command. Note, however, that the SCREEN command automatically clears the screen. When BASIC is started, the display is automatically in text mode (SCREEN 0).

Pixels

Each of the small screen rectangles (more properly, dots) is called a pixel (i.e., a "picture element"). You may color each pixel on an individual basis.

Graphics Coordinates. Each pixel is specified by a pair of coordinates (x,y), where x is the column number and y is the row number. (See Figure 14-6.) Note the following important facts:

1. Rows and columns are numbered beginning with 0 (not 1 as in text mode). In the medium-resolution graphics mode, the rows are numbered from 0 to 199 and the columns from 0 to 319. In high-resolution graphics mode, the rows are numbered from 0 to 199 and the columns from 0 to 639.

2. Coordinates in graphics mode are specified with the column (x-coordinate) first. This is the opposite of the coordinates in text mode. (For example, the LOCATE statement requires the row to precede the column.)

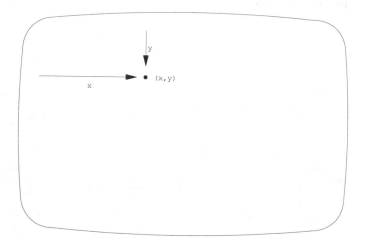

Figure 14-6.
Coordinates in graphics mode.

Relative Coordinates in Graphics Mode

In graphics mode, the cursor is not visible. Instead, the computer keeps track of the last point referenced. This is the point whose coordinates were most recently used in a graphics statement. You may specify the position of new points by giving coordinates relative to the last point referenced. Such coordinates are called **relative coordinates**. Relative coordinates always are preceded by the word STEP. For example, suppose that the last point referenced is (100,75), and that a point is specified by relative coordinates

```
STEP (20,30)
```

This is the point that is 20 units to the right and 30 units up from the last referenced point. See (Figure 14-7.) This is the point with coordinates (120,105).

Similarly, consider the point specified by the relative coordinates:

```
STEP (-10,-40)
```

This is the point that is 10 units to the left and 40 units down from the point (120,105); that is, the point (90,35). (See Figure 14-7.)

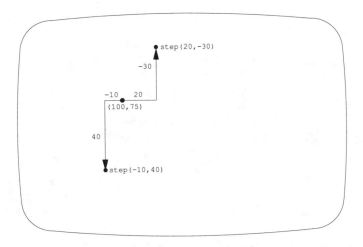

Figure 14-7.
Relative graph-ics coordinates.

Test Your Understanding 1 (Answers on Page 385)

Suppose that the last referenced point is (50,80). Determine the coordinates of the following points.

a.   **STEP (50,50)**

b.   **STEP (-20,10)**

c.   **STEP (10,-40)**

d.   **STEP (-20,-50)**

Colors

To use color in your display, you must first enable color with the SCREEN statement

```
SCREEN 1,0 (means medium-resolution graphics, color ON)
```

You may disable color with the statement

```
SCREEN 1,1 (means medium-resolution graphics, color OFF)
```

Once color has been enabled, you may choose both background and foreground colors. A pixel is considered part of the **background** (at a particular moment) unless its color has been explicitly set by a graphics statement. When you execute CLS, all pixels are set equal to the background color. A nonbackground pixel is said to belong to the **foreground.**

Here are the possible screen colors, numbered 0–15.

```
0 - black          8 - gray
1 - blue           9 - light blue
2 - green         10- light green
3 - cyan          11- light cyan
4 - red           12- light red
5 - magenta       13- light magenta
6 - brown         14- yellow
7 - white         15- high-intensity white
```

Foreground colors may be selected from a palette of four colors. There are two palettes to choose from, palette 0 and palette 1. At any given moment, one of two palettes is in effect. The colors in these two palettes are:

Palette 0	Palette 1
0 - background	0 - background
1 - green	1 - cyan
2 - red	2 - magenta
3 - brown	3 - white

Note that in the case of an EGA, VGA, or MCGA adapter, these palettes may be redefined by assigning different colors to each of the numbers.

Choosing Colors

Background and foreground colors are set using the COLOR statement like this:

```
10 COLOR 12,0
```

This statement sets the background color as light red (color 12) and the palette of the foreground color as 0. These choices remain in effect until they are changed with another COLOR statement.

Test Your Understanding 2 (Answer on Page 385)

Write BASIC statements that select the medium-resolution graphics, set the background color to high-intensity white, and the foreground palette to 1.

Illuminating Pixels. The PSET statement is used to illuminate a pixel. For example, the statement

```
10 PSET (100,150),1
```

will illuminate the pixel at (100,150) in color 1 of the currently chosen palette. Similarly, to turn off this pixel use the statement

```
20 PRESET (100,150)
```

Actually, this last instruction turns on pixel (100,150) in the background color. This is equivalent to turning it off. In using the PSET and PRESET statements, you may specify the pixel in relative form. For example, the statement

```
30 PSET STEP (100,-150), 2
```

turns on the pixel that is 100 blocks to the right and 150 blocks up from the current cursor position, using color 2.

Exercises

Write BASIC instructions to do the following.

1. Select the background color magenta and the foreground color as color 5.

2. Select the background color light red and the foreground color as color 7.

3. Turn on pixel (200,80) with color 1 of the current palette.

4. Turn on pixel (100,100) in red with background color cyan.

5. Set the pixel that is 200 blocks to the left and 100 blocks above the last referenced point. Use color 3.

6. Turn on the pixel that is 100 units to the right of the last referenced point.

7. Set the current palette so that the colors are exactly reversed. That is, assign color 0 to color 15, color 1 to color 14, and so forth.

Answers to Test Your Understandings 1 and 2

1.   a. (100,130) b. (30,90) c. (60,40) d. (30,30)

2.   ```
     10 SCREEN 1
     20 COLOR 15,1
     ```

Lines, Rectangles, and Circles

Straight Lines

You may use the PSET and PRESET statements to design color graphics displays. However, BASIC has a rich repertoire of instructions that greatly
     ```

simplify the task. Consider the task of drawing straight lines. This may be accomplished using the LINE statement. For example, to draw a line connecting the pixels (20,50) and (80,199), use the statement

```
10  LINE (20,50)-(80,199)
```

Example 1.   Draw a triangle in medium-resolution mode with corners at the three points (150,20), (50,100), and (250,130). (See Figure 14-8.)

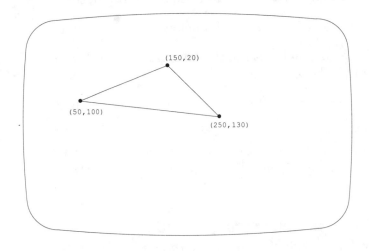

Figure 14-8.
A triangle.

Solution. We must draw three lines: from (150,20) to (50,100); from (50,100) to (250,130); and from (250,130) to (150,20). Here is the program:

```
10 SCREEN 2
20 LINE (150,20)-(50,100)
30 LINE (50,100)-(250,130)
40 LINE (250,130)-(150,20)
50 END
```

Drawing Lines Using Relative Coordinates

To draw a line from the last referenced point to (100,90), use the statement

```
10 LINE -(100,90)
```

To draw a line from the last referenced point to the point 80 units to the right and 100 units above, use the statement

```
20 LINE -STEP(80,-100)
```

Example 2.   Let's reconsider the triangle of Example 1. The point (150,80) is inside the triangle. Draw lines connecting this point to each of the corners of the triangle (see Figure 14-9).

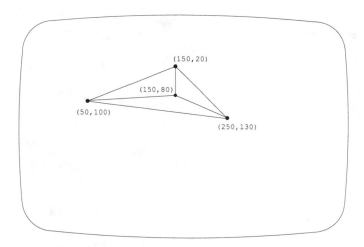

Figure 14-9.
More triangles.

Solution.   The point (150,80) needs to go with three line statements. We use the shorthand form to draw lines from this point to the three corners of the triangle. To make (150,80) the last referenced point, we first PSET it.

```
10 SCREEN 2
20 LINE (150,20)-(50,100)
30 LINE -(250,130)
30 LINE -(150,20)
40 PSET (150,80)
50 LINE -(150,20)
60 PSET (150,80)
70 LINE -(50,100)
80 PSET (150,80)
90 LINE -(250,130)
100 END
```

Using Colors With LINE

You also may specify the color of a line. For example, if you wish to draw the line in statement 10 in color 1 of the current palette, use the statement

```
10 LINE (20,50)-(80,199),1
```

This line is drawn in Figure 14-10.

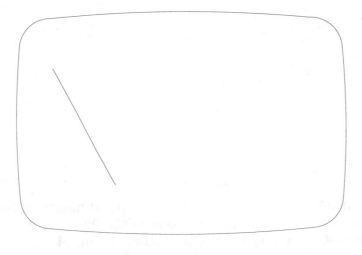

Figure 14-10.
Specifiying the color of a line.

Note that there are lines the computer cannot draw perfectly. Lines on a diagonal are displayed as a series of visible "steps." This is as close as the computer can get to a straight line within the limited resolution provided by the graphics modes. The higher the resolution (that is, the more pixels on the screen), the better your straight lines will look.

Test Your Understanding 1 (Answers on Page 400)

    a. Draw a line connecting (0,100) to (50,75) in color 2.

    b. Draw the triangle with vertices (0,0), (50,50), and (100,30).

Rectangles

The LINE statement has several very sophisticated variations. To draw a rectangle you need to specify a pair of opposite corners in a LINE statement and add the code B (for Box) at the end of the statement. For example, to draw a rectangle, two of whose corners are at (50,100) and (90,175), use the statement

```
10 LINE (50,100)-(90,175),1,B
```

This statement draws the desired rectangle with the sides in color 1 of the current palette (see Figure 14-11a). The inside of the rectangle will be in the background color. You may paint the inside of the rectangle in the same color as the sides by changing the B to BF (B=Box, BF=Box Filled). (See Figure 14-11b.) These instructions greatly simplify drawing complex line displays.

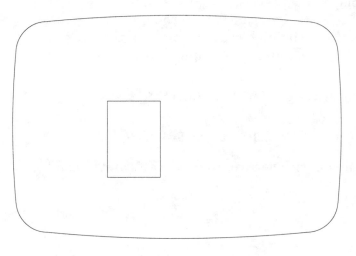

Figure 14-11a.
The B option.

Figure 14-11b.
The BF option.

Test Your Understanding 2 (Answers on Page 400)

a. Draw a rectangle with corners at (10,10), (10,100), (50,100), (50,10).

b. Draw the rectangle of a. and color it and its interior with color 2.

Mixing Text and Graphics

You may include text with your graphics. Use either PRINT or PRINT USING exactly as if you were in text mode. You may use LOCATE to position the cursor at a particular (text) line and column. However, note the following:

1. In medium-resolution graphics mode, you may use only a 40-character line width. This corresponds to the "large" characters. In high-resolution graphics, you may use only an 80-character line width. This corresponds to "small" characters.
2. Text will print in color 3 of the current palette.

In planning text displays to go with your graphics, note that all letters (regardless of line width) are 8 pixels wide and 8 pixels high. For example, the character at the top left corner of the screen occupies pixels (x,y), where x and y both range between 0 and 7.

Example 3.   Write a command to erase text line 1 of the screen in medium-resolution mode.

Solution.   Our scheme for erasing a line is to draw a rectangle over the line, with color equal to the background color (color 0). The first text line of the screen occupies pixel (x,y), where x ranges from 0 to 319 (x equals the column number) and y ranges from 0 to 7 (y equals the row number). Here is the desired statement:

```
10 LINE (0,0)-(319,7),0,BF
```

Circles

GWBASIC has the facility for drawing circles and circular arcs. To draw a circle you must specify the center and the radius, and, optionally, the color. For example, here is the command to draw a circle at center (100,100) and radius 50:

```
10 CIRCLE (100,100),50
```

Since no color has been specified, the circle will be drawn in color 3 (see Figure 14-12).

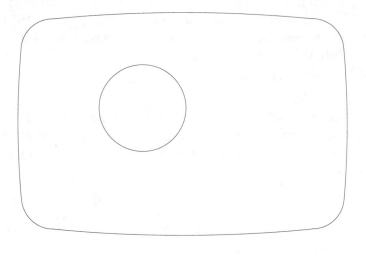

Figure 14-12.
Circle drawn with no color specified.

To draw the same circle in color 1, we use the statement

```
10 CIRCLE (100,100),50,1
```

Note that the circles on the screen are not smooth, but have a "ragged" appearance. This is due to the limited resolution of the screen. If you use high-resolution mode, you will notice that the appearance of your circles improves greatly.

Circular arcs are somewhat more complicated to draw since their description is based on the radian system of angle measurement. Let's take a few moments to describe radian measurement.

Recall the number pi from high school geometry. Pi is a number, denoted by the Greek letter π, that is approximately equal to 3.1415926... (the decimal expansion goes on forever). Ordinarily, angles are measured in degrees, with 360 degrees equaling one complete revolution. In radian measurement, there are 2*pi radians in a revolution. That is:

```
2*pi radians=360 degrees

1 radian=360/(2*pi) degrees
```

If you use the value of pi and carry out the arithmetic, you find that 1 radian is approximately 57 degrees. When describing angles to the computer you must always use radians.

To draw a circular arc, you use the following variation of the CIRCLE statement:

```
10 CIRCLE (xcenter,ycenter),radius,color,
        startangle, endangle
```

where startangle and endangle are measured in radians. For example, to draw a circular arc for the above circle, corresponding to an angle of 1.4 radians and beginning at angle .1 radians, use the command

```
10 CIRCLE (100,100),50,1,.1,1.5
```

The resulting arc is pictured in Figure 14-13.

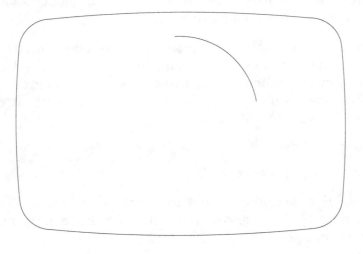

Figure 14-13.
**Arc of a circle,
corresponding
to 1.4 radians,
beginning at
angle 0.1.**

Note that Figure 14-13 does not include the sides of the sector. To include a side on a circular arc put a minus sign on the corresponding angle. (We can't use -0, however (see below). For example, to include both sides in Figure 10.13, use the statement

```
10 CIRCLE (100,100),50,1,-.1,-1.5
```

The resulting arc will look like the one in Figure 14-14.

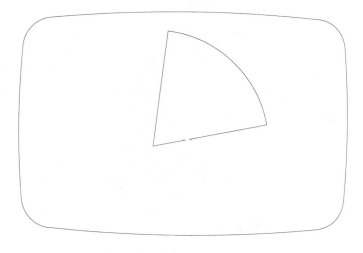

Figure 10-14.
**Sector of a
circle, corre-
sponding to
angle 1.4,
beginning at
angle 0.1.**

Test Your Understanding 3 (Answers on Page 400)

a. Draw a circular arc with radius 60, center (125,75), and going from a starting angle of .25 radians to an ending angle of .75 radians.

b. Draw the same circular arc as in a., but with sides included.

If you have an angle 0 and wish to include a side, just note that the angle 0 and the angle 2*pi are the same. Just replace 0 by 2*pi = 6.28... , and put a minus sign on this new angle!

Aspect Ratio. The CIRCLE statement has an added complication we haven't yet mentioned, namely the aspect ratio. Usually, when you plot circles on graph paper you use the same scale on the x-axis as on the y-axis. For example, if a unit on the x-axis is larger than a unit on the y-axis, your circle will appear as an ellipse stretched out in the x-direction. Similarly, if the unit on the y-axis is larger than the unit on the x-axis, the circle will appear as an ellipse stretched out in the y-direction. So, like it or not, the geometry of circles is intimately bound up with that of ellipses. For this reason, the CIRCLE statement may also be used to draw ellipses.

Consider the following example in high-resolution graphics mode:

```
10 CIRCLE (300,100),100,,,,.5
```

This statement plots an ellipse with center (300,100). (See Figure 14-15.) The extra commas are placeholders for the unspecified color, beginning angle, and ending angle. The x-radius is 100. The number .5 is called the aspect ratio. It tells us that the y-radius is .5 times the x-radius, or 50.

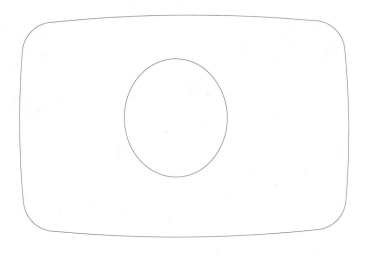

Figure 14-15.
The ellipse
CIRCLE (300, 100),100,,,,.5.

Similarly, consider the statement

```
10 CIRCLE (300,100),100,,,,1.5
```

Here the aspect ratio is 1.5, which is larger than 1. In this case, BASIC assumes that the radius 100 is the y-radius. The x-radius is 1.5 times the y-radius, or 45. The corresponding ellipse is shown in Figure 14-16.

What is the aspect ratio for a circle? Well, that's a tricky question. On first glimpse, you probably guessed that the aspect ratio is 1. And indeed it is if you are looking for a mathematical circle. However, if you draw a circle with an aspect ratio of 1, you will get an ellipse because the scales on the x- and y-axes are different. Let's consider high-resolution graphics mode: The

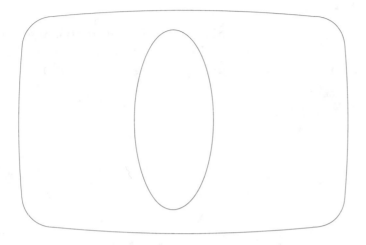

Figure 14-16.
The ellipse
CIRCLE (300,
100),100,,,,1.5.

screen is 640×200 pixels, the ratio of width to height is 200/640, or 5/16. To achieve a circle, you would expect to have to multiply the x-radius by 5/16 to get the proper y-radius; that is, an aspect ratio of 5/16. Well, not quite! TV screens are not square because the ratio of width to height is 4/3. In order to achieve an ellipse that is visually a circle, we must multiply by 5/16 and by 4/3. In other words, the aspect ratio is

```
(5/16) * (4/3) = 5/12
```

Strange, but true. In medium-resolution mode, the aspect ratio giving a visual circle is 5/6. If you use the CIRCLE statement without any aspect ratio, BASIC assumes an aspect ratio of 5/6 in medium-resolution mode and 5/12 in high-resolution mode. With these aspect ratios, circles look like circles. However, the y-radius is quite different from the x-radius!

You can get even finer grained control over circles and ellipses if you apply some mathematics. Suppose that an ellipse (or circle) has its center at the point with coordinates (x0,y0). Suppose that the horizontal half-axis has length A and the vertical half-axis has length B. Then a typical point (x,y) on the ellipse takes the form

```
x = x0 + A*cos(t)

y = y0 + B*sin(t)
```

where t is an angle between 0 and 2*pi radians. The geometric meaning of the angle t is shown in Figure 14-17. The above equations are called the **parametric equations for the ellipse**. They are very useful in drawing graphics.

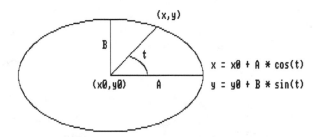

Figure 14-17.
An ellipse in parametic form.

For example, here is a program that draws an ellipse with center (320,100) (the center of the screen in high-resolution mode) by plotting dots in a "sweep" fashion (see Figure 14-18). This graph may be used to simulate the motion of a planet around the sun.

```
1 '*****************************************
2 ' This program depicts the orbit of a
3 ' planet as it travels about the sun
4 ' in an elliptical path.
5 '*****************************************
10 SCREEN 2:CLS:KEY OFF
20 FOR T=0 TO 6.28 STEP .05
30   X=320+200*COS(T):Y=100+30*SIN(T)
```

```
40    PSET (X,Y)
50    FOR K=1 TO 25:NEXT K
70 NEXT T
```

Note that line 50 provides a delay between plotting of consecutive dots.

Figure 14-18.
**Simulating a
planetary orbit.**

Exercises

Write BASIC instructions to draw the following:

1. A line connecting (20,50) and (40,100).

2. A line in color 2 connecting the current cursor position and the point (250,150).

3. A line in color 1 connecting (125,50) to a block 100 blocks to the right and 75 units down from it.

4. A rectangle with corners at (10,20), (200,20), (200,150), and (10,150).

5. The rectangle of Exercise 4 with its sides and interior in color 3.

6. A circle with radius 20 and center (30,50).

7. A circular arc of the circle of Exercise 6 with a starting angle 1.5 and ending angle 3.1.

8. The circular arc of Exercise 7 with sides.

9. Write a program to simulate the movement of a sweep second hand around the face of a clock.

Answers to Test Your Understandings 1, 2, and 3

1.   a. `10 LINE (0,100)-(50,75),2`

    b. `10 LINE (0,0)-(50,50)`
       `20 LINE (50,50)-(100,30)`
       `30 LINE (100,30)-(0,0)`

2.   a. `10 LINE (10,10)-(50,100),,B`
    b. `10 LINE (10,10)-(50,100),2,BF`

3.   a. `10 CIRCLE (125,75),60,,.25,.75`
    b. `10 CIRCLE (125,75),60,,-.25,-.75`

Computer Art

The graphics statements of IBM PC BASIC may be used to draw interesting computer art on the screen. As a taste of what can be done, the program below draws random polygons on the screen. The program is written in high-resolution graphics mode, so that the screen has dimensions 640×200. The program first chooses the number N% of sides of the polygon. The polygon may have up to six sides. Next, the program picks out N%+1 random points (it takes N%+1 points to draw a polygon of N sides). The points are stored in the arrays X%(J%) and Y%(J%), where J% = 0, 1, 2, ..., N%. To generate only closed polygons, we define the point (X%(N%+1),Y%(N%+1)) to be the initial point (X%(0), Y%(0)). The program then draws lines between consecutive points. Figure 14-19 shows a typical polygon.

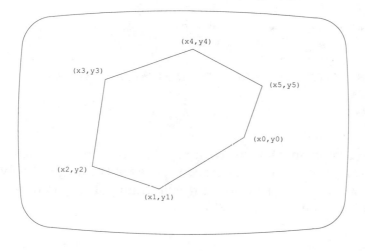

Figure 14-19.
A typical polygon.

The program then erases the polygon and repeats the entire procedure to draw a different polygon. The program draws 50 polygons.

```
10 '*******************************************
11 ' This program draws a number of randomly
12 ' shaped polygons. After each polygon is
13 ' drawn, it is erased, giving a flickering
14 ' effect.
15 ' *******************************************
20 SCREEN 2:CLS:KEY OFF
30 RANDOMIZE VAL(RIGHT$(TIME$,2))
40 FOR M%=1 TO 50
50   C%=1:GOSUB 90'Draw random polygon
60   C%=0:GOSUB 190      'Erase polygon
70 NEXT M%
80 END
90 'Draw random polygon
100 'Determine number of sides
110 N%=INT(5*RND(1) + 1)    'N=# sides <= 6
120 'Compute coordinates of certices
130 FOR J%=0 TO N%
```

```
140    X%(J%)=INT(640*RND(1))
150    Y%(J%)=INT(200*RND(1))
160 NEXT J%
170 X%(N%+1)=X%(0):Y%(N%+1)=Y%(0)
180 'Draw sides
190 FOR J%=1 TO N%+1
200    LINE (X%(J%-1),Y%(J%-1))-(X%(J%),Y%(J%)),C%
210 NEXT J%
220 RETURN
```

Here is a second program that draws a regular polygon (one with equal sides and angles) and then draws inscribed replicas of the original polygon, each of smaller size, until the interior of the original polygon is filled with the inscribed replicas (see Figure 14-20).

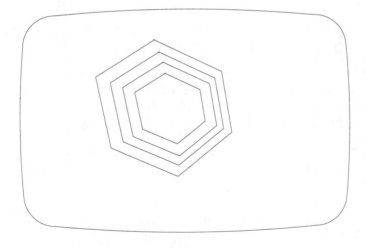

Figure 14-20.
Inscribed polygons.

Here are the mathematics necessary to draw a regular polygon. Suppose that you wish to draw a regular polygon having N sides and inscribed in a circle of radius R and centered at the point (X0,Y0). (See Figure 14-21.) The vertices are then the points (X(J),Y(J)) (J=0,1,2,...,N), where

$$X(J) = X0 + R*COS(2*PI*J/N)$$

$$Y(J) = Y0 + R*(5/12)*SIN(2*PI*J/N)$$

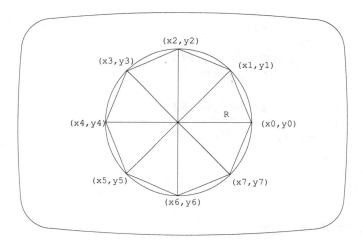

Figure 14-21.
An inscribed polygon.

The factor 5/12 corrects for the aspect ratio, so that the circle in which the polygon is inscribed will appear visually as a circle. The user chooses the value of N (up to 20) for our program. The center of the polygon is the center of the screen (320,100) in high-resolution. Use an initial value of 100 for the radius R, then draw polygons corresponding to the same value of N, but with successively smaller values of R. Shrinking the radius circle in which the polygon is inscribed gives the illusion that the polygon is growing inward. Here is the program:

```
10 '****************************************
20 ' This program draws a sequence of
30 ' inscribed polygons which grow in-
40 ' ward.
50 '****************************************
100 DIM X%(21),Y%(21)
110 INPUT "NUMBER OF SIDES";N%
120 IF N%>20 THEN 110
```

```
130 SCREEN 2:CLS:KEY OFF
140 PI=3.14159
150 FOR R%=100 TO 0 STEP -4
160   GOSUB 190
170 NEXT R%
180 END
185 'Calculate vertices
190   FOR J%=0 TO N%
200   X%(J%)=320+R%*COS(2*PI*J%/N%)
210   Y%(J%)=100+R%*(5/12)*SIN(2*PI*J%/N%)
220   NEXT J%
230   X%(N%+1)=X%(0):Y%(N%+1)=Y%(0)
235 'Draw polygon
240   FOR J%=0 TO N%
250     LINE (X%(J%),Y%(J%))-(X%(J%+1),Y%(J%+1))
260   NEXT J%
270 RETURN
```

Drawing Bar charts

In this section, we'll apply what we have just learned about drawing lines and rectangles to draw the bar chart shown in Figure 14-22.

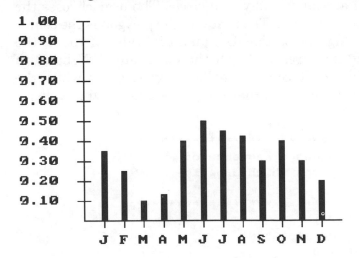

Figure 14-22.
A bar chart.

In setting up any graphics display, some planning is necessary to make the display look "pretty." The main goal in this section is to illustrate the planning procedure.

This display is not too complicated, so let's stick to medium-resolution graphics.

Note that there are ten bars to be displayed. Also, we must put a tick mark under each bar and a letter lined up and centered under the tick mark. Each letter is eight pixels wide, so we can approximate the centering of the letters on the tick marks by placing the tick marks in one of the columns 4, 12, 20, 28,.... (The corresponding letters occupy columns 0–7, 8–15, 16–23, 24–31,....)

Similarly, to center the labels on the vertical axis on the tick marks there, choose the rows for the tick marks from among 4, 12, 20,....

Let's place the vertical axis beginning in row four. This allows us to place the top tick mark in the proper row. There are at most 195 screen rows in which to place the rest of the vertical axis. We must divide the vertical axis into ten equal parts. This suggests that each vertical part is 16 rows high. This causes the vertical axis to be 160 rows high and ends in row 164. We need to leave room for four characters (=32 columns) to the right of the vertical axis as well as the tick marks, and let's not push the labels too far to the left. Finally, the vertical axis must be in one of the columns 4, 12, 20, 28,.... One possibility is to put the vertical axis in column 52. It turns out that this gives a reasonable-looking display.

The horizontal axis begins at the point (52,164). The horizontal axis is divided into 13 equal parts. Let's make each part two characters (=32 columns) wide. This means that the right endpoint of the horizontal axis is $(52+13^*16,164)$.

Here is the section of the program to draw the two axes:

```
100 'Draw axes
110 LINE (52,164)-(52+16*13,164)
120 LINE (52,164)-(52,4)
```

Next, let's draw the tick marks and print the labels. For the vertical axis, we use a PRINT USING statement to format the labels to contain one digit to the right of the decimal point. For the horizontal axis we read the labels into a string array A$(). That is, A$(1)="J", A$(2)="F",.... To print the labels on the horizontal axis we then print the various string array entries. Here is the program segment that draws the tick marks and labels the axes:

```
200 'Draw tick marks
210 FOR J=1 TO 10
220    LINE (47,164-16*J)-(57,164-16*J)
221    LOCATE 21-2*J,1
222    PRINT USING "#.##";J/10;
230 NEXT J
240 FOR J=1 TO 12
250    LINE (52+16*J,164)-(52+16*J,169)
260    LOCATE 23,(52+16*J)/8
270    PRINT A$(J);
280 NEXT J
```

Note the positioning of the labels. The labels on the vertical axis are in rows 1, 3, 5, 7,..., 19. However, the first label is in row 19, the tenth in row one. To achieve the correct positioning we locate the cursor in row 21-2*J. When J is 1, the label is put in row 21-2*1 = 19, and when J is 10, the label is put in row 21-2*10=1. (The labels start from row 21 and back up two rows at a time.)

Similarly, the position of the Jth horizontal label is gotten by dividing the column position, namely 52+16*J by 8 (since a character occupies eight columns). Note that this division always leaves a remainder of four. The LOCATE statement drops any fractional part, so the character is positioned at the character position, which starts just to the right of the tick mark. This is how the positioning was set up.

Now we have drawn everything but the bars. We store the height of the Jth bar in the variable BAR(J). The scale on the vertical axis is from 0 to 1 and the axis is 160 rows high. The height of the Jth bar is BAR(J)*160. The

Jth bar runs from row 164 to row 164-BAR(J)*160. Let's make the bar extend for five columns, two on either side of the tick mark. This means that the Jth bar starts in column

```
52+16*J - 2 = 50+16*J
```

Similarly, the Jth bar ends in column

```
52+16*J + 2 = 54+16*J
```

Here are the instructions to draw the bars:

```
300 'Draw bars
310 FOR J=1 TO 12
320    LINE (50+16*J,164)-(54+16*J,164-BAR(J)*160),,BF
330 NEXT J
```

Finally, we assemble the various pieces into a single program.

```
1 '***********************************
2 'This program draws a bar chart corres-
3 'ponding to fixed data.
4 '***********************************
10 DIM A$(12),BAR(12)
20 CLS:SCREEN 1
30 KEY OFF
40 FOR J=1 TO 12
50    READ A$(J)
60 NEXT J
70 FOR J=1 TO 12
80    READ BAR(J)
90 NEXT J
100 'Draw axes
110 LINE (52,164)-(52+16*13,164)
120 LINE (52,164)-(52,4)
200 'Draw tick marks
210 FOR J=1 TO 10
220    LINE (47,164-16*J)-(57,164-16*J)
221    LOCATE 21-2*J,1
222    PRINT USING "#.##";J/10;
```

```
230 NEXT J
240 FOR J=1 TO 12
250    LINE (52+16*J,164)-(52+16*J,169)
260    LOCATE 23,(52+16*J)/8
270    PRINT A$(J);
280 NEXT J
300 'Draw bars
310 FOR J=1 TO 12
320    LINE (50+16*J,164)-(54+16*J,164-BAR(J)*160),,BF
330 NEXT J
1000 DATA J,F,M,A,M,J,J,A,S,O,N,D
1010 DATA .35,.25,.10,.13,.40,.50,.45,.425,.30,.40,.30,.20
2000 GOTO 2000
```

Drawing Pie Charts

As an application of the CIRCLE command, let's draw the pie chart shown in Figure 14-23.

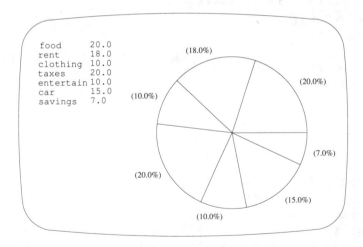

Figure 14-23.
A pie chart.

To draw this pie chart, let's begin by creating an array to contain the various data, and to list the data as shown on the left. We put the category names (Food, Clothing, and so forth) in an array B$( ). The numerical quantities are put in an array A( ). The first part of our program then consists of reading the data from DATA statements and setting up the two arrays. Also, we perform screen initialization by choosing SCREEN 2 (high-resolution graphics mode), and turning the function key display off. Here is the section of the program that accomplishes all these tasks:

```
100 'Program intialization
110   DIM A(7), B$(7),ANGLE(7)
120   DATA food, .20, rent, .18, clothing, .10, taxes, .20,
      entertainment
130   DATA .10, car, .15, savings, .07
140   FOR J=1 TO 7
150      READ B$(J), A(J)
160   NEXT J
170   SCREEN 2:            'high resolution
180   KEY OFF:             'turn off function keys
```

Our next step is to create the left portion of the display. This requires some care and planning. Let's skip the top four lines and begin the display on the fifth line. We set up the numbers in our DATA statements as decimals rather than percentages since the computation of angles that follows is more conveniently carried out in terms of decimals. However, to display percentages we multiply each number A(J) by 100. To get a formatted display we use the PRINT USING statement. Let's put the category description in print zone 1 and the percentage in print zone 2. Here are the instructions corresponding to this section of the program. Pay particular attention to the PRINT statements in lines 240 and 250.

```
200 'Display listed data
210   CLS
220   PRINT:PRINT:PRINT:PRINT
230   FOR J=1 TO 7
240      PRINT B$(J),:      'print and move to 2nd print
```

```
            field
250         PRINT USING "##.#"; 100*A(J)
260    NEXT J
```

Finally, we come to the section of the program in which we draw the pie. The Jth data item corresponds to the proportion A(J) of the total pie. In angular measure, this corresponds to A(J)*(2*PI) (recall that 2*PI radians corresponds to the entire pie). The first slice of the pie begins at angle ANGLE(0), which we set at 0; it ends at ANGLE(1)=A(1)*(2*PI). The second slice begins where the first slice ends; namely, at ANGLE(1). It ends at ANGLE(1)+A(2)*(2*PI), and so forth. Here is the section of the program that draws the various pie slices:

```
300 'Draw Pie
310   ANGLE(0)=0
320   PI=3.14159
330   FOR J=1 TO 7
340     T=A(J)*(2*PI):     't=angle for current data item
350     ANGLE(J)=ANGLE(J-1)+T
360     CIRCLE (450,100),100,,-ANGLE(J),-ANGLE(J-1)
370   NEXT J
```

Note that in line 360 we did not specify a color. Nevertheless, we left space for the color parameter by inserting an extra comma. (The space for the color is an imaginary one between the two commas.) If BASIC calls for a parameter in a certain place, you may usually omit the parameter as long as you leave a place for it. BASIC can't understand your statement if you don't.

You might wonder how we chose the center of the circle at (450,100), and the radius of 100. Well, it was mostly trial and error. We played around with various circle sizes and placements and chose one that looked good! In graphics work, do not be afraid to let your eye be your guide.

For convenience, we now assemble the entire program into one piece:

```
10 ' *************************************
20 ' This program draws a basic pie graph
30 '    for the data given in the program
40 ' *************************************
100 'Program intialization
110   DIM A(7), B$(7),ANGLE(7)
120   DATA food, .20, rent, .18, clothing, .10, taxes, .20,
      entertainment
130   DATA .10, car, .15, savings, .07
140   FOR J=1 TO 7
150     READ B$(J), A(J)
160   NEXT J
170   SCREEN 2:              'high resolution
180   KEY OFF:               'turn off function keys
200 'Display listed data
210   CLS
220   PRINT:PRINT:PRINT:PRINT
230   FOR J=1 TO 7
240     PRINT B$(J),:       'print and move to 2nd print
        field
250     PRINT USING "##.#"; 100*A(J)
260   NEXT J
300 'Draw Pie
310   ANGLE(0)=0
320   PI=3.14159
330   FOR J=1 TO 7
340     T=A(J)*(2*PI):     't=angle for current data item
350     ANGLE(J)=ANGLE(J-1)+T
360     CIRCLE (450,100),100,,-ANGLE(J),-ANGLE(J-1)
370   NEXT J
400 END
```

This program is subject to a number of enhancements, some of which will be suggested in the exercises.

Exercises

1. Alter the program above so that it accepts the data from the keyboard. Allow it to keep asking for data until it receives a data name "@". Allow for up to 20 data items.

2. Modify the above program so that the pie is drawn in color 2 of palette 1. (This will involve some respacing because you are now in medium-resolution and 40-character width.)

Painting Regions of the Screen

Using the graphics commands of BASIC, it is possible to draw a tremendous variety of shapes. For example, Figure 14-24 shows a triangle you may draw using several LINE statements. Figure 14-25 shows a circle drawn using the CIRCLE statement. Underneath each shape is a statement to draw the shape. The boundary lines of each shape are specified in the graphics statements used to draw it. The triangle is drawn in color 2. No color is indicated in the case of the circle, so it is drawn in color 3.

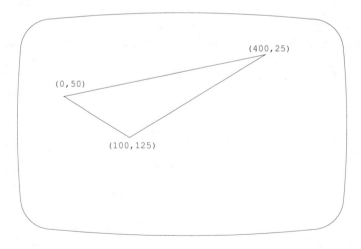

Figure 14-24.
A triangle.

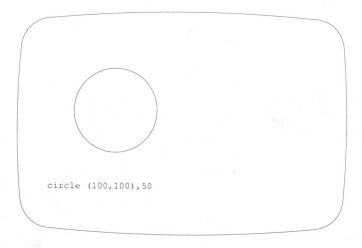

circle (100,100),50

Figure 14-25.
A circle.

The PAINT statement allows you to color the "inside" of a region, just as if the region were in a coloring book and you used a crayon to color it. For example, we may use the PAINT command to paint the interiors of the triangle of Figure 14-24 and the circle of Figure 14-25.

The format of the PAINT command is

```
PAINT (x,y),color,boundary
```

Here (x,y) is a point of the region to be painted, color is the color paint to use, and boundary is the color of the boundary. PAINT starts from the point (x,y) and begins to paint in all directions. Whenever it encounters the boundary color, it stops PAINTing in that direction.

For example, consider the triangle in Figure 14-26. The point (75,75) lies inside the triangle, and the triangle itself is drawn in color 2. Suppose that we wish to color the interior of the triangle in color 3. The appropriate PAINT statement is

```
10 PAINT (75,75),3,2
```

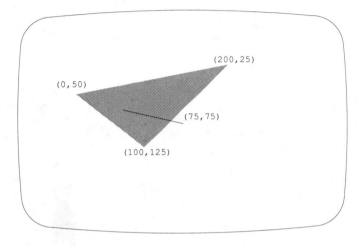

Figure 14-26.
PAINTing the interior of the triangle.

Test Your Understanding 1

Write a statement to color the interior of the circle of Figure 14-25 in color 1.

PAINT is a very straightforward statement to understand. The main difficulty, however, is in specifying a point within the region. Or, to put it more precisely, if we are given a region how do we specify a point within it? Well, that's a mathematical question. I just happen to be a mathematician so I can't resist explaining a little mathematics at this point!

Let's begin by considering the case of the rectangle (x1,y1)-(x2,y2). The center of the rectangle is at the point ((x1+x2)/2, (y1+y2)/2); that is, to obtain the coordinates of the center of the rectangle we average the values of the coordinates of the opposite corners. (see Figure 14-27).

Another way of getting the same answer is to average the values of the coordinates of all four corners: (x1,y1), (x1,y2), (x2,y2), (x2,y1). Now there are four x-coordinates to add up, but we must divide by four. We obtain (2*x1+2*x2)/4 = (x1+x2)/2 and do the same for the y-coordinate.

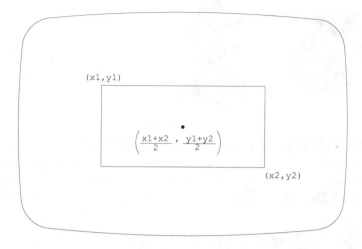

Figure 14-27.
The center of a rectangle.

Let's now consider a triangle with vertices (x1,y1), (x2,y2), and (x3,y3). Suppose that you average the coordinates to obtain

    ((x1+x2+x3)/3, (y1+y2+y3)/3)

This point is called the centroid of the triangle and is always inside the triangle.

Well, what works for 3- and 4-sided figures works in a more general setting. For many figures bounded by straight lines, you may compute a point within the figure simply by averaging the coordinates of the vertices. For which figures does this apply? The simplest such figures are the so-called convex bodies. We say that a figure is convex if, whenever you connect two points within the figure by a line, all points of the line are inside the figure (see Figure 14-28).

A convex figure bounded by line segments is a type of polygon. Suppose that the vertices of such a polygon are (x1,y1), (x2,y2),...., (xn,yn). Then the point

    ((x1+...+xn)/n, (y1+...+yn)/n)

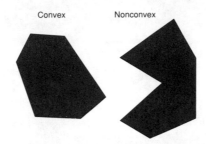

Convex   Nonconvex

Figure 14-28.
**Convex and
nonconvex
figures**.

obtained by averaging the x- and y-coordinates is called the **centroid of
the polygon**. And the centroid is always inside the polygon. So if you wish
to PAINT a convex polygon just compute the centroid. This will give you the
point to use in the PAINT statement!

The Graphics Macro Language

Using the various statements of PC BASIC, you may draw some very complex
screen images. However, the programs can become rather complex. Many
drawings consist only of straight lines in various positions on the screen.
Such drawings may be concisely described and drawn using the Graphics
Macro Language as implemented in the DRAW statement.

To understand the DRAW command, it helps to think of an imaginary
pen you may use to draw on the screen. The motion of the pen is controlled
by a graphics language used by DRAW. The format of the DRAW command
is

```
DRAW <string>
```

Here <string> is a sequence of commands from the graphics language.

In giving commands, you will refer to points on the screen. The action of
many of the commands will depend on the last point referenced. This is the
point most recently referred to in a graphics command associated with

DRAW. The CLS and RUN statements both set the last point referenced to the center of the screen. (This is (160,100) in medium-resolution graphics and (320,100) in high-resolution graphics.)

The graphics commands associated with DRAW are indicated by single letters. The most fundamental is the M command, which has the format

```
DRAW "M x,y"
```

which draws a straight line from the last point referenced to the point with coordinates (x,y). After the statement is executed, the point (x,y) becomes the last point referenced.

Here are two variations on the M command:

1. If M is preceded by N, then the last point referenced is not changed. For example, here is a DRAW command to draw an angle as shown in Figure 14-29 (the vertex of the angle is at (360,100) and the computer is assumed to be in SCREEN 2):

```
10 DRAW "M 500,100 NM 200,50"
```

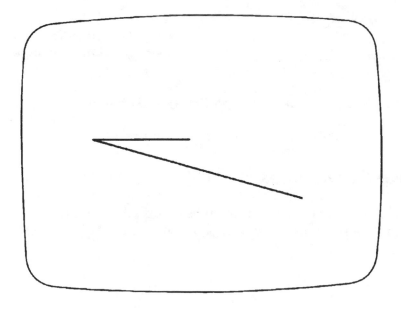

Figure 14-29.
An angle.

2. If M is preceded by B, then the last referenced point is changed but no drawing takes place. The BM command is used to relocate the pen. For example, here is a command to draw the angle of Figure 14-30 with the vertex located at (300,110):

```
10 DRAW "BM 300,110 M 500,100 NM 200,50"
```

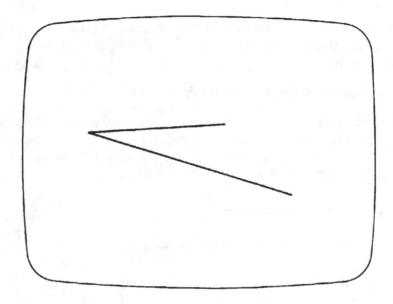

Figure 14-30.
Another angle.

Test Your Understanding 1 (Answer on Page 425)

Use the DRAW command to draw the triangle of Figure 14-24.

Using Relative Coordinates

In our discussion above, all of our coordinates were absolute; that is, we specified the actual coordinates. However, you also may use this form of the M command:

```
M +r,+s
```

It will draw a line from the last referenced point to the point that is r units to the right and s units down. (Down is in the direction of increasing y-coordinates!) In a similar fashion, we may use the commands

```
M -r,+s
M -r,-s
M +r,-s
```

Specifying Coordinates Using Variables

The coordinates in an M command may be specified by variables, <variable1> and <variable2>, respectively. Here is the form of the command:

```
M =<variable1>;,=<variable2>;
```

Note the semicolons and the comma—you need them. For example, to draw a line from the last referenced point to the point specified by the values of the variables A and B, use the command

```
M =A;,=B;
```

By preceding = signs with a + sign, we may use variables to specify a relative coordinate position. For example, to draw the line to the point that is A units to the right and B units down, use the command

```
M +=A;,+=B;
```

Note that the signs of A and B give the actual direction of motion. For example, if A is negative, then the motion will be ABS(A) units to the left.

Figure 14-31 is an example of the sophisticated pictures you can compose using DRAW. Here is a program to create this display:

```
10 ' This program draws the pattern in Figure 10-21
20 SCREEN 1:CLS:KEY OFF
30 FOR R=0 TO 6.3 STEP .1
40   A=160+70*COS(R):B=100+70*SIN(R)
```

```
50    DRAW "NM =A;,=B;"
60 NEXT R
70 END
```

Figure 14-31.
A complex display.

Test Your Understanding 2 (Answer on Page 426)

Use the random number generator to generate 50 pairs of random points. Use DRAW to draw a line associated with each pair.

More About Relative Motions   In most drawing, coordinates are given in relative rather than absolute form. To shorten the lengths of the strings involved in describing such motions, DRAW includes the following commands:

```
U n   - Move n units up
D n   - Move n units down
L n   - Move n units left
R n   - Move n units right
E n   - Move n units northeast
        (n units to the right, n units up)
```

```
F n  - Move n units southeast
        (n units to the right, n units down)
G n  - Move n units southwest
        (n units to the left, n units down)
H n  - Move n units northwest
        (n units to the left, n units up)
```

The effect of these commands is shown in Figure 14-32.

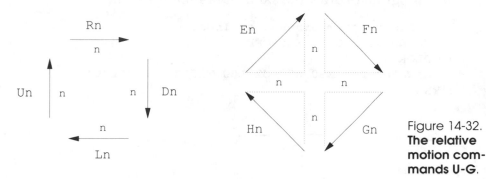

Figure 14-32.
The relative motion commands U-G.

You may use the N and B options with the commands U–G. For example, the command

```
10 DRAW "NU 50"
```

draws a line from the last referenced point upward for 50 units. However, the last referenced point is not updated. Similarly, the command

```
10 DRAW "BU 50"
```

updates the last referenced point to the point 50 units up from the current point. However, no line is drawn.

You also may use variables in connection with the commands U–G. For example, consider the command

```
10 DRAW "U =A;"
```

It draws a line from the last referenced point A units upward. (If the value of A is negative, then the motion will be downward.)

Color.   You may specify color within DRAW by using the command

    C n

Here n is 0, 1, 2 or 3 and refers to a color in the current palette.

Here is a program to draw the sailboat of Figure 14-33:

```
10 ' This program draws a sailboat
20 SCREEN 1,0: CLS: KEY OFF
30 COLOR 7,0
40 DRAW "C1 L60 E60 D80 C2 L60 F20 R40 E20 L20"
50 END
```

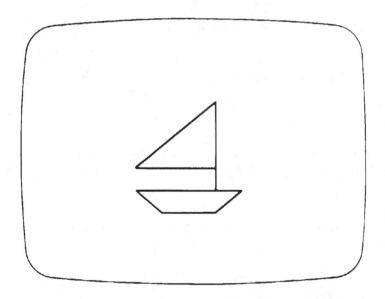

Figure 14-33.
A sailboat.

The background is white, the sail green, and the boat red.

Angle.   You may rotate a figure through an angle that is a multiple of 90 degrees. Just precede the DRAW string (describing the figure in unrotated form) with the command

```
A n
```

Here

```
n=0 : no rotation
n=1 : 90-degree rotation clockwise
n=2 : 180-degree rotation clockwise
n=3 : 270-degree rotation clockwise
```

For example, here is a program that illustrates the sailboat of Figure 14-33 rotated through the various possible angles (see Figure 14-34).

```
10 ' This program draws a rotated sailboat
20 CLS: SCREEN 1: KEY OFF: PSET (160,100)
30 INPUT "ANGLE (0-3)";N
40 DRAW "A=N; BU40 L30 E30 D40 L30 F10 R20 E10 L10"
50 END
```

You may rotate a figure through any angle, clockwise or counterclockwise, using the command TA n. Here n is an angle between -360 and 360 degrees. Positive angles are counterclockwise and negative angles are clockwise. For example, to turn a figure counterclockwise through a 30 degree angle, use the command

```
10 TA 30
```

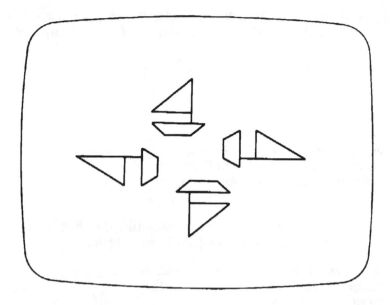

Figure 14-34.
**Rotated sail-
boats**.

Scale. You may automatically scale figures (make them larger or smaller) using the command

    S n

All line lengths are multiplied by n/4. Here n is an integer in the range 1 to 255.

Test Your Understanding 3 (Answer on Page 426)

Write a command to draw the sailboat of Figure 14-33, but at half scale.

Substrings. You may define a string, A$, outside a draw statement and then use it in the form

    DRAW A$

Often, you will wish to use one string several times within a single picture. (This is convenient, for example, if you wish to draw the same figure in several parts of the screen.) You may incorporate a string A$ within a larger string by preceding it with the letter X. For example, here is a statement that draws A$, moves up 50 units, and draws A$ again:

```
10 DRAW "XA$; BU50; XA$"
```

Note that X commands are separated from adjacent commands with semi-colons.

Exercises

1. Write a program to draw the following figure:

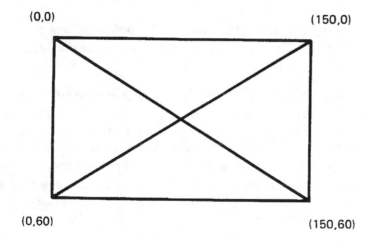

(0,0)   (150,0)

(0,60)   (150,60)

2. Write a program that draws the figure of Exercise 1, but rotates it 270 degrees clockwise.
3. Write a program that draws the figure of Exercise 1, but makes it twice the size.

Answers to Test Your Understandings 1, 2, and 3

1.    ```
10 DRAW "BM 0,50 M 100,125 M 400,25 M 0,50"
```
```

2.
```
20 DIM X(50),Y(50),XX(50),YY(50)
30 CLS: SCREEN 2: KEY OFF
40 FOR J=1 TO 50
50    X(J)=INT(RND*620)): XX(J)=INT(RND*620))
60    Y(J)=INT(RND*200)): YY(J)=INT(RND*200))
70    DRAW "BM =X(J); =Y(J); M =XX(J);=YY(J);"
80 NEXT J
90 END
```

3.
```
10 DRAW "S2 C1 L60 E60 D80 C2 L60 F20 R40 E20 L20"
```

Saving and Recalling Graphics Images

GWBASIC contains commands that allow you to save and recall the contents of any rectangle on the screen. This is extremely convenient in many graphics applications, particularly animation.

Let's begin this discussion with a description of the image to be saved. The image must consist of a rectangular portion of the screen. The rectangle in question may start and end anywhere, and may contain text characters, portions of text characters, or a graphics image. You specify the rectangle by giving the coordinates of two opposite vertices: either the upper-left and lower-right, or the lower-left and upper-right. Thus a rectangle is specified in the same way as in using the LINE statement to draw a rectangle. Here are some specifications of rectangles:

(0,0) – (100,100)

(3,8) – (30,80)

In specifying rectangles, remember to indicate the coordinates in terms of the current graphics mode (either medium- or high-resolution). In either graphics mode, text characters occupy 8×8 rectangles. For example, the character in the upper-left corner of the screen occupies the rectangle (0,0)-(7,7). (Lines of text are always eight pixels high.)

Test Your Understanding 1 (Answer on Page 431)

Specify the rectangle consisting of the second text line of the screen. (Assume that you are in the medium-resolution graphics mode.)

The GET statement allows you to store the contents of a rectangle in an array. You may use any array as long as it is big enough. Suppose that the rectangle is x pixels long and y pixels high, then the size of the array must be at least

```
4 + (2*x+7)*y/32
```

in medium resolution and

```
4 + (x+7)*y/32
```

in high resolution. (Recall that the size of the array is specified in a DIM statement.) For example, suppose that the array is 10 pixels wide and 50 pixels high and is in medium-resolution. The array required to store the rectangle must contain at least

```
4 + (2*10+7)*50/32   or   46
```

elements. We can use an array A() defined by the statement

```
DIM A(46)
```

Once a sufficiently large array has been dimensioned you may store in it the contents of the rectangle using the GET statement, which has the form

```
GET (x1,y1)-(x2,y2), arrayname
```

For example, to store the rectangle (0,0)-(9,49) (this rectangle is 10 by 50) in the array A(), use the statement

```
10 GET (0,0)-(9,49), A
```

To summarize, to store the contents of a rectangle in an array you must:

1. Use a DIM statement to define a rectangle of sufficient size.

2. Execute a GET statement.

You may redisplay the rectangle at any point on the screen by using the PUT statement. For example, to redisplay the rectangle stored in A, use the statement

```
20 PUT (100,125), A
```

This particular statement redisplays the rectangle in A with the upper-left corner of the rectangle at the point (100,125).

To see GET and PUT in action, examine the following program:

```
1 '*****************************************
2 ' This program prints a letter A in the
3 ' 1,1 position. It copies the letter to
4 ' an array and redisplays it at graphics
5 ' location 100,100.
6 '*****************************************
10 SCREEN 1
20 DIM LETTER(9)
30 LOCATE 1,1
40 PRINT "A"
50 GET (0,0)-(7,7),LETTER
60 CLS
70 PUT (100,100),LETTER
```

Line 10 puts BASIC in medium-resolution graphics mode. We are out to store an 8×8 array so we use the above formulas to calculate the required array size, which works out to 9. In lines 30–40 we print a letter A, and in line 50 we store the image in the array LETTER. We then clear the screen. Line 70 recovers the image from the array and places it with its upper-left corner at the point (100,100).

Don't erase the screen yet. Type

```
10 PUT (100,100),LETTER <ENTER>
```

Note that the letter A at (100,100) disappears. If you type the same line again, the A reappears. Use this feature to create the illusion of motion across the screen—suppose that you wish to create the illusion that the letter A is moving across the screen, merely display it and erase it from consecutive screen positions. The screen creates the displays faster than the eye can view them. What you see is a continuous motion of the letter across the screen. Here is a program to create this animation:

```
1 '*****************************************
2 ' This program demonstrates the principles
3 ' of animation by making the letter A
4 ' appear to move across the screen.
5 '*****************************************
10 SCREEN 1
20 DIM LETTER(9)
30 LOCATE 1,1
40 PRINT "A"
50 GET (0,0)-(7,7),LETTER
60 CLS
70 FOR XPOSITION = 0 TO 311
80   PUT (XPOSITION,0),LETTER
90   PUT (XPOSITION,0),LETTER
100 NEXT XPOSITION
```

Note that the XPOSITION runs from 0 to 311. Although the screen is 319 pixels wide, the variable XPOSITION specifies the upper-left corner of the rectangle, which is 8×8. Therefore, 311 is the largest possible value of the variable.

Animation is the backbone of all the arcade games that have become so popular in recent years. We will apply the above principles of animation in designing several computer games later in the book.

Saving a Screen Image on Diskette

Storing large graphics images (such as the entire screen) takes a great deal of memory. To store the entire screen takes more than 16,000 bytes. Compare this with the fact that BASIC can use a maximum of 65,536 bytes. Because graphic images tend to use such large amounts of memory, it is often necessary to save the screen image on diskette. Here is a program for saving the current screen image on diskette under the filename SCREEN:

```
10 DEF SEG = &HB800
20 BSAVE "SCREEN",0,&H4000
```

To recall the stored image to the screen, use the program

```
10 DEF SEG = &HB800
20 BLOAD "SCREEN",0
```

Exercises

1. Specify the rectangle of length 80 and height 40 whose upper-left corner is at (10,10).

2. Specify the rectangle that consists of the first two text columns of the screen in high-resolution mode.

3. Write a dimension statement for the rectangle specified in Exercise 1.

4. Write a dimension statement for the rectangle specified in Exercise 2.

5. Store the current screen contents on diskette.

6. Clear the screen and recall the screen contents stored in Exercise 5.

7. Store a happy face (ASCII character 2) in an array.

8. Display the happy face at the following points:

    a. (0,0)

    b. (50,50)

    c. (0,100)

9. Construct an animation that moves the happy face across the screen in text line 10.

10. Construct an animation that moves the happy face diagonally across the screen from the upper-left to the lower-right corner.

Answer to Test Your Understanding 1

1. (0,8)-(319,15)

VIEW and WINDOW

In this section, we discuss the VIEW and WINDOW statements.

The WINDOW statement allows you to define your own coordinate system on the screen. For example, consider the statement

```
10 WINDOW (-2,0)-(2,100)
```

It causes the screen coordinates to be redefined, as shown in Figure 14-35. Note that the lower-left corner becomes the point (-2,0) and the upper-right conrner becomes the point (2,100). The x-coordinates of the screen run from -2 on the left to 2 on the right. The y-coordinates run from 0 at the bottom to 100 on the top. The point in the middle of the screen is (0,50).

Figure 14-35.
Cartesian coordinates (-2,0)–(2,100).

After using a WINDOW command, all graphics commands work with the new coordinates. For example, suppose that we execute the above WINDOW statement. The statement

```
10 PSET (0,50)
```

turns on the pixel at the center of the screen.

Test Your Understanding 1 (Answer on Page 439)

Assume that the screen coordinates are defined by the WINDOW command of Figure 14-35. Describe the location of these points:

a. (1,75)

b. (-1,100)

c. (2,10)

The WINDOW statement does not disturb the contents of the screen so you may use several different coordinate systems within a single program. Moreover, the placement of text is still governed by the usual text coordinate system (lines 1–25, columns 1–40 or 80), so you can mix text and graphics determined by a WINDOW command.

The WINDOW statement automatically reorders the values of the extreme x- and y-coordinates so that the lesser x-coordinate is on the left, the greater on the right, the lesser y-coordinate is at the bottom, and the greater is on the top. For example, the following WINDOW statements are all equivalent:

```
10 WINDOW (-1,1)-(1,-1)
10 WINDOW (1,1)-(-1,-1)
10 WINDOW (-1,-1)-(1,1)
10 WINDOW (1,-1)-(-1,1)
```

Note that the above statements turn the screen into a portion of a Cartesian coordinate system of the same type used in graphing points and equations in algebra. Note also that increasing values of the y-coordinate correspond to moving up the screen. This is the exact opposite of the normal graphics coordinates in which the pixel rows are numbered from 0 (top of screen) to 199 (bottom of screen). A coordinate system in which increasing values of the y-coordinate correspond to moving down the screen are called **screen coordinates**. You may use the WINDOW statement to create a set of screen coordinates using the SCREEN option. For example, the statement

```
10 WINDOW SCREEN (-2,0)-(2,100)
```

Figure 14-36.
Screen coordinates (-2,0)–(2,100).

creates a coordinate system as shown in Figure 14-36. Note that y-coordinate 0 is now at the top of the screen.

Example 1. Use the WINDOW command to draw an expanding family of rectangles beginning at the center of the screen.

Solution. Let's use a single line statement, namely

```
LINE (-.1,-.1)-(.1,.1),,B
```

to draw a rectangle with center (0,0). However, let's use a sequence of WINDOW commands to redefine the coordinate system so that the radius .1 corresponds to successively larger distances on the screen. That is, we will let the Jth coordinate system be generated by the statement

```
WINDOW (-1/J,-1/J)-(1/J,1/J)
```

for J=1, 2, ... ,10. For the first coordinate system the screen corresponds to (-1,-1)-(1,1). So the distance .1 seems small. (It corresponds to only .05 of the way across the screen). On the other hand, for J=10 the coordinate system corresponds to (-.1,-.1)-(.1,.1), so .1 is halfway across the screen. Here is our program:

```
1  '**************************************
2  '  This program draws a sequence of
3  '  rectangles which nested one inside
4  '  the next.
5  '**************************************
10 SCREEN 2:KEY OFF
20 CLS
30 FOR J=1 TO 10
40    WINDOW (-1/J,-1/J)-(1/J,1/J)
50    LINE (-.1,-.1)-(.1,.1),,B
60 NEXT J
70 END
```

The output of the program is shown in Figure 14-37.

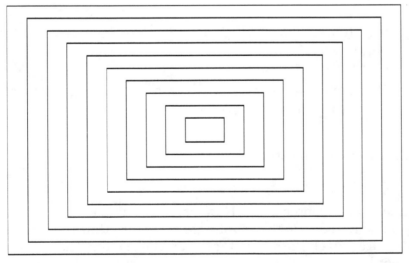

Figure 14-37.
Expanding rect-angles.

The WINDOW statement ignores points corresponding to positions off the screen. This procedure is known as **clipping**.

RUN, SCREEN, and WINDOW with no parameters disable any previous WINDOW command.

VIEW

The VIEW statement allows you to restrict screen activity to a portion of the screen. For example, to restrict all screen activity to the rectangle (20,10)-(100,200) use the statement

```
10 VIEW SCREEN (20,10)-(100,200)
```

This statement turns the rectangle (20,10)-(100,200) in a viewport. While a viewport is in effect you may not plot any points outside the viewport. For example, if a CIRCLE statement refers to a circle that lies partially outside a viewport then only the portion within the viewport is drawn.

If you execute CLS while a viewport is in effect you will erase only the inside of the viewport.

Note that while the viewport applies only to graphics commands, text commands may apply to any position on the screen even though a viewport is in effect. For example, you may use LOCATE and PRINT as if the viewport were not present.

The full form of the VIEW statement is

```
VIEW [SCREEN] (x1,y1)-(x2,y2),[color],[boundary]
```

The [color] option allows you to fill in the viewport with a particular color. The [boundary] option allows you to put a rectangular boundary around the viewport. The value of [boundary] determines the color of the bounding rectangle.

For example, the statement

```
10 VIEW SCREEN (10,20)-(200,100),3,2
```

defines a viewport colored in color 3 with a boundary in color 2, and the statement

```
10 VIEW SCREEN (10,20)-(200,100),,2
```

defines a viewport with a boundary in color 2. The interior of the viewport is the background color.

You may omit the SCREEN parameter to obtain plotting relative to the viewport. For example, consider the statement

```
10 VIEW (10,20)-(200,100)
```

It defines the same viewport as above. However, the point (x,y) in a graphics statement is interpreted to mean (x+10,y+20). In other words, the upper-left corner of the viewport is considered as the corner of the screen. The same clipping rule as for VIEW SCREEN applies: If a point (as computed relative to the viewport) lies outside the viewport, then it is not plotted.

You may disable a viewport using the statement

```
10 VIEW
```

Similarly, using RUN or SCREEN will cancel a viewport.

You may combine VIEW and WINDOW. For example, consider the statements

```
10 VIEW (80,16)-(559,167),,3
10 WINDOW (0,0)-(20,100)
```

They define a viewport in the rectangle (80,16)-(559,167) and then redefine the coordinates within the viewport as the Cartesian coordinates (0,0)-(20,100), so (0,0) corresponds to the lower-left corner of the viewport and (20,100) to the upper-right corner.

On the other hand, consider the statements

```
10 VIEW SCREEN (80,16)-(559,167),,3
10 WINDOW (0,0)-(20,100)
```

Now the WINDOW command refers to the entire screen. (0,0) corresponds to the lower-left corner of the screen and (20,100) to the upper-right corner of the screen. The viewport serves as a mask to clip off all points that (in the coordinates specified by WINDOW) land outside the viewport.

As we'll see in the next section, viewports are ideal for generating business graphics. We'll use a combination of VIEW and WINDOW to create a custom coordinate system on which to draw a bar graph.

Answer to Test Your Understanding 1

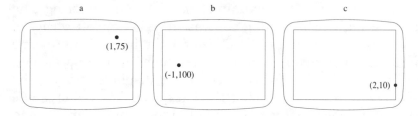

Sound and Music

The IBM PCs and compatibles have a small speaker located within the system unit that you may use to introduce sound and music into your programs. There are three sound commands—BEEP, SOUND, and PLAY. Let's survey the capabilities of each of these commands.

BEEP

The BEEP command is the simplest of the sound commands. It allows you to sound the speaker for 1/4 second. This command gives you no control over the pitch or the duration of the sound.

Here is an example of BEEP in a subroutine that responds to a mistake in input:

```
10 PRINT "YOU MADE A MISTAKE, TRY AGAIN!"
20 BEEP
30 RETURN
```

You also may use a BEEP statement within other statements, as in

```
1 IF X=100 THEN BEEP
```

Professional programs employ sophisticated input routines that subject user input to a number of tests to determine if the input is acceptable. (Is the length correct? Does the input employ any illegal characters?) Here is a simple subroutine of this type: The main program assigns a value to the variable LENGTH, which gives the maximum length of an input string. The subroutine illuminates a box, beginning at location (1,1) (top left corner of the screen) to indicate the maximum field size for the input. The routine then allows you to input characters and to display them in the appropriate position in the illuminated field. For each character displayed part of the illumination disappears. Moreover, using the backspace key restores one character space of illumination. If you attempt to input characters beyond the illuminated field, the routine beeps the speaker.

```
5000 ' *******************************************
5010 ' This subroutine has the user input a string
5020 '    of fixed length into an illuminated box,
5030 '    beeping when the user attempts to input
5040 '    a value that is not legal
5050 ' *******************************************
5060 'LENGTH is the maximum number of characters in
        input string
5070 'COUNT is the current cursor position in the input
        field
5100 ' Initialize, displaying the box
5110    COUNT=1
5120    CLS
5130    LOCATE 1,1
5140    PRINT ""
5150    LOCATE 1,1
5160    FOR I=1 TO LENGTH
5170      LOCATE 1,I:PRINT CHR$(219);
5180    NEXT I
```

```
5190   LOCATE 1,1
5195 ' Scan the keyboard for a character
5200   A$=INKEY$
5210   IF A$="" THEN 5200  :'Wait for key to be struck
5220   IF A$=CHR$(8) THEN GOTO 5300  :'Backspace
5230   IF A$= CHR$(13) THEN 5340      :'Return
5240   IF COUNT=LENGTH+1 THEN 5280   :'Check length
5250   LOCATE 1,COUNT:PRINT A$;       :'Print character
5260   COUNT=COUNT+1
5270   GOTO 5200
5280   BEEP            :'Error
5290   GOTO 5190
5300   COUNT=COUNT-1        :'Remove character from end
5310   IF COUNT=0 THEN BEEP:COUNT=COUNT+1
5320   LOCATE 1,COUNT:PRINT CHR$(219);
5330   GOTO 5190
5340 RETURN
```

SOUND

The second speaker command is called SOUND. This handy little command enables you to access any frequency between 37 and 32767 Hertz (cycles per second, also abbreviated Hz). The duration of the sound is measured in clock ticks, and there are 18.2 clock ticks per second. A numeric expression in the range 0 to 65,535 (that's slightly over one hour) is used. To produce a sound at 500 Hz and make it last for 40 ticks of the clock, use this statement:

```
10 SOUND 500, 40
```

Here is an elementary graphics program that has been enhanced by the SOUND command. It draws fixed triangles and random circles and blinks them in a manner suitable for illuminating a rock concert. SOUND provides some audio accompaniment.

```
10 ' **************************************************
20 ' This program creates a sound and light show
30 '    with random sounds and randomly-placed shapes
```

```
40  ' ************************************************
100 KEY OFF
110 'Turns the key line off
120 SCREEN 1
130 'Switches from text mode to graphics mode
140 FOR I=1 TO 100
150    CIRCLE (RND*250, RND*200), 30
160    'Draws a circle with random coordinates and a
          diameter of 30
170    SOUND RND*1000+37,2
180    'Creates a random sound from 37 to 1037 Hz with a
          duration of 2 clock ticks
190    CLS
200    DRAW "E15; F15; L30"
210    'Draws a triangle
220    SOUND RND*1000+37,2
230    CLS
240 NEXT I
250 END
```

Music on the PC

Next on the level of sound sophistication is the PLAY command. It enables you to turn your IBM PC into a piano and play musical compositions as simple or as complex as you like. (There is even an arrangement of Beethoven's Moonlight Sonata for the PC!)

A few musical facts will help you a great deal in your programming:

1. Just like a piano, the PC uses seven octaves, numbered 0 to 6. Each octave starts with C and goes to B.
2. Octave 3 starts with middle C.
3. The tempo of a song is the speed at which it is played. On the PC, tempo is measured by the number of quarter notes per second. The tempo may range from 32 to 255.

4. The PC allows you to style your notes as normal, legato, or staccato. Normal means that notes are held down for 7/8 of their defined length. Legato means that each note will play for the full time period that you set it to play, while staccato means that each note is held for only 3/4 of the time specified. Legato notes sound "smooth," whereas staccato notes are "crisp."

PLAY

The PLAY command allows you to show your creative musical genius even if you can't play a comb. It uses a language that allows you to write music in the form of strings. Once the music has been transcribed, the PLAY statement allows you to play it on the speaker.

To use the PLAY command:

1. Code the desired musical notes as a string.

2. Use the PLAY command in the form

```
PLAY <string>
```

For example, consider this program. Why not type it in and listen to the results?

```
10 A$="O3L4EDCDEE"
20 PLAY "XA$; E2DDD2EGG2; T255XA$; EEDDEDP2C1"
30 END
```

The program probably makes the music look quite mysterious; however, the musical language is quite simple. Here is a summary:

Notes. Notes are indicated by the letters A to G with an optional #, +, or -. The # or + after a letter indicates a sharp, while - indicates a flat.

For example, the note "A sharp" is written A#; "G flat" is written G-.

Length.   L defines the LENGTH of a note. L1 is a whole note, L2 is a half note, L4 is a quarter note, ..., L64 is a 64th note. The L command defines the length of all subsequent notes until another L command is given. For example, to play the string of notes CDEFG in quarter notes, use this string:

L4 CDEFG

If you wish to define the length of a single note, omit the L and put the number indicating the length after the note. For example, C4 indicates C is held for a quarter note. Subsequent notes are held for an amount defined by the most recent L command.

As in musical notation, a dot after a note indicates that the note is to be held for one-and-one-half times its usual length.

Rest.   P1 is a whole note rest, P2 a half note, and so forth.

Octave.   Initially, all notes are taken from octave 4 (the octave above the one beginning with middle C). The octave is changed by giving the O command. For example, to change to octave 2, the command would be O2. After you give an octave command all notes are taken from the indicated octave unless you change the octave or temporarily overrule the octave (see below). Another method of specifying the octave is by using the symbols > and <. The symbol > means to go up one octave, and the symbol < means to go down one octave.

Test Your Understanding 1 (Answers on Page 444)

Write a string that plays an ascending C major scale in eighth notes, pauses for a half-note, and then plays the same scale descending.

Test Your Understanding 2 (Answers on Page 444)

Write a string that plays the scale of Test Your Understanding 1 in octave 5.

Tempo.   Tempo is the speed at which a composition is played. Tempo is measured in terms of quarter beats per second. Unless you specify otherwise, the tempo is set at 120. You may set the tempo using the T command. For example, to set the tempo to 80, use the command T80. The tempo remains unchanged until you give another T command. The tempo may range from 32 to 255.

Test Your Understanding 3 (Answers on Page 444)

Write a string that plays the scale of Test Your Understanding 1 at a tempo of 80, and at a tempo of 150.

Style.   You may select the style of notes from among: normal, legato, or staccato. The respective commands are MN, ML, and MS. The style chosen remains in effect until it is canceled by another style selection.

Test Your Understanding 4 (Answer on Page 444)

Write a string that plays the scale of Test Your Understanding 1 with legato style and then with staccato style.

Ordinarily, the PLAY command causes BASIC to stop while the specified notes are played. However, you also may use the PLAY command in background mode. In this mode, while the speaker plays the notes BASIC continues executing the program, beginning with the statements immediately after the PLAY statement. The background mode may be started with the command MB. You may return to normal mode (also called foreground mode) with the command MF. If you do not explicitly state the mode, BASIC assumes the background mode.

In coding music you may wish to use the same string a number of times. This occurs, for example, in the case of a refrain. The X command allows you to repeat a string without retyping it. Just store the desired string in a string variable, say A$. Whenever the string is required, type

```
XA$;
```

Exercises

1. Choose a piece of piano music and transcribe it for the PC.

Answers to Test Your Understandings 1, 2, 3, and 4

1.   `10 A$="CDEFGAB O5 C P2 C O4 BAGFEDC"`

2.   `10 A$="O5 CDEFGAB O6 C P2 C O5 BAGFEDC"`

3.   `10 A$="T80 CDEFGAB O5 C P2 C O4 BAGFEDC"`
       `20 A$="T150 CDEFGAB O5 C P2 C O4 BAGFEDC"`

4.   `10 A$="ML CDEFGAB O5 C P2 C O4 BAGFEDC"`
       `20 A$="MS CDEFGAB O5 C P2 C O4 BAGFEDC"`

Fifteen

Some Additional Programming Tools

Introduction

In this chapter we learn about five additional programming tools.

- The INKEY$ variable will give us additional control over input.

- We will learn to control the function keys and use them to trap events.

- We will learn about the concept of extended ASCII codes which supply us with the codes corresponding to various additional keys, such as the function keys and cursor motion keys.

- We will learn to respond to errors without stopping the program.

- Finally, we will learn to run several programs in sequence using the CHAIN statement.

The INKEY$ Function

Many programs depend on input from the operator. We have learned to provide such input using the INPUT and LINE INPUT statements. When the program encounters either of these statements it pauses and waits for input. The program will not proceed unless valid input is provided. The INKEY$ function provides an alternative method of reading the keyboard.

The Keyboard Buffer

When a key is pressed, BASIC interrupts what it is doing and places the corresponding ASCII code in a reserved section of memory called the **keyboard buffer**. The keyboard buffer has space to record a number of keystrokes. The process of recording information in the keyboard buffer usually proceeds so that you don't even realize that the keyboard buffer is there. For instance, in typing program lines BASIC is constantly reading the keyboard buffer and displaying the corresponding characters on the screen. In a similar fashion, an INPUT statement reads the keyboard buffer and displays the corresponding characters on the screen. A carriage return (generated by ENTER) tells the INPUT statement to stop reading the buffer.

As characters are read from the buffer, the space they occupy is released. If the buffer is full and you attempt to type a character, you will hear a beep on the speaker. This is to inform you that until the buffer is read, further typed characters will be lost.

Note that you may type on the keyboard while a program is running. Even though BASIC is busy executing a program it pauses to place your typed characters in the keyboard buffer, and then returns to execution. When the buffer is next read, it will read the characters in the order they were typed. In this way you may "type ahead" of required program input.

The INKEY$ Variable

The INKEY$ function allows you to read one character from the keyboard buffer. When the program reaches INKEY$ it reads the "oldest" character in the keyboard buffer and returns it as a string. This procedure counts as reading the character, so that the character is removed from the buffer. If there is no character in the keyboard buffer, INKEY$ equals the empty string.

INKEY$ has many uses. For example, suppose that you wish your program to pause until some key is pressed. Here is a statement that accomplishes this task:

```
100 WHILE INKEY$=""
110 WEND
```

The program continually tests the keyboard buffer. If there is no character to be read, the test is repeated, and so on until some key has been pressed.

Caution: We have explained the operation of INKEY$ in terms of the keyboard buffer so that you can understand the following trap: If the keyboard buffer is not empty a reference to INKEY$ removes a character. If you use INKEY$ a second time you will be referring to the keyboard buffer anew and the value of the first INKEY$ will be lost. Moral: If you wish to use the value of INKEY$ again, store the value in a string variable as in the statement

```
10 A$ = INKEY$
```

The INSTAT Function

Closely related to the INKEY$ function is the INSTAT function. This function returns TRUE (-1) if there is a character waiting to be read and FALSE (0) otherwise. However, unlike the INKEY$ function INSTAT does not read the character.

Exercises

Suppose that the keyboard buffer is empty and you type A, followed by F, followed by C.

1. What is the value returned by INKEY$?

2. Suppose that the INKEY$ of Exercise 1 has been executed. Suppose that it is followed by the statement

   ```
   10 IF INKEY$ <> "" THEN PRINT INKEY$
   ```

   What letter is displayed on the screen?

3. Write a program to test the keyboard and display the keys pressed. It should display them in a single line, with no spaces between consecutive characters. Have the program terminate when ENTER is pressed, after printing the corresponding character.

The Function Keys and Event Trapping

The function keys are the ten keys labeled F1 through F10 on the left side of the PC keyboard.

The Function Keys As User-defined Keys

Each function key may be assigned a string constant containing as many as 15 characters. When a function key is depressed the corresponding string is input to BASIC. In this way, you may reduce typing standard inputs to single keystrokes. This tends to eliminate errors in typing. For example, suppose that an input statement asked for a response of HIGH, LOW, or AVERAGE. You can define function keys F1, F2, and F3 to be, respectively, the strings

```
F1: HIGH <carriage return>

F2: LOW <carriage return>
```

```
F3: AVERAGE <carriage return>
```

Pressing F1, for example, is then equivalent to responding to the INPUT statement with the string HIGH <carriage return>.

Setting Function Keys. You may assign strings to the function keys in either command or execution mode. To assign <string> to the function key n, use the statement

```
KEY n, <string>
```

Suppose that you wish to assign key F1 the string

```
LIST <carriage return>
```

This may be done using the statement

```
10 KEY 1, "LIST"+CHR$(13)
```

Subsequently, whenever you press key F1 the desired string will be input to BASIC. In particular, if you happen to be in the immediate mode, inputting the string will cause the current program to be listed. You have customized the F1 key to a special application. In a similar fashion, you may customize other keys with commands or keystroke sequences that come up often in your work.

If you assign a null string to a function key (via a command of the form KEY _,""), you will disable the function key.

Note that function-key strings may contain any characters with ASCII codes from 0 to 128, so that control characters may be included within the function key string assignments.

To display the current function-key string assignments, use the command

```
20 KEY LIST
```

The current string assignments will be displayed on the usual text area of the screen (lines 1–24).

In writing or running a program, it is often convenient to have a reminder of the various key string assignments on the screen at all times. This may be accomplished by giving the command

```
30 KEY ON
```

The first six characters of each function-key string will then be displayed in line 25 of the screen. (In case of a line width of 40, only the first five function key strings are displayed.) To turn off the function key display in line 25, use the command

```
40 KEY OFF
```

Test Your Understanding 1 (Answers on Page 455)

a. Write commands to assign the following strings to function keys 1–3.

```
F1 - "ADDITION"
F2 - "SUBTRACTION"
F3 - "MULTIPLICATION"
```

Disable all other function keys.

b. Display the function key assignments in line 25.

Event Trapping

We have described how to input data using INPUT, LINE INPUT, and INKEY$. All of these input methods have the following feature in common: The program decides when to ask for the input. You may use the function keys for a very different form of input.

Suppose you want the program to watch function key F1. The instant F1 is pressed, you wish the program to go to the subroutine in line 1000. This may be accomplished by first turning on event trapping for key F1 via the statement

```
10 KEY(1) ON
```

This tells the program to examine F1 after every program statement is executed. Next, we tell the program that whenever F1 is pushed, go to the subroutine starting in line 1000. We tell the program this in the statement

```
20 ON KEY(1) GOSUB 1000
```

The program will inspect the keyboard buffer at the end of each program statement. When it detects that F1 has been pushed it will go to the subroutine at line 1000.

You may use event trapping to implement a menu, as illustrated in the following example:

Example 1.   Write a program to test addition, subtraction, and multiplication of two-digit numbers. Let the user select the operation via function keys F1 through F3. Let function key F4 cause the program to end.

Solution.   Create four subroutines, corresponding to addition, subtraction, multiplication, and END. Clear the screen and define the strings associated with function keys F1 to F4 to be, respectively, ADD, SUBTR, MULT, and EXIT. Then disable the rest of the function keys. Set up the event trapping lines for function keys F1–F4. Finally, turn the event trapping on.

Select the two numbers to use in our arithmetic. To do this, set up an infinite loop that accesses different random numbers in each repetition. The problem you get depends on how long you take to press one of the function keys; therefore, it is really unnecessary to use the RANDOMIZE command to guarantee nonrepeatability. The program keeps executing the loop until one of the function keys F1–F4 is pressed, then it goes to the appropriate subroutine. Here is the program:

```
1  ' *****************************************
2  ' This program tests addition, subtraction,
3  '   and multiplication of two-digit numbers
4  ' *****************************************
10 'Initialize function keys
20   CLS
30   KEY 1, "ADD"
40   KEY 2, "SUBTR"
```

```
50    KEY 3, "MULT"
60    KEY 4, "END"
70    KEY 5, ""
80    KEY 6, ""
90    KEY 7, ""
100   KEY 8, ""
110   KEY 9, ""
120   KEY 10,""
130   KEY ON
140   ON KEY(1) GOSUB 1000
150   ON KEY(2) GOSUB 2000
160   ON KEY(3) GOSUB 3000
170   ON KEY(4) GOSUB 4000
180   FOR J=1 TO 4
190      KEY(J) ON
200   NEXT J
210   X=INT(100*RND):Y=INT(100*RND)
220   GOTO 210
1000 'Addition
1010    CLS
1020    PRINT "ADDITION"
1030    PRINT "PROBLEM"
1040    PRINT X;"+";Y;" EQUALS?"
1050    INPUT ANSWER
1060    IF ANSWER=X+Y THEN 1070 ELSE 1090
1070    PRINT "CORRECT"
1080    GOTO 1100
1090    PRINT "INCORRECT. THE CORRECT ANSWER IS";X+Y
1100 RETURN
2000 'Subtraction
2010    CLS
2020    PRINT "SUBTRACTION"
2030    PRINT "PROBLEM"
2040    PRINT X;"-";Y;" EQUALS?"
2050    INPUT ANSWER
2060    IF ANSWER=X-Y THEN 2070 ELSE 2090
2070    PRINT "CORRECT"
2080    GOTO 2100
2090    PRINT "INCORRECT. THE CORRECT ANSWER IS";X-Y
2100 RETURN
```

```
3000 'Multiplication
3010    CLS
3020    PRINT "MULTIPLICATION"
3030    PRINT "PROBLEM"
3040    PRINT X;"*";Y;" EQUALS?"
3050    INPUT ANSWER
3060    IF ANSWER=X*Y THEN 3070 ELSE 3090
3070    PRINT "CORRECT"
3080    GOTO 3100
3090    PRINT "INCORRECT. THE CORRECT ANSWER IS";X*Y
3100 RETURN
4000 'Exit
4010    CLS
4020    KEY OFF
4030    FOR J=1 TO 4
4040       KEY(J) OFF
4050    NEXT J
4060 END
```

Figure 15-1 shows a sample run of the above program.

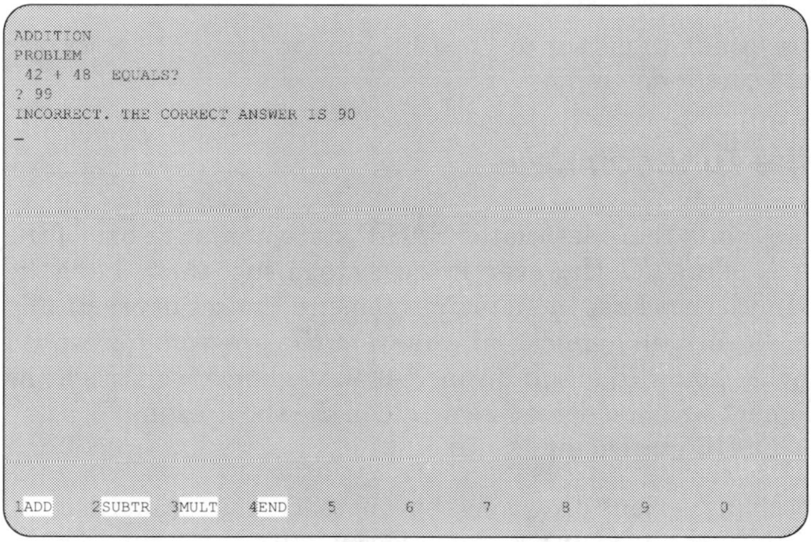

```
ADDITION
PROBLEM
 42 + 48  EQUALS?
? 99
INCORRECT. THE CORRECT ANSWER IS 90
_



1ADD    2SUBTR 3MULT   4END    5      6      7      8      9      0
```

Figure 15-1.
Sample run of the arithmetic program.

There may be certain sections in the program where you want to disallow trapping of function key n. This may be done using either of these statements:

```
KEY(n)  STOP
KEY(n)  OFF
```

You may resume trapping of function key n using the statement

```
KEY(n)  ON
```

If function key n is pressed while a STOP is in effect, the event is remembered. When trapping is turned on the program immediately jumps to the appropriate subroutine. If you use a KEY(n) OFF statement, then function keys are not remembered.

In addition to the function keys you may trap the cursor motion keys. (These are the four keys on the numeric keypad with arrows pointing in the four possible directions of cursor motion.) The commands for trapping these keys are

```
ON KEY(n)  GOSUB
KEY(n)  ON
KEY(n)  OFF
KEY(n)  STOP
```

where n=11 corresponds to cursor up, n=12 to cursor left, n=13 to cursor right, and n=14 to cursor down.

Be Wary of the Function Keys

The function keys and their associated BASIC statements are one of the significant features of the PC. However, it is easy to misuse them. I like the function keys so much that I use them to control menu choices in practically all my programs. In such an application, you want the program to respond to a function key by going to a subroutine. At first glance, you might be tempted to implement such a scheme like we did in the above example, using the ON KEY ... GOSUB statement.

However, in building serious programs this approach has serious defects. For one thing, if you compile your program (as you will almost surely want to do for serious applications programs), any event trapping statements cause extra code to be generated. And the extra code is quite burdensome.

The only way the compiler can check for event trapping is to put a check after each statement in the program. This can easily add several thousand bytes to your program. But that's not the whole story.

All those tests for event trapping will slow your program considerably. This is not to say that event trapping with the function keys is not a valuable feature. It surely is. However, before you use it you should ask yourself: Do I really want the program to test for a function key after each instruction? If you are just implementing choices from a menu the answer should be no!

Exercises

1. Write a statement that disables function key F5.

2. Write a statement that assigns function key F1 the string LIST<carriage return>.

3. Write a program that causes function key F1 to erase the screen and start a new program.

4. Modify the program of Example 1 to disallow function key trapping during the subroutines beginning in lines 1000, 2000, and 3000.

5. Write a statement that traps the cursor up key.

Answers to Test Your Understanding 1

1.   a. `10 DATA ADDITION,SUBTRACTION,MULTIPLICATION`
            `20 FOR J=1 TO 3`
            `30 READ A$(J)`
            `40 NEXT J`
            `50 FOR J=1 TO 10`
            `60 KEY J,A$(J)`
            `70 NEXT J`

    b. `KEY ON`

Extended ASCII Codes

The IBM PC keyboard allows for many more key combinations than the standard set of ASCII codes allows. For this reason the IBM uses extended ASCII codes in addition to the standard ones. An extended ASCII code consists of two numbers: a zero followed by one of the numbers 0–255. Here are some examples of extended ASCII codes:

```
0   15
0   71
0   131
```

The extended ASCII codes are generated from the keyboard as follows:

Table 15-1. **Extended ASCII codes.**

Second Number of Extended ASCII Code	Key(s) Generating Code
15	Shift Tab
16–24	Alt-Q,W,E,R,T,Y,U,I,O,P
30–38	Alt-A,S,D,F,G,H,J,K,L
44–50	Alt-Z,X,C,V,B,N,M
59–68	Function Keys F1–F10 (when disabled as soft keys)
71	Home
72	Cursor Up
73	Pg Up
75	Cursor Left
77	Cursor Right
79	End
80	Cursor Down
81	Pg Down

Table 15-1. (Continued)

82	Ins
83	Del
84–93	Shift-F1-F10
94–103	Ctrl-F1-F10
104–113	Alt-F1-F10
114	Ctrl-PrtSc
115	Ctrl-Space
116	Ctrl-Backspace
117	Ctrl-End
118	Ctrl-PgDn
119	Ctrl-Home
120–131	Alt-1,2,3,4,5,6,7,8,9,0,-,=
132	Ctrl-PgUp

Any ASCII codes that don't appear in the above list may not be generated from the keyboard.

Here is how the extended ASCII codes work: Suppose, for example, that you push the Home key. BASIC inserts its extended ASCII code into the keyboard buffer. The keyboard buffer then contains the two numbers 0 and 71. Run this program as an experiment:

```
10 C$ = INKEY$
20 IF C$ = "" THEN 10
30 PRINT LEN(C$)
40 PRINT ASC(LEFT$(C$,1))
50 PRINT ASC(RIGHT$(C$,1))
60 END
```

In response to the INPUT statement hit the Home key. The program prints out the three numbers 2, 0, and 71. In response to an extended ASCII code, INKEY$ returns the two-character string CHR$(0)+CHR$(71). The first character, CHR$(0), indicates an extended ASCII code. The second character, CHR$(71), indicates the key pushed according to the above table. A few sample runs of the above program are shown in Figure 15-2.

Figure 15-2.
Keystrokes with extended ASCII codes

Using the extended ASCII codes, you may keep track of input from all the keyboard keys.

Test Your Understanding 1 (Answer on Page 460)

Suppose that you press the keys Alt-A followed by End. What will be the contents of the keyboard buffer?

Test Your Understanding 2 (Answer on Page 460)

Write a program that reads a single key from the keyboard buffer. The program should allow you to read a key with an extended ASCII code.

Here is an important note about the function keys: If a function key is enabled, then pressing it causes its associated string to be placed in the keyboard buffer. However, no extended ASCII code will be generated. On the other hand, if a function key is disabled, pressing it will generate the corresponding extended ASCII code. For example, if F1 has the associated string "HELP"+CHR$(13), then pressing F1 puts a string of five ASCII codes in the keyboard buffer, namely the ASCII codes corresponding to the four letters HELP and ASCII code 13. On the other hand, if F1 is disabled, pressing F1 causes the ASCII codes 0 and 59 (the extended code for F1) to be entered into the keyboard buffer.

I prefer to use my function keys by avoiding ON KEY ... GOSUB. To do this, first disable all the function keys as soft keys. I then use a custom input routine that passes on all keyboard characters to an analysis routine. If the key pressed was a function key the analysis routine passes the extended ASCII code in the variable E$. By inspecting E$, I can then direct the program to the appropriate subroutine. In this way, all inputs to my program are treated alike and the savings in memory and run speed are usually considerable.

As an example, consider the following program, which is the command structure we will use to write the bar chart program in Chapter 21. There we will fill in the details of the subroutines in lines 1000–25000.

```
10 KEY OFF
20 MENU$="1 DEF 2 DATA 3 DRAW 4 SAVE 5 RCLL 6 FILE 7 EXIT"
30 FOR J%=1 TO 10:KEY J%,"":NEXT J%
100 'Main Menu Choice-Bar Chart Program
110 'E$ is returned by the input routine, =the second
120 'character of extended ASCII code
130 LOCATE 25,1
140 PRINT MENU$;
150 C=ASC(E$)
160 IF C=59 THEN 1000
170 IF C=60 THEN 2000
180 IF C=61 THEN 3000
190 IF C=62 THEN 4000
200 IF C=63 THEN 5000
210 IF C=64 THEN 6000
220 IF C=65 THEN 7000 ELSE 25000
1000 'Define bar chart parameters
1999 RETURN
2000 'Input bar chart data
2999 RETURN
3000 'Draw bar chart
3999 RETURN
4000 'Save bar chart
```

```
4999 RETURN
5000 'Recall bar chart
5999 RETURN
6000 'Read data file
6999 RETURN
7000 'Exit
7999 RETURN
25000 'Input routine
25999 RETURN
```

Answers to Test Your Understandings 1 and 2

1.   CHR$(0)+CHR$(30)+CHR$(0)+CHR$(79)

2.
```
10 C$ = INKEY$
20 IF C$="" THEN PRINT "NO CHARACTER IN THE BUFFER"
30 IF ASC(LEFT$(C$,1))<>0 THEN 100 ELSE
   C$=RIGHT$(C$,1)
40 PRINT "EXTENDED CODE: 0,";
100 PRINT ASC(RESPONSE$)
200 END
```

Error-Trapping

At the moment our programs have only a single way to respond to an error: The program stops and an error message is displayed. Sometimes the program is stopped with good cause, since a logical error prevents GWBASIC from making any sense of the program. However, there are other instances in which the error is rather innocent: The printer is not turned on, the wrong data diskette is in the drive, or the user provides an incorrect response to a prompt. In each of these situations, it is desirable for the program to report the error to the user and wait for further instructions. Let's learn how to make the program take such action.

Ordinarily, the response to an error is to halt the program. However, an alternative is provided by the

```
ON ERROR GOTO linenumber
```

statement. If your program contains such a statement GWBASIC will go to the indicated line number as soon as an error occurs. For example, suppose your program contains the statement

```
ON ERROR GOTO 10000
```

Whenever an error occurs, the program will go to the routine at the line 10000. The routine can contain an error-trapping routine to:

1. analyze the error;

2. notify the user of the error; and

3. resume the program and/or wait for further instructions from the user.

The ON ERROR GOTO statement is called an error-trapping statement. It may occur anywhere in the program. When you compile the program GWBASIC scans your program for the presence of an error-trapping statement. If it finds an error-trapping line it sets up a code to send your program to the indicated line. In order to minimize BASIC's time to search for an error-trapping statement, you should place an error-trapping statement at the beginning of the program.

To see how an error-trapping routine is constructed, let's consider a particular example. Suppose that your program involves reading a data file, which must be on the diskette in the current drive. The program user may place the wrong diskette in the drive or may not insert any diskette at all. Let's write an error-trapping routine to respond to these two types of errors.

Let's begin our error-trapping routine in line 5000. We begin our program with the error-trapping line

```
ON ERROR GOTO 5000
```

When an error occurs BASIC makes a note of the line number in the variable ERL (error line) and the error number in ERR. It then goes to the routine at the label ErrorHandler. The values of the variables ERL and ERR are at our disposal just like the values of any other variables. Note that ERL returns a line number, but if the statement generating the error does not have a line number, ERL returns the line number of the closest preceding line that has a line number.

In our particular example, there are two types of errors to look out for: File Not Found (error number 53) and Disk Not Ready (error number 71). The first error occurs when the file requested by the program is not on the indicated disk. The second error occurs when either the diskette drive door is open or no diskette is in the drive. The error numbers were obtained from either the list of errors on the summary card at the back of the book or in GWBASIC's reference manual. In the case of each error, the error-trapping routine should notify the user and wait for the situation to be corrected. Here is the routine:

```
5000 'Error trapping routine
5010 IF ERR=53 PRINT "File Not Found"
5020 IF ERR=71 PRINT "Disk Not Ready"
5030 IF ERR<>53 AND ERR<>71 THEN PRINT "Unrecoverable
     Error"
5040 IF ERR<>53 AND ERR<>71 THEN END
5050 PRINT "CORRECT DISKETTE. PRESS ANY KEY WHEN READY."
5060 IF INKEY$="" THEN 5060
5070 RESUME
```

Several comments are in order. Notice that the error-trapping routine only allows recovery in the case of errors 53 and 71. If the error is any other type, the program ends. In the case of error types 53 and 71, the program tells the operator to correct the situation. The program waits until the operator signals that the situation has been corrected. The RESUME then clears the error condition and causes the program to resume execution with the line that caused the error.

Note that we analyzed our errors using ERR. This did not require any use of labels at the lines generating the errors and is thus preferred to using ERL.

RESUME causes the program to resume with the statement that caused the error. The RESUME statement has several useful variations:

RESUME NEXT causes the program to resume with the line immediately after the line which caused the error.

RESUME LABEL causes the program to resume at the indicated label.

In designing and testing an error-trapping routine, it is helpful to be able to generate errors of a particular type. This may be done using the ERROR statement. For example, to generate an error 50 (field overflow) in line 75, just replace line 75 with

```
ERROR 50
```

When the program reaches line 75 it will simulate error 50. The program will then jump to the error-trapping routine to be tested.

Exercises

1. Write an error-trapping routine that allows the program to ignore all errors.
2. Write an error-trapping routine that allows detection of a Type Mismatch error in line 500. The response should be to display the error description and go to line 600.

Sixteen

Computer Games

Introduction

In the last few years computer games have captured the imaginations of millions of people. In this chapter, we will build several computer games which utilize both the random number generator and the graphics capabilities of the IBM Personal Computer. Actually, as we shall shortly see, these games utilize most of what we have learned and provide a good test of our programming prowess.

Several of the games require that we keep track of time, so we begin this chapter with a discussion of BASIC's mechanisms for timing.

Telling Time With Your Computer

In many games we need a clock to time moves. We will start by learning to tell time with the computer.

The MS-DOS operating system has a built-in clock that allows your programs to take into account the time of day (in hours, minutes, and seconds) and the date (day, month, and year). You can use this feature for many purposes, such as timing a segment of a program (see Example 1).

Reading the Clock

The clock keeps track of six pieces of information in the following order:

```
Month (1-12)
Day (1-31)
Year (00-99)
Hours (00-23)
Minutes (00-59)
Seconds (00-59)
```

The date is displayed in the following format:

```
2-15-84
```

The time is displayed in the following format:

```
14:38:27
```

The above displays correspond to February 15, 1984, at 27 seconds after 2:38 P.M. Note that the hours are counted using a 24-hour clock, with 0 hours corresponding to midnight. Hours 0–11 correspond to A.M., and hours 12–23 correspond to P.M. Also note that the year must be in the range 1980–2099.

The clock is programmed to account for the number of days in a month (28, 30, or 31), but it does not recognize leap years.

In BASIC, time is identified using the variable TIME$. To display the current time on the screen, use the command

```
PRINT TIME$
```

If it is currently 5:10 P.M., the computer displays the time in the format

```
17:10:07
```

The :07 denotes 7 seconds past the minute.

BASIC identifies the date using the variable DATE$. To display the current date of the screen, use the command

```
PRINT DATE$
```

If it is currently Dec. 12, 1984, the computer displays

```
12-12-1984
```

Test Your Understanding 1 (Answer on Page 472)

Display the current time and date.

Setting the Clock

You have an opportunity to set the clock when starting the Disk Operating System. The initial DOS display asks you for the date. If you accurately answer this question, the computer will keep the correct date as long as it is operating continuously. Note, however, that the computer loses track of these data as soon as it is turned off. You may also use TIME$ and DATE$ to set the time and date as follows: Suppose that the time is 12:03:17 and the date is 10/31/1984. You type the commands

```
TIME$ = "12:03:17"
DATE$ = "10-31-1984"
```

These commands may be typed whenever the computer is not executing a program and are typed without a line number. These commands may also be used within a BASIC program (with a line number, of course). For example, to reset the time to 00:00:00 within a program, use the statement

```
TIME$ = "00:00:00"
```

In setting the date there are two acceptable variations. First, you may replace some or all of the dashes in the date by slashes. All of the following are acceptable forms of the date:

```
10/31/1984    10-31-1984
10/31-1984    10-31/1984
```

Second, you may input the year as two digits. For example, you can input 1984 as 84. The computer will automatically supply the missing 19.

Test Your Understanding 2 (Answer on Page 472)

Write instructions to set the time to 2 P.M. and the date to Jan. 1, 1989.

Test Your Understanding 3

Set the clock with today's date and time. Check yourself by printing out the value of the clock.

Test Your Understanding 4 (Answer on Page 472)

Write a program that continually displays the correct time on the screen.

Calculating Elapsed Time

The clock may be used to measure elapsed time. You can ask the computer to count 10 seconds or three days. In such measurements it is convenient to have the components (that is, the hours, minutes, seconds, and so on) of the time and date available individually. Let's discuss a method for determining these numbers.

Begin with the string TIME$. Suppose that TIME$ is now equal to

```
"10:07:32"
```

To isolate the seconds (the 32), we must chop off the initial portion of the string, namely 10:07:. We may do this using the statement RIGHT$. The statement

```
RIGHT$(TIME$,2)
```

forms a string out of the rightmost two digits of the string TIME$. This is the string 32. In most applications, we will require the 32 as a number rather than as a string. To convert a string consisting of digits into the corresponding numeric constant we may use the VAL function. That is, to obtain the SECONDS portion of the time as a numeric constant we use the statement

```
SECONDS = VAL(RIGHT$(TIME$,2))
```

In a similar fashion, we may calculate the HOURS portion of the time by extracting the left two characters of the time and converting the resulting string into a numeric constant. The statement to accomplish this is

```
HOURS = VAL(LEFT$(TIME$,2))
```

Finally, to calculate the MINUTES portion of the time we must extract from TIME$ a string of two characters in length beginning with the fourth character. For this purpose, we use the MID$ statement as follows:

```
MINUTES = VAL(MID$(TIME$,4,2))
```

To calculate the MONTH, DAY, and YEAR portions of the date as numeric constants, we use the statements

```
MONTH = VAL(LEFT(DATE$,2))
DAY = VAL(MID$(DATE$,4,2))
YEAR = VAL(RIGHT$(DATE$,4))
```

The ON TIMER statement is even more convenient for calculating elapsed time. Consider the following two statements:

```
ON TIMER(10) GOSUB 200
TIMER ON
```

The first statement tells the computer that whenever the timer is turned on BASIC should count 10 seconds and then go to line 200. The time may be turned on anywhere in the program using a statement like the one on line 20.

Example 1.   In Chapter 7, we developed a program to test mastery in the addition of two-digit numbers. Redesign this program to allow 15 seconds to answer the question.

Solution.   Let us use the clock. After a particular problem has been given we will start the seconds portion of the clock at 0 and perform a loop that continually tests the seconds portion of the clock for the value 15. When this value is encountered, the program prints out "TIME'S UP. WHAT IS YOUR ANSWER?" Here is the program; Lines 50 and 60 contain the loop:

```
1 ' *************************
2 '          ARITH3
3 ' This program provides a
4 ' timed test of addition of
5 ' 2-digit numbers.
6 ' *************************
10 FOR J=1 TO 10:'LOOP TO GIVE 10 PROBLEMS
20    INPUT "TYPE TWO 2-DIGIT NUMBERS"; A,B
30    PRINT "WHAT IS THEIR SUM?"
40    ON TIMER(15) GOSUB 100
50    TIMER ON
60    GOTO 60 'Wait until timer interrupts
100   INPUT "TIME'S UP! WHAT IS YOUR ANSWER";C
120   IF A+B=C THEN 200
130   PRINT "SORRY. THE CORRECT ANSWER IS",A+B
140   GOTO 500: 'GO TO THE NEXT PROBLEM
200   PRINT "YOUR ANSWER IS CORRECT! CONGRATULATIONS"
210   R=R+1:     'INCREASE SCORE BY 1
500 NEXT J
```

```
600 PRINT "YOUR SCORE IS",R,"CORRECT OUT OF 10"
700 PRINT "TO TRY AGAIN, TYPE RUN"
800 END
```

Figure 16-1 shows a sample run of the above program.

```
Ok
run
TYPE TWO 2-DIGIT NUMBERS? 12,25
WHAT IS THEIR SUM?
TIME'S UP! WHAT IS YOUR ANSWER? 37
YOUR ANSWER IS CORRECT! CONGRATULATIONS
TYPE TWO 2-DIGIT NUMBERS? 15,18
WHAT IS THEIR SUM?
TIME'S UP! WHAT IS YOUR ANSWER? 48
SORRY. THE CORRECT ANSWER IS                  33
TYPE TWO 2-DIGIT NUMBERS? _
```

Figure 16-1.
Sample run of the timed arithmetic program.

Test Your Understanding 5 (Answer on Page 472)

Modify the above program so that it allows you to take as much time as you like to solve a problem, but keeps track of elapsed time in seconds and prints out the number of seconds used.

Exercises

1. Set the clock with today's date and the current time.

2. Print out the current time on the screen.

3. Write a program that prints out the date and time at one-second intervals.

4. Write a program that prints out the date and time at one-minute intervals.

Answers to Test Your Understandings 1, 2, 4, and 5

1.
```
10 PRINT TIME$ : PRINT DATE$
20 END
30 RUN
```

2.
```
10 TIME$ = "14:00:00"
20 DATE$ = "1/1/85"
```

4.
```
10 CLS
20 PRINT TIME$
30 FOR J=1 TO 500
40 NEXT J: 'DELAY
50 GOTO 10
60 END
```

Note: This program is an infinite loop and needs to be terminated by pressing the key combination Ctrl-Break.

5. Delete lines 40–100. Change the RETURNs in lines 140 and 200 to GOTOs. Add these lines:

```
40 TIME$ = "00:00:00"
100 INPUT "WHAT IS YOUR ANSWER";C
110 MINUTES = VAL(MID$(TIME$,4,2))
111 SECONDS = VAL(RIGHT$(TIME$,2))
112 PRINT "YOU TOOK",60*MINUTES+SECONDS, "SECONDS"
```

Blind Target Shoot (Text Mode)

The object of this game is to shoot down a target on the screen by moving your cursor to hit the target. The catch is that you only have a two-second look at your target! The program begins by asking if your are ready. If so, you press any key. The computer then randomly chooses a spot to place the target and it lights up the spot for two seconds. The cursor is then moved to the upper left position of the screen (the so-called "home" position). You must then move the cursor to the target based on your brief glimpse of it. You have five seconds to hit the target (see Figure 16-2).

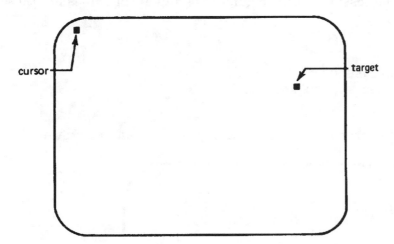

Figure 16-2.
Blind target shoot.

Your score is based on your distance from the target as measured in terms of the moves it takes to get to the target from your final position. Here is the list of possible scores:

Distance From Target	Score
0	100
1 or 2	90
3 to 5	70
6 to 10	50
11 to 15	30
16 to 20	10
over 20	0

You move the cursor using the cursor motion keys on the numeric keypad. We will use event trapping to interrupt the program while the program is running.

Here is a sample session with the game: The underlined lines are those you type.

```
RUN

BLIND TARGET SHOOT
TO BEGIN GAME, PRESS ANY KEY
```

Press any key. The screen clears. The target is displayed. See Figure 16-3.

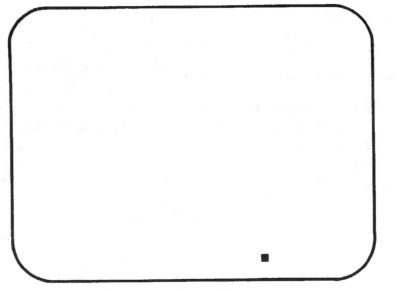

Figure 16-3.
Target displayed.

The screen is cleared and the cursor is moved to the home position (see Figure 16-4a). The cursor is then moved to the remembered position of the target (see Figure 16-4b). Time runs out (see Figure 16-4c).

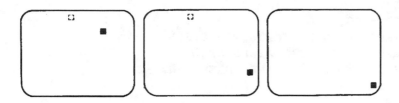

Figure 16-4a.
Cursor moved to home position.

Figure 16-4b.
Cursor moves to position of target.

Figure 16-4c.
Time runs out.

The score is calculated (see Figure 16-5).

YOUR DISTANCE FROM THE TARGET IS 12

Figure 16-5.
Score calcu-lated.

Here is a listing of our program:

```
10 ' ******************
20 ' ** TARGET SHOOT **
30 ' ******************
100 'Title Screen
110     CLS
```

```
120     KEY OFF
130     WIDTH 40
140     RANDOMIZE VAL(RIGHT$(TIME$,2))
150     PRINT "BLIND TARGET SHOOT"
160     PRINT "TO BEGIN GAME, PRESS ANY KEY"
170     IF INKEY$="" THEN 170
180     CLS
190 'Initialization
200     TIME$ = "0:0:0":          'Reset Clock
210     LOCATE ,,0:               'Turn off cursor
220 'Choose target location (targrow,targcol)
230     TARGCOL = INT(40*RND)+1
240     TARGROW = INT(25*RND)+1
250     LOCATE TARGROW,TARGCOL
260     PRINT CHR$(219):          'Display target
270 'Look at target
280     SECONDS = VAL(RIGHT$(TIME$,2))
290     IF SECONDS = 2 THEN 300 ELSE 280
300     'TWO SECONDS ELAPSED
310      LOCATE TARGROW,TARGCOL
320      PRINT " ";:              'Blank out target
330      LOCATE ,,1,1,13
340      PRINT CHR$(11)
350      TIME$ = "0:0:0"
360      X=1:Y=1:
370 'Turn on cursor key trapping
380     ON KEY(11) GOSUB 480
390     ON KEY(12) GOSUB 520
400     ON KEY(13) GOSUB 560
410     ON KEY(14) GOSUB 600
420     KEY(11) ON
430     KEY(12) ON
440     KEY(13) ON
450     KEY(14) ON
460     SECONDS = VAL(RIGHT$(TIME$,2))
470     IF SECONDS = 5 THEN 700 ELSE 460
480 'Cursor Up
490      GOSUB 640
500      PRINT CHR$(30);
510    RETURN
```

```
520 'Cursor Left
530    GOSUB 640
540    PRINT CHR$(29);
550  RETURN
560 'Cursor Right
570    GOSUB 640
580    PRINT CHR$(28);
590  RETURN
600 'Cursor Down
610    GOSUB 640
620    PRINT CHR$(31);
630  RETURN
640 'Turn off cursor motion trapping
650    KEY(11) OFF
660    KEY(12) OFF
670    KEY(13) OFF
680    KEY(14) OFF
690  RETURN
700 'Compute score
710    D = ABS(POS(0)-TARGCOL)+ABS(CSRLIN-TARGROW)
720    CLS
730    PRINT "YOUR DISTANCE FROM THE TARGET IS";D
740    IF D=0 THEN PRINT "CONGRATULATIONS"
750    IF D=0 THEN PRINT "YOU HIT THE TARGET!"
760    SC = 100
770    IF D>0 THEN SC=SC-10
780    IF D>2 THEN SC = SC-20
790    IF D>5 THEN SC = SC-20
800    IF D>10 THEN SC=SC-20
810    IF D>15 THEN SC = SC-20
820    IF D>20 THEN SC = SC-10
830    PRINT "YOUR SCORE IS",SC
840    INPUT "DO YOU WISH TO PLAY AGAIN(Y/N)";B$
850    IF B$ = "Y" OR B$="y" THEN 180 ELSE 860
860    END
```

Exercises

1. Experiment with the above program by making the time of target viewing shorter or longer than two seconds.
2. Experiment with the above program by making the time for target location shorter or longer than five seconds.
3. Modify the program to keep a running total score for a sequence of ten games.
4. Modify the program to allow two players, keeping a running total score for a sequence of ten games. At the end of ten games the computer should announce the total scores and declare the winner.

Shooting Gallery

In this section we develop a game called Shooting Gallery that simulates the shooting galleries of carnivals. The player has a gun that he or she may fire at a moving target (see Figure 16-6). The program keeps track of the hits. The game shows 20 moving targets during one play.

The design of this game incorporates most of what we know. Let's begin by enabling event trapping of the cursor motion keys up, down, right, and left. The right and left motions will tell the program that we wish to move the gun to the right or left. The cursor up key will fire the gun.

This program will be in the medium-resolution graphics mode. The gun will initially be in the center of the last text row of the screen. The first position of the bullet after being fired will be in row 185. We will keep track of the horizontal position of the gun in the variable GUNPOSITION and the vertical and horizontal positions of the bullet in the variables BULLETROW and BULLETCOL. Line 90 initializes GUNPOSITION and BULLETROW.

For the gun we will use the small house-shaped figure (ASCII character 127). The bullet will be a vertical arrow (ASCII character 24) and the target

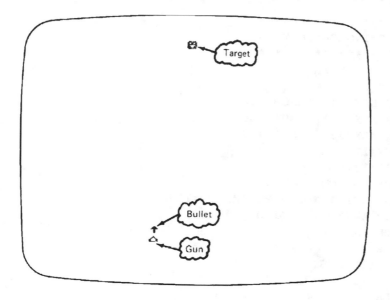

Figure 16-6.
**The game of
shooting gal-
lery**.

will be a happy face (ASCII character 2). All of these figures are to be ani-
mated, so it is necessary to get all of them in appropriate arrays A%, B%,
and C%. Using % means that the arrays will contain integers. Limiting the
type of number that the arrays can contain will speed up program execution.

The program begins by placing the gun in its initial position. There is an
outer loop for 20 targets and an inner loop each step of which moves the
target two columns across the screen and the bullet (if any have been fired)
eight rows up the screen. If you fire the gun (cursor up key), the program is
interrupted and the gun firing routine is called. This displays the bullet in
its initial position. All subsequent motion of the bullet is controlled by the
main loop. The bullet disappears when it reaches the row of the target. The
target disappears when it hits the right edge of the screen. If the bullet and
the target are at the same place at the same time, both disappear and you
are credited with a hit.

The BEEP command is used to sound the speaker when you score a hit.
Also, note the use of the function ABS in line 670. ABS(X) is just X with its
sign removed. For example, ABS(+5) = 5, whereas ABS(-5) = 5.

```
1 ' **********************
2 ' ** SHOOTING GALLERY **
3 ' **********************
10 ' Initialization
20      KEY OFF
30      ON KEY(11) GOSUB 590
40      ON KEY(12) GOSUB 530
50      ON KEY(13) GOSUB 470
60      KEY(11) ON
70      KEY(12) ON
80      KEY(13) ON
90      GUNPOSITION=160:BULLETROW=185
100     DIM A%(100),B%(100),C%(100)
110     SCREEN 1,0
120     CLS
130     PRINT CHR$(2)
140     GET (0,0)-(7,7),A%
150     CLS
160     PRINT CHR$(127)
170     GET (0,0)-(7,7),B%
180     CLS
190     PRINT CHR$(24)
200     GET (0,0)-(7,7),C%
210     CLS
220     PUT (GUNPOSITION,185),B%
230 'Main program loop
240     FOR TARGET=1 TO 20
250          PUT (0,8),A%
260          FOR COLUMN=2 TO 312 STEP 2
270             GOSUB 340:          'Move target
280             GOSUB 380:          'Move bullet
290          NEXT COLUMN
300          IF COLUMN=316 THEN 320
310          PUT (312,8),A%
320     NEXT TARGET
330     END
340 'Move target
350     PUT (COLUMN-2,8),A%
360     PUT (COLUMN,8),A%
370 RETURN
```

```
380 'Move bullet
390     IF BFLAG=0 THEN 460
400     PUT (BULLETCOL,BULLETROW),C%
410     BULLETROW=BULLETROW-8
420     IF BULLETROW<10 THEN GOSUB 670 ELSE 450
430     BFLAG=0
440     GOTO 460
450     PUT (BULLETCOL,BULLETROW),C%
460 RETURN
470 'Move gun 8 steps to right
480     PUT (GUNPOSITION,185),B%
490     GUNPOSITION=GUNPOSITION+8
500     IF GUNPOSITION>311 THEN GUNPOSITION=311
510     PUT (GUNPOSITION,185),B%
520 RETURN
530 'Move gun 8 steps to left
540     PUT (GUNPOSITION,185),B%
550     GUNPOSITION=GUNPOSITION-8
560     IF GUNPOSITION<0 THEN GUNPOSITION=0
570     PUT (GUNPOSITION,185),B%
580 RETURN
590 'Shoot gun
600     IF BFLAG=1 THEN 650
610     BFLAG=1
620     BULLETCOL=GUNPOSITION
630     BULLETROW=177
640     PUT (BULLETCOL,BULLETROW),C%
650 RETURN
660 'Determine if target is hit
670     IF ABS(BULLETCOL-COLUMN)<7 THEN GOSUB 690
680 RETURN
690 'Erase target and bullet
700     PUT (COLUMN,8),A%
710     BEEP
720     SCORE=SCORE+1
730     LOCATE 1,1
740     PRINT "SCORE";SCORE;" hits";
750     COLUMN=314
760 RETURN
```

Exercises

1. Run the above program to get a feel for its operation.
2. Modify the above program so that the bullet speed is increased by a factor of two. (This makes the game easier!)
3. Modify the above program so that the bullet speed is divided by a factor of two.
4. Modify the above program so that every fifth target is a sun (ASCII code 15). Modify the scoring so that hitting a sun counts for five hits.

Tic-Tac-Toe (Graphics Mode)

In this section, we present a program for the traditional game of tic-tac-toe. We won't attempt to let the computer execute a strategy. Rather, we will let it be fairly stupid and choose its moves randomly. We will also use the random number generator to "flip" for the first move. Throughout the program, you will be O and the computer will be X. Here is a sample game. It begins with loading the program as in Figure 16-7. The initial instruction screen in shown in Figure 16-8.

```
Ok
LOAD"TICTAC"
Ok
RUN_
```

Figure 16-7.
Loading tic-tac-toe game.

```
TIC TAC TOE
YOU WILL BE O;THE COMPUTER WILL BE X
THE POSITIONS OF THE BOARD ARE NUMBERED
AS FOLLOWS:

        1            2            3
        4            5            6
        7            8            9

THE COMPUTER WILL TOSS FOR FIRST.
YOU GO FIRST.
WHEN READY TO BEGIN TYPE 'R'
R
```

Figure 16-8.
Sample tic-tac-toe game.

Test Your Understanding 1 (Answer on Page 489)

How can the computer toss to see who goes first?

The computer now draws a tic-tac-toe board. See Figure 16-9.

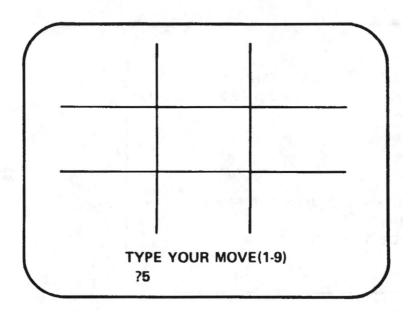

TYPE YOUR MOVE(1-9)
?5

Figure 16-9.
The computer draws a tic-tac-toe board.

The computer now displays your move and makes a move of its own (see Figure 16-10).

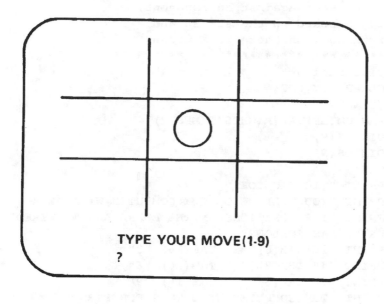

TYPE YOUR MOVE(1-9)
?

Figure 16-10.
**The computer
displays
your move,
and makes
one of its own**.

The computer now makes its move until someone wins or a tie game results.

Here are the variables used in the program:

Z = 0 if it's your move and Z = 1 if it is the computer's.

A$(J) (J=1, 2, ..., 9) contains either O, X, or the empty string, indicating the current status of position J.

S = the position of the current move.

M = the number of moves played (including the current one).
We used a video display worksheet to lay out the board, and to determine the coordinates for the lines and the Xs and Os.

Here is a listing of our program:

```
10 ' ****************************************
20 '                 TIC-TAC-TOE
30 ' This program plays the traditional game
```

```
40 '  of tic-tac-toe against an opponent,
50 '  drawing a board on the screen and
60 '  determining when there is a winner
70 '  ****************************************
1000 'Initialization
1010     CLEAR:KEY OFF
1020     SCREEN 1
1030     RANDOMIZE VAL(RIGHT$(TIME$,2))
1040     DIM A$(9)
1050     DIM B$(9)
1060     CLS
1070     PRINT "TIC TAC TOE"
1080     PRINT "YOU WILL BE O; THE COMPUTER WILL BE X"
1090     PRINT "THE POSITIONS ON THE BOARD ARE NUMBERED"
1100     PRINT "AS FOLLOWS"
1110     PRINT "1";TAB(8) "2";TAB(16) "3"
1120     PRINT "4";TAB(8) "5";TAB(16) "6"
1130     PRINT "7";TAB(8) "8";TAB(16) "9"
1140     PRINT "THE COMPUTER WILL TOSS FOR FIRST"
1150     FOR J=1 TO 2000:NEXT J
1160     IF RND(1) > .5 THEN 1170 ELSE 1210
1170     PRINT "YOU GO FIRST"
1180     FOR J=1 TO 2000:NEXT J
1190     Z=0:                     'Player goes first
1200     GOTO 1240
1210     PRINT "I'LL GO FIRST"
1220     FOR J=1 TO 2000:NEXT J
1230     Z=1:                     'Computer goes first
1240     PRINT "WHEN READY TO BEGIN, PRESS ANY KEY"
1250     IF INKEY$="" THEN 1250
1260     CLS
2000 'Main program
2010     GOSUB 3000:              'Draw game board
2020     FOR M=1 TO 9:                     'M=move #
2030          IF Z=0 THEN GOSUB 5000
2040          IF Z=1 THEN GOSUB 6000
2050          Z=1-Z
2060          IF WIN=1 THEN 2100
2070     NEXT M
2080          PRINT "THE GAME IS TIED"
```

```
2090               FOR J=1 TO 2000:NEXT J
2100      CLS
2110      LOCATE 1,1
2120      INPUT "ANOTHER GAME(Y/N)";R$
2130      IF R$="Y" OR R$="y" THEN 1010 ELSE END
3000 'Draw TIC TAC TOE Board
3010      CLS
3020      LINE (103,8)-(103,191)
3030      LINE (206,8)-(206,191)
3040      LINE (8,70)-(311,70)
3050      LINE (8,132)-(311,132)
3060      RETURN
4000 ' Display current game status
4010      LOCATE 5,7: PRINT A$(1);
4020      LOCATE 5,20: PRINT A$(2);
4030      LOCATE 5,33: PRINT A$(3);
4040      LOCATE 14,7: PRINT A$(4);
4050      LOCATE 14,20: PRINT A$(5);
4060      LOCATE 14,33: PRINT A$(6);
4070      LOCATE 21,7: PRINT A$(7);
4080      LOCATE 21,20: PRINT A$(8);
4090      LOCATE 21,33:PRINT A$(9);
4100 RETURN
5000 'Player's Move
5010      LOCATE 1,1
5020      INPUT "TYPE YOUR MOVE(1-9)";S
5030      IF S<1 OR S>9 THEN 5050
5040      IF A$(S) = "" THEN 5100
5050      LOCATE 1,1
5060      LINE (0,0)-(319,7),0,BF:'Blank out first row
5070      PRINT "ILLEGAL MOVE"
5080      FOR J=1 TO 2000:NEXT J
5090      GOTO 5000
5100      A$(S) = "O"
5110      GOSUB 7000:      'Is game over?
5120      LINE (0,0)-(319,7),0,BF:'Blank out first row
5130      GOSUB 4000:      'Display move
5140 RETURN
6000 'Computer's Move
6010      LOCATE 1,1
```

```
6020      PRINT "Here's my move!";
6030      GOTO 8000:                 'Is there a winning move?
6040      'If not, choose random move
6050      S = INT(9*RND+1)
6060      IF A$(S) = "" THEN 6070 ELSE 6050
6070      A$(S) = "X"
6080      FOR J=1 TO 2000:NEXT J: 'Delay
6090      GOSUB 7000:                'Is game over?
6100      GOSUB 4000:                'Display move
6110 RETURN
7000 'Is the game over?
7010      IF Z = 0 THEN C$ = "O" ELSE C$ = "X"
7020      IF A$(1) = A$(2) THEN 7030 ELSE 7050
7030      IF A$(2) = A$(3) THEN 7040 ELSE 7050
7040      IF A$(3) = C$ THEN 7260
7050      IF A$(1) = A$(4) THEN 7060 ELSE 7080
7060      IF A$(4) = A$(7) THEN 7070 ELSE 7080
7070      IF A$(7) = C$ THEN 7260
7080      IF A$(1) = A$(5) THEN 7090 ELSE 7110
7090      IF A$(5) = A$(9) THEN 7100 ELSE 7110
7100      IF A$(9) = C$ THEN 7260
7110      IF A$(2) = A$(5) THEN 7120 ELSE 7140
7120      IF A$(5) = A$(8) THEN 7130 ELSE 7140
7130      IF A$(8) = C$ THEN 7260
7140      IF A$(3) = A$(6) THEN 7150 ELSE 7170
7150      IF A$(6) = A$(9) THEN 7160 ELSE 7170
7160      IF A$(9) = C$ THEN 7260
7170      IF A$(4) = A$(5) THEN 7180 ELSE 7200
7180      IF A$(5) = A$(6) THEN 7190 ELSE 7200
7190      IF A$(6) = C$ THEN 7260
7200      IF A$(7) = A$(8) THEN 7210 ELSE 7230
7210      IF A$(8) = A$(9) THEN 7220 ELSE 7230
7220      IF A$(9) = C$ THEN 7260
7230      IF A$(3) = A$(5) THEN 7240 ELSE 7320
7240      IF A$(5) = A$(7) THEN 7250 ELSE 7320
7250      IF A$(7) = C$ THEN 7260 ELSE 7320
7260      GOSUB 4000
7270      LOCATE 1,1
7280      PRINT SPACE$(80);
7290      LOCATE 1,1
```

```
7300      PRINT C$ , "WINS THIS ROUND":WIN=1
7310      FOR J=1 TO 2000:NEXT J
7320 RETURN
8000 'Look for a winning move
8010      COUNT = 0
8020      FOR I=1 TO 9
8030            IF A$(I) = "X" THEN B(I) = 1
8040            IF A$(I) = "" THEN B(I) = 0
8050            IF A$(I) = "O" THEN B(I) = -1
8060      NEXT I
8070      COUNT = COUNT+1
8080      IF COUNT = 9 THEN 8180
8090      READ I,J,K
8100      S = B(I)+B(J)+B(K)
8110      IF S =  2 THEN 8120 ELSE 8070
8120      IF B(J) = 0 THEN A$(J) = "X" ELSE 8140
8130      GOTO 8310
8140      IF B(K) = 0 THEN A$(K) = "X" ELSE 8160
8150      GOTO 8310
8160      IF B(I) = 0 THEN A$(I) = "X" ELSE 8070
8170      GOTO 8310
8180      RESTORE
8190      COUNT = 0
8200      COUNT = COUNT + 1
8210      IF COUNT = 9 THEN 8320
8220      READ I,J,K
8230      S = B(I)+B(J)+B(K)
8240      IF S=-2 THEN 8250 ELSE 8200
8250      IF B(J) = 0 THEN A$(J) = "X" ELSE 8270
8260      GOTO 8310
8270      IF B(K) = 0 THEN A$(K) = "X" ELSE 8290
8280      GOTO 8310
8290      A$(I) = "X"
8300      GOTO 8310
8310      RESTORE : GOTO 6080
8320      RESTORE:GOTO 6040
8330      DATA
1,2,3,4,5,6,7,8,9,1,4,7,2,5,8,3,6,9,1,5,9,3,5,7
```

Exercises

1. Modify the above program so that you and the computer may play a series of ten games. The computer should decide the champion of the series.

2. Modify the above program to play 4×4 tic-tac-toe.

Answers to Test Your Understanding 1

Use the random number function and examine its value to see whether it is greater than, less than, or equal to .5. See the listing of the tic-tac-toe program.

Seventeen

Memory Management

Introduction

In this chapter we will explore the memory of the IBM PC and its compatibles. We will describe the way in which numbers and text are stored and the way the memory is organized. Our discussions include:

- The properties of the binary and hexadecimal number systems. As we shall see, binary and hexadecimal arithmetic will arise throughout the book, so we'll begin with a discussion of these important number systems.

- Bits, bytes, and memory addressing.

- How BASIC's various data types are stored in memory.

- Logical operations on bytes and their applications, with particular attention to graphics.

- Some useful memory locations.

Binary and Hexadecimal Numbers

Decimal Representation of Numbers. In grade school we learned to perform arithmetic using the decimal number system. In this system numbers are written as strings of digits chosen from among the ten numbers 0, 1, 2, 3, 4, 5, 6, 7, 8, 9. Here are some examples of these familiar numbers:

```
14312,  -928372,  29831029831902938290
```

Such strings of digits are interpreted according to a system of place value. We proceed from right to left: The digit in the extreme right position represents the number of 1s, the next digit the number of 10s, the next digit the number of 100s, the next digit the number of 1,000s, and so forth. For example, the number 1935 stands for

1	1000s	1*1,000	=	1,000
9	100s	9*100	=	900
3	10s	3*10	=	30
5	1s	5*1	=	5
				____
				1935

The values of the various digit positions, that is, the numbers 1, 10, 100, 1,000,... are all powers of 10:

```
1=100,  10=101,  100=102,  1000=103,  . . .
```

Another way of expressing the number 1935 is

```
1*103 + 9*102 + 3*101 + 5*100
```

Note that we have arranged the digits in their usual order, which corresponds to decreasing powers of 10.

Binary Representation of Numbers. In the binary number system numbers are represented by strings formed from the two digits 0 and 1. Here are some examples of binary numbers:

```
10, 01110000111, 100100100100
```

Just as the decimal number system is based on powers of 10, the binary number system is based on powers of two, for example, the numbers

```
20=1, 21=2, 22=4, 23=8, 24=16,...
```

We interpret a binary number by examining the digits from right to left. The rightmost digit of a binary number corresponds to the number of 1s, the next digit to the number of 2s, the next digit to the number of 4s, and so forth. For example, the binary number 1,101 represents

1 8s	= 8
1 4s	= 4
0 2s	= 0
1 1s (rightmost digit)	= 1
1,101	$= \overline{13}$

Therefore, the binary number 1,101 corresponds to the decimal number 13.

Test Your Understanding 1 (Answer on Page 501)

What decimal number corresponds to the binary number 10101010?

The above calculations for converting a binary number into its decimal equivalent may be tedious. However, the computer can do the work for us. Here is a simple program that performs the conversion:

```
100 'Convert binary to decimal
110 INPUT "NUMBER TO CONVERT";N$
120 E=0:'E=current power of 2
130 D=0:'D=decimal equivalent
```

```
140 L=LEN(N$)
150 IF L=0 THEN 210
160 IF RIGHT$(N$,1) = "1" THEN D=D+2^E:GOTO 180
170 IF RIGHT$(N$,1) <> "0" THEN 230
180 E=E+1
190 N$=LEFT$(N$,L-1)
200 GOTO 140
210 PRINT "Decimal Equivalent=";D
220 GOTO 240
230 PRINT "Input Not In Proper Format"
240 END
```

Figure 17-1 shows a sample run for the above program.

```
Ok
run
NUMBER TO CONVERT? 0110011
Decimal Equivalent= 51
Ok
_
```

Figure 17-1.
Converting from binary to decimal.

Converting From Decimal to Binary. As we have seen, every binary number has a decimal equivalent, however, the reverse is also true: every decimal number has a binary equivalent. For example, consider the decimal number 61. Let's divide it by 2 to obtain a quotient 30 and remainder 1. Write these results in the form

    61 = 30*2 + 1

There is a 2 present now. But the quotient 30 does not yet involve a 2, so we divide the 30 by 2 to obtain the quotient 15 and remainder 0. Write this result in the form

```
30 = 15*2 + 0
```

If we insert this expression for 30 into the expression for 61, we obtain the result

```
61 = (15*2+0)*2 + 1

   = 15*2^2 + 0*2 + 1
```

This is now closer to a representation of 61 by powers of 2, but the 15 does not yet involve 2, so let's now repeat the above procedure using the number 15 instead of 30. First we divide by 2 to obtain a quotient of 7 and a remainder of 1. Next, we write the equation

```
15 = 7*2 + 1
```

and we substitute this equation into our preceding expression for 61:

```
61 = (7*2 + 1)*2^2 + 0*2 + 1

   = 7*2^3 + 1*2^2 + 0*2 + 1
```

This is a better representation of 61. To improve it we repeat the procedure using the number 7:

```
7 = 3*2 + 1

61 = (3*2+1)*2^3 + 1*2^2 + 0*2 + 1

   = 3*2^4 + 1*2^3 + 1*2^2 + 0*2 + 1
```

Repeat the procedure using the number 3:

```
3 = 1*2 + 1

61 = (1*2+1)*2^4 + 1*2^3 + 1*2^2 + 0*2 + 1

   = 1*2^5 + 1*2^4 + 1*2^3 + 1*2^2 + 0*2 + 1
```

This last representation of 61 consists only of powers of 2. From this representation we may read off the binary representation of 61 as the 1 or 0 coefficients of the powers of 2. Read from left to right. The representation is

```
61 (decimal) = 111101 (binary)
```

If you don't believe the computation just proceed in reverse and convert 111101 to its corresponding decimal number. You will obtain 61 as the result.

The above procedure may be programmed for the computer, however, it is necessary to perform division to obtain an integer quotient and remainder. If you use the operation / to perform the division you will obtain a decimal answer and no remainder. For example, the result of 61/2 is 30.5 (rather than the desired quotient 30 and remainder 1). To obtain the desired information it is simplest to use the BASIC operations \ and MOD.

Recall that the operation \ is called integer division and may be used to calculate the quotient of one integer by another. (Remember that an integer is a whole number in the range 32,768 to 32,767. Integer division yields only the integer part of the quotient. For example,

```
 3\2 = 1
16\2 = 8
72\7 = 10
```

The operation MOD allows you to compute the remainder that results from an integer division, for example, 5 MOD 2 yields the remainder of the integer division 5\2. That is 5 MOD 2 equals 1.

Test Your Understanding 2 (Answer on Page 501)
What is the value of $(7\backslash3 + 1)*(18\backslash5 - 1)$?

Test Your Understanding 3 (Answers on Page 502)
What is the value of

a. `17 MOD 7\5`
b. `5^2 MOD 25\2^2`

Using the operations \ and MOD, we may easily convert a decimal number to its binary equivalent. We repeatedly perform integer division by 2. The remainders of the division provide the digits of the binary number proceeding from right to left. Here is a program to perform the calculations:

```
10  '**********************************
20  'This program converts the decimal
30  'number N to its binary equivalent.
40  '**********************************
100 'Main Program
110 INPUT "NUMBER TO CONVERT";N
120 A$ = ""
130 REMAINDER = N MOD 2
140 A$ = RIGHT$(STR$(REMAINDER),1)+A$
150 N=N\2
160 IF N=0 THEN 170 ELSE 130
170 PRINT "The Binary Equivalent Is "; A$
180 END
```

Figure 17-2 shows a sample run for the above program.

```
Ok
run
NUMBER TO CONVERT? 599
The Binary Equivalent Is 1001010111
Ok
_
```

Figure 17-2.
Converting from decimal to binary.

A binary digit (0 or 1) is called a bit. The number 1,011 is four bits long whereas the number 10,010,011 is eight bits long.

Test Your Understanding 4 (Answer on Page 502)

    a. List all possible two-bit numbers.
    b. List all possible three-bit numbers.

In carrying out Test Your Understanding 4 you should have found that there are four two-bit numbers and eight three-bit numbers. There are 16 possible four-bit numbers:

```
0000, 0001, 0010, 0011, 0100, 0101, 0110, 0111
1000, 1001, 1010, 1011, 1100, 1101, 1110, 1111
```

It can be proven in a mathematics text that the number of possible N-bit numbers is equal to 2^N. This fact generalizes the particular cases (N=2,3,4) observed above.

As we shall see, eight-bit and 16-bit binary numbers play a special role in the internal workings of the IBM PC. The number of eight-bit binary numbers is $2^8=256$. They represent the numbers 0 through 255. Similarly, the number of 16-bit binary numbers is $2^{16} = 65536$. They represent the numbers 0 through 65,535.

The IBM PC and all other digital computers use the binary number system for their operation. It may appear as if the computer uses decimal numbers. However, all data must be converted into binary form if the computer is to process it. And this applies to text data and program statements as well as numerical data. Each type of information is translated into binary according to its own translation scheme (more about this later). Computer operations are performed only on binary numbers. When output is required, the computer translates from binary to either numeric or text format.

Hexadecimal Representation of Numbers.   The hexadecimal number system is closely connected with the binary number system and is much easier to work with in many applications. There are 16 possible hexadecimal digits:

0,1,2,3,4,5,6,7,8,9,A,B,C,D,E,F

The digits 0–9 have their usual numerical values and A,B,C,D,E,F have the respective values

10 11 12 13 14 15
 A B   C   D   E   F

A typical hexadecimal number is a string of hexadecimal digits, such as

A1EFF78A

The rightmost digit indicates the number of 1s, the next digit the number of 16s, the next digit the number of 256s ($256 = 16^2$), etc. For example, the above hexadecimal number corresponds to

```
10*16^7 + 1*16^6 + 14*16^5 + 15*16^4 + 15*16^3 + 7*16^2 +
8*16 + 10*1
```

The real advantage of hexadecimal is that it offers a shorthand way of writing numbers in binary. The 16 hexadecimal digits correspond to the following four-digit binary numbers:

Hexadecimal	Binary	Decimal
0	0000	0
1	0001	1
2	0010	2
3	0011	3
4	0100	4
5	0101	5
6	0110	6
7	0111	7
8	1000	8
9	1001	9
A	1010	10
B	1011	11
C	1100	12
D	1101	13
E	1110	14
F	1111	15

A binary number may be blocked off in groups of four digits and translated into hexadecimal according to the above table. For example, consider the 25-digit binary number

```
1111100111001010111100111
```

To convert it into hexadecimal we first block it off into groups of four digits proceeding from right to left:

```
1 1111 0011 1001 0101 1110 0111
```

We complete the leftmost group by adding three zeros on the left:

```
0001 1111 0011 1001 0101 1110 0111
```

Finally, we translate each four-digit group into a hexadecimal digit:

```
0001 1111 0011 1001 0101 1110 0111
  1    F    3    9    5    E    7
```

Therefore the hexadecimal equivalent of the binary number is 1F395E7. It is clearly simpler to work with the hexadecimal form rather than the binary form of the number.

Hexadecimal Numbers in BASIC

Hexadecimal numbers may be used in IBM PC BASIC on a par with decimal numbers. That is, wherever you use a decimal number you may use a hexadecimal number and vice versa. In BASIC a hexadecimal number is indicated with the prefix &H. For example, the hexadecimal number 1A2F is denoted &H1A2F.

It is possible to write a simple program for converting decimal to hexadecimal. However, BASIC has a built-in function that saves us the bother. This function, HEX$, returns a string that is the hexadecimal representation of a given decimal number. For example, we have

```
HEX$(10) equals "A"
```

```
HEX$(30) equals "1E"
```

HEX$ returns a string, which may not be used in calculations. On the other hand, &H1E is a number. As far as BASIC is concerned, &H1E is just another name for 30.

Answers to Test Your Understandings 1, 2, 3, and 4

1. 170

2. 6

3. a. 0

    b. 1

4. a. 00, 01, 10, 11
    b. 000, 001, 010, 011, 100, 101, 110, 111

Bits, Bytes, and Memory

Our first application of the binary and hexadecimal number systems will be to describe the contents and the addressing scheme used in PC memory. At the same time, we will explore the contents of RAM and describe the various data present in RAM while you are using BASIC.

RAM is broken into a series of eight-bit binary numbers called bytes. The size of your RAM is measured in units of 1,024 bytes. One 1024-byte unit is called 1K (for Kilobyte), so a system with 32K of RAM contains 32×1024 or 32,768 bytes. A system with 64K contains 64×1024 or 65536 bytes. Your IBM PC can be expanded to contain as much as 640K, while an AT unit can be expanded to contain as much as 3,072K.

You should think of RAM as divided into a large number of cubbyholes with each cubbyhole containing a single byte. The cubbyholes of RAM are called **memory locations**. The contents of each memory location may be described by two hexadecimal digits (= 8 bits). For example, here are the contents of four memory locations:

    7E 0F FF 81

The memory locations of a computer are numbered, usually beginning with 0. The number associated with each memory location is called its address. For example, in a simple computer system (not the PC) with 4K of RAM, the memory locations have addresses from 0 to 4,095 (decimal). At any particular moment, the contents of addresses 3,001–3,004 might be as follows:

Address	3001	3002	3003	3004

```
Contents   1A       B0       E8      F1
```

The computer makes use of addresses in its internal calculations and for this reason addresses are usually expressed in hexadecimal. Be careful not to confuse an address (a memory location number) with its contents (the data stored in that address).

We observed in the preceding section that 16-bit binary numbers correspond to the decimal numbers 0 through 65,535. On the other hand, 64K = 65,536. Thus, we see that the 16-bit binary numbers provide exactly enough addresses to handle a 64K memory. To address more memory than 64K requires binary numbers longer than 16 bits. Actually, the IBM PC is designed to economically handle 16-bit numbers, so rather than use addresses consisting of, say, 24 or 32 bits, it uses pairs of 16-bit numbers. A typical address on the PC has the form

```
(segment, offset)
```

where `segment` and `offset` are 16-bit numbers having the following meanings:

Bytes are numbered beginning with 0. The byte corresponding to a particular address pair (`segment`, `offset`) is byte number

```
16*segment + offset
```

For example, consider the address pair (00FF,1F58). The segment portion, 00FF, equals 255 in decimal. The offset portion, 1F58, equals 8,024 in decimal. So the particular address pair corresponds to byte number 16*255+8024 = 12,104.

Suppose that we hold the segment portion of an address pair fixed and allow the offset portion to vary. The corresponding address pair runs over a set of 64K consecutive memory locations. Such a section of memory is called a 64K segment. In programming the 8088 chip (in machine language), such 64K segments play an important role.

The following notation is used to denote an address:

```
segment:offset
```

For example, the address in the above example is

    00FF:1F58

Test Your Understanding 1 (Answer on Page 507)

The maximum address theoretically possible is FFFF:000F. To what byte number does this correspond?

If your computations are correct you just found that the PC can address more than one million bytes of RAM.

Addresses Within a BASIC Program

In most BASIC programs you are shielded from dealing directly with specific memory locations. You can name variables, create loops, make decisions, and BASIC automatically keeps track of all the various goings-on in memory. Unfortunately, in some applications it is necessary to access a memory location directly, but BASIC has statements that allow you to do this.

At any given moment, there is a current segment number, which is understood as the segment portion of any needed addresses. You specify this segment number by using the DEF SEG statement. The format of this statement is

    DEF SEG =

This statement defines the segment required for the addresses in the PEEK, POKE, CALL, BLOAD, BSAVE, VARPTR, and USR instructions. (These will all be discussed subsequently.) Once you specify a segment number via a DEF SEG instruction, the segment number remains the same until you change it by another DEF SEG instruction.

When BASIC is initialized, the segment number is set equal to the beginning address of the BASIC interpreter (DS in the above memory map). Unless you change this segment number via a DEF SEG instruction, all addresses in BASIC are assumed to have the beginning of the BASIC interpreter as their segment number. After giving a DEF SEG instruction you may return the segment number to its initial setting with the instruction

```
DEF SEG
```

(The segment number is omitted.)

To read the contents of a memory location, you may use the PEEK statement. It has the format

```
x = PEEK(offset)
```

This statement assigns the contents of :offset to the numerical variable x, where is the number assigned by the most recent DEF SEG instruction. The contents of a memory location are given as an integer between 0 and 255. For example, the instruction

```
10 CONTENTS = PEEK(35873)
```

assigns the contents of memory location :35873 to the numerical variable contents.

Test Your Understanding 2

Use the PEEK instruction to determine the contents of the first four memory locations in which the BASIC interpreter is stored. (Remember that the results of the preceding Test Your Understanding were provided in hexadecimal, whereas PEEK gives its results in decimal.)

You may store a number in a memory location using the POKE instruction that has the format

```
POKE offset, contents
```

For example, consider the instruction

```
10 POKE 5000, 217
```

It stores the number 217 in location :5000. The contents assigned to a memory location must be an integer between 0 and 255.

The PEEK and POKE instructions give you untold power; however, you must use them with care. Be sure not to POKE into a memory location that contains part of the BASIC interpreter, DOS, or any other "nonuser" area of memory because you may cause your program to crash!

The various dots of light that comprise the screen display at any given moment are stored, in coded form, in a section of memory. The monochrome display interface uses 4K of memory beginning at &HB000:0000, whereas the color/graphics interface uses 16K beginning at &HB800:0000 and proceeding for 16K bytes. You may write in these memory locations and see what happens. Here is a program that accomplishes this in the case of the color/graphics interface, in medium-resolution graphics mode. The program requests a memory offset. It then stores 255 in the corresponding memory location. Visually, this corresponds to four dots in a row. The position of the dots corresponds to the memory offset selected.

```
1 '****************************************
2 'This program pokes a bit pattern directly
3 'into screen memory.
4 '****************************************
10 KEY OFF
20 SCREEN 1
30 DEF SEG = &HB800
40 LOCATE 1,1
50 INPUT OFFSET
60 CLS
70 POKE OFFSET,255
80 INPUT "Again (Y or N)";A$
90 IF A$="Y" OR A$="y" THEN 40
100 END
```

In many graphics applications it is most efficient to manipulate displays by writing into, or reading directly from the screen memory.

If you consult the memory map provided above you can see the relative positions of your variables, strings and arrays within the memory. You may locate the exact position of any one of these program elements using the VARPTR instruction. For example, suppose that your program uses the variable ALPHA. The instruction

```
10 X = VARPTR(ALPHA)
```

sets X equal to the offset of the first byte of memory that is used to store ALPHA. The assumed segment is always the beginning of the BASIC interpreter and is not affected by DEF SEG instructions. We will discuss (at a later time) the precise manner in which variables are stored and we will use the VARPTR instruction to snoop on some variables in action.

Answers to Test Your Understanding 1

1. `1,048,575`

How Data Is Stored in Memory

In the previous section we discussed the memory of the PC and how the various memory locations are identified by addresses. Let's now turn to the actual contents of the memory locations and discuss how BASIC stores various sorts of data in RAM. We should begin by saying that all locations of RAM and ROM contain binary numbers. What we are really after, however, is the way in which various kinds of data, such as integers, single-precision numbers, double-precision numbers, and strings, are represented as binary numbers.

Positive and Negative Integers

An integer is a whole number in the range -32,768 to 32,767. An integer is stored in RAM as a 16-bit binary number. Let's spend a moment discussing the layout of such storage.

The bits of a binary number are numbered as in the diagram below:

```
bit number 15 14 13 12 11 10  9  8  7  6  5  4  3  2  1  0
   bit         1  0  1  0  1  1  0  1  1  0  1  0  0  1  1  1
```

Bit 0 is called the least significant and bit 15 the most significant.

A 16-bit binary number is called **a word**. Storage of a word requires two (eight-bit) bytes. Now here is the confusing part: The two bytes are stored in consecutive memory locations with the least-significant bits in the first byte and the most-significant bits in the second byte. This may seem perfectly natural but there is some confusion. Consider the following 16-bit number in hexadecimal form: 1A3F. (Remember that each hexadecimal digit corresponds to four bits.) The most-significant eight bits correspond to 1A and the least-significant to 3F. Therefore, this 16-bit number is stored in memory as

    3F 1A

And, indeed, if you use DEBUG to look at memory you will see the bytes displayed in this order. Before you interpret a 16-bit number from RAM, remember to reverse the order of the bytes!

Test Your Understanding 1 (Answer on Page 512)

Here are two consecutive bytes in memory:

    A3 1F

To what decimal number does this correspond?

In our discussion so far we have avoided any mention of negative numbers in binary and hexadecimal. Let's fill in that gap. BASIC uses only the 15 least-significant bits (bits 0 through 14) to represent a positive number. The most-significant bit (bit 15) is always 0 for a positive number (see Figure 17-3). This coding method allows representation of $2^{16} = 32,768$ binary numbers, corresponding to the decimal numbers 0 through 32,767.

```
bit 15 = 0
```

```
0 b b b b b b b b b b b b b b b
```

Figure 17-3.
**A positive
16-bit
number.**

```
b = bit which is 0 or 1
```

The most-significant bit (bit 15) is used to indicate the sign of the number. Perhaps the most obvious way of indicating the sign would be to have bit 15 = 0 to represent a positive number and bit 15 = 1 to represent a negative number. However, this is not what is done. Instead, negative numbers are indicated using the so-called two's-complement.

To form the two's-complement of a binary number proceed as follows:

1. Change every 0 bit to a 1 and vice versa.
2. Add 1 to the resulting number.

For example, to form the two's-complement of 0110 we first reverse each bit to obtain

```
1001
```

We then add 1 to this last number—do this by converting to decimal, performing the addition, and then reconverting to binary. However, it is easy to add directly in binary. Just add corresponding places from right to left as if you were adding decimal numbers and follow these rules:

```
0 + 0 = 0
```

```
0 + 1 = 1
```

```
1 + 1 = 0 and carry the 1 to the next place
```

For example, we have

```
   1001
+     1
  _____
   1010
```

Thus, the two's-complement of 0110 is 1010.

Here is the connection between two's-complements and negative numbers: a negative number -n is represented in binary by the two's-complement of n, considered as a 16-bit number. For example, the binary number 0110 equals the positive decimal number 6. The binary representation of -6 is obtained as follows: First, consider 0110 as the 16-bit number

```
0000 0000 0000 0110
```

Now form the two's-complement:

```
1111 1111 1111 1001
        +    1
─────────────────────
1111 1111 1111 1010
```

So -6 is represented by the binary number 1111111111111010.

Here is an easy way to recognize a negative integer directly from its binary representation: A negative always has its high-order bit equal to 1; moreover, you may recover the original number by taking the two's-complement a second time. For example, the two's-complement of 1111111111111010 is

```
0000 0000 0000 0101
        +    1
─────────────────────
0000 0000 0000 0110
```

So we retrieve our original number 0110.

Test Your Understanding 2 (Answer on Page 512)

Determine the number represented by the binary number

```
1111 1111 1001 1100
```

Test Your Understanding 3 (Answers on Page 512)

Determine the binary representation of
  a. 32767
  b. -32767

The two's-complement of an integer n may be calculated in decimal notation using a very simple procedure:

```
[two's complement of n] = 65536 - n
```

For example, the two's-complement of 6 is equal to 65,530, and it is easy to check that in binary it is equal to

```
1111111111110101
```

Test Your Understanding 4 (Answers on Page 513)

a. Store the number -15 in memory location 30,000.

b. Use a PEEK instruction to display the contents of memory location 30,000. What are the contents? Can you explain the results?

The two's-complement procedure may seem to be an obscure way of representing negative numbers but it is designed to aid in performing arithmetic among binary numbers with the greatest possible speed.

ASCII Characters

The IBM PC has 255 displayable characters. Each of these characters is given an ASCII code, which is an integer between 0 and 255. A character is represented in memory by this ASCII code and therefore occupies exactly one byte. For example, here is how the string "This is a test." is stored in memory:

```
T     h    i    s         i    s         a    t    e    s    t    .
84   104  105  115   32  105  115   32   97   32  116  101  115  116  46
Decimal
54    68   69   73   20   69   73   20   61   20   7    4    65   73   74   2E
Hexadecimal
```

So the given string is stored in memory as the consecutive bytes

54,68,69,73,20,69,73,20,61,20,74,65,73,74,2E

Test Your Understanding 5 (Answer on Page 513)

How is this display stored in memory?

```
Line 1
Line 2
Line 3
```

Single-Precision Numbers and Variables

A single-precision number is stored in a "scientific notation" requiring four bytes, regardless of the size of the number. The actual algorithm used for the storage is rather complicated and is designed for efficiency in carrying out computations rather than the convenience of the programmer. One of the four bytes is used to store an exponent, which is used as a scaling factor. The other three bytes are used to store a scaled version of the number, called the mantissa. We will omit a precise description of the storage algorithm at the end of this chapter.

Double-Precision Numbers

Double-precision numbers are stored using eight bytes: The first byte is the exponent, exactly as for single-precision numbers and the next seven bytes are used for the mantissa. The fact that 56 bits are used for the mantissa rather than 24 allows for the greater number of digit precision in double-precision numbers.

Answers to Test Your Understandings 1, 2, 3, 4, and 5

1. 8099

2. −1540

3. a. 0111 1111 1111 1111

b. `1000 0000 0000 0001`

4.   a. **POKE** `-15,3000`

b. What you see is the decimal equivalent of the two's-complement of -15.

5.   In decimal, the list of ASCII codes is

```
76, 105, 110, 101, 32, 49, 13,
76, 105, 110, 101, 32, 50, 13,
76, 105, 110, 101, 32, 51, 13
```

Operations on Bytes

In many applications (we shall see a few shortly) it is necessary to perform operations directly on the bits of a byte. In this section we will introduce you to these operations.

Shift and Truncate Operations

It is often required to move all the bits of a byte to the left or to the right. Such operations are called, respectively, a left shift and a right shift. For example, consider this byte:

`1101 0110`

If we apply a left shift, we obtain the byte

`1010 1100`

Note that the rightmost bit is a zero and the original leftmost bit has been "pushed off the end."

Similarly, a right shift applied to the original byte yields

`0110 1011`

Note that the leftmost bit is replaced by a zero and the original rightmost bit is "pushed off the end."

How can operations such as those just described be carried out in BASIC? Before we describe a method, let's remember that the binary number system is based on powers of two. If we multiply a decimal number by 10 we shift all the digits to the left one place. Similarly, in the binary number system, if we multiply a number by two, we shift the bits to the left one place. Moreover, if we divide a binary number by two (integer division), we then shift the digits to the right by one bit.

In the case of multiplication by two, there may be a bit shifted into bit position nine. We may rid ourselves of this bit by using MOD 256. (The remainder of division by 256 is exactly the rightmost eight bits.)

Here is how to perform shifts on the value of the integer variable A%:

```
Left Shift: 2*A% MOD 256

Right Shift: A%\2
```

The above use of the MOD operation may be generalized. The remainder on dividing by 2^N is precisely the rightmost N bits. The bits beyond N are replaced by zeros. This process is called **truncation.**

Test Your Understanding 1 (Answer on Page 518)

Write an instruction that shifts the value of A% to the right three bits.

Test Your Understanding 2 (Answer on Page 518)

Write an instruction that truncates the most significant three bits of the value of B%.

Logical Operations on Words

BASIC has a number of built-in operations that you may perform on 16-bit quantities (integers).

NOT.   The NOT operation reverses all the bits of a number. For example, consider the number

```
NOT 0000 1010 1111 0101
```

We may compute this number by changing every 0 to a 1 and every 1 to a zero. The result is

```
1111 0101 0000 1010
```

In BASIC, we may apply the NOT operation to any integer, written in either decimal or hexadecimal form. The NOT operation converts the number to binary form, performs the above computation, and reconverts the number to decimal form. For example, let's compute NOT 18. We have

```
18 decimal = 0000 0000 0001 0010 binary
```

so that

```
NOT 18 = 1111 1111 1110 1101 binary

       = -19 decimal
```

AND.   The operation A AND B produces a 16-bit number from the 16-bit numbers A and B. More precisely, if A and B are 16-bit quantities, then

```
A AND B
```

is the 16-bit number obtained as follows: Compare A and B bit by bit. For a given bit position, if both A and B have a one, then the corresponding bit of A and B is a one. If either A or B has a zero, the corresponding bit of A AND B is a zero. For example, consider the 16-bit quantities

```
A = 1101 1011 1000 0000
```

```
B = 1001 0001 0011 1111
```

Then

```
A AND B = 1001 0001 0000 0000
```

If A and B are integers given in decimal form, we may also apply the operation AND. The answer will be a decimal number that is obtained by computing A and B using the respective binary representations of A and B. (In using these binary representations, remember that a negative number is represented in two's-complement form.) For instance, suppose that A = 3 and B = 5. Then

```
A = 0000 0000 0000 0011

B = 0000 0000 0000 0101

A AND B = 0000 0000 0000 0001
```

That is,

```
5 AND 3 = 1
```

OR.   The operation A OR B produces a 16-bit number from the two 16-bit numbers A and B. More precisely, if A and B are 16-bit quantities, then

```
A OR B
```

is the 16-bit number obtained as follows: Compare A and B bit by bit. For a given bit position, if either A or B have a one, then the corresponding bit of A OR B is a one. If both A and B have a zero, the corresponding bit of A OR B is a zero. For example, consider the 16-bit quantities

```
A = 1101 1011 1000 0000

B = 1001 0001 0011 1111
```

Then

```
A OR B = 1101 1011 1011 1111
```

If A and B are integers given in decimal form, we may also apply the operation OR. The answer will be a decimal number that is obtained by computing A and B using the respective binary representations of A and B.

(Again, in using these binary representations, remember that a negative number is represented in two's-complement form.) For instance, suppose that A = 3 and B = 5. Then

    A = 0000 0000 0000 0011

    B = 0000 0000 0000 0101

    A OR B = 0000 0000 0000 0111

That is

    5 OR 3 = 7

XOR.   The operation A XOR B is called the exclusive OR of A and B and produces a 16-bit result from the two 16-bit numbers A and B. If A and B are 16-bit quantities, then

    A XOR B

is the 16-bit number obtained by comparing A and B bit by bit. For a given bit position, if A and B have different bits, then the corresponding bit of A and B is a one. If A and B have the same bits, the corresponding bit of A XOR B is a zero. For example, consider the 16-bit quantities

    A = 1101 1011 1000 0000

    B = 1001 0001 0011 1111

Then

    A XOR B = 0100 1010 1011 1111

If A and B are integers given in decimal form, we may also apply the operation XOR. The procedure is similar to that described in our discussion of AND and OR.

Caution.   Do not confuse the use of AND, NOT, OR, and XOR within numerical operations and the use of the corresponding words to construct statements in conditional (IF-THEN) instructions. For example, note the use of AND in the expression

```
A>1 AND B<3
```

In this case, the AND serves as a logical connector. The statement given is true only if both of the statements A>1 and B<3 are true. In a similar fashion, we may consider statements of the form

```
NOT (A>1)

(A>1) OR (B<3)

(A>1) XOR (B<3)?
```

The first of these statements is true provided that the statement A>1 is not true. The second of the statements is true if either of the statements A>1 or B<3 is true. The third statement is true provided that the statements A>1 and B<3 are both false or true.

Answers to Test Your Understandings 1 and 2

1.   `A%=A%\8`

2.   `A%=(A%*8)\8`

Some Applications of Byte Operations

In this section, we will apply some of what we have learned about binary numbers and bytes. We will present three applications:

1. We will construct a capitalization function.
2. We will present some advanced graphics tricks using GET and PUT. These tricks will aid in displaying animations.

3. We will explain the mechanics of designing custom characters for screen display.

A Capitalization Function

You may have noticed that BASIC turns alphabetic characters within a program listing into capital letters. For example, if you type a program statement containing the letter a, a subsequent listing of the statement will display the letter as A. Let's write a program to perform such a conversion.

Of course, we may convert lowercase letters into capital letters using a series of IF...THEN statements of the form

```
IF A$="a" THEN A$="A"
```

(Here A$ is a string variable containing the letter to be capitalized.) However, such a program would contain many statements, occupy a great deal of memory, and run very slowly. There is a much better way.

To discover the secret relationship between uppercase and lowercase letters, let's look at their respective ASCII codes. Here is a portion of the ASCII table:

Letter	ASCII Code	Letter	ASCII Code
A	65	a	97
B	66	b	98
C	67	c	99
.	.	.	.
.	.	.	.
.	.	.	.
Z	90	z	122

What is the relationship between a letter and its corresponding capital? Well, a quick look at the table shows that the ASCII code of a uppercase letter is 32 less than the ASCII code of the corresponding lowercase letter. And 32 corresponds to one of the bit positions in a byte, namely bit 5. This is no accident, but a result of good planning! Consider the binary equivalents of the ASCII codes for A and a:

```
65 decimal = 00000000 01000001 binary

97 decimal = 00000000 01100001 binary
```

Note that they differ only in the 32's place, namely bit 5. Similarly, consider the ASCII codes for B and b:

```
66 decimal = 00000000 01000010 binary

98 decimal = 00000000 01100010 binary
```

Again the only difference is in bit 5. By subsequent examination of the other letter pairs, we come up with the following rule:

To Convert a Letter From Lowercase to Uppercase: Change bit 5 in its ASCII code from 1 to 0.

And the change in bit 5 may be accomplished by ANDing the ASCII code with 00000000 11011111 = 223 decimal. Here's why: For all bits except bit 5, we are ANDing with a 1. If the ASCII code has a 1, the ANDing will have a 1; if the ASCII code has a 0, the ANDing will have a 0. In other words, all bits other than bit 5 will remain unchanged. On the other hand, bit 5 is ANDed with a 0 so it will certainly result in a 0. In particular, if bit 5 is a 1 (lowercase), it is converted to a 0 (uppercase).

On the basis of our discussion, we may finally construct a function FNA$(X$), which converts the character X$ into a uppercase letter if it was lowercase and otherwise leaves X$ alone:

```
DEF FNA(X$) = CHR$(ASC(X$) AND 223)
```

This function starts with a string X$ (any string will do) and computes the ASCII code of its first character. (This is the ASC(X$) part.) The ASCII code is then ANDed with 223 and the resulting ASCII code is converted back into a character. You should test this function out with some examples of characters X$. Here is a program to carry out the tests.

```
 1 '*****************************************
 2 'This program tests the capitalization
 3 'function FNA$(X).
 4 '*****************************************
10 DEF FNA$(X$) = CHR$(ASC(X$) AND 223)
20 INPUT "CHARACTER=";X$
30 Z$=FNA$(X$)
40 PRINT "THE CONVERTED CHARACTER IS "; Z$
50 INPUT "TRY ANOTHER CHARACTER (Y/N)";REPLY$
60 IF FNA$(REPLY$)= "Y" THEN 20
70 END
```

Figure 17-4 shows a sample run for the above program.

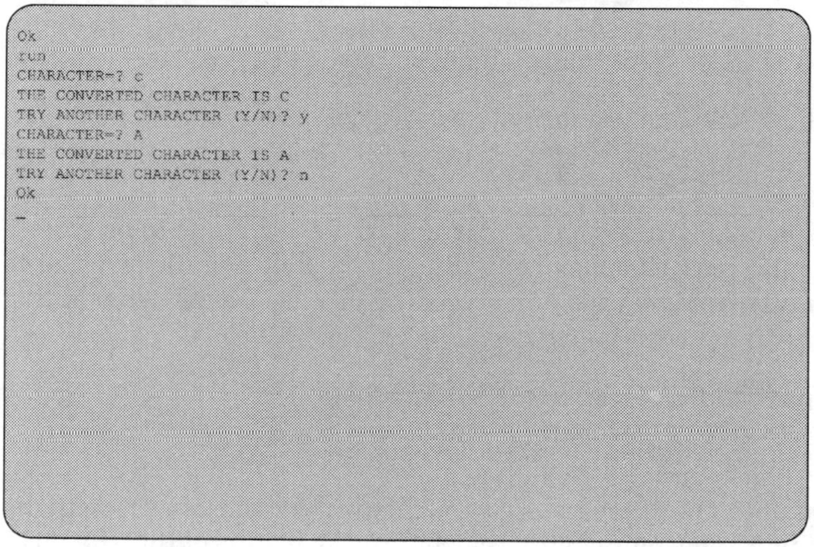

```
Ok
run
CHARACTER=? c
THE CONVERTED CHARACTER IS C
TRY ANOTHER CHARACTER (Y/N)? y
CHARACTER=? A
THE CONVERTED CHARACTER IS A
TRY ANOTHER CHARACTER (Y/N)? n
Ok
_
```

Figure 17-4.
Capitalizing letters.

This program is interesting in several respects. First, it allows you to try out the capitalization function FNA(X$). Second, it shows you how the function may be used in practice. Observe the instructions in lines 50–70. Line 50 asks if you wish to type another character. It asks for a reply of Y or N. Most people will not even think much about it and respond with y or n. Good program design should allow for such responses. One way of doing this is to ask separately if REPLY$ = Y or if REPLY$=y. A much cleaner approach is the one taken in line 60. We replace REPLY$ by FNA$(REPLY$). This converts a reply of y into Y. Then a single question suffices in line 70.

Test Your Understanding 1

Modify the above program so that it leaves X$ unchanged if it begins with a non-letter character (A–Z, a–z).

Some Further Tricks With GET and PUT

In Chapter 12 we introduced the GET and PUT statements which can be used for transporting images from place to place on the screen. There are several features of these commands which we have yet to discuss.

Remember that GET has the format

```
GET (x1,y1)-(x2,y2), <array>
```

where (x1,y1) and (x2,y2) are opposite corners of the rectangle to be stored, and <array> is an array that has been dimensioned of a sufficient size to hold the rectangular image. (See our preceding discussion for determining the size of the array.)

Remember that the PUT statement has the form

```
PUT (x,y), <array>
```

This statement puts the image stored in <array> on the screen with its upper-left corner at the point with coordinates (x,y). Actually, the PUT command offers five modes of displaying the image on the screen. These five modes are indicated by the words

```
PSET
PRESET
XOR
OR
AND
```

The last words should be familiar from our discussion of them earlier in this chapter. Their function in connection with the PUT command is similar to their use in the operations we described.

PUT with the PSET option displays the image in exactly the form in which it was stored. This is done independently of the data that was on the screen. This option is invoked with the command

```
PUT (x,y), <array>, PSET
```

PUT with the PRESET option displays the image in the array, but in inverse color. A pixel that was stored in color 3 will be displayed in color 0 (background color); color 2 will be displayed in color 1; color 1 will be displayed in color 2; and color 0 will be displayed in color 3. On a monochrome display, the PRESET option will simply reverse the roles of background and foreground. The PRESET option is invoked with the command

```
PUT (x,y) <array>, PRESET
```

PUT with the AND option displays the recorded image by ANDing it with the image already at the indicated position on the screen. This ANDing takes place pixel by pixel. A pixel is displayed only if the pixel was previously displayed. The AND option is invoked with the command

```
PUT (x,y), <array>, AND
```

PUT with the OR option displays the recorded image by ORing it with the image already at the indicated position on the screen. This ORing takes place pixel by pixel. A pixel is displayed if either the pixel was previously displayed or the array has the pixel displayed. The OR option is invoked with the command

```
PUT (x,y), <array>, OR
```

PUT with the XOR option displays the recorded image by XORing it with the image already at the indicated position on the screen. This XORing takes place pixel by pixel. In the XOR option a pixel is displayed provided that it is displayed in exactly one of the original screen images and the display image. In particular, a pixel currently displayed on the screen and displayed in the current image will not be displayed. If you PUT the same image twice using the XOR option, then you will restore the screen to its original state. This property of the XOR option is especially useful for animations, since you may move an image across the screen and restore the background to its original state. The XOR option is invoked with either of the commands

```
PUT (x,y), <array>, XOR

PUT (x,y), <array>
```

(The XOR option is the default option. That is, if you use PUT without specifying an option, then the XOR option is assumed.)

The precise color assignments used with the AND, OR, and XOR options are rather complicated and are summarized in the following charts.

AND Color Assignment

Current Color	0	1	2	3
PUT Color				
0	0	0	0	0
1	0	1	0	1
2	0	0	2	2
3	0	1	2	3

OR Color Assignment

Current Color	0	1	2	3
PUT Color				

0		1	2	3	3
1		1	1	3	3
2		2	3	2	3
3		3	3	3	3

XOR Color Assignment

Current Color	0	1	2	3
PUT Color				
0	0	1	2	3
1	1	0	3	2
2	2	3	0	1
3	3	2	1	0

Let's illustrate the action of each of the options PSET, PRESET, AND, OR, and XOR using the following example. Suppose that A% is an eight-pixel by eight-pixel array that contains the letter A, obtained from a previous GET operation (see Figure 17-5). Further, suppose that we use a PUT to place this image on a portion of the screen, which currently has the image in Figure 17-6. The results of each of the various options are described in Figure 17-7.

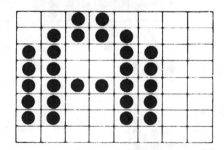

Figure 17-5.
**The contents of
A%.**

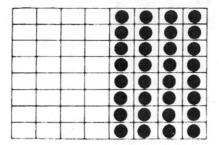

Figure 17-6.
**The back-
ground.**

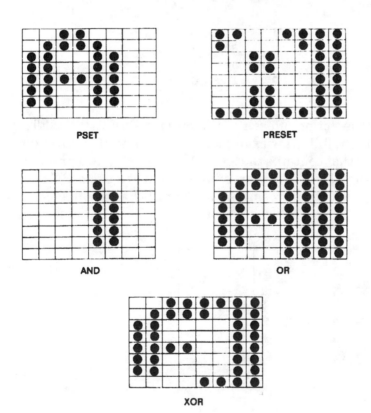

PSET

PRESET

AND

OR

XOR

Figure 17-7.
**The results of
PUT with various
options.**

Designing Custom Characters

We may combine our recently acquired knowledge of bytes and binary numbers with the PUT command to design custom characters for the screen. Here's how: A character in graphics mode is displayed in a rectangle eight pixels wide and eight pixels high. Note that it does not matter whether the character is displayed in medium-resolution or high-resolution mode. The rectangle is always 8×8. For example, Figure 17-8 contains the pixels displayed for the letter A.

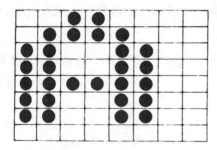

Figure 17-8.
The letter A.

Each character may be described by a series of bytes, corresponding to the various rows of the rectangle. This description is simplest in high-resolution graphics mode. In this case each pixel corresponds to a single bit proceeding from left to right. For example, Figure 17-9 shows the bits corresponding to the letter A.

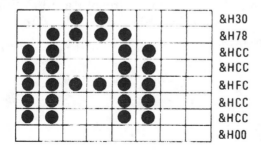

Figure 17-9.
The bits corresponding to the letter A.

Note that each row of the rectangle corresponds to a single byte, or two hexadecimal digits. In hexadecimal, the letter A may be represented by the bytes

&H03, &H78, &HCC, &HCC, &HFC, &HCC, &HCC, &H00

When you perform a GET, the bytes are arranged in the array as follows:

A%(0) = the width of the rectangle

A%(1) = the height of the rectangle

A%(2), A%(3),... contain the bytes corresponding to the pixels, with two bytes per array element.

For example, the results of GETing the letter A to the array A% yield the following array contents:

```
A%(0)  =  8
A%(1)  =  8
A%(2)  =  &H7803
A%(3)  =  &HCCCC
A%(4)  =  &HCCFC
A%(5)  =  &H00CC
```

Note the order in which the bytes appear. As usual, the byte to the left (the one containing the higher-order bits) is the byte after the byte to the right.

The above discussion applies to high-resolution graphics mode in which each pixel corresponds to one bit. In medium-resolution graphics mode a pixel may be in any one of four colors, numbered 0, 1, 2, 3. In binary these choices are coded using two bits:

00 = color 0
01 = color 1
10 = color 2
11 = color 3

Each row of the rectangle now contains two bits per pixel, or 16 bits. That is, each row of the rectangle corresponds to one 16-bit integer. In terms of the array, the first row will now completely fill A%(2), the second A%(3), and so forth.

We have just described how the GET statement fills an array. With this information, we may omit the GET statement entirely. We may fill an array with the data corresponding to a display without first creating the display on the screen. To do this:

1. Use graph paper to draw the pixels of the display.

2. Convert the rows of the display into binary.

3. Convert the binary numbers into hexadecimal.

4. Fill the 0th array element with the display width, the 1st array element with the display hieght.

5. Fill the array elements beginning with the 2nd with the hexadecimal numbers of step 3. (Be sure to put the later hexadecimal digits on the left of a 16-bit word.)

6. The array is now ready for PUTing.

Let's illustrate this procedure by creating an array that displays the capital Greek letter phi:

We begin by reducing the letter to pixels, as shown in Figure 17-10.

Next, we code the various rows into binary and then hexadecimal form:

row #	binary number	hexadecimal number	array element
1	0000 0000	00	0
2	0010 0000	20	32
3	0111 0000	70	112

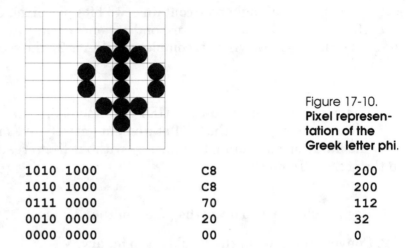

Figure 17-10.
**Pixel representa-
tation of the
Greek letter phi.**

4	1010 1000	C8	200
5	1010 1000	C8	200
6	0111 0000	70	112
7	0010 0000	20	32
8	0000 0000	00	0

We may summarize our results in this BASIC program:

```
1 '****************************************
2 'Create and display the letter "PHI"
3 'formed from pixels stored in an array.
4 '****************************************
10 'at position (100,100).
20 DIM A%(9)
30 A%(0)=8: A%(1)=8: A%(2)=0
40 A%(3)=32: A%(4)=112: A%(5)=200
50 A%(6)=200:A%(7)=112: A%(8)=32: A%(9)=0
60 SCREEN 2:CLS
70 PUT (100,100), A%
80 END
```

Replacing the Graphics Character Set

The ASCII character set (ASCII codes 0–127) is stored in ROM, coded in exactly the fashion we have described above for high-resolution graphics mode. That is, each character is described by a sequence of eight bytes. This table of bytes begins at memory location F000:FA6E. Here is a program that fills the array A% with the appropriate data from the table for any character you specify:

```
1 '*****************************************
2 'This program looks up the pixels for a
3 'character and stores the resulting
4 'bytes in an array.
5 '*****************************************
100 'Main Program
110 DIM A%(10)
120 A%(0)=8
130 A%(1)=8
140 DEF SEG = &HF000
150 INPUT "CHARACTER TO LOAD";C$
160 OFFSET=8*ASC(C$)+&HFA6E
170 FOR J=0 TO 7
180       B$(J)=HEX$(PEEK(OFFSET+J))
190       IF LEN(B$(J))=1 THEN B$(J)="0"+B$(J)
200 NEXT J
210 FOR J=0 TO 3
220       A%(J+2) = VAL("&H" + B$(2*J+1) + B$(2*J))
230 NEXT J
240 DEF SEG
250 END
```

The above program may be used as a subroutine in various character alteration operations. For example, you may create characters that are vertically enlarged by including duplicates of the bytes corresponding to the various display lines. Here is a program that enables you to load an array with a character that is the expansion of a specified character by a given factor:

```
1 '***********************************
2 'This program creates an array that
3 ' contains the pixels for the enlarge-
4 ' ment of a user-defined character by
5 ' a user-defined factor F.
6 '***********************************
100 DIM A%(10),B%(200)
```

```
110 INPUT "FACTOR OF ENLARGEMENT";F
120 INPUT "CHARACTER";C$
130 GOSUB 300:
150 B%(0)=8
160 B%(1)=8*F
170 FOR J=0 TO 7
180    FOR K=0 TO F-1
190       B%(F*J+K+2)=A%(J+2)
200    NEXT K
210 NEXT J
220 END
300 'Load character into array
320 A%(0)=8
330 A%(1)=8
340 DEF SEG = &HF000
360 OFFSET=8*ASC(C$)+&HFA6E
370 FOR J=0 TO 7
380    B$(J)=HEX$(PEEK(OFFSET+J))
390    IF LEN(B$(J))=1 THEN B$(J)="0"+B$(J)
400 NEXT J
410 FOR J=0 TO 3
420    A%(J+2) = VAL("&H" + B$(2*J+1) + B$(2*J))
430 NEXT J
440 DEF SEG
450 RETURN
```

You may print out the character in the array B%() by using a PUT statement. This is illustrated in Figure 17-11.

```
factor of enlargement? 3
string? Enlarged three times
Ok
```

Enlarged three times

Figure 17-11.
**Displaying an
expanded char-
acter.**

Test Your Understanding 2

Use the above program to display a letter A that is three times the usual
height.

Some Graphics Tricks

In this section we discuss various enhancements to the LINE and PAINT
statements that require knowledge of binary and hexadecimal numbers.

Enhancements to LINE

Recall the format of the LINE statement:

```
LINE (x1,y1)-(x2,y2),color,box
```

Here color is one of the colors 0–3, box is either the letter B (= open box) or
the letters BF (= filled box), and (x1,y1) and (x2,y2) are the coordinates of
the endpoints of the line. After the box parameter you may add the parameter
style, which determines the line style. Using this option you may draw an
incredible variety of line styles, including dotted and dashed lines. Figure
17-12 shows some of the possibilities. Figure 17-13 shows some of the possible
box fill options.

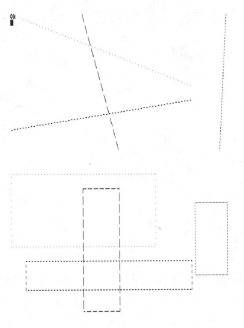

Figure 17-12.
Line styles.

Figure 17-13.
Box styles.

If you make use of the style option, you must code the style as a 16-bit number input to the program as a hexadecimal number. The LINE command refers to this style designation as it plots the pixels of the line. It starts with the leftmost bit. If the bit is a one, it plots the pixel. If it is a zero, then it does not plot the pixel. For the next pixel LINE looks at the second bit of the style designation, and so forth. After 16 pixels, LINE begins over with the leftmost bit. For example, here is a style designator for a dashed line with eight pixels plotted followed by eight pixels not plotted.

```
11111111 00000000
```

In hexadecimal this style designation is denoted &HFF00. Here is a line that contains a long dash (11 pixels) followed by a one-pixel space, followed by a dot and another space (see Figure 17-14):

```
binary style designation = 11111111 11111010

hexadecimal style designation = &HFFFA
```

&HFFFA.

———————————————————————————————— Figure 17-14.
A line of style

To connect the points (50,75) and (100,100) with a line of style &HFFFA, use the statement

```
10 LINE (50,75),,,,&HFFFA
```

Note that you must use the correct number of commas as placeholders for the color and box parameters.

Test Your Understanding 1 (Answer on Page 538)

Describe the line with style designation &HAAAA.

You may use the style designation with the B parameter, in which case the required rectangle is drawn with its sides in the requested style. However, you may not use the style designation with the BF parameter. If you do, you will generate a syntax error.

Enhancements to PAINT

As you will recall, the PAINT statement allows you to paint a region of the screen with a particular color. In many graphics applications, you may wish to "crosshatch" the region with a particular pattern rather than a solid color. For example, you may wish to shade a region with horizontal lines, with vertical lines, or with a rectangular mesh. BASIC allows you to accomplish such shading with ease.

Recall that the format for PAINT is

```
PAINT (x,y), paint, boundary
```

Here (x,y) is a point in the region to be painted, paint is the color the region is to be painted, and boundary is the color of the boundary of the region.

The PAINT enhancement allows the paint parameter to be a string expression describing the figures to be used in shading the region. The string expression may contain as many as 64 bytes. The entire string describes one shading figure. To determine the shading figure, we convert the bytes of the string into binary to obtain an array of the form

```
1 0 0 1 0 1 1 0     byte 1
0 0 1 1 0 0 0 1     byte 2
1 0 0 1 0 1 1 0     byte 3
```

These bytes are translated into pixels in the usual way. In high resolution, the bits are translated into pixels on a one-to-one basis. A 1 means that the pixel is displayed and a 0 means that the pixel is not displayed. In medium resolution, two bits represent one pixel, with the two-bit combination representing one of the four possible colors for the pixel. For example, in high resolution the above array stands for the shading character shown in Figure 17-15.

Figure 17-15.
A shading character represented by a given array.

If this shading character is used, then the region to be painted will be filled with shapes of this sort, starting at the point (x,y) and working out to the boundaries.

The above three bytes are specified in hexadecimal as

&H96
&H31
&H96

To construct the corresponding paint string, we must convert these bytes into string form using the CHR$ function. That is, the desired paint string is

```
CHR$(&H96) + CHR$(&H31) + CHR$(&H96)
```

The paint string option is extremely powerful. For example, we may shade a region using horizontal lines two pixels apart as follows:

```
1111 1111  byte 1 = &HFF
0000 0000  byte 2 = &H00
0000 0000  byte 3 = &H00
```

paint string = CHR$(&HFF) + CHR$(0) + CHR$(0)

Here is a short program that draws a circle and paints the interior using the last paint string.

```
1 '*****************************************
2 'This program draws a circle and paints the
3 'interior using a specified paint string.
4 '*****************************************
10 KEY OFF
20 SCREEN 2,0
30 CIRCLE (100,100),75
40 PAINT (100,100), CHR$(&HFF) + CHR$(0) + CHR$(0)
50 LOCATE 1,1
60 END
```

Test Your Understanding 2 (Answer on Page 538)

Write a paint string that will allow shading with vertical lines spaced one pixel apart.

Answers to Test Your Understandings 1 and 2

1. The hexadecimal digit A equals 10, which in binary is 1010. So the given line style consists of

```
dot-space-dot-space-dot-space-dot-space-dot-space-
dot-space-dot-space-dot-space.
```

2.   `CHR$ (&HAA)`

Plotting Characters in Graphics Mode

My first business graphics program required me to draw a coordinate system. That was a simple enough task using the LINE statement. I calibrated the axes using tick marks, just as I was accustomed to do in lecturing my calculus students. Still no problem. However, next came the job of labeling the various tick marks. The results were very unsatisfying because I couldn't center the labels on the tick marks.

For example, if I wished to label a vertical tick mark as 4.00, I could rarely get the label exactly centered on the tick mark! The reason was that the tick mark was drawn using graphics coordinates and the labels were being plotted with text coordinates. Each character is eight pixels wide and BASIC automatically starts characters at positions whose x-coordinate (graphics coordinate) is divisible by eight. If that placement happens to result in a chart that looks good, fine. If not, too bad!

In response to my frustration, I developed the routine PLOTSTRING, which places a string at a particular graphics coordinate. In the following routine, the string is s$. I allow for two types of placement: point and center. In the first type you specify a set of graphics coordinates (x1,y1). The routine will plot s$ with the upper left corner of the first character of s$ at the point (x1,y1). For center placement you specify two points, (x1,y1) and (x2,y2). The routine then centers s$ within the rectangle (x1,y1)-(x2,y2).

I had so much fun with this routine that I decided to allow for vertical display of strings. There are four possible options, specified by the parameter c%:

```
c%=1: place at point, horizontal
c%=2: place at point, vertical
c%=3: center, horizontal
c%=4: center, vertical
```

PLOTSTRING uses the subroutine of the preceding section to read the pixels of a character into an array A%, using the table in ROM.

Here is a listing of the routine PLOTSTRING:

```
28000 '**************PLOTSTRING*******************
28005 'This routine allows precise placement of a string
28010 ' in graphics mode.
28015 ' (x1,y1),(x1,y2) are graphics coordinates
28020 ' s$=string to be placed
28025 ' c%=1:place string horizontally, with left corner
of 1st
28030 '       character at (x1,y1)
28035 ' c%=2:place string vertically, with left corner of
1st
28040 '       character at (x1,y1)
28045 ' c%=3:center string horizontally in the
28050 '         field (x1,y1)-(x2,y2)
28055 ' c%=4:center string vertically in the
28060 '         field (x1,y1)-(x2,y2)
28065 'Maxwidth=largest allowable x-coordinate
28070 'Maxheight=largest allowable y-coordinate
28075 '****************MAIN ROUTINE*****************
28080    IF C%=1 OR C%=2 THEN X=X1:Y=Y1
28085    ON C% GOSUB 28195,28275,28245,28320
28090    RETURN
28095 ****************SUBROUTINES****************
28100 'Load character into array
28105    A%(0)=8
28110    A%(1)=8
28115    DEF SEG = &HF000
28120    OFFSET=8*ASC(C$)+&HFA6E
28125    FOR J=0 TO 7
28130      B$(J)=HEX$(PEEK(OFFSET+J))
28135      IF LEN(B$(J))=1 THEN B$(J)="0"+B$(J)
28140    NEXT J
28145    FOR J=0 TO 3
28150      A%(J+2) = VAL("&H" + B$(2*J+1) + B$(2*J))
28155    NEXT J
28160    DEF SEG
```

```
28165    RETURN
28170 'Place character at particular coordinates
28175 'Character =c$, coordinates (x,y)
28180    GOSUB 28100
28185    PUT (X,Y), A%
28190    RETURN
28195 'Place string in field beginning at particular coor-
dinates
28200 'Field begins at (x,y), string in S$
28205    WHILE S$ <> ""
28210      IF X>MAXWIDTH THEN 28235
28215      C$=LEFT$(S$,1):S$=MID$(S$,2)
28220      GOSUB 28170: 'place character
28225      IF X<0 THEN 28235
28230      X=X+8
28235    WEND
28240    RETURN
28245 'Center string s$ in field defined by coordinates
(x1,y1)-(x2,y2)
28250    IF X1>X2 THEN SWAP X1,X2: IF Y1>Y2 THEN SWAP
Y1,Y2
28255    L=LEN(S$): C=INT((X2-X1)/8): IF L>C THEN
S$=LEFT$(S$,C)
28260    X=X1+(X2-X1+1)/2-8*LEN(S$)/2+4:Y=Y1+(Y2-Y1+1)/2-4
28265    GOSUB 28195
28270    RETURN
28275 'Display string s$ vertically beginning at coordi-
nate (x,y)
28280    WHILE S$ <> ""
28285      IF Y+7>MAXHEIGHT THEN 28315
28290      C$=LEFT$(S$,1):S$=MID$(S$,2)
28295      IF Y<0 THEN 28305
28300      GOSUB 28170: 'place character
28305      Y=Y+8
28310    WEND
28315    RETURN
28320 'Center string s$ vertically in field (x1,y1)-
(x2,y2)
28325    IF X1>X2 THEN SWAP X1,X2: IF Y1>Y2 THEN SWAP
Y1,Y2
```

```
28330      L=LEN(S$): C=INT((Y2-Y1)/8): IF L>C THEN
S$=LEFT$(S$,C)
28335      Y=Y1+(Y2-Y1+1)/2-8*LEN(S$)/2:X=X1+(X2-X1+1)/2-4
28340      IF X<0 THEN X=0 : IF Y<0 THEN Y=0
28345      GOSUB 28275
28350      RETURN
```

PLOTSTRING gives you very precise control of text display in graphics mode. However, you will notice that characters are displayed somewhat more slowly that if you use the PRINT statement. This perceptible difference in speed disappears if PLOTSTRING is used in a compiled program. However, even when using the BASIC interpreter the difference in the appearance of your graphics is worth the slight delay.

You may test PLOTSTRING with a program of the form

```
10 INPUT "S$";S$
20 INPUT "C%";C%
30 IIntroduction to the IBM PC40 IF C%=3 OR C%=4 THEN
INPUT
   "x2,y2";x2,y2
50 CLS
60 GOSUB PlotString
70 END
```

Extending the PC's Character Set

In text mode, the PC has 255 characters available. The first 128 ASCII codes 0–127 correspond to the usual displayable characters and control codes. ASCII codes 128 through 255 correspond to the graphics characters. The graphics characters are available only in text mode, however. If you try to print CHR$(175), say, when in SCREEN 1 or SCREEN 2, you will get garbage. However, IBM allows you to define you own character set corresponding to the unused ASCII codes. Here's how:

1. Define the characters in terms of bytes as we have already described. Write them in a list, with eight bytes to a character.

2. Find a section of memory that is unused. (See below for a way to do this.)

3. Use POKE to store the list of bytes in consecutive memory locations.

4. POKE into memory locations 0000:7C through 0000:7F the offset and segment address of the first location you used.

5. The first character in your list now corresponds to ASCII 32+128=161, the second to ASCII 33+128=162, and so forth.

For example, let's duplicate the ordinary displayable characters in ASCII codes 161–255. The ROM character table begins at F000:FA6E, so we poke 6E into 0000:007C, FA into 0000:007D, 00 into 0000:007E, and F0 into 0000:007F. Now ASCII code 161 is a space (= the same as ASCII code 32), ASCII code 193 is an A, and so forth.

Of course, the real power of the above procedure is that you may design your own character sets. It doesn't matter whether you wish to display Russian, Hebrew, or a set of scientific symbols because your IBM allows you to customize your character set to your needs.

Eighteen

Data Structures in BASIC

What Is a Data Structure?

In the preceding chapters, we have written many programs to accomplish a variety of tasks. Typically, these programs combined two features: First, each of them worked with data. In some the data were a list of numbers or words; in others they were the data describing the status of a game. Second, each program performed some sort of manipulation of the data. In some, arithmetic was performed, in some the data were analyzed and decisions made based on the analysis; in yet others, the data were manipulated to simulate the plays of a game.

One of the key steps in designing a program is to represent the task the program is to perform in terms of data. In the most elementary programs, this representation is a direct translation of the tasks the program is to perform. However, in dealing with more complex programs, there are typically a number of different ways in which the data may be represented. In designing your program you must construct a data representation that accurately mirrors the application you are describing and that allows the most efficient manipulation of the data to produce the outputs desired.

A representation of a set of data is called a **data structure**. In this chapter, we will discuss some of the most common data structures encountered in programming and how to implement these structures in BASIC.

Elementary Data Structures

The simplest data structures in BASIC are the variables of a specific type, namely integer, single precision, double precision, and string variables. By choosing which type of variable represents a given quantity, you are making a design decision in specifying a data structure for your program.

In addition to variables, BASICA includes arrays of various types: Integer, single precision, double precision, and string. In the previous chapters, we have used arrays to represent lists of various types. In what follows, we will show how arrays may be used to represent other data structures.

Records

A **record** is a collection of related variables of the same or different types. For example, consider an entry in a personnel file that consists of a four-digit ID (an integer), the person's name (an integer), and his/her department code (a string). We could just define three different variables to represent this data. However, to indicate that the data are to be considered as a group, we assign variable names with a common prefix, PERS, namely: PERS_ID% = the integer ID, PERS_NAME$ = the name of the person, PERS_DEPT$ = the department code. The collection of three related variables:

```
PERS_ID%
PERS_NAME$
PERS_DEPT$
```

is an example of a record. Of course, we work with the variables of this data structure just as we would any other variables. However, using a common prefix for the variable names helps us to organize three pieces of related data.

In many applications, it is necessary to handle lists of records. For example, in the above illustration, we would want to have a list of personnel department records for each of 100 employees. This can be accomplished by creating arrays defined by the statement:

```
10 DIM PERS_ID%(100), PERS_NAME$(100), PERS_DEPT$(100)
```

Such a collection of arrays is called a set of **parallel arrays**. Each collection consisting of corresponding entries for each of the arrays is one record. In total, the three arrays consist of a collection of 100 records.

Sets

A set is a collection of objects. For our purposes, let's initially consider sets of integers. The number of objects we can conveniently allow in our sets (at least with the implementation we have in mind) will be limited in BASICA to 15 or fewer.

Here are some typical sets we are considering:

```
{1, 4, 7} = the set consisting of 1, 4, and 7

    {5} = the set consisting of 5

 c  {} = the null set consisting of no numbers.
```

Sets are very useful for describing many applied situations. And sets constitute a very useful data structure to have when developing programs. Some computer languages, most notably Pascal, have a built-in set data type. This is not the case for BASICA. However, we can very easily create a data structure to describe sets. Namely, we identify each set with one of the integers $0, 1, ..., 32767 = 2^{16}-1$.

Here's how: Each such number can be represented by a binary number containing 16 or fewer digits. A given binary number corresponds to the set containing the numbers corresponding to 1's. For instance, the number

```
10010000
```

has 1's in its fifth and eighth places, reading the digits from the right. It corresponds to the set {5, 8}. The number

```
01010101
```

has 1's in its first, third, fifth, and seventh places and so corresponds to the set {1,3,5,7}. The number 0 has no 1's and corresponds to the null set.

By regarding numbers as integers, we may define a set of integers as an integer in BASICA.

It may not seem that we have done anything. After all, integers were already in BASICA. What we have done (which is new) is the decision to interpret an integer as a set. There are a number of operations that can be performed on sets. Suppose that A% and B% are sets. Then we have the operations union, intersection, difference, and complement defined as follows:

```
A% union B% = the set consisting of elements that belong
to either A% or B%.

A% intersection B% = the set consisting of elements that
belong to both A% and B%.

A% difference B% = the set consisting of the elements of
A% that are not in B%.

A% complement = the set consisting of all elements that
are not in A%.
```

For example, suppose that

```
A% = {1, 2, 3},  B% = {3 , 5, 7, 8}.
```

Then we have

```
A% union B% = {1, 2, 3, 5, 7, 8}

A% intersection B% = {3}

A% minus B% = {1, 2}

A% complement = {4,5,6,7,8,9,10,11,12,13,14,15,16}
```

In terms of the binary numbers corresponding to A% and B%, the operation of union corresponds to the bitwise operation OR, the operation of intersection corresponds to the bitwise operation AND, the minus corresponds to the bitwise operation XOR, and the complement corresponds to the bitwise operation NOT. So we may perform the various set operations in terms of bit manipulations. Here are DEF FN statements defining a set of BASICA functions for performing these operations.

```
10 DEF FNUNION%(A%,B%) = A% OR B%
20 DEF FNINTERSECTION%(A%,B%) = A% AND B%
30 DEF FNMINUS(A%,B%) = A% XOR B%
40 DEF FNCOMPLEMENT%(A%) = NOT A%
```

Suppose that C% is an integer representing a set. Given an integer I%, we often wish to determine whether or not the integer is in the set C%. We will construct a function that equals 0 (FALSE) if not and -1 (TRUE) if so. Then the desired function IN is given by the following definition:

```
50 DEF FNIN(I%, C%) = - (2^I% AND B%)
```

For example, here is a statement that tests to determine whether or not 5 is in the set C%:

```
60 IF FNIN(5,C%) THEN PRINT "5 is in the set C%"
```

Our description above of sets restricts us to numbers. However, we can represent any set as a set of nonnegative integers by assigning integers to stand for elements of the set. For example, to deal with sets of colors, we can assign the integers 0, 1, 2,... to the colors, say 0 = RED, 1 = BLUE, 2= YELLOW, and so forth. Then the above functions allow us to deal with sets of colors, such as:

```
{RED, YELLOW, BLUE}
```

In a similar way we can use abstraction to represent any set as a set of nonnegative integers.

Queues

A **queue** is a changing list of data elements in which elements are deleted from the beginning of the list (the **head**) and added to the end of the list (the **tail**). An example of a queue is a waiting line of people buying tickets at a movie theater. The head of the queue is the first person in line; the tail is the last person in line.

In many applications, it is necessary to describe a queue within a BASICA program. One way of doing this is to represent the queue as an array QUEUE(). The index of the array stands for the position in line, with lower indices closer to the head. In addition to the array, we need two variables, HEAD% and TAIL%, that give the index of the head and tail, respectively.

For example, if HEAD% is equal to 5 and TAIL% is equal to 12, then QUEUE(5) is the first entry in the queue and QUEUE(12) is the last entry.

To add an entry to the queue, set QUEUE(TAIL%+1) equal to the new entry and set TAIL% equal to TAIL%+1.

To delete an entry from the queue, set HEAD% equal to HEAD%-1.

Of course, an array must have a predeclared size. In the implementation of a queue just described, it is necessary to decide beforehand the maximum size that the queue can attain and declare the array equal to this size. Furthermore, as entries are added to the queue, you will eventually come to the last entry of the array. At this point, it will be necessary to move the contents of the array upward into the entry space freed by entries that have been already deleted from the queue. We leave it as an exercise to write a subroutine that accomplishes this queue adjustment.

Stacks

A **stack** is a changing list of data entries where new entries are added to the beginning of the stack (the **top of the stack**) and are deleted from the top of the stack. A stack is like a stack of dishes in which new plates are placed on top of the pile and plates are removed from the top of the pile. Stacks are very important in representing the operation of arithmetic in computers. In BASICA, a stack may be represented by an array STACK() and a variable STACKTOP%, which gives the index of the top of the array. As entries are added to the stack, the array variable corresponding to the top of the stack is assigned and the variable STACKTOP% is increased by 1. To remove an entry from the stack, just decrease STACKTOP% by 1.

Graphs

Another data structure that is commonly used in applications is that of a **graph**. This data structure is a geometric one consisting of a certain number of nodes (represented by dots), and certain connections of nodes by lines. An example of a graph is an airline route map. The nodes are the cities served by the airlines and the connections are the routes flown (see Figure 18-1).

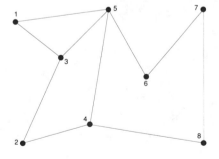

Figure 18-1.
A graph

In BASICA, we can represent the data contained in such a map as a two-dimensional array ROUTES(), where the size in each dimension equals the number of nodes (cities served). We set ROUTES(I%,J%) equal to -1 (TRUE) if there is a direct connection between city I% and J%; otherwise ROUTES(I%,J%) is equal to 0 (FALSE). Here is a BASICA statement that tests whether city 2 has a direct route to city 5:

```
10 IF ROUTES(I%,J%) THEN PRINT "City 2 has a direct route
to city 5."
```

Data structures like ROUTES() can be used in programs that plan deliveries for a fleet of trucks, make reservations for a car rental company, and so forth.

Other Data Structures

In our discussion above, we have introduced a number of different data structures. These were by no means exhaustive. However, they were representative. In each application, it is necessary to represent whatever situation occurs, be it verbal, numerical, graphic, or logical, as a data structure. This often takes imagination and cleverness to create the right data structure from the elementary data structures that BASICA allows. But this is one of the smost fun-filled and creative parts of programming.

Nineteen

Using a Printer From BASIC

Introduction

Until now we have used the printer in a rather simple fashion for listing programs and for printing output. In this chapter we discuss some of the fine points of printer usage, including:

- Printer command sequences.

- An introduction to printer graphics.

- A graphics screen dump that will print the contents of the screen in either of the two graphics modes.

Each printer is different. Printer capabilities and the techniques for accessing them vary widely among manufacturers and even among models by a single manufacturer. The discussion of this chapter applies only to the following printers:

IBM 80-character-per-second Graphics Printer
IBM Color Printer
EPSON FX/80 or FX/100
EPSON LX/80
EPSON LQ 1500

Note that most dot matrix printers have an IBM or Epson compatibility mode which allows them to work with the command sequences described in this chapter. Consult your owner's manual to determine whether your printer has such a mode and, if so, how to enable it.

Printing Fundamentals

The IBM/EPSON printers accomplish printing by means of a print head with nine wires arranged vertically. A character is sent to the printer as an ASCII code, which is an integer from 0 to 255. Some ASCII codes represent printable characters and some represent commands. In response to a printable ASCII character, the electronics of the printer cause the wires of the print head to "fire" in particular combinations that have been prepro-grammed. For a given character the print wires fire 12 times. After each firing the print head is advanced by 1/12 of a character (1/120 inch). The result is a set of dot patterns arranged within a rectangular grid nine dots high and 12 dots wide. For example, in Figure 19-1 we show the dot pattern corresponding to the letter A.

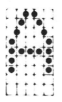

Figure 19-1.
The letter A.

The above sequence of print-head firings happens extraordinarily fast; too fast, in fact, for the eye to observe. Because the print head prints a set of dots within a rectangular matrix, this type of printer is called a dot-matrix printer. One advantage of a dot-matrix printer is its great speed. The IBM Dot-Matrix Printer, the IBM Graphics Printer, and the EPSON MX/80, MX/100, and LX/80 are all capable of printing 80 characters per second. The EPSON FX/80 and FX/100 are capable of 160 characters per second. The EPSON LQ 1500 has both a high-quality and draft mode. In draft mode, it can print at 200 characters per second.

However, speed is not the only virtue of these printers. They are capable of some incredibly sophisticated printing assignments. Before we begin to tell you about the various possibilities, let's discuss the way in which the printer receives and interprets information.

Printer Communications

The IBM PC communicates with the printer through a parallel port, which is cabled to a connector at the rear of the system unit. If you have a monochrome display interface, then the parallel port is mounted on the monochrome display interface card. If you are using the color/graphics interface, then you must get your parallel port on some other card. The parallel port of the PC is connected to the rear of the printer via a rather heavy cable, which you may purchase from your local computer dealer. (The same cable works for all the printers we are discussing.)

When you send data to the printer (say, via an LPRINT statement), here is what happens:

1. The data, in the form of a sequence of one-byte ASCII codes, are deposited in a section of the PC's memory called the **printer buffer.** This is a holding area for data awaiting transmission to the printer.

2. At intervals, the printer requests data. (Don't worry about how it does this.)

3. In response, the computer sends a number of bytes from the printer buffer, taking care to note which bytes were sent.

4. When the printer receives the bytes, it deposits them in its own buffer, to await printing.

5. Whenever the print mechanism needs a character to print, the printer looks to the buffer for a byte.

6. If the buffer is not empty, the printer takes the next byte in line.

7. The byte is decoded. It may correspond to a command or to a printable character.

8. The printer takes action on the byte. Either the command is executed or the character is printed.

9. Steps 5–8 are repeated until the printer's buffer becomes almost empty.

10. The printer then tells the computer to transmit more data and the process begins again with step 3.

The above procedure happens so quickly that you are unlikely to be aware of it. However, it is helpful to understand what is happening "under the hood" if you are to understand the operation (or nonoperation) of the printer commands.

Some Elementary Printer Commands

The most rudimentary printer command is the carriage return-line feed sequence. A carriage return is a command to return the print head to the leftmost end of the print line. A line feed advances the paper by one line. The carriage return-line feed sequence is used at the ends of most lines to reposition the print head for the beginning of the next line. In fact, the statements LPRINT and LPRINT USING automatically insert the carriage return-line feed sequence, unless you suppress it by using a semicolon at the end of the statement, as in

```
10 LPRINT A$;
20 LPRINT USING "##.##";A,B,C;
```

A carriage return is indicated by ASCII code 13 or ASCII code 141. A line feed is indicated by ASCII code 10. In theory, then, a carriage return-line feed sequence should be generated by the string

```
CHR$(13)+CHR$(10)
```

However, there is a slight catch. IBM PC BASIC automatically adds the CHR$(10) whenever it sees CHR$(13). So the carriage return-line feed sequence may be generated with the command

```
10 LPRINT CHR$(13);
```

If you wish to send a carriage return without a line feed, you must use ASCII code 141.

You may use the carriage return without the line feed to produce some interesting print effects. For example, you may backspace and then overprint some characters. Here is a program that prints the string "BASIC", then backspaces to the beginning of the string and overprints each letter with a /.

```
10 LPRINT "BASIC";
20 LPRINT CHR$(8);
30 LPRINT "/";
40 LPRINT TAB(30) "PASCAL"
50 END
```

In the above example, we used the carriage return to go back to the beginning of the line. However, in some overprint operations you may wish to go back only a single space. This may be accomplished with the backspace command. You may backspace the print head one character with ASCII code 8:

```
10 LPRINT CHR$(8);
```

Here is a program that prints the string BASIC and overprints each character with a /.

```
1 '*****************************************
2 'This program prints the word BASIC and
3 '  then overprints it with slashes.
4 '*****************************************
10 LPRINT "BASIC";
20 LPRINT CHR$(141); :'Carriage return, no line feed
30 LPRINT "/////"     :'Overprint and carriage return-line
feed
```

A word of caution: Try this program:

```
10 LPRINT "BASIC";
```

When you try to run it, nothing seems to happen. Actually, the string BASIC is sent to the printer's buffer. However, it is held there until the buffer fills up. (Printing partial buffers is inefficient.) You may force release of the printer buffer by giving a carriage return-line feed sequence. For example, the program

```
10 LPRINT "BASIC"
```

will result in immediately printing the string BASIC, since the automatic carriage return-line feed sequence has not been suppressed.

Just as the line feed command allows you to advance the paper by one line, the form feed command allows you to advance the paper to the beginning of the next page. Form feed is indicated by ASCII code 12.

Printing Mailing Labels

You may use your printer to print mailing address labels; here's how. You can buy peel-off labels on continuous form backing. These labels are available in several layouts, including one and three labels across. Let's assume that we are dealing with labels three inches wide and 15/16 inches high, with a 1/16-inch vertical space between labels. At six lines to the inch vertical spacing, each label has room for five lines. The sixth line space is to the beginning of the next label. The layout of two consecutive labels is shown in Figure 19-2. (Of course, one or more of the lines can be blank.)

```
Line 1
Line 2
Line 3
Line 4
Line 5


Line 1
Line 2
Line 3
Line 4
Line 5
```

Figure 19-2.
**Two consecu-
tive labels**.

I usually use labels three inches wide. Since the print on the printer is ten characters to the inch, this allows up to 30 characters per line. When I use labels that are two across, the first label begins in print column 1, and the second begins in print column 50. (These numbers depend on the particular label.)

Below are three programs that do various label printing tasks. The first program allows printing multiple copies of a single label, using forms containing only one label across. The second program performs the same task for forms containing two labels across. I use these programs for generating address labels for people I communicate with often. I also use such labels when I travel. I address the labels to my home address and regularly mail papers home, rather than carry them with me for the duration of the trip.

The third program takes addresses from a mailing list and prints a set of corresponding labels on forms containing one label across. It is assumed that the file containing the addresses is a random access file in which each record contains five fields (one per label line) each containing 20 characters.

Here are the three programs:

Copies of a Single Label, One Across

```
10   DIM L$(6)
20   INPUT "NUMBER OF COPIES";NUMBER
```

```
30   FOR J=1 TO 5
40     PRINT "LINE";J;
50     INPUT L$(J)
60   NEXT J
70   FOR K=1 TO NUMBER
80     FOR J=1 TO 6
90       LPRINT L$(J)
100    NEXT J
110  NEXT K
120  END
```

Copies of a Single Label, Two Across

```
10   DIM L$(6)
20   INPUT "NUMBER OF COPIES";NUMBER
30   FOR J=1 TO 5
40     PRINT "LINE";J;
50     INPUT L$(J)
60   NEXT J
70   FOR K=1 TO NUMBER
80     FOR J=1 TO 6
90       LPRINT L$(J) TAB(50) L$(J)
100    NEXT J
110  NEXT K
120  END
```

Print Labels From a Mailing List

```
10   DIM L$(6)
20   INPUT "FILE NAME OF MAILING LIST";FILENAME$
30   OPEN FILENAME$ AS #1
40   FIELD #1, 20 AS L$(1), 20 AS L$(2), 20 AS L$(3), 20 AS
L$(4),
     20 AS L$(5)
50   IF EOF(1) THEN 110
60   GET #1
70   FOR K=1 TO 6
80     LPRINT L$(J)
90   NEXT K
```

```
100  GOTO  50
110  CLOSE
120  END
```

Exercises

1. Modify label program two so that it prints copies of a label three across. (Assume that the labels begin in print columns 1, 31, and 61.)
2. Modify label program one so that it allows addition of serial numbers in the lower right corner of the label, on line five. Write the program so that it generates 100 labels with the serial numbers 100,...,199.
3. Modify label program three so that it generates labels from the mailing list using forms containing two labels across.

Printer Command Sequences

Your printer is capable of a great many options with regard to type style, print spacing, page length, and so forth. This section presents an organized look at the various command sequences available to you.

Certain printer commands are given by means of a single ASCII code. For example, a carriage return is given with ASCII code 13. However, certain printer commands are given as a sequence of ASCII codes. For such commands, the sequence of codes begins with ASCII code 27 (= Escape). This ASCII code tells the printer that the following ASCII codes are to be interpreted as part of a command rather than as printable characters. For example, consider the sequence of ASCII codes

```
27,  78,  3
```

It instructs the printer to skip three lines at the end of the page. This allows you to skip over the perforation between consecutive sheets of paper. You may communicate this sequence of ASCII codes to the printer as you would any other ASCII codes, using the LPRINT statement

```
LPRINT CHR$(27);CHR$(78);CHR$(3);
```

Line Spacing

The following commands are available for adjusting the vertical line spacing:

Action	Command Sequence
Set line spacing to 1/6 inch	27, 50
Set line spacing to 1/8 inch	27, 48
Set line spacing to 7/72 inch	27, 49
Set line spacing to n/72 inch	27, 65, n, 27, 50[1]
	27, 65, n[2]
Set line spacing to n/216 inch[1]	27, 51, n
Set line spacing to n/216 inch[1] for current line only.	27, 74, n
Default setting: line spacing = 1/6 inch	

---

1 IBM printers only.

2 Non-IBM printers only.

Figure 19-3 shows some samples of various vertical line spacings.

```
Line  Spacing 8 /72  inches
Line  Spacing 10/72  inches
Line  Spacing 12/72  inches
Line  Spacing 14/72  inches

Line  Spacing 16/72  inches

Line  Spacing 18/72  inches


Line  Spacing 20/72  inches


Line  Spacing 22/72  inches


Line  Spacing 24/72  inches
```

Figure 19-3.
Examples of vertical line spacing.

Page Length and Layout

This group of commands allows you to set the length of the page and the amount of space to skip in order to avoid the perforations in continuous forms.

Set page length to n lines	27, 67, n
Set page length to n inches[1]	27, 67, n, 0
Leave n lines blank at bottom of page (=skip perforation)[1]	27, 78, n
Cancel skip perforation[1]	27, 79

Default setting: Page length = 66 lines = 11 inches

Notes:

a. You must set the page length before giving the Skip Perforation command.

b. The Skip Perforation command causes the number of printed lines to be decreased by the specified skip. For example, a skip of 10 lines and standard page length will cause pages to consist of 56 lines followed by 10 blank lines.

c. You may wish to adjust the paper so that any skip is evenly distributed between the bottom of a page and the top of the following one.

d. The beginning of the page is set when the printer is turned on. Any form feed commands make reference to the latest vertical line spacing and the latest page length information in spacing to the top of the next page.

Print Style

The IBM/EPSON printers are capable of a number of print styles, including emphasized, double strike, double width, compressed, underlined, and subscript/superscript. We may group these attributes as follows:

Group A: Normal
   Compressed
   Emphasized
Group B: Double Strike
   Subscript
   Superscript
Group C: Double Width
Group D: Underline

You may combine attributes by selecting at most one attribute from each group. For example, you may select print that is simultaneously compressed, subscript, and double width. However, you may not select print simultaneously compressed and emphasized.

Figure 19-4 shows some samples of the various print styles possible with your printer.

```
This is the standard type font.
This line is emphasized.
This line is double-struck.
This line is double width.
This line is condensed.
This line is italics.
```

Figure 19-4.
**Various print
styles.**

Here are the print commands that govern the various print styles:

Emphasized print ON	27, 69
Emphasized print OFF	27, 70
Double strike ON	27, 71
Double strike OFF	27, 72
Subscript ON[1]	27, 83, 1
Superscript ON[1]	27, 83, 0
Subscript/Superscript OFF[1]	27, 84
Compressed ON	15
Compressed OFF	18
Double-width ON (current line only)	14
Double-width OFF	20

Underline ON[3]   27, 45, 1

Underline OFF[1]   27, 45, 0

Notes:

   a. The double-width style prints five characters to the inch, but is the same height as standard print.

   b. The compressed print style prints 132 characters per eight-inch line.

Tabs

Set horizontal tabs   27, 68, n1, n2,...,nk,0
at columns n1,n2,...,nk

Horizontal tab   9

Cancel horizontal tabs   27, 68, 0

Set vertical tabs   27, 66, n1, n2, ...,nk, 0
at columns n1,n2,...,nk

Vertical tab   11

Cancel vertical tabs   27, 66, 0

Exercises

Write a command that sets the following parameters of the printer.

---

[3] Not available with the IBM dot-matrix printer or Epson MX/80.

1. Vertical line spacing to 9/72 inches.

2. Vertical line spacing to eight lines per inch.

3. Vertical line spacing to 12 lines per inch.

4. Vertical line spacing to six lines per inch, double spaced.

5. Set horizontal tabs at columns 5, 10, 15, and 30.

6. Set the page length to 33 lines per page.

7. Suppose that you wish to print six lines per inch, triple spaced. Write commands to set the appropriate page length and vertical line spacing.

Print the sentence THIS IS A TEST. in the following type styles:

8. emphasized

9. compressed

10. double width

11. double strike

Print the following expressions:

12. $X2$

13. $H2O$

14. $ex = 51.3$

Printer Graphics

In this section we will discuss the graphics capabilities of the IBM/EPSON printers.

As we have mentioned, the print head has nine wires arranged vertically. In the graphics mode only the top eight of these wires are used. Figure 19-5 shows the eight wires used in the graphics modes and numbers them, from bottom to top, with the numbers 0 through 7.

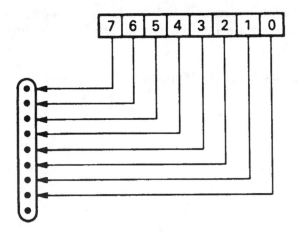

Figure 19-5.
The print head wires.

Each print wire corresponds to a single printed dot. You may request the print head to print any combination of dots corresponding to the eight wires used in graphics mode. Figure 19-6 shows a number of typical dot patterns.

A dot pattern is specified as a single byte, with wire 0 corresponding to bit 0, wire 1 corresponding to bit 1, and so forth. The most significant bit corresponds to the top print wire. Figure 19-6 indicates the bytes corresponding to each of the given bit patterns.

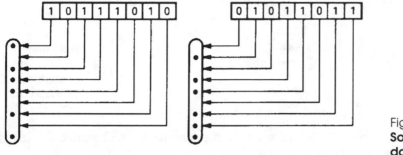

Figure 19-6.
**Some typical
dot patterns**.

Test Your Understanding 1 (Answer on Page 575)

Determine the bytes corresponding to the following dot patterns:

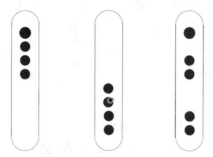

Test Your Understanding 2 (Answers on Page 576)

Determine the dot patterns corresponding to the following bytes:

a. `&HFF`
b. `&H0F`
c. `&H1A`

You may specify more complex dot patterns by representing them in terms of a number of eight-dot vertical patterns like those above. For example, consider the following dot pattern that forms the letter A in Figure 19-7.

Figure 19-7.
The letter "A" as formed from pixels on an IBM or Epson dot matrix printer.

It is formed of a grid 11×8 and may be represented as 11 vertical eight-bit dot patterns. Figure 19-8 shows the dot patterns with their corresponding byte representations.

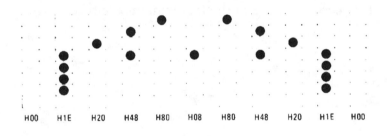

Figure 19-8.
Dot patters with their corresponding byte representations.

Test Your Understanding 3 (Answer on Page 576)

Determine the dot configuration determined by the bytes

&HFE, &H01, &H00, &H01, &H00, &H01, &H00, &HFE

Test Your Understanding 4 (Answer on Page 576)

Determine the bytes corresponding to the following dot configuration (a mathematical symbol meaning "sum").

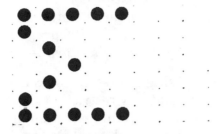

Horizontal Dot Placement

There are three graphics modes, with the following horizontal dot densities:

Medium Resolution: 480 dots per eight-inch line
High Resolution: 960 dots per eight-inch line
Ultra High Resolution[4]: 1920 dots per eight-inch line

In medium resolution adjacent dots have a noticeable horizontal space between them. In high resolution this space is eliminated. In ultra-high resolution adjacent dots actually overlap. For each density, you may, in principle, print any eight-dot vertical pattern in each of the horizontal dot positions on a line (see below for an exception). For example, in medium-resolution mode, you may print 480 vertical eight-bit patterns per eight inch line.

---

4 IBM Graphics Printer.

Actually, it is possible to mix graphics patterns with text. For example, you might print a line consisting of 50 standard printed characters (at ten characters to the inch = five inches), followed by 120 graphics patterns (at 60 per inch = two inches), followed by ten standard printed characters.

As with most things in life, increasing the resolution comes at a price. If you wish to use high resolution without any restrictions in dot placement, you can print only at half the speed of medium resolution. A similar statement goes for ultra-high resolution. If you wish to retain the speed, you must live with some restrictions in dot placement. In order for high resolution to run at full printer speed, you cannot print two dots that are horizontally adjacent to one another. In ultra-high resolution you can print dots only in every third horizontal dot position.

In order to initiate a printer graphics mode it is necessary to give an escape sequence that tells the computer:

1. The graphics mode.

2. The speed.

3. The number of vertical eight-bit graphics patterns forthcoming.

These three data items are expressed by a four-byte code:

        27 m n1 n2

where m is a byte denoting the graphics mode/speed and n1 and n2 are bytes that, together, indicate the number of vertical eight-bit graphics patterns to come. Here are the meanings of m, n1, and n2:

m = 75 : 480 dots per eight-inch line

m = 76 : 960 dots per eight-inch line, half speed

m = 89 : 960 dots per eight-inch line, full speed, no
                adjacent dots

m = 90 : 1,920 dots per eight-inch line, full speed; can
print only every third dot

n1 = the remainder obtained when the number of graphics
patterns is divided by 256

n2 = the number of graphics patterns divided by 256
(integer part)

Thus, n1 and n2 satisfy this relationship:

```
<number of graphics patterns> = 256*n2 + n1
```

For example, suppose that you wish to print 400 graphics patterns in medium-resolution mode. Divide 400 by 256. The quotient is 1 and the remainder is 144. That is,

```
400 = 256*1 + 144
```

Therefore, n2 = 1 and n1 = 144. The command that specifies 400 graphics patterns in medium-resolution mode is then given by the sequence of bytes

```
27, 75, 144, 1
```

As a second example, suppose that we wish to print the letter A, given as the sequence of nine graphics patterns, as specified in the hexadecimal bytes

```
&H1E    &H20    &H48    &H80    &H08    &H80    &H48    &H20
&H1E
```

Further, suppose that we wish to use low speed, high-resolution mode. Since 9 = 0*256 + 9, we have n1 = 9 and n2 = 0. We initiate the desired printing pattern with the sequence of bytes

```
27, 76, 9, 0
```

We follow these bytes with the bytes representing the nine graphics patterns. Here is a program that prints the desired nine graphics patterns:

```
10 LPRINT CHR$(27);CHR$(76);CHR$(9);CHR$(0);
20 LPRINT CHR$(&H1E);CHR$(&H20);CHR$(&H48);CHR$(&H80);
30 LPRINT CHR$(&H8);CHR$(&H80);CHR$(&H48);CHR$(&H20);
40 LPRINT CHR$(&H1E);
50 END
```

Note that we did not allow any carriage returns in any of the LPRINT statements. Furthermore, note that we specified the graphics patterns in hexadecimal rather than decimal. This is because it is easier to go from the actual dot pattern to hexadecimal. Translating the hexadecimal into decimal would provide room for errors. Finally note that we sent each hexadecimal byte to the printer via a CHR$ statement. You might wonder why we don't just LPRINT the hexadecimal bytes directly, as in, say

```
10 LPRINT &H1E
```

This approach will not work, however, for it sends the printer the number &H1E. BASIC automatically translates this number into its decimal equivalent 31. BASIC then sends the printer the decimal digits 3 and 1, coded as ASCII codes. What gets sent are the two bytes &H33 and &H31. This is not the same thing as sending the hexadecimal byte &H1E.

The above program is extremely hard to read. A better approach is as follows:

```
10 INIT$= CHR$(27)+CHR$(76)+CHR$(9)+CHR$(0)
20 A$ = CHR$(&H1E)+CHR$(&H20)+CHR$(&H48)+CHR$(&H80)+CHR$
          (&H8)+CHR$(&H80)+CHR$(&H48)+CHR$(&H20)+CHR$(&H1E)
30 LPRINT INIT$;
40 LPRINT A$;
50 END
```

As a further example, let's draw a box as shown in Figure 19-9. The

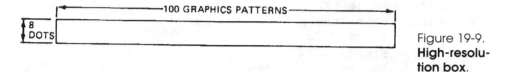

Figure 19-9.
**High-resolu-
tion box.**

box is 100 graphics patterns wide in high resolution. The bottom of the box is drawn by print wire 0 and the top by print wire 7. We may draw this box out of two graphics patterns, one consisting of all eight dots (for both ends) and a second consisting of only the top and bottom dot. The hexadecimal equivalents for these dots are, respectively, &HFF and &H81. (Check this!) Here is a program that draws the box.

```
10  INIT$=CHR$(27)+CHR$(76)+CHR$(100)+CHR$(0)
20  SIDE$=CHR$(&HFF)
30  MIDDLE$=CHR$(&H81)
40  LPRINT INIT$;
50  LPRINT SIDE$;
60  FOR J=1 TO 98
70     LPRINT MIDDLE$;
80  NEXT J
90  LPRINT SIDE$;
100 END
```

Note that you may mix ordinary text and graphics. For example, let's print the phrase WRITE YOUR ANSWER IN THE BOX. immediately to the left of the box, and the phrase STOP immediately to the right. Our printed line should look like the one shown in Figure 19-10.

WRITE YOUR ANSWER IN THE BOX ⊏━━━━━━━━━━━━━━━━⊐ STOP

Figure 19-10.
**A printed line
requesting use
to write an
answer in the
box.**

Here is a program to print this line:

```
10   LPRINT "WRITE YOUR ANSWER IN THE BOX.";
20   INIT$=CHR$(27)+CHR$(76)+CHR$(100)+CHR$(0)
```

```
30    SIDE$=CHR$(&HFF)
40    MIDDLE$=CHR$(&H81)
50    LPRINT INIT$;
60    LPRINT SIDE$;
70    FOR J=1 TO 98
80       LPRINT MIDDLE$;
90    NEXT J
100   LPRINT SIDE$;
110   LPRINT "STOP"
120   END
```

This program prints the desired line and does a carriage return to the next line. (There is no semicolon on line 110.)

Note that line 10 prints in ordinary text, lines 40–100 in high-resolution graphics mode. Line 110 returns to ordinary text. It is not necessary to give any special command to return to text mode. After the specified number of graphics patterns, the printer automatically reverts to ordinary text. Any special print modes (emphasized, subscript, compressed, etc.) in effect before entry into graphics mode remain in effect on return to text mode.

If you print two consecutive lines of graphics with default line spacing (1/8 inch), you will notice that there is a small blank area between them. You may eliminate this space, making a continuous graphics pattern. The secret is to use 8/72-inch spacing. (This corresponds to nine lines to the inch as opposed to the default eight lines per inch.) You may set this spacing using the command

```
LPRINT CHR$(27);CHR$(65);CHR$(8);CHR$(27);CHR$(50);
    (IBM Graphics Printer)
LPRINT CHR$(27);CHR$(65);CHR$(8);
    (others)
```

You may print as many consecutive graphics lines as you wish. However, if you then wish to return to printing text, remember to reset the vertical line spacing.

Exercises

1. Write a program to print the following symbol:

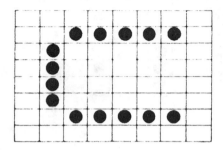

2. Write a program to print the following line:

THIS IS A TEST ▭ ▭ ▭

3. Write a program to draw a box 500 dots long and 80 dots high in high resolution graphics mode.

Answers to Test Your Understandings 1, 2, 3, and 4

1. a. &H11

    a. &H0F

    c. &HFA

2.

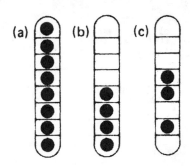

3.

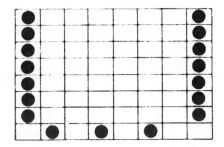

4.   &HC6, &HAA, &H92, &H8s, &H82, &H99, &H00, &H00

A Graphics Screen Dump

Let's use what we have learned to write a program that prints the contents of the screen in either medium- or high-resolution graphics mode. Our program is designed as a subroutine to be called within another program. Once you have the desired image on the screen, just call this subroutine and it will print the contents of the screen, pixel by pixel.

To start, let's assume that we are dealing with an image in high-resolution graphics mode. The image is then 640 pixels wide and 200 pixels high. We don't wish to impose any restrictions on printing of adjacent dots, so we are stuck with printing in medium-resolution graphics mode. Of course, this allows us only 480 dots across a line, not enough to print a line of the screen. The solution to this dilemma is to print the screen sideways. The lower left corner of the screen will be printed at the upper-left-side of the paper. The upper left corner of the screen will correspond to the upper right corner of the paper (see Figure 19-11).

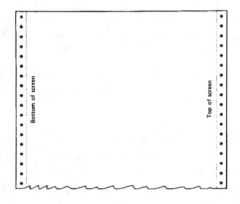

Figure 19-11.
Screen printed sideways.

Our basic idea is to use the GET statement to read pixels of the screen, from bottom to top, in columns eight pixels wide (see Figure 19-12).

Each GET statement will yield a single byte, one bit for each of the eight pixels. This byte will be sent to the printer and printed as a graphics pattern. Each row of graphics patterns on the printer will correspond to a single column of eight pixels. Since the screen is 640 pixels wide, we will need to break the screen into 80 columns.

At 1/9-inch per column, the screen will print as 80/9 = 8.9 inches down the page. On the other hand, the width of the printed image is 200 dots, or 200/60 = 3.3 inches. As you can see, the perspective is quite distorted. The image is almost three times as long as it is high. To make up for this deficiency, let's print each graphics pattern twice. This will expand the printed

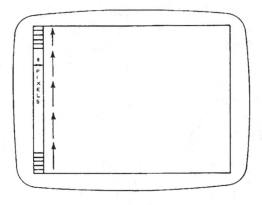

Figure 19-12.
**Eight-pixel wide
column**.

image across the page to 400 dot = 400/60 = 6.7 inches. This is close to the
usual 4 to 3 ratio between the horizontal and vertical measurements of the
screen.

To center the image vertically on the page, we begin with one inch of space
at the top of the page. Since the image will be approximately 8.9 inches down
the page, this leaves about a one-inch space at the bottom, which centers
the image. Across each printed line, we are using 6.67 inches. To center the
image, we must have a space of approximately .9 inches on each side of a
line. Since there are ten characters to the inch, we leave a nine-character
space at the beginning of the line.

One last problem before we write our program: BASIC automatically
inserts carriage returns at the end of every line. In fact, unless you tell it
otherwise, it assumes that a line has ended after 80 characters sends a
carriage return-line feed sequence. In our graphics screen dump, we will be
sending several hundred "characters" per line. (As far as BASIC is concerned,
each byte sent is a "character.") We must somehow disable this automatic
feature. This may be done using the WIDTH instruction. The statement

```
WIDTH "LPT1:",255
```

tells BASIC to assume an infinite line width for the printer. This statement
disables the automatic carriage return-line feed.

After all these considerable preliminaries, here is our screen dump program:

```
1 '**********************************************
2 'This program is a subroutine which can be
3 'incorporated into a program to print the
4 'contents of a graphics screen (SCREEN 1 or
5 'SCREEN 2).
6 '**********************************************
1000 'IBM GRAPHICS PRINTER VERSION
1010 'Initialization
1020 DIM Z%(2)
1030 WIDTH "LPT1:",255
1040 'Print Screen
1050 LINESPACE9$=CHR$(27)+CHR$(65)+CHR$(8)
1060 LINESPACE6$=CHR$(27)+CHR$(65)+CHR$(12)
1070 GRAPH400$=CHR$(27)+CHR$(75)+CHR$(144)+CHR$(1)
1080 LPRINT LINESPACE9$;
1090 FOR J%=1 TO 9
1100    LPRINT
1110 NEXT J%
1120 FOR COL%=0 TO 79
1130    LPRINT SPACE$(9);
1140    LPRINT GRAPH400$;
1150    FOR ROW%=199 TO 0 STEP -1
1160       GET (8*COL%+7,ROW%)-(8*COL%,ROW%),Z%
1170       LPRINT CHR$(Z%(2))+CHR$(Z%(2));
1180    NEXT ROW%
1190    LPRINT
1200 NEXT COL%
1210 FOR J%=1 TO 10
1220    LPRINT
1230 NEXT J%
1240 LPRINT LINESPACE6$;
1250 RETURN
```

We have explained the reason behind most of the program already. However, lines 1130 and 1140 deserve some comment. The pixels corresponding to (COL%+7,ROW%)-(COL%,ROW%) go across the column COL%

at row ROW%, proceeding from right to left. These pixels are stored in the array Z%. Recall the manner in which GET stores this information. Z%(0) contains the width of the rectangle being stored, in this case eight; Z%(1) contains the height of the rectangle being stored, namely 1; Z%(2) contains the first eight pixels of the first row of the rectangle. In this case, the entire rectangle has only eight pixels. Z%(2) contains precisely the information we want, and the information is stored with the most-significant bit corresponding to the rightmost pixel. (The order of storage is guaranteed by the order in which we have stated the endpoints of the rectangle in line 1130.)

A few further comments.

1. The above program is written for the IBM Graphics Printer. To use the program on the EPSON printers, replace lines 1050–1060 with

    ```
    1050  LINESPACE9$=CHR$(27)+CHR$(65)+CHR$(8)
    1060  LINESPACE6$=CHR$(27)+CHR$(65)+CHR$(12)
    ```

2. The above program is written to be used in high-resolution graphics mode (SCREEN 2). We leave the modifications necessary to print the screen in medium-resolution graphics mode for the exercises.

Exercises

1. Type in the screen print program and use it to print a graphics image in high-resolution graphics mode.
2. Modify the screen print program for use with medium-resolution graphics mode. (Recall that in this mode GET returns two bits for each pixel instead of one.)
3. Modify the routine to print sections of the screen.

Twenty

Input the Professional Way

Introduction

In this chapter we take a closer look at the input process and develop routines to allow for "bullet-proof" input of data. In particular, we develop routines to:

- Input a character restricted to a particular set.

- Input a string of limited length.

- Input a number of particular type and within an allowable range.

Why You Need an Input Routine

When you saw the title of this chapter, you probably thought: "I know about input. I can use INPUT and LINE INPUT to handle my programs' input needs." Well, I have some bad news. If you want to write professional-level programs, the BASIC input statements INPUT and LINE INPUT leave much to be desired.

For example, suppose that your program has just set up a menu with choices to be input by the user, and suppose that INPUT is used to accept the user response. BASIC responds to a type mismatch (string instead of number) with the prompt

    Redo from start?

This usually wrecks the carefully planned screen layout you have just created.

INPUT accepts as numerical input any number legal in BASIC, such as 1.7839E-18. For each input to your program, it is your responsibility to check that numbers are of the required type (say, positive or an integer between 1 and 10). But how do you prevent the program user from inputting a number such as 1E40, which is beyond the limits allowed by BASIC? Before you can analyze the input, BASIC declares an overflow error. And you can't RESUME after an overflow!

As for string input, you usually must control the length of input (say, a name cannot have more than 20 characters). Or, suppose that a question calls for a Y or N response. Your program should also accept y or n and reject all other letters.

As you can see from the above recitation, input is a complicated business. And, if you wish to write professional level programs, you must be able to control your input so that you force the user to provide input the program can use. That's the purpose of an input routine.

In this chapter, I'll describe an input routine I've developed that avoids all the problems mentioned above. It is a complex routine, but you'll have no trouble understanding it. It was more complicated to build than it is to comprehend. And now that the work's done, you can use it in your own programs.

Our input program is called INPUT and is composed of three main routines, called KEYIN, SCREENIN, and NUMBERCK.

KEYIN reads the keyboard, one character at a time. On the basis of user-supplied information, KEYIN accepts certain characters and rejects others. You may request KEYIN to change input to all uppercase letters.

SCREENIN is a screen entry routine, which displays input characters in a specific field on the screen. SCREENIN allows some character editing and passes on extended ASCII codes for further analysis.

NUMBERCK is a routine that analyzes a string to determine if it is in an acceptable format to be converted into a number. If possible, NUMBERCK performs the conversion and passes the number back to the main program. NUMBERCK also determines whether the converted number is an integer.

Together, these three routines allow you to input data to your program knowing that you are in total control.

Inputting Characters

As the first part of our professional input package, let's build the routine KEYIN, which inputs characters from the keyboard. KEYIN continually inspects the keyboard buffer to determine if a key has been pressed. If so, the keyboard buffer is read via INKEY$ and the result is put into the variable C$. Next, KEYIN determines if the key corresponds to an extended ASCII code. (Is the length of C$ two?) If so, C$ is replaced by its second byte.

After reading the keyboard buffer, KEYIN goes to one of two analysis sections to determine whether the character is acceptable. There is one analysis section for ordinary ASCII codes and one for extended ASCII codes.

In general, the acceptable characters will vary with the section of the program. For one input you may wish to accept only the characters Y, y, n, or N; for another, you may wish to accept only the digits 1,2,3,4,5; and so forth. There is a variable CALLER that identifies a set of acceptable characters. For each value of CALLER used, you must define six values:

```
MINKEY(CALLER), MAXKEY(CALLER),
SPECIALKEY$(CALLER)

EXTMINKEY(CALLER), EXTMAXKEY(CALLER),
EXTSPECIALKEY$(CALLER)
```

The first three values correspond to ordinary ASCII codes and the second three to extended ASCII codes. For example, suppose that CALLER=1 and

```
MINKEY(1)=32, MAXKEY(1)=127,
SPECIALKEY$(1)=CHR$(8)+CHR(13)+CHR$(27)
```

Then KEYIN will accept any character with an ASCII code from 32 to 127 inclusive (these are the displayable, nongraphics characters), as well as the special characters CHR$(8) (backspace), CHR$(13) (carriage return), and CHR$(27) (Esc). Further, suppose that

```
EXTMINKEY(1)=59, EXTMAXKEY(1)=68,
EXTSPECIALKEY$(1)=""
```

Then KEYIN will accept extended ASCII codes 59 through 68 (function keys F1 through F10) and no other extended ASCII codes.

Test Your Understanding 1 (Answer on Page 588)

What are the values of the six variables if KEYIN is to accept all displayable, nongraphics characters, as well as the four cursor motion keys?

Actually, there is a seventh variable that can depend on the particular CALLER, namely CAPSON(CALLER). If CAPSON=-1 then KEYIN converts letters to uppercase; if CAPSON=0 then KEYIN returns the character as input. If conversion to uppercase is requested, then it is performed in line 26195. This uses the function for uppercase conversion, which we developed in the preceding chapter.

Test Your Understanding 2 (Answer on Page 588)

What are the values of the seven variables if KEYIN is to accept numerical input and all extended ASCII codes?

Test Your Understanding 3 (Answer on Page 588)

What are the values of the seven variables if KEYIN is to accept the two responses Yes and No (as indicated by the characters Y and N)?

If you type an unacceptable character, KEYIN beeps the speaker and waits for another character.

We have made certain assumptions in writing KEYIN. First, we assume that the arrays MINKEY(), MAXKEY(), SPECIALKEY$, EXTMINKEY(), EXTMAXKEY(), and EXTSPECIALKEY$() are dimensioned in the main program. Their size should be dictated by the number of different types of input required by the program.

Second, the variables TRUE=-1 and FALSE=0 are assumed to be assigned in the main program. Using TRUE and FALSE, we can write statements such as

```
IF EXTENDED=TRUE THEN . . .
IF MENUEND=FALSE THEN . . .
```

Using TRUE and FALSE makes programs so much more readable, I include these definitions at the beginning of every program that I write.

Here is the routine KEYIN:

```
26000 '****************KEYIN********************
26005 '
26010 'This routine reads a character from the keyboard
26011 'and accepts or rejects it based on the caller's
26012 ' specifications.
26020 'Subroutine variables:
26025 '    CALLER = number of caller
26030 '    MINKEY(CALLER)=minimum ASCII code for CALLER
26035 '    MAXKEY(CALLER)=maximum ASCII code for CALLER
26040 '    CAPSON(CALLER)=Convert to CAPITALS?
26045 '    SPECIALKEYS$(CALLER)=String containing any
26050 '             special acceptable keys for CALLER
26055 '    EXTMINKEY(CALLER)=minimum extended ASCII
26056 '             code for CALLER
26060 '    EXTMAXKEY(CALLER)=maximum extended ASCII
26061 '             code for CALLER
26065 '    EXTSPECIALKEY$(CALLER)=special extended
26066 '             ASCII codes for CALLER
26070 ' The above arrays must be dimensioned in the
26075 ' main program. The array values must be assigned
26080 ' in the main program. The values of TRUE and
26085 ' FALSE must also be assigned in the main
26090 ' program.
26095 '    C$=the character returned
26100 '    EXTENDED=-1 if C$ is the second byte of an
26101 '                     extended ASCII code,
26105 '             = 0 otherwise
26110 'Input character string from INKEY$
26115    C$=INKEY$
26120    IF C$="" THEN 26115: 'Wait for input
26125    C=ASC(C$)
26130    IF LEN(C$)=2 THEN EXTENDED=TRUE ELSE
         EXTENDED=FALSE
26135    IF EXTENDED=FALSE THEN 26155
26140    C$=RIGHT$(C$,1)
26145    C=ASC(C$)
26150    GOTO 26205
26155 'Ordinary ASCII Codes
26160 '  Test for range
26165      IF C>=MINKEY(CALLER) AND C<=MAXKEY(CALLER) THEN
```

```
26185
26170 '   Handle special characters
26175       IF SPECIALKEY$(CALLER)="" THEN 26240 :'No
            special characters
26180       IF INSTR(SPECIALKEY$(CALLER),C$)=0 THEN 26240
26185 '  Convert to capitals if necessary
26190       IF CAPSON(CALLER)=FALSE THEN 26255
26195       IF C>96 AND C<123 THEN C$=CHR$(C AND 223)
26200       GOTO 26255
26205 ' Extended ASCII codes
26210 '   Test for range
26215 IF C>=EXTMINKEY(CALLER) AND C<=EXTMINKEY(CALLER)
      THEN 26255
26220 '   Handle special characters
26225       IF EXTSPECIALKEY$(CALLER)="" THEN 26240
26230       IF INSTR(EXTSPECIALKEY$(CALLER),C$)=0 THEN
            26240
26235       GOTO 26255
26240 ' Illegal character
26245       BEEP
26250       GOTO 26115: 'Try again
26255 RETURN
```

To try out KEYIN, use a program of this type:

```
10  TRUE=-1:FALSE=0
20  DIM MINKEY(5),MAXKEY(5),EXTMINKEY(5),EXTMAXKEY(5)
30  DIM SPECIALKEY$(5),EXTSPECIALKEY$(5),CAPSON(5)
40  MINKEY(1)=0:MAXKEY(1)=0
50  SPECIALKEY$(1)= "1234567890-+Ee "
60  EXTMINKEY(1)=0:EXTMAXKEY(1)=0
70  EXTSPECIALKEY$(1)=CHR$(59)+CHR$(60)
80  CAPSON(1)=TRUE:CALLER=1
90  KEY OFF:FOR J=1 TO 10:KEY J,"":NEXT J
100 GOSUB 26000
110 IF EXTENDED=TRUE THEN PRINT "EXTENDED ASCII CODE"
120 PRINT ASC(C$),C$
130 INPUT "Again (Y or N)";A$
140 IF A$="Y" OR A$="y" THEN 80
150 END
26000 (INCLUDE KEYIN SUBROUTINE HERE)
```

This program allows for five different callers (only one is actually used). The acceptable characters for CALLER 1 are the digits 0–9, and the characters +, -, E, space, and the extended ASCII codes 59 and 60 (functions keys F1 and F2). Note that if you type e, it is converted to E since CAPSON(1)=TRUE. The program prints out the ASCII code of the character and the character itself and then awaits another character. You should run this program to convince yourself that KEYIN does, in fact, work.

Answers to Test Your Understandings 1, 2, and 3

1.  ```
    MINKEY(1)=32:MAXKEY(1)=127:SPECIALKEY$(1)=""
    EXTMINKEY(1)=0:EXTMAXKEY(1)=0:EXTSPECIALKEY$(1)=
    CHR$(72)+CHR$(75)+CHR$(77)+CHR$(80)
    ```

2.  ```
    MINKEY(1)=0:MAXKEY(1)=0:SPECIALKEY$(1)="1234567890-+E."
    EXTMINKEY(1)=0:EXTMAXKEY(1)=127:EXTSPECIALKEY$(1)=""
    CAPSON=-1
    ```

3.  ```
    MINKEY(1)=0:MAXKEY(1)=0:SPECIALKEY$(1)="YN"
    EXTMINKEY(1)=0:EXTMAXKEY(1)=127:EXTSPECIALKEY$(1)=""
    CAPSON=-1
    ```

Inputting Strings and Numbers

Now that we have a character input routine, let's extend our sights and build routines that input strings and numbers.

The routine SCREENIN uses KEYIN to accept input from the keyboard and displays it at a specified position on the screen. When you call SCREENIN, you must specify, in addition to the values needed by KEYIN, the values

```
XFLD=column position where output is to begin
YFLD=row where output is to be displayed
LNGTH=maximum number of characters allowed
```
```

By specifying the allowable characters for KEYIN, you may control the characters that are allowed in your display. You may use the backspace key to erase a character, just as in the BASIC editor. ENTER signifies the end of output, and Esc causes the display field to be erased and the cursor to be positioned at the beginning of the field. (In order for these keys to have the functions indicated, however, you must define the corresponding keys to be acceptable to KEYIN.)

Any extended ASCII code automatically ends input.

The end of input is indicated by setting the variable INPUTEND=TRUE. When input has ended, SCREENIN reads the display field using the SCREEN function. SCREEN(row,column) equals the ASCII code of the character at position (row,column). The resulting string is stored in the variable S$. If input was ended by an extended ASCII code, then EXTENDED is set equal to true and E$ contains the second character of the extended code. Note that S$ does not include any reference to an extended ASCII code.

You will note in several places the statements

```
LOCATE ,,0
LOCATE ,,1
```

The first turns the cursor off and the second turns the cursor on. I have found that watching the cursor motion is very annoying, especially when using SCREEN. In order to preserve my sanity while using SCREENIN, I turned off the cursor whenever cursor motion proved annoying.

Here is the code for SCREENIN. Note that the code for KEYIN is required to operate SCREENIN. (We numbered KEYIN beginning with 26000 with this in mind.)

```
25000 '******************SCREENIN********************
25005 ' This routine inputs data as a string S$ from the
         keyboard.
25010 ' It allows input to have the following parameters:
25015 ' LNGTH = maximum length of input string
25020 ' XFLD = cursor column for beginning of input field
25025 ' YFLD = cursor row for input field
```

```
25030 'CALLER = number of caller
25035 'CAPSON(CALLER) = -1 if letters are to be capital-
                          ized for CALLER
25040 '                 = 0 otherwise
25045 'FLDBEG = first character position in field
25050 'FLDEND = last character position in field
         (calculated)
25055 'S$=Contents of the field from beginning up to space
         before cursor
25060 'T$=contents of the field from the cursor to the end
         of the field
25065 'At end of routine, the contents of the field are
         returned in S$
25070 'LASTPOS=position currently occupied by last
         character
25075 'If a key with an extended ASCII code is pressed,
25080 'it ends processing the current field. The
25085 'contents of the field are returned in S$ and
25090 'the second byte of the extended ASCII code in E$.
25095 '************************************************
25100 '
25105 '******MAIN ROUTINE******
25110 '
25115    S$="":E$="":INPUTEND=FALSE:KEYHIT=FALSE
25120    FLDEND=XFLD+LNGTH-1:CSR=XFLD
25125    GOSUB 25450:'Compute initial LASTPOS
25130    LOCATE YFLD,XFLD
25135    WHILE INPUTEND=FALSE
25140      GOSUB 26000:'Input character
25145      IF EXTENDED=TRUE THEN 25225
25150    GOTO 25185
25155    WEND
25160    GOSUB 25365:'Read screen
25165    S$=S$+T$
25170    RETURN
25175 '************************************************
25180 '
25185 '****** Subroutines ******
25190 '
25195 'Handle ordinary ASCII codes
```

```
25200      KEYHIT=TRUE
25205      IF C$=CHR$(8) THEN   25260: 'Backspace
25210      IF C$=CHR$(13) THEN 25295: 'ENTER
25215      IF C$=CHR$(27) THEN 25310: 'Esc
25220      IF C$>=CHR$(32) THEN 25340:'Handle
       displayable character
25225 'Handle extended ASCII codes
25230      E$=C$
25235      INPUTEND=TRUE
25240      GOTO 25155
25245 'Reject character
25250      BEEP
25255      GOTO 25155
25260 'Handle Backspace
25265      IF LASTPOS<XFLD THEN 25245
25270      GOSUB 25365:'Read field
25275 IF CSR<>XFLD THEN CSR=CSR-1:PRINT CHR$(29)+T$+
       CHR$(32); ELSE PRINT T$;
25280      LOCATE YFLD,CSR
25285      LASTPOS=LASTPOS-1
25290      GOTO 25155
25295 'Handle ENTER
25300      INPUTEND=TRUE
25305      GOTO 25155
25310 'Handle ESC (Erase field)
25315      LOCATE YFLD,XFLD
25320      PRINT STRING$(LNGTH,32);
25325      LASTPOS=0:CSR=XFLD
25330      LOCATE YFLD,XFLD
25335      GOTO 25155
25340 'Display character
25345      PRINT C$;
25350      IF LASTPOS<CSR THEN LASTPOS=CSR
25355      IF CSR=FLDEND THEN PRINT CHR$(29); ELSE CSR=CSR+1
25360      GOTO 25155
25365 'Read field from screen
25370      LOCATE ,,0
25375      S$="": T$=""
25380      IF LASTPOS=0 THEN 25420
25385      FOR J%=XFLD TO CSR-1
```

```
25390        S$=S$+CHR$(SCREEN(YFLD,J%))
25395      NEXT J%
25400      FOR J%=CSR TO LASTPOS
25405        T$=T$+CHR$(SCREEN(YFLD,J%))
25410      NEXT J%
25415      LOCATE ,,1
25420      RETURN
25425 'Erase field
25430      LOCATE YFLD,XFLD:CSR=XFLD:LASTPOS=0
25435      PRINT STRING$(LNGTH,32);
25440      LOCATE YFLD,XFLD
25445      RETURN
25450 'Compute LASTPOS (For inital non-blank field)
25455      LASTPOS=FLDEND:CSR=XFLD
25460      GOSUB 25365:'Read field
25465      WHILE RIGHT$(T$,1)=CHR$(32)
25470        T$=LEFT$(T$,LEN(T$)-1)
25475        LASTPOS=LASTPOS-1
25480      WEND
25485      RETURN
25490 'Clear keyboard buffer
25495      DEF SEG=0:POKE1050,PEEK(1052)
25500      DEF SEG:'Clear keyboard buffer
25510      RETURN
```

You may test SCREENIN using a program of the following sort.

```
10   TRUE=-1:FALSE=0
20   DIM MINKEY(5),MAXKEY(5),EXTMINKEY(5),EXTMAXKEY(5)
30   DIM SPECIALKEY$(5), EXTSPECIALKEY$(5),CAPSON(5)
40   MINKEY(1)=0:MAXKEY(1)=127
50   SPECIALKEY$(1)= ""
60   EXTMINKEY(1)=0:EXTMAXKEY(1)=0
70   EXTSPECIALKEY$(1)=CHR$(59)+CHR$(60)
80   CAPSON(1)=TRUE:CALLER=1
90   FOR J=1 TO 10:KEY J,"":NEXT J
100  CLS
120  XFLD=5:YFLD=10:LNGTH=20
```

```
130 GOSUB 25000
140 END
25000 (INSERT CODE FOR SCREENIN)
```

This program allows input of any ordinary ASCII codes and F1 and F2. Figure 20-1 shows a sample run for the above program.

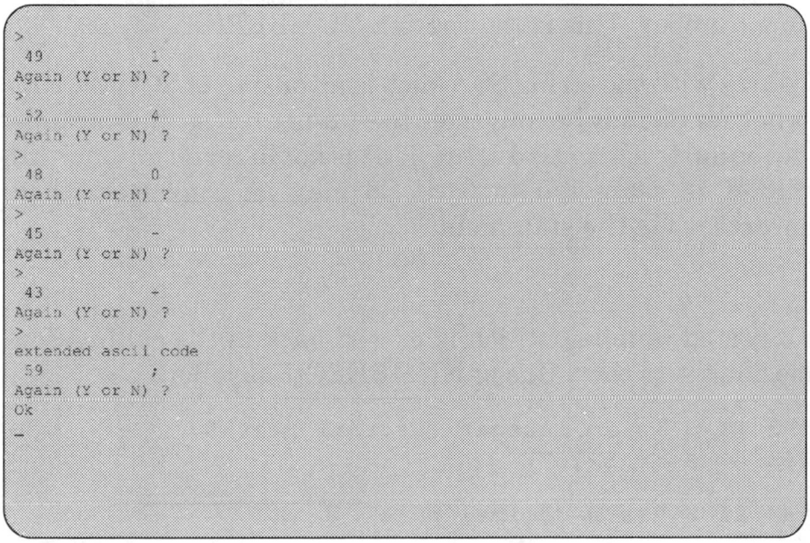

Figure 20-1.
Test of the SCREENIN routine.

Note that SCREENIN returns all input in string form. But suppose that your input is a number? You can, of course, convert a string such as "1234" to the number 1,234 using the VAL function; i.e., VAL("1234") is equal to 1,234. However, some care must be exercised. VAL accepts any string at all. It scans the string to determine the first character that shouldn't be in a number, ignores all characters from there on, and converts the initial string into a number. Thus, for example,

```
VAL("1NUMBER")=1
VAL("NUMBER")=0 (the null string is converted into 0).
```

Using KEYIN, we can set up a CALLER that allows our string to contain only the characters

```
1,2,3,4,5,6,7,8,9,0,+,E, and space
```

This goes a long way toward disallowing incorrect input. However, what about the following strings?

```
"1.2.3", "1EEE", "1.0E++", "1.783E.78-"
```

All contain only characters acceptable to KEYIN with the above CALLER. Clearly, we need a routine that checks whether a string is in proper format to be converted to a number. This is the routine NUMBERCK.

NUMBERCK starts with the string S$, which is an output of SCREENIN, and determines whether S$ may be converted to a number. If so, the variable NUMBERCK is set equal to a negative value. If S$ is not in correct numerical format, NUMBERCK is set equal to 0. If S$ may be converted, then NUMBERCK converts it via the statement

```
S=VAL(S$)
```

So S holds the converted number, which is passed back to the calling program. The routine then sets the value of NUMBERCK as follows:

```
NUMBERCK=-3 if S is an integer (decimal part=0,
     -32768 <= S <= 32767)

NUMBERCK=-2 if S has 0 decimal part

NUMBERCK=-1 if S has a non-zero decimal part
```

The routine NUMBERCK takes no action if S$ cannot be converted, other than to set the value of NUMBERCK equal to 0. It is up to the calling program to take any action, such as requesting the user to repeat the input.

Here is the code for the routine NUMBERCK.

```
27000 '**********NUMBERCK**********
27005 'This routine checks the format
27006 'of the string S$ to determine if it may
27007 'successfully be converted to a number.
27008 'It returns the result of the check in
27009 'the variable NUMBERCK.
27020 'NUMBERCK = 0: S$ not in numerical format
27025 '          =-1: S$ may be converted into a single-
```

```
                  precision real
27030 '          =-2: S$ may be converted with 0 fractional
                  part
27035 '          =-3: S$ may be converted to an integer
27040 'If conversion is possible, S contains the
27045 'converted real,S$ the corresponding string.
27050 '************MAIN ROUTINE***************
27055 'Initialize and handle leading sign
27060     N$="":NUMBERCK=TRUE:DIGIT$="1234567890."
27065     DECPT=FALSE:EXPNT=FALSE:SIGN=FALSE
27070     IF S$="" THEN 27210
27075     T$=LEFT$(S$,1)
27080     IF T$="+" OR T$="-" THEN N$=T$:S$=MID$(S$,2)
27085     IF S$="" THEN NUMBERCK=FALSE:GOTO 27210
27090     IF INSTR(DIGIT$,LEFT$(S$,1))=0 THEN
          NUMBERCK=FALSE:GOTO 27140
27095 WHILE S$ <> "" :'Loop strips spaces and checks
      format.Result in N$
27100     T$=LEFT$(S$,1):S$=MID$(S$,2)
27105     IF T$=" " THEN 27135: 'Delete space
27110     IF (T$="+" OR T$="-") AND RIGHT$(N$,1)<>"E" THEN
          NUMBERCK=FALSE:GOTO 27135
27115     IF T$="." THEN IF DECPT=TRUE  OR EXPNT=TRUE THEN
          NUMBERCK=FALSE ELSE N$=N$+T$:DECPT=TRUE
27120     IF T$="+" OR T$="-" THEN IF SIGN=TRUE OR
          EXPNT=FALSE
          THEN NUMBERCK=FALSE ELSE N$=N$+T$:SIGN=TRUE
27125     IF T$="E" THEN IF EXPNT=TRUE THEN NUMBERCK=FALSE
ELSE
          N$=N$+T$:EXPNT=TRUE:DECPT=TRUE
27130     IF T$<>"." AND T$<>"+" AND T$<>"-" AND T$<>"E"
          THEN N$=N$+T$
27135 WEND
27140 'Check for overflow(<10^-38 or >10^38)
27145     N%=INSTR(N$,"E")
27150     IF N%=0 THEN 27190
27155     IF N%=1 THEN NUMBERCK=FALSE:GOTO 27210
27160     S$=LEFT$(N$,N%-1):S1$=MID$(N$,N%+1)
27165     S=VAL(S$)
27170     IF S=0 THEN D=0 ELSE D=INT(LOG(ABS(S))/LOG(10))
```

```
27175      IF S1$<>"" THEN D=D+VAL(S1$)
27180      IF D<-37 OR D>37 THEN NUMBERCK=FALSE
27185 'Perform the conversion
27190      IF NUMBERCK=TRUE THEN S=VAL(N$)
27195      IF NUMBERCK=TRUE AND S=INT(S) THEN NUMBERCK=-2
27200      IF NUMBERCK=-2 AND S>=-32768! AND S<=32767 THEN
           NUMBERCK=-3
27205      S$=N$
27210 RETURN
```

The three routines KEYIN, SCREENIN, and NUMBERCK allow you to put your input on a professional basis: to control what comes in to your program and to deal with it in a totally controlled manner.

Twenty-one

Planning and Developing Large Programs

Introduction

In the early parts of this introduction to BASIC, you learned the syntax of the most rudimentary BASIC statements and how to combine such statements into programs. Our first programs were reasonably short and their logic fairly simple. This chapter provides some tips on building larger programs. We will center our discussion on a concrete program, a Bar Chart Generator, such as is found in many business graphics packages. In this chapter, we will design and implement this program and learn something about handling large programs in the process.

Planning THE BAR CHART GENERATOR

In developing a large-scale program, above all else, careful attention to program design is essential. You must have a clear idea of what you want your program to do: What outputs will it produce? From what inputs?

One of the principal defects in BASIC is that it allows you to sit down and start writing a program without much thought or planning. (And I'll bet many of you thought that was an advantage!) You may be able to get away without planning if you are writing a small program. But as soon as the program requires the interplay of a number of different subroutines, producing differing outputs and affecting various program variables, program planning becomes a necessity.

Let's outline the planning process for THE BAR CHART GENERATOR.

What Is the Program to Do?

A Bit About Bar Charts.   Examine the graph in Figure 21-1. It is a typical bar chart. You should note the following features of the graph. The chart graphically depicts three sets of data, with one set of bars corresponding to each set of data. We distinguish among the different data sets by the shading of the bars.

The bars are set in a coordinate system, a rectangular box whose edges are labeled with information necessary to read the chart. The bottom horizontal edge of the coordinate system is called the x-axis. Just below this axis are labels that describe the various bars.

The vertical, left edge of the coordinate system is called the y-axis. Along the y-axis is a numerical scale that allows you to determine the numerical heights of the bars.

The x-axis and y-axis are labeled with titles, as is the entire graph. Note that the y-axis title is arranged vertically to the left of the scale, centered vertically on the coordinate system. The x-axis title is centered under the coordinate system, just below the x-axis labels. The chart title is centered above the coordinate system.

Each of the three sets of data has a title, displayed to the right of the coordinate system. To the left of each title is a square containing a sample of the shading type corresponding to the particular data set.

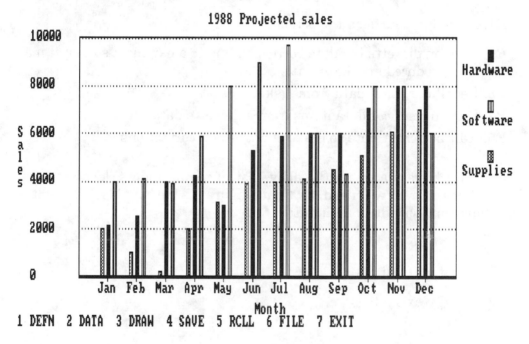

Figure 21-1. **A typical bar chart**.

We have just taken a quick tour of a bar chart. Now we can state our goal.

Goal. Construct a program, called THE BAR CHART GENERATOR, that displays bar charts corresponding to user-supplied data.

Before we can achieve our goal, we need to learn a great deal about programming. However, let's proceed with the first step in program development: Program Planning.

To plan our program, we begin by making a list of the specific functions that the program is to perform. This is our list of program requirements:

R1. Draw bar charts on the screen.

R2. Save on diskette the data corresponding to a bar chart so that it may be reproduced at a later date.

R3. Recall bar chart data from diskette.

R4. Read numerical data items from a diskette data file.

R5. Edit bar chart data to make changes and corrections.

Once we have drawn up the above list of requirements, let's see what inputs our program will need. Examine Figure 21-1; each visual element of the chart corresponds to an input:

I1. Chart title

I2. x- and y-axis titles

I3. x- and y-axis labels

I4. Bars

   a. Provision for several sets of bars, reflecting different data series.
   b. Bars of different data series need to be distinguished by different shading.
   c. Each set of bars needs an identifying title.

In examining the above list, we ask: How many sets of bars should we allow? How many bars should we allow? Let's allow up to three sets of bars, with at most 20 bars per set. Using these numbers we can display all the data on a single screen. This will make the data entry portion of the program easier. In any case, these numbers are too generous. There is no way to fit $3 \times 20 = 60$ bars on the screen at once. The bars will overlap. However, there are applications where you want to display, say, 20 bars of a single series or 12 bars each of a set of three data series. Our numbers are large enough to accommodate these choices.

Now that we know what the program is to do and what inputs are required, let's think of how the program will work. I don't mean that you should sit and start to code at this point. Rather, you should ask yourself how the user will use this program. Actually, picture the user sitting down at the computer and ask yourself: What does he or she do to use this program? When I thought about this question, I pictured the user choosing from a menu of various actions, as displayed on a function key display. This leads us to define a sequence of actions that corresponds to the function keys.

F1–Define bar chart parameters
F2–Enter x-axis labels and numerical data
F3–Draw the chart based on current data
F4–Save chart
F5–Recall chart
F6–Enter data from a data file
F7–Exit

At this point, we start to see the structure of the program emerging. There must be seven main routines, one corresponding to each of the seven function keys. Note that the requirement R5 (Editing capability) does not appear as a routine. As we'll see, it's easiest to build the editing directly into data entry routines, F1 and F2.

In addition to the seven basic routines, we will need a control routine, which allows us to choose from among the various functions by pressing the appropriate function key. Our program will need a number of arrays and many of the variables will require particular initial values. It is convenient to have a particular part of the program, called the initialization, which handles all such definitions.

Based on our discussion, we may now sketch out our program:

```
'Initialization
'Control Routine
'Define Bar Chart Parameters
'Input Data
'Draw Chart
'Save Chart
'Recall Chart
'Read Data File
'Exit
```

Well, there's the program plan! We've left plenty of room to fill in the various program lines. And, as we'll see, there are several other routines that are required by the seven fundamental routines. However, the above sketch will be our guide.

The Initialization and Control Routines

In various sections, we have developed a number of routines that perform particular tasks for the bar chart generator. In order for these routines to work together, we need a control routine that allows us to select among them. When we planned the program, we designated seven main functions for the bar chart generator:

Define Bar Chart Parameters—Specify the coordinate system and its various labels and the number of series of data.

Input Data—Input the numerical data corresponding to the various bar heights, and string data naming the various bars.

Draw Bar Chart—Use the graphics capabilities of the PC to draw the bar chart.

Save Bar Chart—Save in a diskette data file the parameters and data corresponding to a particular bar chart.

Recall Bar Chart—Recall a bar chart that has been saved on diskette.

Read Data File—Read numerical bar chart data that has been saved in a diskette data file produced by another program.

Exit—Stop executing the program and return to BASIC.

Each of these seven functions corresponds to a routine. The code for the first routine begins in line 1000, for the second in line 2000, and so forth. We call a particular function by pressing a function key: The nth function is called by pressing function key n. Our control routine calls KEYIN, the character input routine, and allows only function keys F1–F7 as input. The control routine responds to an allowable function key by performing the requested function. Note that each of the function routines ends by sending control back to the control routine.

Here is the code for the control routine.

```
900 '*****************CONTROL ROUTINE*******************
905 'E$ is returned by the input routine, = the second
910 'character of extended ASCII code
915 KEY OFF:CLS
920 IF E$<>"" THEN 945
925 LOCATE 25,1
930 PRINT FKEY$;
935 CALLER=5:GOSUB 25000
940 GOTO 920
945 C=ASC(E$):EXTENDED=FALSE
950 IF C=59 THEN 1000 :'Bar Chart Definition
955 IF C=60 THEN 2000 :'Data Input
960 IF C=61 THEN 3000 :'Draw Bar Chart
965 IF C=62 THEN 4000 :'Save Bar Chart
970 IF C=63 THEN 5000 :'Recall Bar Chart
975 IF C=64 THEN 6000 :'Read Data File
980 IF C=65 THEN 7000 :'Exit
985 CALLER=5:GOSUB 25000:'Await instructions
```

This routine presupposes that the function keys are disabled as soft keys and that the function key line fkey$ has been specified somewhere. And this brings me to the subject of program organization.

I like to organize my programs (especially the large ones) in a particular order. You may have noticed that the program fragments often had what seemed like "dangling lines" at the beginning, before the documentation. This is because those lines, while necessary to run the particular fragment, really belong in another section of the program, the INITIALIZATION. Here is my INITIALIZATION for the bar chart generator.

```
10  '**********INITIALIZATION ROUTINE**********
100 'Dimension Statements
200 'Data Statements
300 'Common Statements
400 'Error Trapping Line
500 'DEF statements
600 'Define parameters for input routine
700 'Initialization of variables
702     TRUE=-1:FALSE=0
704     FOR J%=1 TO 10
706        KEY J%,""
708     NEXT J%
710     FKEY$="1 DEFN  2 DATA  3 DRAW  4 SAVE  5 RCLL
        6 FILE  7 EXIT"
712     XFLD=1:YFLD=1:LNGTH=0
714     MENU$(1)="BAR CHART DEFINITION"
716     MENU$(2)="TITLE? "
718     MENU$(3)="DATA SERIES 1 TITLE? "
720     MENU$(4)="DATA SERIES 2 TITLE? "
722     MENU$(5)="DATA SERIES 3 TITLE? "
724     MENU$(6)="Y AXIS RANGE:MINIMUM? "
726     MENU$(7)="Y AXIS RANGE:MAXIMUM? "
728     MENU$(8)="Y AXIS STEP? "
730     MENU$(9)="X AXIS TITLE? "
732     MENU$(10)="Y AXIS TITLE? "
734     MAXHEIGHT=199
736     MAXWIDTH=639
```

Note that INITIALIZATION begins with five categories of statements (not all used): DIM, DATA, COMMON, ON ERROR, and DEF. These are the "nonexecutable" statements of the program. When the program encounters these statements, it merely makes a definition, sets aside space, or makes a note of a fact to be used later. It is a good idea to put all these statements in one part of the program. For one thing, they are easy to find if, say, you want to increase the size of an array or to insert a new function definition. A second, more compelling reason for grouping these statements together is that the BASIC Compiler requires that all nonexecutable statements precede all executable statements. Rather than try to rearrange the statements after the program is written, you should develop the discipline to create the INITIALIZATION portion of the program as you go along by placing any statements that belong to the INITIALIZATION at the start of a module. After all the modules are constructed, you may assemble the initial statements into the INITIALIZATION.

Note that, in addition to nonexecutable statements, INITIALIZATION contains variable initializations. You should get in the habit of initializing all variables. I know it's easy to get lazy, especially when dimensioning small arrays. However, if you only need an array with three elements, why use ten? Memory is precious. Conserve it. Also, give your variables descriptive names. It is true that they will take up more space in the BASIC interpreter. However, if you plan to compile your program, a descriptive name will lead to no longer a program than a single-letter name. (I assume that most large programs will ultimately be compiled.)

To each function key corresponds a routine of the program. Each of the routines is constructed pretty much like the main program. Start with lists of requirements (outputs) and inputs. From these describe the routine in a series of steps. Each step becomes a subroutine. In each routine, you will note a "main routine," which is really like an outline of the routine. Then there are subroutines that carry out the details of the routine. The process of designing a program consists of starting from a main outline, then proceeding to subroutines containing the next level of detail, and then to sub-subroutines containing the next level of detail, and so forth. This procedure is called **top-down design**.

I construct each subroutine separately and test it with sample data. It's a good idea to debug the small routines first. That way, when a bug arises at the next level, you may usually assume that the trouble is that the output from one subroutine isn't the proper input to another. (That's not always the problem, but in a surprising number of instances, it is!)

After you are sure that the subroutines are working properly, assemble them into a routine and follow the same test procedure again.

When you develop subroutines, don't worry about line numbers. Start all subroutines with line 10 (or 100 or 1000). Add and delete lines at will. After the subroutine is debugged, use the RENUM command to adjust the line numbers so that the subroutine will fit into its intended routine.

When all the main routines are debugged, assemble them into the main program and combine miscellaneous lines to form the INITIALIZATION section. That's all there is to it!

I don't mean to say that the above approach is the only one that can be used to successfully develop large programs. But it's one that works for me. Why not try it? I'm sure that you'll discover convenient variations and improvements. Programming is as much an art as a science. And there is room for artists of all schools.

The DRAW BAR CHART Module

Our bar chart program will be built from a number of separate pieces, collected as subroutines and sequenced by a controlling program. In this section, let's concentrate on the design of the portion of the program that actually draws the bar chart from the data. (We'll worry about data input later.)

Let's assign variables to some of the important quantities that our program must reference.

Our requirements, drawn up on page 600, state that the program should allow for display of up to three separate sets of data. The number of different sets (or series) of data will be contained in the variable SER%. SER% will equal either 1, 2, or 3. Each set of data may contain as many as 20 data items. (This will allow up to 3×20 or 60 sets of bars. This is the maximum that our screen layout can accommodate.)

The data for the bar chart will be contained in an array DTA$(N%,J%). Here N% is the number of the data set and J% is the number of the data item within the particular data set. Here is a typical set of data:

	Data Series 1	Data Series 2	Data Series 3
Jan	1580	38.35	48.55
Feb	1312.11	1450.00	12.11

For example, DTA$(2,1)="38.35". The month designations on the left are called labels and will be stored as the zero elements in the array. For example, DTA$(1,0)="Jan".

You may wonder why we are using a string array to store the data rather than a numerical array. There are two good reasons. First, a string array allows us to store the labels in the same array as the data. Second (and more important), a numerical array makes BASIC reformat our numbers. For example, 1,450.00 is converted to the number 1,450. Of course, we can reformat our numbers on output with PRINT USING, but it is by far easier not to keep track of formats and simply store the data as a string, exactly as it was input. When we use the data for numerical purposes, we will convert them to numerical form using the VAL function.

Let's draw our bar chart in high-resolution graphics (SCREEN 2). We will confine our bar chart to the portion of the screen (80,16)-(559,169). This gives us a 152×480 region for our chart. It also leaves the top two lines and the bottom four lines of the screen for titles. Also, we have room for labels eight characters wide on either side of the graph.

The problem of displaying the labels involves the precise placement of text in graphics mode, which we solved in the preceding chapter using the routine PLOTSTRING. Let's include PLOTSTRING as part of our program and use it to display the various titles.

The coordinate system for the bar chart will be described by the following parameters.

```
YMIN    = the beginning y-value on the y-axis
YMAX    = the final y-value on the y-axis
XMAX    = maximum number of data items in a data series
GRID$   = Y if horizontal grid lines are to be
          displayed
        = N otherwise
```

Our program begins by defining the above screen area as a viewport. Next, we use WINDOW to define the coordinate system (0,YMIN)-(XMAX+1,YMAX) on the viewport. Note that we use XMAX + 1 (rather than XMAX) so that the value XMAX is within the viewport, leaving space for the last bar.

The width of the bars will be (XMAX+1)/120. This makes each bar four pixels wide. (The viewport is 480 pixels wide.) We will store half of this number, or (XMAX+1)/240, in the variable BW (=bar width). We will draw a bar by locating the center of the lower edge and drawing the sides of the bar at a distance of BW on either side of the center. At each of the integer positions along the x-axis, we will center the bar corresponding to data series 2. We will place the bar for data series 2 eight pixels to the left and the bar for data series 3 eight pixels to the right. We store this data in the array ADJ():

```
ADJ(1) = -(XMAX+1)/60 (8 pixels to the left)
ADJ(2) = 0 (center)
ADJ(3) = (XMAX+1)/60 (8 pixels to the right)
```

Here is the program:

```
3000 '**************DRAWBAR ROUTINE***************
3005    CLS
3010    KEY OFF
3015    SCREEN 2:SER%=3
3020    YMIN=VAL(YMIN$)
3025    YMAX=VAL(YMAX$)
3030    YSTEP=VAL(YSTEP$)
3035    IF YMIN>YMAX THEN SWAP YMIN,YMAX
```

```
3040      IF YMIN=YMAX THEN 3095
3045      IF YSTEP=0 THEN 3095
3050      GOSUB 3105:'Computer SER%
3055      STYLE$(1)=CHR$(&HFF):STYLE$(2)=CHR$(&HAA):
          STYLE$(3)=CHR$(&H99)+CHR$(&H55)
3060      BW=(XMAX+1)/240
3065      ADJ(1)=0:ADJ(2)=(XMAX+1)/60:ADJ(3)=-(XMAX+1)/60
3070      GOSUB 3195:'Write Titles
3075      GOSUB 3305:'Write x-axis labels
3080      GOSUB 3360:'Write y-axis labels
3085      GOSUB 3415:'Draw coordinate system
3090      GOSUB 3435:'Draw bars
3095      E$="":GOTO 920:'Return to control routine
3100  **************SUBROUTINES****************
3105  'Compute SER%
3110      FOR N%=3 TO 1 STEP -1
3115         XMAX(N%)=20:J%=0
3120         DATAEND=FALSE
3125         WHILE DATAEND=FALSE
3130            IF DTA$(N%,20-J%)<>"" THEN DATAEND=
                TRUE:XMAX(N%)=XMAX(N%)+1
3135            XMAX(N%)=XMAX(N%)-1:J%=J%+1
3140            IF J%=21 THEN DATAEND=TRUE
3145         WEND
3150      NEXT N%
3155      IF XMAX(3)<=0 THEN SER%=2
3160      IF SER%=2 AND XMAX(2)<=0 THEN SER%=1
3165      IF SER%=1 AND XMAX(1)<=0 THEN SER%=0
3170      XMAX=XMAX(1)
3175      FOR J%=1 TO 3
3180         IF XMAX< XMAX(J%) THEN XMAX=XMAX(J%)
3185      NEXT J%
3190      RETURN
3195  'Write titles
3200      LOCATE 5,72:PRINT SER1TITLE$;
3205      IF SER%=1 THEN 3225
3210      LOCATE 9,72:PRINT SER2TITLE$;
3215      IF SER%=2 THEN 3225
3220      LOCATE 13,72:PRINT SER3TITLE$;
3225      LINE (599,23)-(606,30),,B
```

```
3230     PAINT (603,27),STYLE$(1)
3235     IF SER%=1 THEN 3265
3240     LINE (599,55)-(606,62),,B
3245     PAINT (603,60),STYLE$(2)
3250     IF SER%=2 THEN 3265
3255     LINE (599,87)-(606,94),,B
3260     PAINT (603,93),STYLE$(3)
3265     X1=80:X2=559:Y1=0:Y2=7:C%=3:S$=TITLE$
3270     GOSUB 28000
3275     Y1=191:Y2=184:S$=XTITLE$
3280     GOSUB 28000
3285     X1=0:X2=7:Y1=16:Y2=167:C%=4
3290     S$=YTITLE$
3295     GOSUB 28000
3300     RETURN
3305 'Write x-axis labels
3310     K=480/(XMAX+1)
3315     FOR J%=1 TO XMAX
3320         L=79+K*J%
3325         M%=4*LEN(DTA$(0,J%))
3330         LINE (L,167)-(L,170):'Tick marks
3335         X1=L-M%:X2=L+M%-1:Y1=171:Y2=178:C%=1
3340         S$=DTA$(0,J%)
3345         GOSUB 28000
3350     NEXT J%
3355     RETURN
3360 'Write y-axis labels
3365     IF YSTEP=0 THEN 3410
3370     M=(YMAX-YMIN)/YSTEP
3375     FOR J%=0 TO M
3380         S$=STR$(YMIN+J%*YSTEP)
3385         X1=8:X2=79
3390         Y1=167-J%*152/M-4
3395         Y2=Y1-7:C%=1
3400         GOSUB 28000
3405     NEXT J%
3410     RETURN
3415 'Draw coordinate system
3420     VIEW (80,16)-(559,167),,1
3425     WINDOW (0,YMIN)-(XMAX+1,YMAX)
```

```
3430      LINE (0,0)-(XMAX+1,0):'Draw x-axis
3435 'Draw bars
3440      FOR N%=1 TO SER%
3445          FOR J%=1 TO XMAX(N%)
3450              IF DTA$(N%,J%)="" THEN 3470
3455              HT=VAL(DTA$(N%,J%))
3460              LINE (J%+ADJ(N%)-BW,0)-
                  (J%+ADJ(N%)+BW,HT),,B
3465              PAINT (J%+ADJ(N%),HT/2),STYLE$(N%)
3470          NEXT J%
3475      NEXT N%
3480 'Draw grid lines
3485      FOR J%=0 TO (YMAX-YMIN)/YSTEP
3490          H=YMIN+J%*YSTEP
3495          LINE (0,H)-(XMAX+1,H),,,&H8888
3500      NEXT J%
3505      RETURN
```

Note that the initial lines (below line 3000) provide some data you may use to test the program. Note also that we have indicated subroutines to insert titles, but we'll work out those routines in the next section.

One further point. Note the array STYLE$(). It defines the various shading types for the bars. STYLE$() is used in the PAINT statement in line 3465. STYLE$() is the style string that produces the various shadings in the bars of Figure 21-1.

Exercises

1. Test the above bar chart program by running it with the given test data.

2. Modify the above bar chart program so that the screen image is saved in a diskette file.

3. Recall the image stored in Exercise 2.

Defining a Bar Chart

Our bar chart program has two program modules that require keyboard input—the chart definition module and the data entry module. Let's now build these two modules using the input routines developed in Chapter 20.

The Define Bar Chart Parameters Module

By pressing a function key, you will be able to start the bar chart definition module. This part of the bar chart program allows you to enter the bar chart parameters into predetermined fields on the screen. When you start the chart definition module, the screen is cleared and the program creates a display like the one in Figure 21-2.

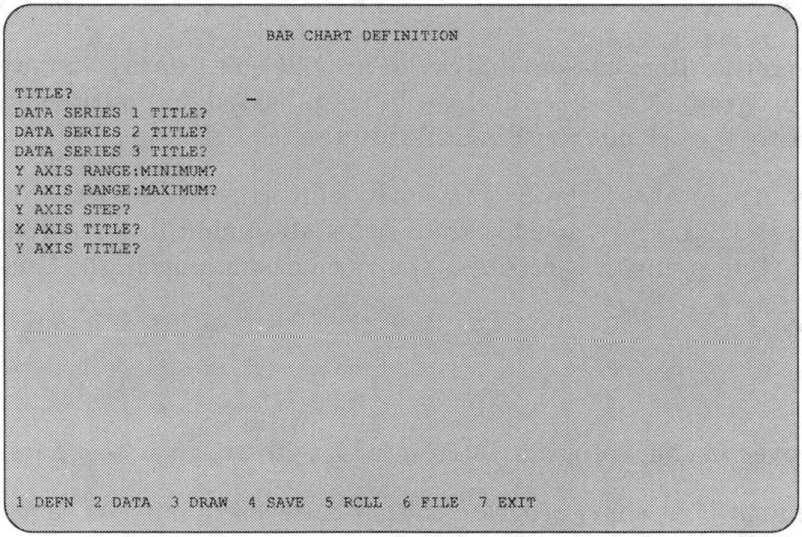

```
                    BAR CHART DEFINITION


TITLE?                              _
DATA SERIES 1 TITLE?
DATA SERIES 2 TITLE?
DATA SERIES 3 TITLE?
Y AXIS RANGE:MINIMUM?
Y AXIS RANGE:MAXIMUM?
Y AXIS STEP?
X AXIS TITLE?
Y AXIS TITLE?






 1 DEFN   2 DATA   3 DRAW   4 SAVE   5 RCLL   6 FILE   7 EXIT
```

Figure 21-2.
Bar chart definition menu.

The program is requesting the following pieces of data:

```
TITLE$ = chart title (at most 50 characters)
SER1TITLE$ = data series 1 title (at most 10
               characters)
SER2TITLE$ = data series 2 title (at most 10
```

```
                   characters)
SER3TITLE$ = data series 3 title (at most 10
                   characters)
YMIN$ = minimum displayable y-value in string form
YMAX$ = maximum displayable y-value in string form
YSTEP$ = value of each subdivision along the y-axis
        in string form
XTITLE$ = Title for x-axis (at most 10 characters)
YTITLE$ = Title for y-axis (at most 10 characters)
```

The program allows you to use the cursor up and down keys to move from line to line of the menu. In each line, the cursor is positioned in the first position of the input field. You may type your input into the field, using the backspace and Esc keys for editing. When an extended ASCII code (cursor motion key or function key) is detected, the program reads the field at the current cursor position and assigns the value S$, returned by the input routine, to the appropriate program variable. In the case of inputs to be converted into numbers, the program calls on NUMBERCK to check for numerical format. If the format test fails, then the value of S$ is not assigned to the program variable and the field is erased. If a function key is pressed, then it causes the program to read the current field, assign the program variable (if possible), and then GOTO the main control program, which we assume begins in line 900.

Here is our program:

```
1000 '**********BAR CHART PARAMETERS INPUT**************
1005 SCREEN 0:CLS:LOCATE 25,1:PRINT FKEY$;
1010 'Display template
1015 LOCATE 1,1:PRINT TAB(27) MENU$(1);
1020 FOR J%=2 TO 10
1025    LOCATE J%+2,1
1030    PRINT MENU$(J%);
1035 NEXT J%
1040 MENUEND=FALSE
1045 GOSUB 1170:'Display current parameter values
1050 XFLD=25:YFLD=4
1055 WHILE MENUEND=FALSE
1060    LOCATE YFLD,XFLD
```

```
1065    IF YFLD=4 THEN CALLER=1:LNGTH=50
1070    IF YFLD>4 AND YFLD<7 THEN CALLER=1:LNGTH=10
1075    IF YFLD>7 AND YFLD<11 THEN CALLER=2:LNGTH=10
1080    IF YFLD>10 THEN CALLER=1:LNGTH=10
1085    GOSUB 25000: 'Call input routine
1090    IF YFLD>7 AND YFLD<11 THEN GOSUB 27000:'Numberck
1095    IF YFLD>7 AND YFLD<11 AND NUMBERCK=FALSE THEN
        GOSUB 25425:GOTO 1085
1100    IF YFLD=4 THEN TITLE$=S$
1105    IF YFLD=5 THEN SER1TITLE$=S$
1110    IF YFLD=6 THEN SER2TITLE$=S$
1115    IF YFLD=7 THEN SER3TITLE$=S$
1120    IF YFLD=8 THEN YMIN$=S$
1125    IF YFLD=9 THEN YMAX$=S$
1130    IF YFLD=10 THEN YSTEP$=S$
1135    IF YFLD=11 THEN XTITLE$=S$
1140    IF YFLD=12 THEN YTITLE$=S$
1145    IF E$=CHR$(80) THEN IF YFLD<12 THEN YFLD=YFLD+1
1150    IF E$=CHR$(72) THEN IF YFLD>4 THEN YFLD=YFLD-1
1155    IF INSTR(FUNCTION$,E$)>0 THEN MENUEND=TRUE
1160 WEND
1165 GOTO 900: 'Return to control routine
1170 'Display current parameter values
1175    LOCATE 4,25:PRINT TITLE$
1180    LOCATE 5,25:PRINT SER1TITLE$
1185    LOCATE 6,25:PRINT SER2TITLE$
1190    LOCATE 7,25:PRINT SER3TITLE$
1195    LOCATE 8,25:PRINT YMIN$
1200    LOCATE 9,25:PRINT YMAX$
1205    LOCATE 10,25:PRINT YSTEP$
1210    LOCATE 11,25:PRINT XTITLE$
1215    LOCATE 12,25:PRINT YTITLE$
1220    RETURN
```

Note that we have defined CALLERs 1 and 2 to correspond to the text input and numerical input, respectively. The only extended ASCII codes allowed are Cursor Up (E$=CHR$(72)) and Cursor Down (E$=CHR$(80)) and the function keys F1–F7, which return you to the main control routine in line 900.

The Data Input Module

The data input module is the part of the program in which you enter the numerical values for the various bars and the corresponding identifying labels, which will be displayed below the bars. This module is very similar to the bar chart definition module. When it is called, it clears the screen and creates a display like the one in Figure 21-3.

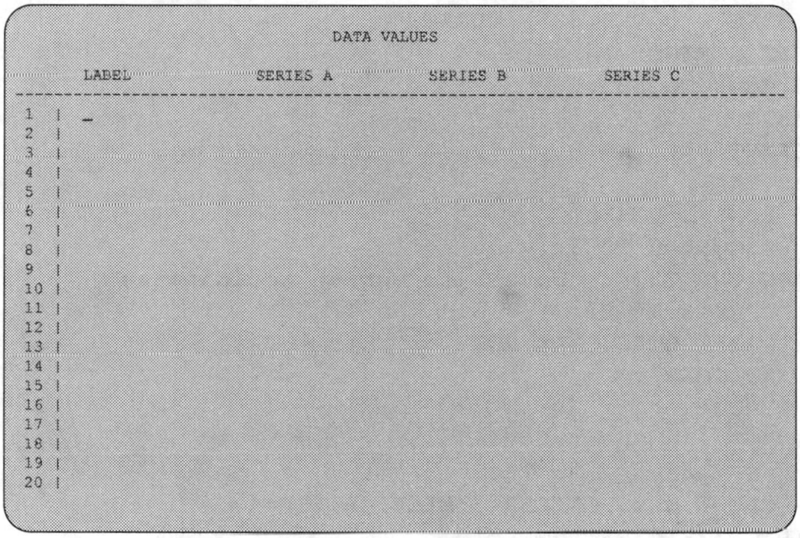

Figure 21-3.
The data input matrix.

You type your data into the various positions in the matrix. The cursor motion keys move you around within the matrix. Function keys F1–F7 return you to the main control routine in line 900.

Here is the code for the data input module.

```
2000 '**********DATA INPUT ROUTINE**********
2005 SCREEN 0:CLS:LOCATE 25,1:PRINT FKEY$;
2010 LOCATE 1,1:GOSUB 2055:'Display spreadsheet
2015 ROW%=1:COL%=0
2020 DATAEND=FALSE
2025 WHILE DATAEND=FALSE
2030    GOSUB 2335:'Locate cursor
2035    GOSUB 2150:'Input data
```

```
2040 WEND
2045 GOTO 900:'Return to control routine
2050 ***************SUBROUTINES******************
2055 'Display spreadsheet
2060 CLS
2065 LOCATE 1,34
2070 PRINT "DATA VALUES"
2075 PRINT
2080 PRINT TAB(8) "LABEL";TAB(26) "SERIES A";TAB(44)
     "SERIES B"; TAB(62) "SERIES C"
2085 PRINT STRING$(80,45);
2090 FOR J%=1 TO 20
2095 LOCATE J%+4,1
2100   PRINT J%; TAB(5) "|";
2105 NEXT J%
2110 FOR ROW%=1 TO 20
2115   FOR COL%=0 TO 3
2120     GOSUB 2335:'Convert to screen coordinates
2125     LOCATE R%,C%
2130     PRINT DTA$(COL%,ROW%);
2135   NEXT COL%
2140 NEXT ROW%
2145 RETURN
2150 'Input data
2155 IF COL%=0 THEN CALLER=3 ELSE CALLER=4
2160 XFLD=C%:YFLD=R%:LNGTH=10
2165 GOSUB 25000
2170 IF S$="" THEN 2195
2175 IF CALLER=3 THEN NUMBERCK=TRUE
2180 IF CALLER=4 THEN GOSUB 27000
2185 IF NUMBERCK<0 THEN DTA$(COL%,ROW%)=S$
2190 IF NUMBERCK=FALSE THEN GOSUB 25425:GOTO 2330
2195 IF INSTR(FUNCTION$,E$)>0 THEN DATAEND=TRUE:GOTO 2330
2200 IF E$=CHR$(72) THEN 2230:'Cursor up
2205 IF E$=CHR$(75) THEN 2245:'Cursor left
2210 IF E$=CHR$(77) THEN 2260:'Cursor right
2215 IF E$=CHR$(80) THEN 2275:'Cursor down
2220 IF E$=CHR$(71) THEN 2290:'Home (To position 1,1)
2225 IF E$=CHR$(79) THEN 2310:'End (To position 20,3)
2230 'Cursor up
```

```
2235 IF ROW%>1 THEN ROW%=ROW%-1
2240 GOTO 2330
2245 'Cursor left
2250 IF COL%>0 THEN COL%=COL%-1
2255 GOTO 2330
2260 'Cursor right
2265 IF COL%<3 THEN COL%=COL%+1
2270 GOTO 2330
2275 'Cursor down
2280 IF ROW%>0 THEN ROW%=ROW%+1
2285 GOTO 2330
2290 'Home (To position 1,1)
2295 COL%=1
2300 ROW%=1
2305 GOTO 2330
2310 'End (To position 20,3)
2315 COL%=3
2320 ROW%=20
2325 GOTO 2330
2330 RETURN
2335 'Compute screen coordinates
2340 R%=ROW%+4
2345 C%=18*COL%+8
2350 LOCATE R%,C%
2355 RETURN
2360 RETURN
```

Note that it was necessary to define two new CALLERs, CALLER 3 and CALLER 4, since this module allows you to use all six cursor motion keys, whereas the bar chart definition module only allows you to use Cursor Up and Cursor Down.

Note how easy it was to force the program user to give correct input. That's the whole point of using an input routine rather than BASIC's prepackaged input statements.

The Other Modules

Let's now describe the other modules of the program.

Save Bar Chart Module

This module saves the titles and data corresponding to a barchart using a sequential data file.

```
4000 '**********SAVE BAR CHART*************
4005 CLS:SCREEN 0
4010 PRINT "SAVE BAR CHART"
4015 INPUT "NAME OF FILE";FILENAME$
4020 OPEN FILENAME$ FOR OUTPUT AS #1
4025 WRITE #1, TITLE$
4030 WRITE #1, SER1TITLE$
4035 WRITE #1, SER2TITLE$
4040 WRITE #1, SER3TITLE$
4045 WRITE #1, YMIN$
4050 WRITE #1, YMAX$
4055 WRITE #1, YSTEP$
4060 WRITE #1, XTITLE$
4065 WRITE #1, YTITLE$
4070 FOR N%=1 TO 3
4075    FOR J%=1 TO 20
4080       WRITE #1, DTA$(N%,J%)
4085    NEXT J%
4090 NEXT N%
4095 CLOSE #1
4100 LOCATE 25,1:PRINT FKEY$;
4105 E$=""
4110 GOTO 900
```

Recall Bar Chart Module

This module recalls from a sequential file the titles and data for a bar chart. It is assumed that the file has been created using the format specified by the SAVE BAR CHART module.

```
5000 '**********RECALL BAR CHART*************
5005 CLS
5010 PRINT "RECALL BAR CHAR"
5015 INPUT "NAME OF FILE";FILENAME$
5020 OPEN FILENAME$ FOR INPUT AS #1
5025 INPUT #1, TITLE$
5030 INPUT #1, SER1TITLE$
5035 INPUT #1, SER2TITLE$
5040 INPUT #1, SER3TITLE$
5045 INPUT #1, YMIN$
5050 INPUT #1, YMAX$
5055 INPUT #1, YSTEP$
5060 INPUT #1, XTITLE$
5065 INPUT #1, YTITLE$
5070 FOR N%=1 TO 3
5075   FOR J%=1 TO 20
5080     INPUT #1, DTA$(N%,J%)
5085   NEXT J%
5090 NEXT N%
5095 CLOSE #1
5100 GOTO 3000: 'Display bar chart
6000 '**********READ DATA FILE**********
6005 '(Exercise for the reader)
6010 E$="":GOTO 900
```

Read From Data File Module

This module allows the user to import data items from a sequential data file into a part of the bar chart input matrix.

```
6000 '**********READ DATA FILE**********
6005 '(Exercise for the reader)
6010 E$="":GOTO 900
```

Conclusion

We have now constructed all of the routines of the BAR CHART GENER-ATOR. In order to achieve a running program, it is only necessary to collect all of the pieces into one program and the standard subroutines (KEYIN, SCREENIN, PLOTSTRING, etc.). This is a straightforward affair. If you have created the pieces in separate files, you may unite them using BASIC's MERGE command. The only snag is to collect the various pieces of the INITIALIZATION routine, which occurs at the beginning of the program. For your reference, we include a completed listing of the initialization routine.

```
10  '**********INITIALIZATION ROUTINE**********
100 'Dimension Statements
105     DIM MINKEY(5),MAXKEY(5),EXTMINKEY(5),EXTMAXKEY(5)
110     DIM CAPSON(5),SPECIALKEY$(5),
        EXTSPECIALKEY$(5),DTA$(3,20)
115     DIM MENU$(11),A%(10),B$(10),XMAX(3)
200 'Data Statements
300 'Common Statements
400 'Error Trapping Line
500 'DEF statements
600 'Define parameters for input routine
602     MOTION$=CHR$(71)+CHR$(72)+CHR$(75)+CHR$(77)+CHR$
        (79)+CHR$(80)
604     MOTION1$=CHR$(72)+CHR$(80)
606     FUNCTION$=CHR$(59)+CHR$(60)+CHR$(61)+CHR$(62)
               +CHR$(63)+CHR$(64)+CHR$(65)
608 '   **Text input(CALLER=1)**
610     MINKEY(1)=32:MAXKEY(1)=127:SPECIALKEY$(1)=
        CHR$(8)+CHR$(27)
612     CAPSON(1)=0
614     EXTMINKEY(1)=0:EXTMINKEY(1)=0
616     EXTSPECIALKEY$(1)=MOTION1$+FUNCTION$
618 '   **Numerical input (CALLER=2)**
620     MINKEY(2)=0:MAXKEY(2)=0:SPECIALKEY$(2)=
        "1234567890-+ E."+CHR$(8)+CHR$(27)
622     CAPSON(2)=-1
```

```
624      EXTMINKEY(2)=0:EXTMAXKEY(2)=0
626      EXTSPECIALKEY$(2)=MOTION1$+FUNCTION$
628 '    **Text input(CALLER=1)**
630      MINKEY(3)=0:MAXKEY(3)=127:SPECIALKEY$(3)=""
632      CAPSON(3)=0
634      EXTMINKEY(3)=0:EXTMINKEY(3)=0
636      EXTSPECIALKEY$(3)=MOTION$+FUNCTION$
638 '    **Numerical input (CALLER=4)**
640      MINKEY(4)=0:MAXKEY(4)=31:SPECIALKEY$(4)
         ="1234567890-+ E."
642      CAPSON(4)=-1
644      EXTMINKEY(4)=0:EXTMAXKEY(4)=0
646      EXTSPECIALKEY$(4)=MOTION$+FUNCTION$
648 '    **Control Routine(CALLER=5)**
650      MINKEY(5)=0:MAXKEY(5)=0
652      CAPSON(5)=0
654      EXTMINKEY(5)=0:EXTMAXKEY(5)=0
656      EXTSPECIALKEY$(5)=FUNCTION$
700 'Initialization of variables
702      TRUE=-1:FALSE=0
704      FOR J%=1 TO 10
706        KEY J%,""
708      NEXT J%
710      FKEY$="1 DEFN  2 DATA  3 DRAW  4 SAVE  5 RCLL
         6 FILE  7 EXIT"
712      XFLD=1:YFLD=1:LNGTH=0
714      MENU$(1)="BAR CHART DEFINITION"
716      MENU$(2)="TITLE? "
718      MENU$(3)="DATA SERIES 1 TITLE? "
720      MENU$(4)="DATA SERIES 2 TITLE? "
722      MENU$(5)="DATA SERIES 3 TITLE? "
724      MENU$(6)="Y AXIS RANGE:MINIMUM? "
726      MENU$(7)="Y AXIS RANGE:MAXIMUM? "
728      MENU$(8)="Y AXIS STEP? "
730      MENU$(9)="X AXIS TITLE? "
732      MENU$(10)="Y AXIS TITLE? "
734      MAXHEIGHT=199
736      MAXWIDTH=639
```

In this chapter, we have presented an approach to the development of large BASIC programs. It has the virtue of being an organized approach, which you can follow to develop even the most complex programs. With experience, you will surely develop refinements of your own.

INDEX

Don't Waste Any Time!

Order the *Diskette to Accompany IBM PC and Compatibles, Fourth Edition* by Larry Joel Goldstein

Make learning to use your IBM PC, XT, AT, PS/2, or compatible as fast and easy as possible. Avoid the tedium (and potential errors) of keying in the more than 100 programs that are included in the book. At your own pace, work through and examine all the word processing, bar generation, form letter generation, list management, and computer games programs described in the book.

To order the disk, clip or photocopy this whole page and fill in the coupon below. Send it with your check or money order for $20 (U.S. funds), or use your MasterCard or Visa. (Maryland residents add 5% sales tax.)

- -

Send to:

Goldstein Software
21231 Georgia Avenue
Brookeville, MD 20833

Please send me____copies of the *Diskette to Accompany IBM PC and Compatibles, Fourth Edition* by Larry Joel Goldstein at $20 each. $_____is enclosed.

Name _____

Address _____

City _____

State _____ Zip _____

Country _____

Charge My Credit Card Instead

__ VISA   __ MasterCard

Account number _____

Expiration Date _____

Signature _____